A Child Goes Forth

A Curriculum Guide for Preschool Children

Sixth Edition

Barbara J. Taylor
Professor of Family Sciences
Director, Early Childhood Education Laboratories
Brigham Young University

Burgess Publishing Company
Minneapolis, Minnesota

Acquisitions Editor: Richard M. Abel
Development Editors: Mary Hoff, Nancy Crochiere
Art Director: Judy Vicars

Cover photography: Danny Novak

Printed in the United States of America

Library of Congress Cataloging in Publication Data

Taylor, Barbara J.
A child goes forth.

Includes bibliographies and index.
1. Education, Preschool—Curricula. I. Title.
LB1140.4.T388 1985 372.19 84-23087
ISBN 0-8087-3663-9

Burgess Publishing Company
7108 Ohms Lane
Minneapolis, MN 55435

J I H G F E D C B

To Young Children Everywhere

There was a child went forth every day,
And the first object he look'd upon, that object he became,
And that object became part of him for the
    day or a certain part of the day,
Or for many years or stretching cycles of years.

Walt Whitman
From "Autumn Rivulets"
in *Leaves of Grass*

Contents

Preface

In Walt Whitman's poem "Autumn Rivulets," a child becomes part of all he sees and does. Children of all ages are curious, imitative, and growing, and the title A CHILD GOES FORTH reflects this involvement of children with the world around them. Part of what has made A CHILD GOES FORTH a successful text for early childhood education courses is the book's emphasis on the individuality of each child. My philosophy is that all facets of a child's personality—social, intellectual, spiritual, physical, and emotional—are interrelated, and that a relaxed, unstructured atmosphere is most conducive to effective learning.

The revised sixth edition of this curriculum planner for teachers of preschool children retains the strengths of the previous editions while adding information that makes the book more up-to-date, comprehensive, and challenging. The book is still full of practical and meaningful tasks, activities, and games for youngsters. It also remains a useful guide for parents.

Reflecting current changes in preschool curricula, the sixth edition of A CHILD GOES FORTH covers ages 2 through 5 years. To help in understanding and meeting the needs of different age groups, the book now includes developmental characteristics for each age group and shows how these relate to planning, curriculum, and general expectations.

The bibliography has been updated; however, classic references or earlier editions have sometimes been used because of their importance to the field or thorough coverage of certain topics.

I have approached lesson planning in a more flexible way, shifting the emphasis away from behavioral objectives. A new format, suggesting four specific groupings, lends well to planning, and can be extended or varied as appropriate.

I encourage centers to move toward the two-teacher model with both teachers having primary responsibility for planning and guiding different parts of the day. Each can then rotate in the role of lead or support teacher easily and efficiently.

Because hands-on experience is so important in learning, adults as well as children need opportunities to practice. Each chapter gives suggestions for applying the principles taught in that chapter. These applications will be more valuable to some teachers, parents, or settings than to others. The applications are not intended to be assurances of learning, but merely to direct thinking into productive channels. Applications that are inappropriate can be modified or deleted, or more appropriate ones can be substituted.

The importance of nutrition for growth, development, and learning in young children is becoming more and more evident. For this reason, Chapter 10 has been expanded to include basic information about nutrition, how it influences behavior, ways to involve children in food preparation, and how to help them enjoy eating and mealtimes.

I hope that this new edition will motivate all adults to plan well, teach effectively, and reap the joy that comes from being a part of the lives of young children.

Professors Patty W. Cox of Abilene Christian University and Marjorie L. Oelerich of Mankato State University reviewed the manuscript, and their helpful comments are gratefully acknowledged.

A Child Goes Forth

1
Planning the Curriculum

Bring the hoop, and bring the ball,
Come with happy faces all;
Let us make a merry ring,
Talk and laugh, and dance and sing;
Quickly, quickly, come away,
For it is a pleasant day.

MAIN PRINCIPLES

To plan properly for young children, one needs to:

1. Know their developmental characteristics at each age level
2. Know how they learn best
3. Discard any misconceptions
4. Provide well-rounded experiences
5. Respect and value children
6. Take the privilege and responsibility seriously

Adults who work with young children are really involved with the "pot of gold at the end of the rainbow." Young children are tender, malleable, trusting, lovable, curious, and teachable. It is as if the teacher or parent were seated at the potter's wheel about to take the clump of clay and mold it into a thing of beauty and value. At the same time, the adult does not have the privilege of molding a child into a preconceived idea of "perfection;" rather, he must help the child to capitalize on his individual talents and abilities so he can live happily and healthily in his world and feel good about himself and his contribution.

Before planning a curriculum for young children, several important questions must be considered. What are the children like? How do children learn best? Are there misconceptions about behavior or learning styles? What components should be included daily or at frequent intervals to give children a well-rounded view of their world? What is the role or responsibility of the teacher? What does a good lesson plan look like?

WHAT YOUNG CHILDREN ARE LIKE

In previous editions of this text, the main focus has been on preschool children, typically identified as 3- and 4-year-olds. In order to have a broader base for teaching young children, this edition has been expanded to include 2-year-olds and 5-year-olds. After all, what the child is and does as a 2-year-old certainly is reflected in what he is and does as an older child. Likewise, how a child reacts as he moves into the "school" world will also depend on how he has spent his earlier years.

At the onset, the reader must be cautioned about individual differences of children in age, family backgrounds, and opportunity. The following paragraphs note some expected behavior or developmental characteristics of children at ages covered within the scope of this book. Just knowing whether behavior is typical of an age can help the adult in planning for and understanding children. For more characteristics, see Appendix A and also pages 27–34, 85, 116–117, and 133.

2-Year-Olds

At 2 years of age, children depend on someone for satisfaction of needs, for personal support, and for entertainment. They may show no particular interest in a toy until it is moved by another child or adult. Usually the attention span is short. (The difference between "attention" and "interest" span will be discussed later.) These children play mostly alone or in the presence of an adult, and may even walk on or over another person without acknowledging his presence. They enjoy music, finger plays, stories, and art activities, but in a much more limited sense than older children. They may have "tantrums" (also to be discussed later).

Language is limited; 2-year-olds understand much more than they are able to verbalize

A good teacher respects the child as an individual.

but may use some words or short sentences. They also have their own words for objects or wants, which only someone who knows them well will understand.

At 2 years of age, children are gaining better control over large muscles—they run, jump, throw, and climb in immature and uncoordinated ways. Getting their way is accomplished mostly by physical action—taking things (often as though the other person were not there) or hurting someone (although they do not understand how the other person feels). They are great imitators, curious, and full of energy.

3-Year-Olds

Children at 3 years of age are not secure enough to be independent; they still like to be close to an adult and often imitate the actions of others. They enjoy assisting in small chores. Their interests are expanding, and they spend more time in certain activities. At this age, children begin to play by other children (parallel play) but may have little or no interaction. They are definitely doers and no longer watchers and enjoy participating in music, stories, art, and other activities. They enjoy the security of routines but may begin to test limits.

The 3-year-old's use of language increases rapidly. Often conversation with another child will be "collective monologue," that is, each child will await his turn to talk and then speak only of his thoughts and not in response to the other person. He enjoys talking, sounds of words, and nonsense topics. He is becoming more verbal in getting his way, but still uses some physical means. Ability to distinguish reality from fantasy is limited—everything is possible, and the 3-year-old attempts to demonstrate rather than verbalize ideas.

Large muscles are increasing in strength and coordination; however, agility is lacking. Use of small muscles is still limited even though increasing all the time. Lack of eye-hand coordination and of precision in small muscle use makes it tiring for a 3-year-old to stay with small muscle activities (puzzles, pegboards, or scissors). Growth is tapering off, causing dawdling over food and poor appetite.

4-Year-Olds

At 4 years of age, children make definite strides for independence, and, for the most part, are assertive and boastful. They express caring behavior toward others. Their interests are much broader than previously; they can spend long periods of time with an activity. Language is used increasingly in interaction with others, to gain desired things, and in self-expression. Many questions are asked, and serious answers are wanted with verbiage.

These children play cooperatively with others. They want more realistic "props" and may assign roles for each member. Play may continue from one day to another. They are now adept at using tools and utensils—hammers, saws, scissors, and paint brushes. They may even decide in advance what the finished product will be; however, they are still more interested in the process than the product. Attention is gained by showing off, expressing displeasure, and being aggressive or loud. Gross and fine muscles are becoming better coordinated, but large muscles are still preferred over small ones.

Some distinction is being made between reality and fantasy at this age; however, there is still some confusion. When such actions as displays of superhuman strength or impossible feats are viewed on television, 4-year-olds insist they can be performed.

5-Year-Olds

Children at 5 years of age are more independent, dependable, self-assured, and conforming than younger children but like approval from others. They are protective toward younger siblings. They prefer to play with children of the same sex and age, and their play is cooperative, sustained, and more complex than formerly. Eye-hand coordination, gross and fine muscle movements, and ideas work cooperatively. Body control is good; they can throw and catch a ball, jump rope, skip, and use their skills to interact with other people. They use scissors with more precision than younger children and enjoy making things. They love stories and school and can remember sequences of numbers or letters. Although 5-year-olds tend to be obedient, cooperative, and empathetic, they also brag about accomplishments, exaggerate, and enter into short quarrels. They understand and use language freely in expressing their feelings and in complying with requests. They differentiate better between truth and make-believe and can verbally explain some differences. They still enjoy dramatic play but are interested in the "real" world.

Summary

From the above descriptions, specific differences can be noted among children between ages 2 and 5; however, the match between a child and his age characteristics is another thing. Some fit so well that the movement from one age to the next is evident; others pass casually through the stages. Along with individual differences are periods when development is more continuous and smooth than others. When children are in a period of rapid development, behavior is less stable than when development is slower. For instance, the behavior of 2- and 4-year-olds, who are in periods of rapid development, reflects more negativism or egocentrism than that of 3- and 5-year-olds.

Young children from financially, educationally, nutritionally, or experientially restricted backgrounds would probably not fit into the above age characteristics as easily as other children. They may have the same tendencies toward these characteristics, but yet not have the opportunity to explore, experience, or be motivated or encouraged.

A quick note about "attention" and "interest" mentioned earlier. *Webster's New World Dictionary* makes the following distinctions: "Attention: the ability to give heed or observe carefully." "Interest: a share or participation in something." It may be said that young children have short attention spans. That is very logical if they are expected to observe carefully. Participating or sharing in an experience is very different. Young children are not observers—they are participators. If their attention or longer involvement is desired, active involvement rather than "showing" is required. Here is an example of how the interest span of a group of 2-year-olds was lengthened:

Balls of dough-clay were placed in front of each child. Without delay, it was tasted, pinched, and smelled. This wasn't too exciting or interesting. As two children started to leave the table, the teacher brought out some flour sifters and flour. The children turned back to the activity. Sifting flour was fun for a few minutes; rolling the flour into the dough also took some concentration. Again a couple of the children were ready to leave. The teacher placed a small rolling pin in front of each child. Nothing was said, but eager hands reached for the pins. Now the children were tasting, pinching, flouring, and rolling. This continued for several minutes. Then, as disinterest began to set in, the teacher placed cookie cutters and a pan on the table. Again, the eager fingers and minds were diverted back to the activity. All in all, the children stayed at the activity for a length of time that was notable, especially considering their age and "short" interest span.

What was it that kept the children interested? New and varied materials, attention from the teacher, peers, or success? Each of these components must have added to the experience.

Children of different ages have varying abilities and interests. The wise adult looks for the things that attract and sustain children in activities. After all, if children are going to perform well in the academic world, they need to concentrate and to see an activity to finality.

Several children may share the same interests. For example, Tetsuya had an insatiable concern with dinosaurs. The teacher felt that the topic was beyond preschoolers, uninteresting, and difficult to teach. Finally, convinced that the only way to halt Tetsuya's constant questions was to teach about dinosaurs, she located some good dinosaur pictures, acquired a few large replicas, drew some large pictures for the bulletin board, and encouraged role playing. Much to her surprise, all the children were so interested that they compared replicas to the pictures, learned the names of the particular dinosaurs, and became involved in good, constructive dramatic play in the block area. Never underestimate the interest of a child! Also, the teacher did not try to "tell" the children about the dinosaurs—she provided involvement.

HOW YOUNG CHILDREN LEARN BEST

In early European history, children were treated like adults, were dressed like adults, worked like adults, and were considered adult in all ways except size. They were expected to carry their full share of responsibility in providing for the family. In some cases, children performed tasks that adults could not: they crawled in small openings while working in mines, spent long hours in the fields, and survived on less food and sleep.

In the past century, observation and research have revealed that children are not miniature adults. They have feelings similar to adults, such as fear, joy, and pain, but their learning patterns are different from those of adults. Piaget, the Swiss epistemologist, formulated a model for the stages of intellectual development in children as follows (1974):

Stage 1: Sensorimotor (0 to 24 months of age)
Stage 2: Preoperational (2 to 7 years of age)
Stage 3: Concrete operations (7 to 11 years of age)
Stage 4: Formal operations (11 years of age on)

The first, or **sensorimotor,** stage involves learning through the five senses, the emerging ability to control one's body movements, and a combination of both. Children under 2 years of age mouth and touch everything, listen intently, have a keen sense of smell, and notice even the smallest thing on the floor. They are into everything in or out of reach. They crawl into small or dangerous spaces without fear; nothing is safe from them.

The second, or **preoperational,** stage is the focal point in early childhood education, representing expansion of the first stage. During the years of 2 to 7, children are somewhat self-centered and still oriented toward learning through the senses and body skills. They broaden their scope of activity from the home base to other individuals and experiences. Their best learning is done through hands-on experiences. They live in a "here-and-now" world and need concrete experiences—things that they can explore through the five senses and opportunities to interact with things that are real and present. They imitate, question, and practice. From birth, they have been thinkers; during the second stage they begin to handle abstract concepts, although the ideas of past and future are difficult for them.

In addition to concrete experience and sensory involvement, children in this stage learn best when language is used to increase vocabulary and ideas, when opportunities to practice problem-solving are provided, when activities are appropriate for their level of development (not too easy or too difficult, but challenging), and when they have interactions with other children and adults. Other aspects to consider are individual readiness, opportunities, materials, support, freedom to explore, degree of involvement, variety of experiences, and repetition. Practice, guidance, and motivation are important to children as they learn about themselves and their environment. Hopefully, most of their experiences will be positive so they have self-confidence.

Positive experiences increase self-confidence.

The third and fourth stages (**concrete** and **formal operations**) are beyond the scope of this book; however, the reader may find value in investigating these later stages. Many child development texts or articles in professional journals would be good sources of information.

Helping children develop good work habits is also important in learning. In a recent article, Stipek (1983) compiled several studies relating to work habits and has formulated the following basic conclusions:

> The children who learn most are those who persist at tasks rather than giving up as soon as the task becomes difficult, who pay attention to the task and select tasks that offer some challenge rather than the easiest available or ones that they could not possibly do, and who work on a task alone without unnecessary request for help. . . . The teachers of children with good work habits gave fewer directions, responded to children's questions more, and offered unrequested information less (pp. 25, 28).

Thus, developing good work habits depends on three things: the child, the task, and the adult.

Children need opportunities to work on their own and feel rewarded from their own efforts. They may need some guidance in the tasks undertaken, but the most rewarding thing is how they feel personally. They should feel good because of their efforts and results. The adult must plan well. This is simplified by knowing what to expect of children in general and each child in particular. The adult should expect children to succeed and convey confidence in and to them. The adult should meet their needs rather than his own by being unobtrusive and nondirective. The children should be allowed to take the initiative. Praise that comes from the adult should be more related to attempts and progress than to final outcomes. According to Stipek, a teacher or parent who rewards "less-than-optimal performance" prevents children from developing an understanding of a relationship between effort and performance. For example:

A group of preschool children were involved in a planting experience. They had a bucket of dirt, individual containers, spoons, bulbs, seeds, and a small watering can. Unnoticed by the children, the teacher became distracted. The children busied themselves with the task at hand. Shaun filled his container. Then, realizing it might not be a good idea just to lay the bulbs and seeds on the top of the dirt, he emptied his container. This time he put the seeds and bulbs in the bottom and filled the jar with soil. Thoughtfully, he looked at the jar. Evidently deciding that this also was not the best idea, he spooned the dirt out until he reached the bulbs and seeds. The bulbs were easily retrieved, but the seeds became a problem. Carefully, he spooned the dirt onto the table. At first he tenderly stirred the dirt with his spoon but finally resorted to using his fingers to pick out the seeds one by one. Then he remembered how they had used cotton balls when they sprouted seeds previously. He got some small, white cotton balls from the shelf, lightly dampened them at the sink, and returned to the activity. He picked up each seed and placed it on a cotton ball. This time, as he filled his jar, he was very precise in placing the dirt, bulbs, and seeds. When the jar was full, he patted the dirt gently and slowly poured water from the can. His masterpiece was finished! By now the teacher had returned and was quietly observing the different skills and methods of the children. Shaun showed her his jar and told her of his different attempts at planting the bulbs and seeds and how he had finally succeeded. One could tell from the look of satisfaction on his face that Shaun was pleased with his planting experience. The teacher's smile and interest confirmed his ability to solve his problem.

MISCONCEPTIONS ABOUT BEHAVIOR AND LEARNING STYLES

In general, when 2-year-olds are mentioned, first thoughts are of behavior: age plus negativism equal the "terrible 2s." While negative behavior might be expressed more vigorously at 2 years than at most other ages, this is not the only age when a person is negative. Many people know adults who have never passed this stage. Because negativism is so often associated with the young child, this concept will be briefly explored here.

At 2 years of age, children are striving for independence but lack the knowledge and skill to get it. They may constantly use the word "NO!", even when they want the opposite; they may become rigid or limp all over, use aggressive behavior, such as biting, kicking, and scratching, run away, or worst of all, throw a tantrum. They cannot verbalize feelings or desires, so they revert to behavior—with vigor. To them, negativism is felt, but may often be short-lived. It does get results. Instead of ignoring or playing down the behavior, adults often force more negativism before attending to the behavior. The 2-year-olds then see that negative behavior has to be increased in intensity or duration in order to get results.

Hurlock (1964) has an early but still applicable and interesting discussion on negativism. She states that this tendency can result from aggressive discipline, intolerance toward normal childish behavior, refusal by the child to carry out requests when and how the adult requires, adult interference, inconsistent training, early toilet training, or reaction of people to different tempos. Negativism begins at about 18 months of age, reaches a peak between 3 and 6 years of age, and then recedes rapidly. The decline results partly from social influences, partly because children learn that compliance is to their advantage, and partly because parents learn to show more respect for the children. Negativism is usually more frequent and more severe in poorly adjusted children but also appears in well-adjusted children. Between the ages of 4 and 6 years, children change resistance from physical to verbal forms. They also pretend not to hear or understand, refuse to see the point, insist on reopening issues, complain or act irresponsibly about requests or responsibilities. As for the value of negativism, Banham (1952) states:

> They [contrasuggestability, negativism, and obstinacy] are forms of behavior that are unsatisfactory in themselves, but that at least show vitality, motivation, and the beginnings of selective sensitivity to a complex social situation. They indicate that the child is capable of developing social and emotional attachments and antagonisms. . . . Children become exces-

> sively obstinate when demands are made that are impossible for them to execute, when the demands are humiliating, unfair, or exceedingly disagreeable or painful. Obstinate contrariness is a compensatory adaptive reaction, only partially successful, in the interest of self-preservation, growth, and development. It is likely to change to cooperative behavior when the child finds something he can do that will bring satisfaction to him while complying with the wishes of those for whom he cares.

This is an old reference, but still has application and gives good food for thought.

The above paragraph notes that negativism is a part of the young child's life, but duration, intensity, and frequency depend in large measure upon the response of the adult. Through behavior, adults can increase or decrease negativism by planning for and interacting with young children. Adults must see that issues are resolved without causing children to suffer loss of face, without trying to win a power struggle, and through a loving relationship. When these are thoughtfully done, not only will the "terrible 2s" be changed to the "terrific 2s," but other ages and stages will be less stressful for both children and adults. In a broad generality, many adults try to do too much for a child at each age when the child is trying to become more and more independent, that is, a person in his own right with needs, abilities, and desires.

Like negativism, other aspects of behavior such as independence, confidence, security, conformity, and conflict recur throughout the child's life cycle, becoming notable again during adolescence and young adulthood. For example:

In a group of children 2 through 5 years of age, the children are planning a field trip to a nearby park. Each child is to prepare his own lunch, assist in a group assignment, and report to his group for transportation. **Glenn,** age 2, has great difficulty getting peanut butter spread on his bread and wrapping his cookie and raisins without eating or dropping them. He spends his entire time and energy trying to get his lunch ready. Finally, he gives up in disgust, sweeps his food onto the floor, throws himself down beside it, and begins to cry. Teachers are frantically trying to get organized so they can spend as much time at the park as possible. Nobody notices Glenn, and his frustration intensifies. **Su Li,** a 3-year-old, has difficulty preparing her lunch, but finally shoves all the items in the sack with a "thank-goodness-that's-done" attitude. She moves on to her group assignment: stories and songs with visual aids. She wants to take more books than she can carry, and she doesn't care about the topic or number. Songs are even harder to select. She keeps going to the visual aids, grabbing a handful, running to pile them on the books, and returning for more. Other children in her group are also trying to make selections, as well as returning some of the things Su Li has taken. Finally, her patience ends. She picks up the stack of visuals and books and literally throws them at her peers. Nobody notices her frustration, either. Then there is **Vhari,** a capable 4-year-old. She prepares her lunch easily, sacks the paper cups, napkins, can opener, and clean-up materials (her group assignment). She sits down to wait for the others. She waits—and waits—and waits. She, too, becomes disgusted and starts hurrying the slow lunch preparers, gives orders to the group projects, and then starts hassling the teachers. Being ignored by all, she sits in her locker, sulks, and declares, "It is a dumb idea to go to the park, anyway." **Charles,** a contented boy of 5 years, enjoys making his lunch (especially licking the peanut butter off his hands and knife), nonchalantly puts a toy or two away, waters the plant, puts on his favorite hat, wanders around the room, and then goes to his group. It is time to go, and nothing has bothered him in the least. He likes to go to the park.

If you were the teacher of this group, what preparations would you make so the frustration level of each child could be reduced or eliminated entirely and yet allow the children to take some initiative and responsibility in the trip?

Glenn: Use a different kind of sandwich spread. Peanut butter is hard to spread on fresh bread. Let him wash a stick of celery or carrot. Cookies and raisins could be put into a small plastic bag rather than being wrapped. An adult nearby could have been very helpful in offering suggestions and aid if necessary.

Su Li: She seemed satisfied with her lunch preparation. Her problem was with the books and visual aids. It would have been helpful if she had been told which part of the assignment was hers. Throwing the things made her upset with her group and them upset with her. What a way to start on a trip!

Vhari: She was able to prepare her lunch and get her assignment ready with ease. This gave her extra time to heckle the other children. After all, when you are 4 years old, you are somewhat capable, but also somewhat bossy. She could have been encouraged to help less experienced children (such as Glenn) fix their lunches. She could have handled the book and song assignment much better than did Su Li. Waiting didn't get her any reward, so maybe sulking or loud, negative remarks would!

Charles: Good old Charles! Nothing upset him. He relished every minute of every activity. He was anxious and eager but not aggressive or intimidated. He got things done in his own sweet time. He probably thought the trip preparations were just great!

With the exception of Charles, the apparent differences in behavior of each child were reactions to the circumstances in which they were placed: the level of challenge or difficulty, clarity of task definition, support and guidance offered or lacking, and interaction with others.

Now as to some **misconceptions** about how children learn, early childhood educator Elkind (1978) has thoughtfully brought to focus five important misunderstandings of adults.

1. Children are most like adults in their thinking and least like them in their feelings.
2. Children learn best while sitting still and listening.
3. Children can learn and operate according to rules.
4. *Acceleration* is preferable to *elaboration*.
5. Parents and teachers can raise the IQ of children.

Adults who have been around young children a lot will recognize these five points as myths and react accordingly. Adults whose experience with young children is limited, however, will have to be observant to avoid these pitfalls.

COMPONENTS FOR A WELL-ROUNDED VIEW OF THE WORLD

Creative planning for young children is essential. Opposing the belief that children younger than 5 or 6 years of age waste time until they are old enough to enter formal school, research in the field continues to indicate the importance of formative years. Early educators and researchers such as Montessori and Gesell felt that (1) development was a process of "unfolding" related to maturation and (2) the rate of unfolding was determined genetically. More recently, educators and researchers have come to believe that a stimulating and planned environment can influence the learning capabilities of young children, especially those from deprived environments.

Although some children are prepared for group experience earlier than others, there is some general agreement that children are ready for peer contacts around the age of 3; however, more and more children are being placed in group care at age 2 or younger. Factors other than chronological age must be considered in evaluating the total social, emotional, spiritual, physical, and intellectual needs of each child. How secure does the child feel in the home? Is his physical development within the expected range for his age? Does he have opportunities to be with children his own age? How does he respond to strangers (peers, adults)? What is the relationship between the child and his parents? Are significant happenings in the home (new baby, recent move) disturbing to him? What could the child gain from a group experience that he could not get at home? Would costs or arrangements cause a hardship on the family? How would this experience affect the whole family? As these questions suggest, a group experience must

Many children under 2 years of age are now in group care.

be entered into with caution; the child must be given time to adjust, whether he does it slowly or rapidly.

Either daily or frequently, the young child should participate in various curricula on a developmental level that is appropriately challenging and interesting. Other provisions include individual concentration and play as well as group involvement; periods of activity and periods of quiet; indoor and outdoor play; and opportunities for physical, social, emotional, intellectual, and moral development. The focus should ever be on helping each child to acquire a healthy self-concept and to reach his potential more fully.

Goals for teachers and children should be short- and long-range. Whatever the duration, careful planning and foresight are necessary. Good teaching does not just happen.

To determine realistic and appropriate goals, the individual child's characteristics are considered first, then the philosophy or model used at the school. Setting goals without considering the children first is ineffective and is the same as saying, "We'll mold the children to fit the program." More important to say is, "Children *are* the program, and we'll plan to meet their needs." Also goals for one group or year very possibly would not be effective for another group or year.

Some activities should bring the children together as a group.

The following are examples of goals for children in a center:

- Development of a good self-image, a wholesome attitude toward their bodies, and a good start toward reaching their potential
- Provision of opportunities to develop their whole personalities through: (1) firsthand experience in social relationships, (2) physical development of large and small muscles, (3) acceptable outlets for emotions, and (4) stimulating experiences that encourage them to think, analyze problems, and arrive at different possible solutions
- Stimulation of language development through listening and speaking opportunities
- Development of an awareness and use of their five senses

Firsthand social relationships develop the child's personality.

- Encouragement of independence
- Assistance in exploring their environment and in satisfying their curiosity
- Help in establishing good work habits
- Positive experiences with other children
- Meeting their individual and group needs
- Development of a positive attitude toward teachers, school, and learning in order to build a tie between home and school
- Provision of some experiences to supplement, not substitute for, those that take place in the home

ROLE OF THE TEACHER

For convenience throughout this text, the teacher is referred to as "you" or "she," the child as "he." Unfortunately, men have had a certain reluctance to enter an occupation that has been traditionally "female." Men in the field of education are often teaching older children or in administrative positions. Young children need and want male teachers. Hopefully a trend toward more men teaching young children will increase.

Teaching is a great responsibility. Being a teacher of young children is even more important. Teachers should take their stewardship seriously by building good relationships with and among staff, parents, and children, being professional at all times, and keeping confidences. Snap judgments should not be made without facts. Frequent and friendly contacts with parents are essential.

The number of teachers required to operate a center efficiently depends on the number and ages of the children, physical facilities, experience of the teachers, and local regulations, when applicable; however, at least *two* trained teachers are needed per group. More are required when a group is composed of only 2-year-olds or more than 16 children. (State and local requirements vary, but the recommended maximum is 24 children per group, with the ideal number being between 16 and 20 for children ages 3 through 5.)

Why is one trained teacher insufficient to handle a group of young children? How can a center afford two trained teachers per group? "Trained" does not necessarily refer to a four-year college degree in early childhood education. Training can be obtained through trade tech, working for an associate degree or child development associate (CDA) credential, or on-the-job training. A new, relatively inexpensive self-training packet developed at Brigham Young University takes the student step by step through eight workbooks with audiotapes and also has a slide-tape presentation that is very helpful in seeing and understanding the components in operating a good center. (For additional information on teacher roles and operating a good center, see Cahoon, Larsen, and Taylor reference at end of chapter.)

The program works best with two distinct teacher roles—the "lead" teacher and the "support" teacher. (A third teacher would also be assigned the role of "support" teacher.) As the name suggests, the lead teacher "leads out" in an activity, taking the major responsibility for planning, organization, and actual teaching. Support teachers assist the lead teacher. Although the roles differ in specific assignments, they are of equal importance. All teachers must have the training necessary to function competently in either role and to rotate roles easily and successfully.

For a brief clarification of the two roles, consider Teacher A (TA) and Teacher B (TB) in the same classroom. Today, TA has planned the opening time, snack, and art. TB has planned the group theme time, outside activity, and language time. (For complete lesson plans, see Appendix C.)

A brief outline defining the two roles follows:

Time	Activity Period	Description	Materials Needed	Teacher
______	Opening	Free choice	(Complete this	A
______	Gathering	Theme-setting	column	B
______	Activity	Outdoor	according to	B
______	Gathering	Snack	activities	A
______	Gathering	Language	planned)	B
______	Activity	Creative art		A
______	Closing			A/B

TA takes the initiative to set up free play activities. Both teachers participate with the children as needed. At clean-up time, TA follows through; TB assists at the beginning and then moves to group time so she will be ready as the first children arrive. She begins some interesting activities. The children put away their toys and join TB. When TA is through with clean-up, she joins the children in the group and assists with incidentals while TB presents. At the conclusion of this period, both teachers help the children get ready to go outside. TB accompanies them while TA sets up the snack, with the help of two children, after which all three also go outside. To be ready when the children arrive at snack, TA precedes them into the classroom and assists them as needed. TB brings in the stragglers and joins the other children at the snack table. As this activity concludes, TB moves with the first children to another group time for stories and songs. TA clears away the snack, prepares the tables for art activities, then joins the group in progress. During art, both teachers move freely among the children, giving verbal support, physical help, or manipulating the materials when appropriate. At the end of the day, both teachers help the children make the transition from school to home.

Clearly, two teachers are needed to work individually or cooperatively according to the needs of the children or the experiences planned. On another day, the teachers could change roles, with TA planning and presenting the curriculum areas that TB had done the previous day, or one teacher might keep the same role for a longer period of time. The best teaching occurs when plans are made well in advance of the teaching day; a week ahead gives plenty of time to gather materials, make contacts, and solidify ideas. This new two-teacher model eliminates the teacher-aid model where one person had the teaching responsibility and the other had a less important role. Each teacher now takes primary responsibility for some activities.

The basic inner qualities of the teacher are more influential on the learning of the young child than any other single factor (Elkind 1970); therefore, the teacher must accept the following responsibilities:

To herself:

To grow professionally; to be progressive and creative
To remain in good physical and emotional health
To be enthusiastic, loving, and patient
To know, understand, and value herself

To the children:

To build good relationships with them
To determine and meet their needs through appropriate experiences
To enjoy being with them
To respect them as individuals and encourage independence and self-control
To help them build a good self-image
To assist them toward reaching their potential

To the parents:
To build a good relationship with them; to value them and their ideas
To provide good counseling; to assist in planning for the well-being of the child
To keep them informed about school practices and activities, thereby bridging the gap between home and school

To other staff members:
To build a good relationship with and among them
To support and value them and their ideas
To share ideas and knowledge
To encourage their professional growth

To the community:
To be active in solving its problems
To participate in local professional early childhood organizations
To disseminate information about the importance of growth, development, and education for the young child

SUGGESTIONS FOR TEACHERS

- Make sure the setting is child-centered. Give support when needed, but allow each child the time and opportunity to explore and solve problems. Put his needs before your own.
- Know how many children are in the group daily, where they are, what they are doing, and where the other teachers are.
- See that behavior limits, when necessary, are set, understood, and maintained. Be consistent without being inflexible.

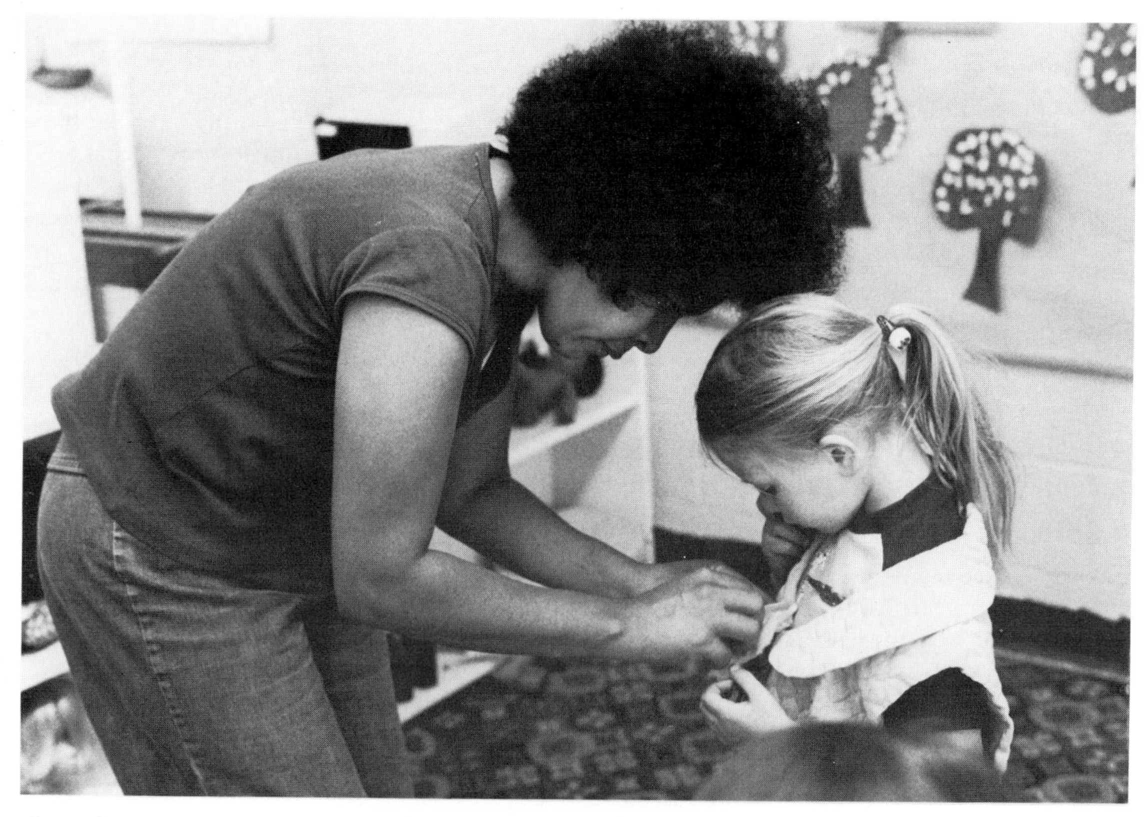

A teacher interacts with each child many times during the day.

- Use your voice as a teaching tool. A soft, pleasant voice receives better response than a loud, gruff one or a high-pitched, overly excited one.
- Make sure your words and actions indicate the same thing. When it is time to go inside, for instance, tell the children and then go inside yourself.
- Use verbalization as a technique to gain cooperation from the children. Help them to understand what is expected of them. Speak with confidence.
- Get on a child's physical level when speaking to him by either kneeling, stooping, or sitting on a low chair or the floor.
- Get adequate rest and proper nutrition.
- Leave your problems outside the center.
- Dress appropriately for the job, the weather, and activities.
- Be prompt. Have things organized and ready when the children arrive. Control is difficult to regain if children get ahead of you.
- Keep current by reading professional periodicals, books, and pamphlets and by attending professional workshops and conferences to aid you in becoming a more effective teacher.
- Plan ahead. Make sure the next activity is ready before warning children to finish their current involvement.
- When another teacher is handling a situation, do not interfere unless your help is requested.
- Be a good housekeeper both indoors and outdoors. Keep the center clean and attractive; however, avoid being so involved that the children are unsupervised.
- Be totally aware of what is going on. Just furnishing a warm body is insufficient.
- Strike a balance between giving needed one-to-one attention and keeping peripheral awareness of other activities.
- Share your experiences and ideas with other staff members.
- In all ways be a good support and lead teacher.
- Be honestly enthusiastic about being with the children.
- Relax and smile!

WHAT TO PLAN

First, each child in the group must be considered individually. What are his needs and interests? What have his past experiences been, and how has he met them? What are the ages of the children? Recall the general characteristics of each age between 2 and 5 years. Some teachers prefer the children in a group to be within one year of the same age. They think that children of similar chronological age already have enough differences, and planning is easier when the age span is narrow. Other teachers prefer to group the children vertically with a wide age span (sometimes called family grouping), because the older children can be models for the younger ones, more variation in planning is possible, and experiences are more challenging to both children and teachers. Vertical grouping also provides enough children for a group when enrollment is small.

Second, plans should include varied experiences: interpersonal relationships, sensory experiences, exploration of natural and physical surroundings, intellectual stimulation, development of large and small muscles, and many opportunities to hear and use language. Most young children prefer a regular routine, depending on repetition of activities for security. Nonetheless, they enjoy variety and occasionally accept changes.

Plans should be simple, especially when the children are very young or new, but specific. Interrelating ideas and using real objects are important. Ideas presented should be interesting and challenging.

The day should be divided into specific periods and provide for active, quiet, indoor, outdoor, and group and individual play. Suggested blocks of time include "opening

Time is provided for individual play.

time," "group time," "activity time," and "closing time." Examples of each will be given in the following section.

Third, consider the curriculum itself. Why do you want to teach a certain topic? What do the children already know about it? Are the concepts true and on an appropriate developmental level? Are there some new terms to introduce and define? What are the most effective ways of teaching? What materials will you need? Remembering that children learn best through doing, will firsthand experiences be sufficient? After you have taught the topic, how can you determine if the children have learned anything?

Many ask whether the use of written plans causes rigidity. The answer is no. Flexibility comes in implementing the plan. The more thorough the plan, the less the chance of leaving some important details uncovered. Planning extra or optional activities increases teacher confidence, allows for flexibility, and prevents teacher distress when planned activities take less time than expected, are not well received, or are clearly inappropriate for the group that day, based on such variables as mood, weather, or absenteeism. Also, if the teacher who made the plans is absent, the other teachers can easily carry on if the plans are in sufficient detail. Posting a copy of the daily plan makes staff members and parents aware of the activities of the day. When a teacher has only mental plans, other teachers may find difficulty interpreting or supporting them.

When two teachers are planning together, as in the earlier example of Teacher A and Teacher B, one of three approaches to the written plan is possible:

1. One teacher is established as the lead teacher for that day or week. She then combines her plans with the activities planned by the support teacher and writes them up.
2. A planning form is posted, and both the lead and the support teachers fill in their activities. This may lead to less coordination and continuity, however, than if one person fills in the form.
3. The two teachers plan together and fill out the form as the plan evolves. This approach is preferred.

Fourth, a daily evaluation should be planned with specific points to cover. Strengths and weaknesses in the program are noted, and the progress of each child is evaluated frequently. Discussing events immediately after departure of the children enhances planning skills, the ability to evaluate objectively, and relationships with other staff members.

A GOOD LESSON PLAN

A lesson plan is used as a guide and not as an end in itself. Planning is an ongoing procedure designed to meet the needs of young children. The process includes three general stages of preassessment, teaching, and evaluating, as mentioned above. A complete lesson plan has seven components: theme, preassessment and findings, ideas to be emphasized, schedule of the day, items for special attention, evaluation, and follow-through for parents.

On the day the lesson plan is to be taught, the teachers sit down together, before the children arrive, and review the activities and responsibilities so that everything is fresh in their minds.

Theme

The main purpose for selecting a topic is to provide direction and continuity. The theme chosen should interest the children and add variety and dimension to their lives. The theme itself suggests the best ways to put over the concepts. Because all areas of curriculum do not lend support to all topics, ways of supporting the theme must be chosen wisely, with some activities that reinforce the topic and some that are diversions from it. Rather than a one-shot overdose, the topic is used again later on. On occasion, it is possible to build on a theme or have it continue several days or a week, depending on the interests of the children.

For some suggested curriculum topics, see Appendix B.

Preassessment and Findings

Once a theme is selected, the next step is to find out what the children already know about it. Children with prior knowledge are used to help inform the others. Each child is taken just beyond his present knowledge.

Preassessment is made before developing a plan and is done casually or formally. The casual approach yields general information; the formal, specific. Here are two examples of preassessment on shapes:

1. **Casual.** Approach individual children or a small group and ask them if they know any shapes. If so, which ones? On a table, place items in the different shapes you

DAILY PLANNING OUTLINE

Teacher/Planner ______________________ Date __________

THEME

PREASSESSMENT AND FINDINGS

IDEAS TO EMPHASIZE

SCHEDULE OF THE DAY

Time	Activity Period	Description	Materials Needed	Teacher

ITEMS FOR SPECIAL ATTENTION

EVALUATION

FOLLOW-THROUGH FOR PARENTS

plan to teach. See what the children say about them or do with them. With this method you are trying to see if the children can name shapes without the shapes being present; then you are supplying the actual shapes and seeing if this gives the children clues. Observe, listen, and take notes.

2. **Formal.** Prepare some of the desired shapes. Then individually ask each child to hand you a specific shape. Also ask him to look around the room and tell you if he can find things in the room that are of the same shape. Can he give the right name for each shape and point out an example?

In the preassessment section of the planning sheet are written the specific methods to be used and results or findings. Preassessment is employed to acquire significant information, not merely to reaffirm what was to be taught in the first place. If the preassessment and the rest of the plan do not connect, it will be necessary to start over.

Ideas to Emphasize

The central ideas, which are a direct result of the preassessment, bind the theme and the activities together. Known ideas are used as a foundation on which to add new ideas. The latter should be in the form of simple, true statements based on the developmental level of the children. The number of new ideas depends on the amount and depth of information to be taught.

Schedule of the Day

This part of the planning sheet covers five headings and reflects the teacher's creativity, thoroughness, and versatility.

Under the first subheading, the amount of time allowed for the activity is listed. This is tentative, and the teacher should be ready to lengthen or shorten the activity as the interests of the children become evident. Also, the activities are listed in order of occurrence. Overplanning is advisable but with enough flexibility so that an activity can be saved until another day. Someday you will be happy that you had some extra activities scheduled.

Under the second heading, the activity period is listed. On the planning sheet, only the title of the activity is needed: "opening," "gathering," "activity play time," or "closing."

The opening helps the child make the transition from home to center. This time is used to welcome the child and help him to feel comfortable and to become involved in the group. The length of this period varies according to the check-in procedure, the interest of the children, the number of staff, and the total plans for the day.

Activity play time and gathering time occur one or more times each per day. An all-day program can alternate between these two periods or have longer blocks of time each time they are scheduled. These periods occur in whatever sequence is most appropriate for the particular center. Activity play time is mainly a child-centered period and is designed to allow children the time and materials to explore, discover, interpret, test, and satisfy their curiosity. The teacher carefully plans and sets out materials so the children have choices between activities.

Gathering time is when the children are brought together for a teacher-directed activity. Its main purpose is to teach concepts or skills in an organized way either indoors or outdoors. The first gathering time usually includes the theme and sets the tone for the whole day. *Caution:* this is not to be used for general announcements. As with other activities, the length of gathering time is flexible enough to involve the amount of time that is profitable to the children. Group activities may include stories, finger plays, songs, concept teaching, a visitor, a demonstration, preparation for another activity (field trip or visitor), science experience, food preparation, snack, music, or any other activity in which children participate as a group. The children should not be expected to sit for long periods of time but should have the opportunity for involvement. This period is usually planned and conducted by the lead teacher.

Finally comes closing time—the last few minutes of the day as the children prepare to return home. Often, the children are involved in a small informal group that is undisturbed as each child leaves. When someone calls for the child, he gathers together his belongings and checks out with a teacher. In some ways, closing time is similar to gathering time, except at the end of the day concepts can be reviewed rather than introduced, and children are prepared emotionally for leaving. For some centers, this method of closing would not meet the needs of children or parents, especially when children leave at staggered times. In such instances, the lead teacher participates with the children while the support teacher assists each child to leave the group and ready himself for departure. Closing time is more than a filler; it helps each child wind down and make a peaceful exit.

Under the third heading is space to define the activity. The amount of information placed here varies. Some teachers like details, others jot ideas or a word or two. Enough information should be given to describe the activity. The teacher also should check over the entire plan to make sure that some activities reinforce the main ideas, some provide experiences to stimulate development in the various areas, some encourage group or individual participation, and some are held in reserve, just in case they are needed.

Under the fourth heading are listed the materials needed. The absence of an important tool, object, aid, or prop may bring disaster to an activity. Listing needed items here helps the teacher to think through the activity in its entirety and also aids her as she gathers the materials for the day.

The last column in this section gives the name of the teacher responsible for the activity. This saves any confusion or question and also helps the lead teacher to see how well balanced the responsibilities are. Having the same teacher scheduled to supervise two activities in a row could cause problems for both teachers and children.

Items for Special Attention

Items may or may not be listed here daily, but the reminder is invaluable when needed. The staff may need to carefully watch a certain activity (a transition, for example) or a certain child (perhaps one has been especially listless lately). A reminder to recontact someone for a future activity, such as a field trip or a visitor, can be written here. A note can be made to rearrange the indoor or outdoor areas, to order more supplies for an activity (wood for the woodworking table for Thursday), or to check the drain on the water table before filling it with water and boats. This space is not used for personal reminders.

Evaluation

Now is the time to see how well the day was planned, how well the children responded, how well the staff performed, and what changes can be made when the plan is used again. Notes can be written right on the plan as reminders to make any additions, deletions, or modifications.

To be most effective, as noted previously, the evaluation is held as soon as possible after the children leave the center. All the staff who worked with the children that day are included, if possible. At times just the lead and support teachers participate.

On the lesson plan will have been written some ideas that would be valuable to discuss. They may be in the form of questions or statements and are merely reminders of things considered important when the plan was prepared. They give a starting point to the discussion and, hopefully, help make the evaluation meaningful. The time allotted for this process varies, but 15 to 30 minutes of concentrated time handles most items. Productivity of the evaluation and not the clock decides the length.

To get the staff in a constructive mood, discussion should begin with things that went well. Open-ended questions, that is, ones that require thinking, recalling, observing, and interpreting, help effective evaluation. For example, compare these two questions:

"Did the children like the activities today?" "Which activities did the children seem to enjoy the most today?" The first question calls for a "yes" or "no" answer, the second for careful thought and response.

Things that did not go well are also discussed, continuing until ideas come up on how they can be done differently, avoided, or turned into learning experiences instead of failures.

The progress of each child should be assessed frequently. Looking at one or two children per week may be sufficient, or there may be a child who needs more consideration. The children should be the focal point of the center.

Follow-Through for Parents

This section gives space to consider the parents and the home while planning. Some teachers prefer to send home a note daily telling what has transpired during the day; some prefer a weekly or monthly newsletter; still others post a lesson plan daily and remind the parents to read it. Whatever the method, the closeness between home and center is vital, and the child is the connecting link.

A little time and effort are needed to prepare a message for the parents but are worthwhile. When the parent brings or picks up the child, a common topic can be shared, but the teacher's message should never be a tool of interrogation. Rather, it should keep parents informed and encourage valuable feedback so that misconceptions, comments, or interests of the children can be used in future planning.

For additional practice in lesson planning, the end of each of the following chapters (exclusive of Chapter 12) has a list of activities pertaining to the curriculum topic, which make up the components of a lesson plan on "boxes." In Appendix C is a compilation of ideas, resulting in a usable lesson plan.

ESPECIALLY FOR PARENTS

As parents, you are interested in what your child is learning and doing at school. Home visits, individual parent conferences, group parent meetings, observations by and

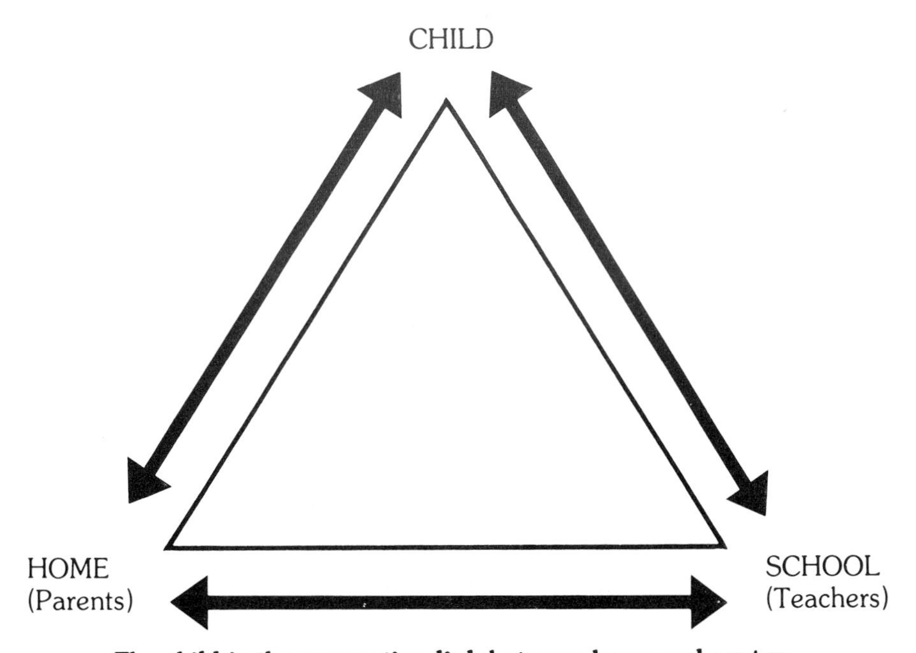

The child is the connecting link between home and center.

with the teacher, and participation are some of the elements that bring school, home, and child together. When you do have contact with the teacher, strive for a quality relationship. You should feel valued, useful, wanted, and appreciated. An occasional phone call or communication by mail is important if personal contacts are infrequent.

Select a group experience only after careful and thorough investigations and many visits to the center when the children are present. Ask yourself the following clarifying questions: Are the goals and philosophy of the center compatible with ours? Will our child grow and develop successfully under a particular program? Are the teachers well trained? What are their personal characteristics? Are they patient and understanding? Are they stable mentally, physically, socially, and emotionally? Are the needs of the children of prime concern? Is there provision for active as well as quiet play? Is language an important factor? Also ask other questions that are important to you and to the particular child you wish to enroll. Do not be in a rush. Give this matter careful consideration.

Perhaps your community does not have a center for young children, or perhaps the one in your community does not support your philosophy. Suppose you simply choose to have your children remain at home during the early years. How could the information in this chapter be of use to you?

First, as parents, you have been with your child under a great many different circumstances and know him very well. If you are objective—and flexible—you will be the greatest teacher your child will ever have. You will be his guide and model.

Second, you will have many opportunities to observe your child—his needs, his interests, his growth and development, his interactions with people and materials, his fears, and all other factors that contribute to his total self.

Third, you will be able to respond to him on a one-to-one basis, which is often difficult in a school setting. As spontaneous questions or experiences occur, you can satisfy his individual questions and create learning situations just for him. You can spend some quality time with him each day.

Fourth, you can help him understand about his community by taking him with you. Before leaving home, briefly, but casually, talk about where you are going and what you will do there. He isn't excess baggage; he is an eager learner.

Fifth, you can preassess the child's knowledge in various areas. Because you are planning for your own child, you can increase his knowledge and help him integrate that knowledge into his world.

Sixth, some parents want to share special experiences with their children, such as going to the zoo, visiting the train station or airport, or riding a horse. They should have the privilege. Some experiences are automatically eliminated from a school setting because of cost, distance, danger, or liability.

Seventh, if you see that your child is avoiding certain situations, such as art, books, or social contacts, you can plan some enjoyable, stimulating experiences to encourage him in these activities.

Eighth, you can help your child become independent and dependable by sharing in family responsibilities.

Ninth, through your daily living, you can demonstrate your religious and philosophical values of life.

Tenth, through seeing your child as a total person—not segmented into areas of development or by skills—you can help him build self-confidence and self-control.

A group experience during the child's early years does not insure either his acceptance or rejection from the country's leading universities or businesses. Some children do very well in group experiences and others do poorly. Alternative methods of "educating" young children are available. Parents need to consider carefully what the child's attendance or absence from a group before compulsory school age will mean to the child, the parents, and the entire family.

APPLICATION OF PRINCIPLES

1. Observe one child at each age between 2 and 5 years. Record evidence of abilities in physical, social, emotional, and intellectual development. Compare your findings with information in Appendix A. Remember that each child grows individually, but that each child passes through a pattern.
2. Give an example of attention span and of interest span. How do they differ?
3. List some ways to help children develop good work habits.
4. Explain Elkind's five important misunderstandings that adults have about how children learn.
5. Develop a list of five important goals for children at a child care center.
6. How do lead and support teachers interchange roles?
7. Identify and explain the seven elements of a good lesson plan. Write a lesson plan and compare it with one in Appendix C. Use and evaluate your plan.
8. Explain how relations between home and school can be strengthened.

References

Cahoon, Owen W., Jean M. Larsen, and Barbara J. Taylor. *To Teach Young Children.* Provo, Utah: Brigham Young University, 1983. Self-training packet available from Media Marketing, JACH, 84602.

Elkind, David. "The Case for the Academic Preschool: Fact or Fiction?" *Young Children* 25 (January 1970): 132–140.

______. "Misunderstandings About How Children Learn." *Today's Education,* March 1972, pp. 125–126.

Stipek, Deborah J. "Work Habits Begin in Preschool." *Young Children* 38 (May 1983): 25–31.

Sources on Age Characteristics

Banham, K. M. "Obstinate Children Are Adaptable." *Mental Hygiene,* 36 (1952): 84–89.

Eliason, Claudia F., and Loa T. Jenkins. *A Practical Guide to Early Childhood Curriculum.* 2d ed. St. Louis: C. V. Mosby, 1981.

Fowler, Marie. "What To Expect of the Fours and Fives." Leaflet no. 1. Washington, D.C.: Association for Childhood International, n.d.

Hurlock, Elizabeth B. *Child Development.* 4th ed. New York: McGraw-Hill, 1964.

Hymes, James L., Jr. *Teaching the Child Under Six.* 3d ed. Columbus, Ohio: Charles E. Merrill, 1981.

Lundsteen, Sara Wynn, and Norma B. Tarrow. *Guiding Young Children's Learning.* New York: McGraw-Hill, 1981.

McClinton, Barbara S., and Blanche G. Meier. *Beginnings: Psychology of Early Childhood.* St. Louis: C. V. Mosby, 1978.

Piaget, Jean. *The Child and Reality: Problems of Genetic Psychology.* Translated by Arnold Rosin. New York: Viking, 1974.

Ramsey, Marjorie E., and Kathleen M. Bayless. *Kindergarten: Programs and Practices.* St. Louis: C. V. Mosby, 1980.

2
The Value of Play

Rub-a-dub-dub, three men in a tub
And who do you think they be?
The butcher, the baker, the candlestick maker
All going out to sea!

MAIN PRINCIPLES

1. Play is a child's world. It is his prime educator.
2. Play enhances the physical, social, emotional, and intellectual development of the young child.
3. A child needs opportunity for play that is active and quiet, spontaneous and planned, indoors and outdoors, and done alone and with peers.
4. Adults can promote the young child's play experiences.

Why do some people question the value of play opportunities for young children? Are they so product- and time-conscious that they want the children to get past the stage of playing and get on to the stage of "learning"? Anyone who has watched or worked with young children realizes the importance of firsthand experiences. A child may seem to be wasting time at play, but to the child, play *is* his work, his way of learning about his environment. Consider how development is furthered through play experiences.

DEVELOPMENT DURING YEARS 2 THROUGH 5

Physical Development

Physical changes in the young child are more obvious than changes in other areas of development. Through physical increase, the child gains independence, develops body skills and coordination, masters his environment, and learns to cooperate. Numerous studies have shown the important relationship between a child's physical skills and his self-concept. When he feels competent, he is willing to attempt new and different experiences.

The young child's body is used as a "vehicle of expression." Through body movements, he learns spatial relationships and bilateral movements. He learns about motion, speed, and force. Many of these activities are symbolic and are satisfying at the time and also in later learning.

Some academic learning difficulties (specifically, reading problems) have been attri-

Through play, the child develops body skills and gains independence.

buted to lack of early physical development. Regarding psychomotor skills, Dr. Carl Delacato (1959) says a child who does not learn to crawl at the appropriate time misses important body usage necessary for academic success.

Caplan (1973) reviewed two studies that included gross motor opportunities for young children. Theory stated that if physical activities had been skipped in earlier years, the upper levels of the brain would be prevented from functioning fully. One study aimed at teaching each child a sense of laterality (internal awareness of the right and left sides of one's body) and of directionality (up, down, behind, and so on). The second study dealt with gross motor activities. Results for both studies supported the same findings: vast progress was made in academic learning and physical poise in children who had participated in structured gross motor activities.

While some educators stress perceptual motor programs, others issue cautions:

> It is our opinion that these [perceptual motor programs] must be recognized for what they are—programs to increase perceptual-motor efficiency. Grandiose claims that they increase academic success are not well founded. By giving children opportunities for both physical outlets and successful experiences, these programs probably have subsidiary effects on social and emotional development, including the concepts children have of themselves. They serve as an effective means of early identification of children with disabilities or developmental lag—*if* teachers are trained in careful screening. For children so identified, a concentrated perceptual-motor program is probably effective. For children who are functioning well, however, such programs probably serve no purpose. Although some would claim that they "do no harm and may do some good," such programs do take up most of the time usually allocated for attention to children's physical development. We believe this time could be better spent in a program that builds skills while encouraging creative responses, exploration, problem solving, and social cooperation. (Lundsteen and Tarrow 1981)

Growth follows a plan, but progression in maturation is individual. "If suitable environmental stimuli are provided exactly when the child's powers are ready for them, the learning is more intense and inclusive than when each one is offered at a later time. Thus we say there are sensitive periods during which greater plasticity for gaining control of one's body and learning are in operation" (Caplan 1973).

For the most part, and mainly because of inadequate space indoors, most large muscle activities are performed outside. However, some provision should be made for indoor large muscle play, giving consideration to space needs, type of equipment, appropriate activities, and noise level. Children should play outdoors each day, even during inclement weather, but sustained large-muscle development is difficult when it is wet or cold. On such days children profit from large-muscle activities. A portable jungle gym, ladders, and boxes can be brought in or a sheet thrown over furniture. Set up the limits—the stick horses can be ridden in one room, but not throughout the building—and watch the enjoyment!

Social Development

Social skill learning, a complex task, can be fostered through play. Some skills are self-related and some are interpersonally related. Every child wants to participate with other children, and the first few years are the most important for practicing social living.

Numerous studies have shown the importance of social development. One found that children entering first grade in 1971 were less socially oriented in play activities than those entering in the late 1920s; this was partially explained by the later group's greater exposure to mass media and smaller family size (Barnes 1971). Several studies show a correlation between playfulness in the parent-child relationship and a child who is more socially inclined. Studies over several decades show the relationship between the absence of pleasure and the failure to develop normally. Some years ago, Dr. Rene Spitz observed that infants in a foundling home developed severe psychological disturbances, even though physical care was adequate. This behavior has been noted in other institutional settings but can be contrasted with that of infants in a nursery attached to a women's penitentiary where the mothers came regularly to feed, bathe, and play with their babies. The backgrounds of the penitentiary mothers included delinquency, prostitution, and low mentality and were far more unfavorable than those noted in Spitz's study; however, their infants developed along normal patterns because of the socialization and mothering effect (Piers and Wallach 1975). In their research on the quality of parents' play with an infant, Singer and Singer (1977) conclude:

> It follows that the mother or father who can get "in touch" with her or his own playfulness, imaginative resources and childhood joys is much more likely to offer the child richer opportunities for development than the adult who merely provides good physical care and love

Social skills are learned by playing with other children.

for the child without exposing him to the whimsy and joy of make-believe. Love, however deeply felt, needs playful actions and words, which engage the child's attention and encourage imitation.

Caplan (1973, p. 75) says: "Social development can be measured in terms of a child's mobility, communication ability, self-care, self-directed activity, and social attitudes and behavior." He continues:

Both pleasure and learning are benefits of play.

Play helps a child try out his social skills. Children have a strong need to get and give love. In their play, young children also find outlets for such wishes as a desire to dominate, destroy, display their prowess, make noise, or make a mess. The child who in real life finds it difficult to construct, to repair damage, to help, or to give of himself to others, can find many opportunities to do so in make-believe play, as well as in reality through cooperative play with others. There is really nothing mysterious about the power of play. Play is basic to all normal, healthy children. It provides pleasure and learning and a minimum of risks and penalties for mistakes. Because it enables them to escape from the restraints and frustrations of the real world, play provides children with greater opportunity to experiment and care and more possibilities for the full exercise of the imagination.

Maturation is a factor to consider in assessing a child's readiness for specific types of play activities. It sets limitations on his skills, experience, and techniques.

Emotional Development

Some adults have little patience with and understanding of a child's emotional development. That is one reason why play opportunities are so important for young children. Through play, children learn trust and confidence in themselves, in others, and in their environment. They recognize their self-worth and develop inner satisfaction. Instead of feeling helpless in many situations and showing fear or rage, they reduce or gain mastery over these feelings and formulate acceptable age-related emotional releases. In play they can exercise rule-making and direction-following; both are important for interaction with others and for later learning.

Play is a medium through which children can express their positive or negative feelings. For a time they do not have to conform to adult ways and can have relief from high expectations in childlike ways. Whenever a child has a successful experience, his feelings of self-worth and ability increase. Success also releases him from a sense of powerlessness. He actually can control and manipulate his environment.

"When people fail a child, play may be his only salvation. Play remains one of the most reliable factors in personality building and self-education during the child's earliest years. Through his play, a child lays the base for his development of a wholesome personality and the ability to function satisfactorily in the world in which he lives" (Caplan 1973).

In her book *Play in Childhood* (1967), Lowenfeld says: "Lack of ability to play is not natural and is not an inborn characteristic. It is neurosis and should be reckoned with as such." She continues:

> Play is an essential function of the passage from immaturity to emotional maturity. Any individual without the opportunities for adequate play in early life will go on seeking them in the stuff of adult life. Emotional satisfactions which the mind missed at the period to which they properly belong do not present themselves later in the same form. Forces unrealized in the childhood become an inner drive forever seeking outlet and lead men to express them no longer in play (since this is regarded as an activity of childhood), but in competition, anarchy, and war.

During the ages from 2 to 4, the child is less inhibited than he will ever be. His self-image during this period depends upon his play. He is very egocentric and he desires power. According to Caplan (1973): "One may well shudder to think what would happen if there were no time for this basic ego-centric play. We are convinced that if children did not have this period of ego play, drive and will power would be adversely affected in adulthood." And further: "Healthy personality development is tied to each child's own biological time clock, to his endowment, and his very early life experiences."

Intellectual Development

Many people think intellectual development must be taught through structured academic experience. They think that children must be taught early to perform the three Rs. Some teachers are so anxious to look good and to prepare children for the next grade that they are introducing topics earlier and earlier. Hymes calls this the "dribble down disease" (1981, p. 25). Caplan (1973) says that "there is extreme danger in prematurely pushing symbols during the child's first three years of life since this can curtail the spontaneity and non-verbal experimentation of early play." Why are adults not just as concerned about training children in the basics of life? Have they ever stopped to think that children who are helped to live fully as 3-, 4-, 5-, 6-, or whatever-year-olds will be happier and more productive throughout their entire schooling and lives? Young children may read, write, or do arithmetic, but do they know how to play?

The preschool period is not a valueless waiting time. Much is to be gained from play experiences: sustained attention and deep concentration, so necessary for reading; imagination, which assists the child in "innovative ways of perceiving and dealing with reality" (Read 1976); curiosity to explore, examine, and discover; initiative to try one's own ideas; opportunity to use memory in relating, recalling, and thinking; a chance to play and organize; leadership and group participation; a larger repertoire of responses; language development; creativity; acquisition of knowledge; self-enhancement; flexibility; understanding of one's personal problems; and the ability to exercise divergent thinking.

"Play is viewed as insufficient by itself to assure cognitive development, but it can be viewed as a means to foster this development" (Weikart 1971). Play must include aspects appropriate to and within the developmental level of each child in order to nurture development.

In his article, "Misunderstandings About How Children Learn," Elkind (1972) identifies five misconceptions of adults. He states:

> To be sure, IQ is affected by environment, but most middle-class children have probably grown intellectually about as rapidly as their endowment permits. Further enrichment is not likely to have marked effects upon their intellectual ability, although it may affect how

Play stimulates imagination and language development.

> they make use of this ability. Children who have been intellectually deprived can, however, make sufficient gains in intellectual performance as a consequence of intellectual enrichment.

How can children or adults be expected to make good decisions based on logic, cause and effect, value, or consequences if opportunities are not provided throughout their lives to exercise judgment, originality, and independence? Development and use of the ability to think divergently are essential.

Feitelson (1972) supervised college students conducting "play teaching" sessions with children from homes where play activities had not been encouraged. After nine weekly one-hour sessions, significant changes were seen in interest span, intensity of play, and initiative in creative play.

Studying the effects of guidance on the play behavior of preschool children in Japan, Suzuki (1971) observed a group of children who played under a structured curriculum and a group who played without instruction. The two groups used the same toys and room. Attributes such as liveliness, consistency, and enjoyment improved in both groups; however, the group without instruction was superior in creativity.

Dr. Raymond Hock of Drake University believes that preschool and early elementary school children should be given many opportunities to do creative work in areas that include music and nature, rather than being taught to read. He states that too-early emphasis on reading could cause overdevelopment of the left side of the brain, which deals with linear and logical concepts, as opposed to the right side, which deals with creative, intuitive, and metaphorical concepts. He thus concludes that early readers may be less creative than later readers.

In his article, "Education Is Play," Courtney views cognitive development as being fostered through choice and decision-making. To him these activities allow the child to practice self-direction, independence, and internal control.

"Since studies demonstrate a close relationship between play behavior and cognitive development in the child, the earlier a child starts to play, the sooner his education begins. Unfortunately, the relaxed learning climate of play is short-lived" (Seefeldt 1976).

Lawrence K. Frank, author and lecturer on human growth and development, has this to say about play and learning:

> With his sensory capacities, the child learns not only to look but to see, not only to hear but to listen, not only to touch but to feel and grasp what he handles. He tastes whatever he can get into his mouth. He begins to smell what he encounters. He can and will, if not handicapped, impaired or blocked, master these many experiences through continual play . . . the most intensive and fruitful learning activity in his whole life cycle. (1968)

The teacher or parent should accept the challenge of designing and providing appropriate play activities that enhance the child's intellectual development. Most kinds of opportunities, such as dramatic, sensory, or scientific exploration, are meaningful but especially so are creative or artistic endeavors. Deciding *what* to do and *how* to do it sharpen the child's intellect. These activities also provide for exercise of the brain, eye, hand, and other parts of the body.

Because most of this text is aimed at curriculum that is generally done indoors (although it could and should be used outdoors as well), the reader is referred to individual chapters (especially to Chapter 3 and the section on dramatic play) to see how play activities enhance the various areas of development.

OUTDOOR PLAY

Often teachers use outdoor equipment and space with less planning than for indoor activities. Stationary equipment is always available and may become the only activity on the playground unless some other focal point is provided daily, such as climbing apparatus arranged in a new or stimulating way, sturdy tools for gardening, games, musical activities, stick horses, and wheel toys.

Role of the Teacher

The teacher's role outdoors is similar to that in other areas:

- To provide for the individual child and his needs
- To "pace" the area to be inviting and stimulating
- To set up and maintain necessary limits
- To be flexible in her teaching
- To provide a variety of experiences in the fresh air
- To stimulate and encourage children to explore
- To appreciate the interests and enthusiasm of the children
- To enjoy being with them

Good planning is necessary for maximum utilization of the playground and its equipment. The area can be beautiful yet functional, with space for freedom of movement. Needs of the children can be provided for without a great deal of cost.

The children should play outside independently, but not unsupervised. Equipment and activities should provide opportunities to make decisions, try ideas, work, and play with others without fear of harm or destruction. The focal point should be obvious to the children and should attract them to it, either to use as provided or to stimulate their creativity.

Values for Children

Large-Muscle Development

The young child needs the proper equipment to help him exercise his large muscles. One of the most versatile is a good assortment of sturdy boxes and boards that can be moved easily and arranged in a manner stimulating to the interests and abilities of the children. Equipment constructed to take the abuse of energetic bodies should be colored brightly to attract attention. A board can be used directly on the ground for beginners, then raised to various levels as imaginations and skills dictate. One minute the board may be a road, the next, a bridge to crawl under. Boxes should be large enough for children to climb into, onto, or over. Boards and boxes can be combined into interesting obstacle courses. If funds are limited, large cardboard boxes can be obtained from floral, appliance, furniture, or grocery stores.

A jungle gym or climbing apparatus of some kind should be included in the equipment. One that presents a variety of possibilities for activity is best. Such equipment stimulates imagination and exercises muscles as well.

A paved area should be provided for wheel toys. Tricycles and wagons can be used separately or jointly. Most pedal cars are difficult for preschoolers because the pedals and steering are not coordinated as they are on a tricycle. Some 5-year-olds are ready to ride a two-wheel bike but must constantly be reminded about safety (stopping, running into people and obstacles, going into traffic, and so on).

Swings have little to offer children between ages 2 and 5 (although the adult gets pushing practice). The 2-year-old is not coordinated enough to pump the swing; therefore, he gets no exercise and must depend upon someone to push him. Accidents occur, also, because children walk into the path of the swing, or the swinging child decides to let go. Moreover, swinging takes a child away from group or active play. He has opportunities elsewhere (at home or in a park) for this type of experience. The 5-year-old, however, uses the swing in more advanced ways: pumping while sitting or standing, resting on his stomach, and twisting and turning in more cooperative and creative ways than the younger child.

While large-muscle and cooperative activities are encouraged in young children, competitive games are best avoided, because the young child lacks the physical skills and

Outdoor equipment includes a climbing apparatus. Adult supervision is mandatory.

emotional stability to make such competition a growth-promoting experience. Young children enjoy some appropriate outdoor games but every child should not be required to stay and play for a long period of time.

The following suggestions may be used to enhance large-muscle development:

- A broom handle (or even a string) can be placed between two chairs or posts and the child encouraged to go under or over it at various heights.
- Tires or tubes help children release excess energy. Large truck or airplane tubes are exciting to roll in, climb through, jump on, and bounce on.
- Stick horses provide good exercise at a low price. They can be stored in tall garbage cans when not in use.
- Either blocks built for outdoor use or large barrels add interest to the playground.
- Large wooden or plastic carriers used by milkmen make good stacking and storage units.
- Parachutes (or large sheets) provide fun and muscle practice.
- The play yard can be explored for such treasures as nests, insects, and rocks.

The play yard gives a child an opportunity to explore.

- The bottom and side beneath the handle of a gallon plastic container can be cut out to make a scoop for scoop ball. Partners throw and catch a ball or beanbag.
- A rope can be tied in a high place, such as a tree or frame of a swing. Knots are made at two- or three-foot intervals, so the child can sit on one knot while reaching for the next higher one and pulling himself up. Careful supervision is required.
- A steering wheel attached to a large wooden frame initiates interaction.
- Equipment can be put in different combinations or locations. In warm weather, materials and activities generally used inside can be taken outside.
- Woodworking will be discussed in Chapter 3.

Social Interaction or Dramatic Play

The theme and complexity of play depend on the age of the child. The 2-year-old child plays silently and alone. Variations continue up to the 5-year-old, who chatters incessantly, needs other children, and may initiate and continue elaborate play over a period of time lasting from minutes to days.

Much equipment discussed in this chapter stimulates socialization and group and dramatic play. Children often initiate an unusual use for a piece of equipment. For example, two children were building with large blocks when one discovered that his arrangement looked "like a horse!"

Role playing takes on a new and vigorous light outdoors. The entire playground is the stage. A rowboat, for instance, provides hours of imaginative and cooperative play. It can be brightly painted and strategically placed, with some holes drilled in the bottom to facilitate drainage. Other similar possibilities are an old car frame, a tractor, or a cockpit from Army surplus.

Sensory Experiences

Experiences with water are more fully undertaken outside than is possible inside. When weather permits, water makes an occasion special. Many parents object to their children's playing with water at home; opportunities should be provided at the center. Precautions are taken, of course, to see that children are properly dressed for this activity

On a hot day, the slide can be cooled with water from a hose.

in bathing suits, boots, or cover-ups. Washing doll clothes and hanging them outside is one interesting water experience for children. Another is "painting" with water; still another is sailing boats. Even watering plants is fun. (*See* chapters 3 and 6 related to water experiences.) On a hot day, it is refreshing to let the hose run on the slide, cooling it and adding an extra "zip" as the children slide down. A wading pool filled with water at the end of the slide adds zest to the experience but must be closely supervised. Outside is often the one place that water can be used in the housekeeping area, so free use should be encouraged.

Sand is another item that is better used outdoors. It holds many possibilities, especially with the addition of props such as strainers, spoons, molds, buckets, shovels, cars, and various toys.

Learning About Nature

The landscaping around the playground area can be planned to stimulate children's interest in nature. Shrubs of differing sizes, colors, and characteristics can be planted either in the ground or in large tubs. A large tree for climbing is desirable if available. Check with a gardener or landscape architect to ensure that leaves, berries, shrubs, and other plantings are not poisonous or harmful to children if chewed, eaten, or touched. Planned experiences, such as feeders and animals, and unplanned ones, such as the weather and bugs, add to the environmental learning of the children.

Planning the Area

The playground should provide large areas of space away from equipment. A garden or digging area provides many opportunities for children to use proper tools, to plant, and to harvest. Free-flowing paths are inviting to fast-paced youngsters, too. They resemble curves found on modern highways.

As a result of playing and building outdoors, a child adds to his experiences. Crates and large wooden cartons (pop, beer, milk) are fun to build with, as are old tires, wooden and metal frames, and boards. The weight of the object should challenge but not tax the ability of a child. He will also learn about cooperation, interdependence, balance, size, and gravity. Through use of his body, he will develop skills and dexterity.

The following list contains suggestions for types of areas and items for an outdoor play area.

animals
areas: domestic (Chapter 3), open, private, planning, running
barrels
bedspread over box
blocks (hollow)
boards for crawling, jumping, bouncing
boxes (large packing)
cars (doors removed)
climbers (wood, metal), rings, ropes, poles, platform
clocks
cockpit
easels
fishing net
gardening equipment
gas pump
inner tubes
ladders (horizontal or perpendicular made of rope, wood, or metal)
levers
nets over frames
parachute
playhouse
pulley
pumps (water, tire)
punching bag
radios
ramps
ropes (use with caution)
sand tools
sawhorses
signs (road)
slides
sounds: pleasant, varied
storage
storm drain pipe
surfaces: grass, dirt, asphalt
swing (tire)
tent
terrarium
wheel toys (wagons, tricycles)
water
woodworking equipment

CUMULATIVE LESSON PLAN

Make a small community out of boxes. Add props such as cars, people, and animals.

ESPECIALLY FOR PARENTS

Providing outdoor equipment for children is sometimes costly in terms of money and space. However, an effort should be made to see that your child has daily outdoor experiences that develop large and small muscles, encourage social interaction or dramatic play, provide sensory stimulation, and include learning opportunities. If the equipment

A tree for climbing is desirable to increase strength and coordination in large muscles.

is not available at home, take your child to a park or a playground where he can have these experiences. Outdoor experiences at home are preferable because of the convenience. A child has more opportunities there for spontaneous, sustained play, and you may go about your task with an eye on the activities or even a chance to play at times.

Home equipment can include one or more items from each of the following groups (note that some of the items appropriately fit in more than one category):

For Muscle Development

- boards
- boxes (wood or cardboard)
- climbing equipment (including ladders)
- digging equipment
- pulleys
- ropes
- sand toys
- stick horses
- trees
- tricycles
- wagons
- wheel toys
- woodworking tools

For Social Interaction or Dramatic Play

- creative art materials
- dolls
- dishes
- dress-up clothing (hats, shoes, and other articles)
- open and private areas
- playhouse
- sand toys
- trucks, cars
- trunk or suitcases
- water and toys
- wheel toys

For Sensory Stimulation

- aesthetic design (color, arrangement, variety)
- flowers
- garden plot
- sand
- sounds of nature
- water

Play materials listed earlier in the chapter can also be used at home.

APPLICATION OF PRINCIPLES

1. Role play with a partner: one is a parent, the other a teacher. The parent seriously says, "If I wanted my child to play, I would keep him at home. I sent him to school to *learn*." The teacher is to describe how the play of young children enhances their physical, social, and emotional development.
2. Discuss the values of outdoor play for young children. Should teachers plan outdoor activities or let the children find their own activities? Evaluate both possibilities.
3. Suggest a variety of occupations and activities that could be used in the dramatic play center. What will you need? How could you support these activities with other areas of your curriculum (pictures, songs, stories, field trips, visitors)?
4. At group time, encourage children to act out one of their favorite stories.
5. At the eye level of the children, place pictures of children enacting adult roles (cooking, gardening, other occupations).

References

Barnes, K. "Preschool Play Norms: A Replication." *Developmental Psychology* 5 (1971): 99–103.

Caplan, Frank, and Theresa Caplan. *The Power of Play.* Garden City, N.Y.: Anchor Press, 1973.

Courtney, R. "Education Is Play." *Childhood Education* 49 (1973): 246–250.

Delacato, Carl H. *Treatment and Prevention of Reading Problems.* Springfield, Ill.: Charles C Thomas, 1959.

Elkind, David. "Misunderstandings About How Children Learn." *Today's Education,* March 1972, pp. 125–126.

Feitelson, D., "Developing Imaginative Play in Pre-school Children as a Possible Approach to Fostering Creativity." *Early Childhood Development and Care* 1(1972): 181–195.

Frank, Lawrence K. "Play Is Valid." *Childhood Education* 44(March 1968): 433–440.

Hymes, James L. *Teaching the Child Under Six.* Columbus, Ohio: Charles E. Merrill, 1981.

Lowenfeld, Margaret. *Play in Childhood.* New York: John Wiley, 1967.

Lundsteen, S., and N. Tarrow. *Guiding Young Children's Learning.* New York: McGraw-Hill, 1981.

Piers, Maria W., and Lorraine B. Wallach. "Playways to Learning." *Parents Magazine* 50(June 1975): 23–25, 58.

Read, Katherine. *The Nursery School.* Philadelphia: W. B. Saunders, 1976.

Seefeldt, Carol, ed. *Curriculum for the Preschool-Primary Child: A Review of the Research.* Columbus, Ohio: Charles E. Merrill, 1976.

Singer, Dorothy G., and Jerome L. Singer. *Partners in Play.* New York: Harper & Row, 1977.

Spitz, R. A., and Wolf, K. M. "Anaclitic Depression: An Inquiry Into the Genesis of Psychiatric Conditions in Early Childhood, II." In *The Psychoanalytic Study of the Child,* vol. 2, edited by A. Freud et al. New York: International University Press, 1946, pp. 313–342.

Suzuki, Y. "The Study of Physical Play in Preschool Children: An Analysis of the Characteristics of Child Behavior." *Bulletin of Yamagata University* 5 (1971): 31–48.

Weikart, David, Linda Rogers, Carolyn Adcock, and Donna McClelland. *The Cognitively Oriented Curriculum.* Washington, D.C.: National Association for the Education of Young Children, 1971.

3
Creative, Artistic, and Sensory Expression

Roses are red, violets are blue.
Sugar is sweet—and so are you!

MAIN PRINCIPLES

1. Raw materials and uninterrupted time for artistic expression are valuable in the child's development.
2. The teacher plays an important role in planning and providing art experiences for the young child.
3. Children learn from experiences that allow them to express their ideas and feelings.

Nothing is quite so delightful as seeing a young child wholly absorbed in creative self-expression. He may be creative when he moves to music, engages in dramatic play, exercises large muscles, or prepares food. This chapter is devoted to creative, artistic, and sensory expression. Music and other forms of creativity are covered in later chapters.

Not all children enjoy things that are "messy," but the need for expression is still there. The teacher is responsible for seeing that children have many opportunities for self-expression, that these ways are acceptable in society and meet developmental needs, and that children feel good about them.

VALUES FOR CHILDREN

Sensory experiences are very important to the young child; through these experiences, he learns about his world.

Independence

Keeping materials and supplies where children can get and return them stimulates independence. When interest is high, it should be satisfied. If children feel inclined to

Self-expression through sensory experience teaches a child about the world.

make a picture, play a record, or enter into dramatic play, and if "props" are at their disposal, they make the transition smoothly rather than having to wait for help or for another time.

Through the use of creative materials, children express their individuality and learn social techniques, such as sharing and cooperating.

Ronald, 3 years old, was given several different opportunities at school to finger-paint. He thoroughly enjoyed each experience. The request came from home to "quit finger-painting at school because Ronald finger-paints in everything at home—especially his food at mealtime!" Here was a child who needed more, not fewer, sensory experiences.

Aesthetic Appreciation

By setting a good example, having a wholesome attitude and atmosphere, encouraging the children, and giving them honest praise, adults help them appreciate the beauty surrounding them. If children develop appreciation for aesthetics at a young age, their environment becomes more meaningful. By taking an interest in what children do, adults help them see the unusual in the usual and hear that which they have not heard before. This builds an awareness of the environment.

Teachers who live in a community where paintings can be borrowed from a local source, such as a library or university, should plan often to change the paintings in the classroom. Teachers can teach about famous art work by pointing out the colors, the lines, and the meanings, but this must be done on a level children understand and appreciate.

Be unlike the teacher who thinks all pictures have to be done exactly the same or they won't be displayed.

Satisfaction and Enjoyment

The conversation of young children during creative or dramatic play is enlightening. They should be encouraged to give verbal comments: "It's gushy!" "It holds onto my fingers." "It scratches!" "Look how funny I am in this floppy old hat!"

Adults encourage creativity by showing interest in the child's efforts.

Two essentials for gaining the most value from the use of creative materials are time and space. Time is so important in the lives of young children—even though they seem to waste it at times. They need time to investigate and to live through each experience in their own way. They also need space in which to move; traffic lanes, cramped quarters, or competition with the clock or other experiences discourages children at the outset.

When children know that they can complete an activity without interruption, they are more likely to be interested in it. Analyze this episode: Several children were finger-painting; some entered eagerly into the activity while others watched. Ann debated whether or not to get involved. Some of the children finished and left the table. Ann gingerly put one finger into the mixture. It seemed acceptable; she put her finger in again and quietly pondered. She was about to involve herself when the teacher came with a sponge and told her they were through for the day. She rushed Ann away from the table and finished cleaning it herself. Wouldn't it have been better for Ann if she had been allowed to stay longer, or if she had been encouraged to help in cleaning the table?

Creative expression can help children realize that they are worthwhile people, have good ideas, and can do things in different ways. Adults stifle creativity in young children through remarks such as: "What is that?" "Nobody draws like that." "You're doing it the wrong way." Adults encourage creativity when they take pride in what the child does. "The colors are beautiful!" "This part is especially nice—the lines go around and around."

Betty carefully guarded her finger painting as she tenderly carried it to the car. A few moments later an angry young uncle stormed into the classroom with the painting and shouted, "If you think you're going to put that junk in my car and mess up the upholstery, you're sadly mistaken!" Betty ran after him with tears in her eyes but made no comment; she was heartbroken. One wonders how long it was before she tried finger painting again.

David sat quietly waiting for his father. As his father appeared, David proudly displayed his picture. The father studied the picture appreciatively, nodded his head, and smiled. After a short pause, the child looked at his father and asked, "Well, what is it, Dad?" as if the father saw much more in the painting than the child did. The father pointed out several appealing parts of the picture. Think how much more David was encouraged to pursue creative activities than was Betty.

Emotional Release

Artistic expression can be a means of soothing feelings; sliding hands through slippery finger paint, boldly pounding clay from one form to another, or building in the block area can be relaxing to most young children. Beating a drum, playing a role in the domestic area, or moving to music are also creative ways for children to relieve pressures.

John was especially aggressive one day. He had had several distressing incidents. He got a stick horse and galloped around and around the play yard. When he returned, he said, "I feel better now. Let's go read a story." Russ had been frightened by a dog on his way to school. At the finger painting table, he made a resemblance of the dog and then quickly rubbed it out with the remark, "He can't bark at me now." Susan picked up a doll and rocked it, saying, "You'll feel better if I sing to you and hold you close." She had experienced these same feelings when an understanding adult had come to her rescue.

Good Work Habits

Even work habits involve creative expression. Wiping up finger paint made from soap flakes adds a new and exciting dimension. Lisa felt that staying clean was important. She would stand near the creative tables and watch the children as they enjoyed using the materials. She automatically wiped her already clean hands on her clothes. Whenever cleanup was initiated, she was the first to get a sponge. To her, it was unacceptable to get dirty but it was very acceptable to clean up. This was her introduction to creative materials.

Children enjoy participating, and valuable learning experiences can be gained from doing so. They need to be involved in the whole cycle of an activity. They should be encouraged to mix, to use, to clean up, and to prepare materials for storage. This may take longer, but the satisfaction is priceless. Children develop good work habits if they get the right cues from adults.

An art experience should not be confused with an exercise in following directions. The art experience allows children the freedom of creating. If you want to know if children can follow directions, then tell them to color the ball red and the pumpkin orange.

Recall the importance of good work habits in helping young children learn. Also recall how the behavior of the teacher helps children establish good patterns.

Muscle Development

Through self-expression, children can develop gross and fine muscles. The large ones are exercised through such activities as woodworking, movement to music, and active play. Small-muscle activities include cutting and pasting, working with collage, coloring with large crayons or chalk, drawing, making puzzles, or manipulating other table toys, such as pegboards or small blocks. For young children, activities that encourage use of large (gross) muscles should predominate over those that encourage use of small (fine)

Dexterity and eye-hand coordination require use of small muscles.

muscles. Some children enjoy using their small muscles; these activities are provided for dexterity and eye-hand coordination, but young children should not be required to stay with this type of activity for any length of time.

Exploration

Through the use of raw materials, children often learn to think for themselves. Those who wait for other children or adults to tell them what to do or when to do it profit from experiences with such materials, which can be used in many creative ways. Use of the material is more important than the finished product. The creation of the very young child changes name and focus as the materials are used. A 5-year-old may decide in advance what his creation will be and then set out to accomplish it, but one should not be surprised or disappointed if it, too, changes from the original plan.

Children enjoy repetition of materials and activities—not to limit their experiences, but as opportunities to further explore, manipulate, and exercise their imaginations and initiative. When new ideas or materials are introduced to children, plans for repeated use should be included. One exposure is not enough.

Some children may want to watch an activity before entering into it. Watching is also a way a child learns. Adults must feel comfortable in recognizing that some children join an activity readily while others need to watch first. Some children need help in discarding erroneous concepts about their abilities.

A recent study indicated that creativity increases in preschool children until the age of 5, when a sharp decrease begins. Contributing to this decrease are parental influence, need for conformity, patterning, adherence to unrealistic standards, peer pressure, and commercial materials. Television also plays a role in shaping the child's image of reality and interferes with his creativity (Gotz 1978).

Divergent thinking should be encouraged in children. They should be helped to discover different ways to use or assemble different objects. They will have many times when thinking is directed (convergent), so they need opportunities to exercise their brains in divergent ways.

When children feel free to explore, they find many creative uses for "junk" or other items found in the environment. Many are discarded items, such as cardboard, candy papers, containers, eggshells, labels, string, and tickets. You be the supplier; let the child be the designer and builder.

ROLE OF THE TEACHER

Attitude

A teacher should have a wholesome, accepting attitude toward the use of creative and artistic materials. If she has the attitude that using art materials is a waste of time or messy, the children adopt the same philosophy.

In one center, a substitute teacher went to assist. As creative materials were being prepared for the day, she asked: "Why not use this bucket of earth clay, which is already prepared?" Several teachers agreed with the one who replied, "Our children don't like clay." The substitute persisted, volunteering to supervise, and the teachers agreed. As the children entered the center, they drifted to the clay table. There the substitute teacher was rolling and pounding the clay and remarking that it was cool, soft, and so forth. Many of the children sat down at the clay table and remained for a long period of time. Others stayed a short time, but during the period all of the children had been to the clay table. The conversation was delightful. At the end of the day, the teachers remarked, "We don't understand why the children went to the clay table. They haven't liked it before." The magical thing that drew the children was the attitude of the substitute

Children and teachers combine conversation and creativity.

teacher. The children felt her enjoyment and enthusiasm and wanted to share these feelings with her. At evaluation, the other teachers confessed that none of them enjoyed the messiness or the feel of clay. No wonder the children "didn't like it." Even though they had not expressed their dislike verbally to the children, the teachers had convinced them that something was wrong with the experience.

Proper Materials

Materials should be appropriate to the developmental level of the children. Large sheets of paper, large brushes, and jumbo crayons are easiest for children to use. Children enjoy making large, free-arm movements as they develop eye-hand coordination and show interest in the various uses of materials.

Covering the table with newspaper or plastic before an activity begins is a great aid at cleanup time. Simply roll up the paper containing the excess paint, clay, paste, or other spilled materials and place the roll in the waste container. A sponge quickly and easily cleans plastic; an old shower curtain or canvas under creative materials is also a time and energy saver.

Materials should help to release feelings, not create frustrations. At one center, several children were enjoying pegs and boards. Guido was not as adept as the others and soon became discouraged. Then he became frustrated and pushed the pegs and boards onto the floor. Painting at the easel or playing in the block area would have better met his needs.

One windy day, Suheil wanted to make a kite. He went to the shelf, got paper and yarn, then joined a teacher at the woodworking table. He carefully measured and hammered until he was satisfied. He then covered the frame with paper and tied on the yarn. Richard, age 3, had watched Suheil's actions and tried to follow Suheil's procedure—first paper and yarn and then a trip to the woodworking table. Richard was not successful with the hammer, so he picked up a screwdriver and tried to push the small nails into the wood. When that failed, he tried to wrap the paper around the stick, again without

Proper materials are essential for creative expression. Large brushes are easiest for children to use when painting.

success. He got a pair of scissors and tried to cut the paper into a smaller piece. The scissors did not work, so he tore the paper into small pieces and threw them on the floor. Totally disgusted, he grabbed Suheil's kite and ran outside with it, Suheil running closely behind him. Obviously, Suheil had more experience and skills than Richard. Making the kite was a satisfying experience for Suheil but quite the opposite for Richard. Often young children *want* to do things; they have the ideas but not the abilities. Suheil used proper materials and tools for his ideas and abilities. Richard thought he could also make a kite but was limited in his physical and mental capacities. He would have been more satisfied playing in the block area or painting at the easel where less precision is required. A perceptive teacher could have helped him avoid discouragement and frustration.

Placement of Materials

The placement of equipment for self-expression is most important. Messy materials should be near a water supply, in a well-lighted area out of the traffic pattern. Interruption by others passing by is discouraging to a child.

Materials placed on low shelves or cupboards are readily accessible and assist children to be independent. Seeing materials often encourages their use. Of course, dangerous materials or activities require close teacher supervision.

The children should be allowed to help prepare the materials as much as possible. Children can easily make earth clay, dough clay, paint, and other media, and they should

Some activities should be near a water supply and out of the traffic pattern.

be expected to help clean up. Swishing a sponge around on a tabletop, a plastic cover, or a tray is fun.

Because most children like to take their creations home, a place should be provided where art work can dry. If space is limited, a portable rack can be used and then folded out of the way. Some art work can remain at the center overnight to dry; however, children do like to take it home the day they make it, if possible.

Concern for the Individual

Each child comes from a different background with various experiences. He should be met at his level and helped to increase his experiences with the materials. He may be hearing double messages—one at home and one at the center. For example:

Finger painting is done with pudding at the center one day. When the child has pudding served at home, he remembers how much fun it was to put his hands in it, so he proceeds to do so. The parent becomes very upset and gives the child a lecture about eating with utensils (not fingers) and not wasting his food. The next time pudding finger paint is provided at the center, the child refuses to participate for fear he will receive the lecture again. The teacher finally discovers the problem. She explains to the child that sometimes things are done differently at home than at the center; a child can understand this idea. This time the pudding will be used for an art activity and it will be all right to feel it and be "messy." Another day the pudding will be a snack (the teacher should follow through with this very soon). The teacher also should take the initiative to explain the reasoning to the parent, who may still feel that food is for eating, but can be a little more tolerant of the teacher's view.

As children express themselves with creative materials, the teacher encourages discussion of their work by such honest statements as, "That's my favorite color you're using," or "This is an interesting design." But she should comment with the children in mind, not with her own need to be busy or feel important. From conversation, the teacher can gain insight into the children's ideas and feelings, as well as sustain them in activities.

The teacher should empathize on the child's level. Judging a child's work by adult standards tends to make one critical. The child needs understanding and encouragement.

Enriching Materials

When young children draw, they sometimes eliminate an important part of the picture. They draw things as they appear to them. When a child's firsthand experiences have been limited, some things have greater importance than others. In order to clarify misconceptions or omissions, the wise teacher provides stimulating props and ideas. For instance, if a rabbit with huge ears, a small body, and no legs appears in a child's drawing, the teacher appropriately brings a rabbit into the center and lets the children see it and learn about it firsthand. Maybe one child only recalls seeing a rabbit with its legs tucked up under its body, which may explain why his drawing looks as it does. Maybe he was impressed with the size and shape of the rabbit's ears and has not given any thought to the rest of the rabbit's body. Or, maybe a rabbit scratched him, and he wants to make sure it does not happen again, so he hides the paws.

Teachers often are too limited in their art activities. Even though children like some repetition, the same experiences day after day tend to discourage participation. On the other hand, using some experiences two or three days in a row may encourage their use.

Goals and Objectives

Creative experiences must be well planned and executed. Using an activity to consume a block of time is unacceptable. Goals and objectives should be clearly defined and within reach of the children. Providing teacher-centered materials for children detracts from the experience and may even discourage further participation.

Besides other reasons, a creative art period can be provided just for fun. Activities do not always have to promote the objectives of the day.

Availability

Even when she does not actively participate, a teacher lends support to activities by her presence. If given the opportunity, most children solve their problems without adult interference.

When possible, more than one art activity should be provided so that the children can have a choice. Some children enjoy some experiences more than others, while some go to as many activities as are provided. Some activities should be planned that encourage independence.

Limits

Limits must be clearly defined and consistently maintained. Each head teacher may designate different limits; so all teachers must become aware of the limits of their individual group. One teacher may confine finger painting to paper while another one may permit finger painting on tabletops or the glass in windows or sliding doors.

Children look to adults for guidelines; when guidelines are unclear or lacking, the children become confused. At a table the children were rolling and pounding clay; that became boring quite soon. A teacher sat by the children but did not converse much with them. The boredom grew. Soon one child put some clay on the teacher's hand. No response was forthcoming, so he continued pressing pieces of clay up her arm. Still no response. Other children started doing the same thing. Next, the clay went on her face and finally in her hair. The teacher sat motionless but petrified! The lead teacher noticed what was happening and moved to the clay table. She talked with the children about keeping the clay on the table. Later, in privacy, the lead teacher asked the other teacher how the situation had evolved and how she felt about it. The reply was, "I didn't know what to do. I didn't like the clay put on me, but I just didn't know what to do, so I didn't do anything! What can I do if the same thing happens again?" An interesting discussion followed about setting and maintaining limits for the children.

Concern for Process or Product?

In our complex society, it is possible to become too product- and time-conscious. Too often parents are heard outwardly encouraging their children to "make something" to account for at least part of their time.

One child received daily urgings from her mother to make something while at the center. This weighed heavily upon the child's mind. Upon entering school one morning, she walked directly to the easel, grabbed a brush, dipped it in red paint, and made two large lines across the paper. As she left the easel, she was heard to say, "There, I've made a picture for Mother and now I can do what I want!"

One center was having difficulty with some product-minded parents. The parents were pressuring the children—and the center—into making something to take home each day. The teacher recognized that the children were not enjoying the materials as much as previously. She therefore arranged for the children to finger-paint directly on the plastic tabletops. On another day, a large piece of butcher paper was placed on the floor, and the children made a group mural. (What conversation and cooperation!) When it came time to go home, the children had no products. Explaining the rationale to the parents helped them understand about pressuring their children. Shortly thereafter, the children again enjoyed the materials without feeling they had to "make something."

Patterns, Stereotyped Cutouts, Coloring Books

Patterning of any kind should be eliminated from art experiences for young children. It stifles rather than encourages creativity. Children draw things as they see them. Lines made by others are meaningless, and young children have difficulty staying inside lines created by someone else.

Coloring books stifle creativity in young children, cause frustration again because of need to stay in lines, discourage drawing because the child cannot draw as well as the model, require muscle skills which most young children do not have, and are often limited in size. Adults should never use coloring books or predrawn figures with young children and call them "art" projects. Coloring books may provide teachers with good sources for visual aids, however.

One mother was called to a conference with a kindergarten teacher because her child "refused to color anything" given to him by the teacher. Everything provided was stereotyped and provided no interest for the child, who had always been encouraged at home to draw his own pictures.

Some adults entertain children by drawing for them. Then when the child draws, he becomes easily frustrated because his pictures do not have the realism of the adult "artist." He refuses to attempt drawing because he compares his work to that of the adult.

Summary of the Teacher's Role

As stated by Hoover in *Art Activities for the Very Young:* "Our object is providing experiences which will expand their horizons of understanding and manipulative skills. But, most important of all, we are developing the creative potential which we know exists within each one of our children." (P. 88)

The teacher is responsible for providing materials, attitudes, and an atmosphere conducive to self-expression. Benefits from such expression are endless.

For an easy and quick overview of the activities presented in this chapter and their values to the children, see the chart on page 56.

VALUES OF SPECIFIC ACTIVITIES FOR PRESCHOOLERS

Key: ● Best ■ Average ▲ Least

ACTIVITIES \ VALUES	SENSORY EXPERIENCE	EXPLORATION	SATISFACTION & ENJOYMENT	SELF-EXPRESSION	MANIPULATION	EMOTIONAL RELEASE	EXERCISE IMAGINATION & INITIATIVE	GOOD WORK HABITS	LEARNING EXPERIENCE	SKILL & CONCENTRATION	EYE-HAND COORDINATION	HARMONY, RHYTHM & BALANCE	INSIGHT INTO OWN FEELINGS	DEVELOPS LARGE MUSCLES	DEVELOPS SMALL MUSCLES
BLOCKS Large	▲	●	●	■	■	●	▲	▲	▲	■	■	●	●	●	▲
Small	■	●	■	■	■	▲	▲	▲	■	■	●	■	■	▲	●
CHALK	▲	▲	▲	▲	▲	▲	▲	■	▲	▲	■	▲	▲	▲	■
CLAY	●	●	■	●	●	●	●	●	■	■	■	▲	●	●	■
COLLAGE	●	●	●	●	●	●	●	●	■	■	■	▲	■	▲	●
CRAYONS	▲	▲	▲	▲	▲	▲	▲	■	▲	▲	■	▲	▲	▲	■
CUTTING & PASTING	■	■	■	■	■	■	■	●	■	●	●	▲	▲	▲	●
DOMESTIC AREA	■	●	●	●	■	●	●	●	●	■	■	▲	●	■	■
PAINTING Easel	■	●	■	■	●	■	■	●	■	■	■	▲	■	●	■
Finger	●	■	●	●	■	●	■	●	■	▲	■	▲	●	■	■
Sponge or block	■	●	■	■	●	■	■	●	■	■	■	▲	■	■	●
Miscellaneous	■	■	■	■	■	■	■	●	■	■	■	▲	■	■	■
SAND	●	■	■	●	●	■	●	●	●	■	■	▲	■	●	■
STRINGING	▲	▲	■	▲	■	▲	■	■	▲	●	●	■	▲	▲	●
WATER	●	●	●	●	●	●	●	●	●	■	●	■	●	●	●
WOOD-WORKING	●	●	●	●	●	●	●	●	●	●	●	■	●	●	■

SUGGESTED EXPERIENCES

Blocks

Blocks are important in the education of young children both at home and at school.

Types and Use

Blocks are of many different kinds: large and hollow with handle openings, solid, unit, dimensionally proportioned, plastic, cardboard, vinyl, or fabric. Some are intended for use on the floor, others for use on tables. They are made in different sizes, shapes, and colors. Children enjoy putting blocks together to make new shapes or color combina-

Some blocks are hollow with openings for easy handling.

tions. Dramatic play is often enhanced with the addition of "props" to blocks. Two areas in the center may be joined together with the use of blocks (blocks and trucks, blocks used to enclose a reading area, and so on).

Good planning should go into the purchase of blocks. Green and Woods, (1963), in *A Nursery School Handbook,* tell us: "All blocks should be designed to fit together mathematically, each size twice as long or wide as the preceding size. Not only will they serve better purposes in building, but they will stack compactly when not in use. All types of blocks should be either shellacked or waxed. This finish will be more practical than paint."

A teacher was anxious to promote block play with a group of 4-year-old children. The space in the room was limited, so she moved out part of the furniture and the domestic equipment. The first day after the equipment was gone, the children all asked, "Who took our stove?" "Where did the refrigerator go?" They wandered around aimlessly. The second day, they noticed a stack of large blocks in the corner and began using the blocks in their play. By the end of the week, they had experienced many joys from using these blocks. They worked cooperatively and came up with some rather ingenious ideas—including making furniture. The use of blocks was no longer a problem.

Role of the Teacher

Physical arrangements. Plenty of space and uninterrupted time are necessary for good block play. As in the above example, equipment can be moved to another area or room if necessary to provide sufficient floor space. Because of the noise they create, blocks are used on a rug or carpet if at all possible. This protects the blocks from damage when they tumble down and keeps the children's knees from a cold or hard surface.

Blocks should be out of the traffic pattern. For several days, two children had tried to build a block fence to house some new farm animals. Every time they got ready to play with their creation, someone either knocked it down or they had to pick it up. This day they were determined to have success. Quickly they gathered up the needed blocks and animals. They selected a different spot and set out to build. Soon one child after another rushed past and down went the blocks. In total disgust, they complained to the next child, who replied, "I didn't mean to—but I just had to get in to the toilet." The children had selected the most vulnerable spot in the room—right in front of the bathroom door!

A unit of time should be allotted to utilize a completed structure. At one center, day after day the children played that they were going to Africa to catch zoo animals. One child had recently been to a nearby zoo and had shared his ideas. Seeing how sustained the play was, the teacher began the basic structure so the children could finish it and get on with their trip to Africa. Otherwise, they never would have been able to play—they would always be building!

The teacher should be conscious of the time and warn the children in advance to end the activity at the appropriate time. Sometimes good constructive play can be continued and some other activity shortened or eliminated. Simply saying "It's almost time to pick up the blocks" or "It will soon be time for snack" gives the children an opportunity to prepare to end the activity. If possible, the structure is left up for later play.

Supervision. The teacher should indicate to the children what the guidelines are for the block area. She should be nearby, but need not actively participate. Her verbal support is often enough to sustain activity in this area.

When structures get too tall or wobbly, a positive suggestion redirects the activity. Statements such as "Build as high as your nose" or "It's time to start another stack" are usually readily accepted by the children. Safety is important. The teacher should show appreciation for a structure but avoid overemphasis, never giving the children the idea that they must make certain structures in order to gain approval.

To interest children in the block area, a teacher may have to provide a "pace-setter,"

Children experience many joys from using blocks. The activity should be given plenty of time and space.

that is, an eye-catcher or attention getter. It should not be elaborate—just attract the children. One day it may be a tall or complex structure; another day a farm or single block road leading to transportation vehicles.

As noted previously, children should be involved in cleanup. If shelves are low, near the building area, and have predrawn shapes, the children generally are willing to help put the blocks away. A teacher might say, "You pick up that size and I'll pick up this size," which gets the cleanup underway. The block area is watched carefully, and as interest begins to decrease or the children start being destructive, the teacher immediately steps in and helps the children decide whether they want to continue to play constructively, or if it is time to put the blocks away. To bring a child back from another area to help pick up blocks is not the most effective idea. When children take many blocks off the shelf at one time, the task of replacing them looks insurmountable. Here the teacher uses her initiative and wisdom in directing the children.

Clay

Use of Material

Clay is a medium ruling out failure. A child expresses his own idea through rolling, pounding, pinching, or however he desires. He can either retain or destroy his creation. The experience can be solitary or social.

Earth clay must be prepared in advance of its use, and children delight in helping. Some teachers feel that a center cannot be successfully operated without a large bucket of earth clay readily available for experimentation and release of feelings.

Earth clay is most effective when the children use their hands freely. Cookie cutters, rollers, and other objects detract from the sensory experience.

With dough-clay, however, the child may use cookie cutters and rollers for a more realistic experience; the medium closely resembles cookie dough. Dough is not used as a substitute for clay, but as an additional material. It provides sensory and manipulative experience but does not stimulate the same kind of creativity as clay.

Role of the Teacher

The teacher should refrain from patterning for the children; she can manipulate the materials, encourage conversation, and give support, but her role should be minor. She should listen for enlightening and interesting conversation about the way the children think.

To stimulate the interests of the children in the clay area, one teacher discussed building a bird's nest and then helped the children gather leaves, twigs, string, and other materials. They took these materials to the clay table and there learned a great deal by making nests. (The clay will not be reusable because of the added materials.)

Limits should be explained to and understood by the children. If each child is to

Cookie cutters are used with dough-clay for a realistic experience.

clean up his own space when he is finished, he should be told in advance. "Here's a sponge to wipe up where you have been working." Also let the children know if the product is to be saved or if all the clay will be placed back in the container for another time.

Clay can be inexpensive and last a long time if stored properly. Earth clay should be stored in a covered earthen jar or metal container. It can be molded into a large ball and covered with damp towels or cloths if it is to be used again soon. For longer storage, impressions made with the thumb are filled with water. Too much water causes the clay to become moldy. Dough clay should be stored in air tight containers.

For recipes for different kinds of clay, see Appendix D.

Collage

Webster's New World Dictionary defines collage as "a kind of surrealist art in which bits of flat objects, as newspaper, cloth, pressed flowers . . . . are pasted together in incongruous relationship for their symbolic or suggestive effect." Collages stimulate the imagination of children and increase their interest in the feel of different textures and combinations.

Gigi, age 4, exercised her ingenuity with materials provided. She used straws for arms and legs, a sponge for a head, heavy twine for hair, different fabrics for a blouse and skirt, and small pieces of foam for shoes. Such imagination!

A variety of materials and plenty of time are needed for collage.

Role of the Teacher

The teacher's role for this activity is similar to previous ones. She provides a number of different things, which the children use as their imaginations dictate. The number of different materials supplied at one time depends upon the ages and development of the children involved. Young children adequately handle three or four materials, while older children delight in a larger selection. The children also need access to scissors, paste, something to paste on, and plenty of time.

Suggested Teaching Aids

Building Materials
Cellotex
bark
fiberboard
foam insulation
gravel
linoleum
Popsicle sticks
rocks
sand
sandpaper
sawdust, shavings
screening
tongue depressors
washers
wire
wood

Fabrics
burlap
carpet
chiffon
corduroy
cotton
denim
felt
fur
interfacing
knits
leather
muslin
net
satin
silk
taffeta
velvet
wool
yarn

Food Products
beans
cereals
corn (dry, popped, or unpopped)
eggshells
macaroni
rice
rigatoni
salt (colored)
seeds
shellroni
spaghetti

Paper and Paper Substitutes
aluminum foil
blotters
boxes (small)
cardboard
  boxes
  corrugated
  food box
  shirt form
catalogs
cellophane
confetti
construction
crepe
cups (candy)
doilies
egg cartons
gift cards
greeting cards
gummed labels
magazines
newspapers
plates
reinforcements
stamps
straws
tape
tissue
towels
tubes
wallpaper
waxed

Plastic
doilies
egg cartons
flowers
foam
food containers
hair rollers
straws
Styrofoam
toothpicks

Sewing
beads
buttons
elastic
lace
ribbon
rickrack
sequins
spools
string
tape
yarn

Miscellaneous
acorns
bottle caps
brads
cans
clothespins
corks
cotton balls
excelsior
feathers
flowers (dried or fresh)
glitter
hairpins
jars, lids, rings
jewelry
keys
leaves
net sacks
packing material
paper clips
pipe cleaners
Q-tips
shells
shoelaces
sponges
twigs, sticks
weeds
wrappers (gum, candy)

Teaching Suggestions

Some individuals strongly object to the use of food as creative material, in some cases because food is being "wasted." Others think this use extends the child's imagination and exploratory ability. Individual teachers need to decide if and how they will use food in teaching.

Junk can be made into beautiful pictures. Lots of boxes, tubes, and materials of all kinds and sizes should be on hand. Appropriate cutting tools are needed as are good strong ways to attach objects (glue, staples, and other materials). Color and embellish the product. Through this kind of creative play, children learn skills, dexterity, scale, and balance. The intellect is stimulated to decide what items to use, where to place them, and how to attach them. The following procedures are suggested:

- Place materials between two sheets of waxed paper and then press with a warm iron to seal the design (especially good for crayon shavings and leaves).
- Paste materials on cloth or wallpaper instead of paper for a different experience.
- Apply colored tissue paper (with liquid starch as the adhesive) on nonwaxed paper plates for an interesting experience involving color.
- Using heavy paper and strong glue, let children make a collage with noodles, corn flakes, and similar materials.
- Glue small boxes (match, food, or other) together for an interesting design.
- Take small pieces of wood and let the children arrange and paste them onto another piece of wood or cardboard.
- Cut pictures out of magazines and let the children paste them on a sheet of paper. Encourage the children to do their own cutting when possible. You might have pictures for the children to arrange in groups (food, color, things to wear).

Cutting and Pasting

Cutting is difficult for many young children; however, if they are provided with good scissors, they learn to use and enjoy them. Make sure the blades cut, are free from paste or other materials, and are the appropriate size for small hands and fingers. Every center should have some left-handed scissors, which are available from a number of sources. Manufacturers are also producing plastic scissors with inserted metal blades, handles with four holes for adult assistance, and scissors with a spring action. Try a number of kinds to see what features best meet the needs of your children: left- or right-handed, sharp or dull tips, metal or plastic blades, serrated or smooth blades.

Most 3-year-olds are unable to use scissors; some 4-year-olds can use them in rather immature ways; most 5-year-olds are able to follow lines and cut. Once Stephen, age 3, learned to cut, that was all he wanted to do. He was proud of the sack of scraps he had cut. While still difficult for him to accurately follow lines, especially the curvy ones, he loved his own scissors and had some magazines that were just his own, but he could not cut up Mom's magazines, fabrics, books, or the evening paper.

The following activities are suggested:

- Color dry salt with powdered tempera. Brush paste on paper; then sprinkle salt over the paste. A salt shaker makes a good container.
- Take a black sheet of construction paper and cut holes in various sizes, shapes, and places. Paste tissue over the holes to make "stained glass windows."
- Get fabric samples from a decorator or use remnants. Paste objects on them to make beautiful wall hangings.
- Cut designs from paper or fabric. Paste on cans or jars for nice gifts.
- Tear or cut strips from magazines. Have children paste them in interesting designs.
- Fold paper. Cut or tear designs in it.
- Make a mural of the community, having children make and cut shapes for their homes, churches, and other important landmarks.

- Provide scraps of paper and paper bags. Children can make paper bag puppets or masks.
- Paste objects on paper plates.
- Use materials such as those listed for collage.
- Paste colored paper or magazine pictures on tubes, rollers, or boxes.
- Cut pictures from magazines and have the children make their family (determine how many children they need, what sizes, what color of hair, and so on).
- Have the children paste shapes, ribbons, or floral tape into a plastic meat tray. They can also paste textures in the bottom (straw for a cow, fabric for a cat, leaves for a bird) and then paste on a picture of an animal who would live there.
- Decorate large (gallon) plastic jugs with paper, fabric, or marking pens.
- Paste single color objects on same color paper (for snow pictures use white paper, wadded white tissue, felt, Styrofoam, popcorn, doilies, cotton balls, salt, and so on).
- Drip glue on dark paper. Sprinkle on salt or glitter.
- Draw a large body on a large brown bag and let the child use his imagination to decorate it (for a gingerbread boy, provide such items as rickrack and fabric scraps).

Dramatic Play

At the Valley View Center, the teachers wondered how to stimulate interest in the neglected dramatic play area. To get into the refrigerator, the children had to lean over the table. Guests had to stand. The dolls were stacked in the cradle as if it were a storage bin. The cooking and eating utensils were mismatched, cracked, and wrinkled. At a serious glance, the teachers decided the activity lacked space and interest. Much needed were some attractive dress-up articles for both sex roles, reduction in the number of dolls, new dishes and utensils, and more space! When these changes were made and a colorful tablecloth was added, this became the most popular area!

Values for Children

Children often reenact what they see or hear at home. To them, this reenactment is realistic living, not dramatic play, and helps them understand the adult world. Anything is possible; a child can be the mother, father, baby, street sweeper, engineer, doctor, or whatever he likes. Roles may even change rapidly. Such play should be encouraged. Studies have indicated that playful children are more advanced in their ability to think divergently than their nonplayful counterparts (Lieberman 1965).

Most young children enjoy this area of expression. When interest begins to dwindle, a few props may be added, such as food boxes, dress-up clothes, or career equipment. A store can be built with blocks, boxes, and boards, or the area can be transformed to represent the locale of different occupations in the community (gas station, hair salon, library, and so on).

Water in this area has a magical attraction, but limits must be set as to where the water can be obtained and used.

Role of the Teacher

"Teacher, please tie this scarf around my head so I can have long, flowing hair, and put on the record of the soft, slow music so I can be Sleeping Beauty." This was the request of Martha, a 5-year-old. She had imagination and motivation but needed the teacher's help with props. Other children joined her, but lacked her vision and expression.

Dramatic play occurs in any area: domestic, block, sand, art, snack, language arts, or anywhere children are. Either teachers or children can be the initiators, but the actual activity should be child-centered. A story may trigger an activity, or the teacher can initiate dramatization of a story the children have just heard. A field trip is reinforced by dramatizing it upon return.

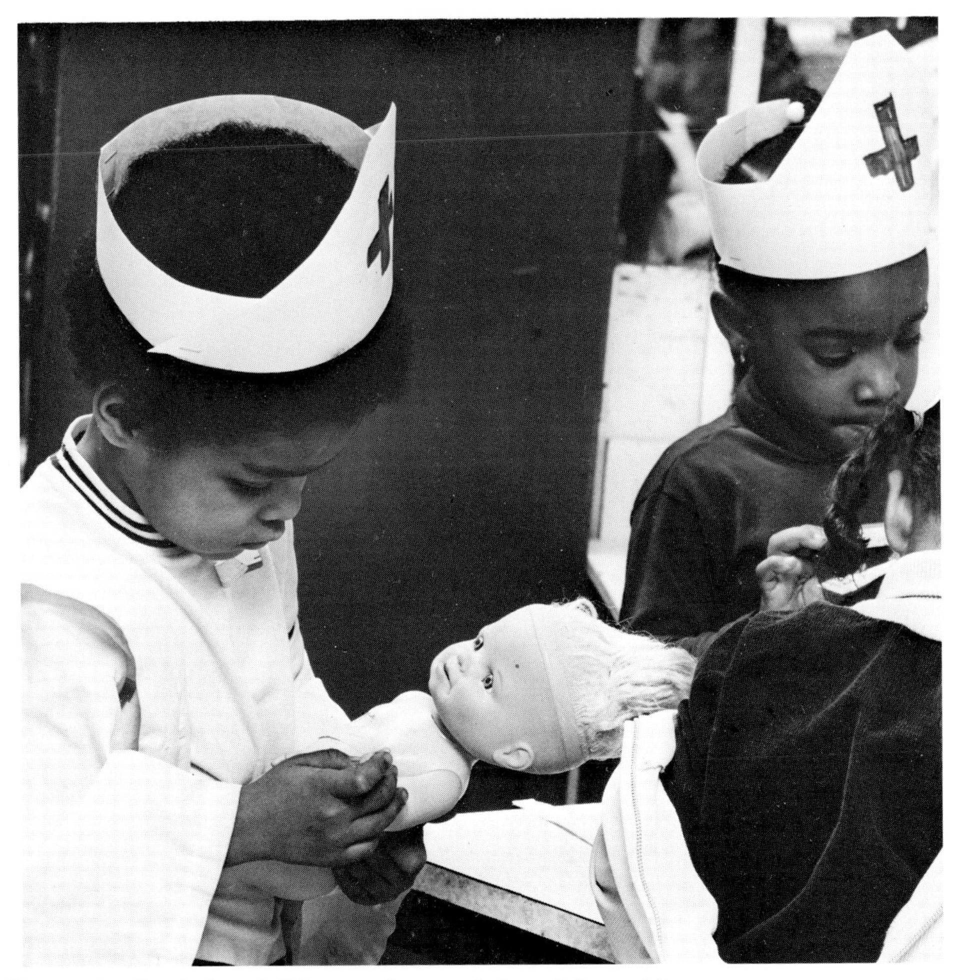

Dramatic play helps children understand the adult world.

How the teacher feels and prepares for dramatic play is very important in encouraging or discouraging participation. Children are usually anxious for such experiences. Still they want and like the approval of the teacher, which can be shown by her actions, such as providing two or more similar toys for cooperative play or by rearranging the equipment.

Children sometimes dramatize unfamiliar, fearful, or familiar themes. Simon and Ann were playing in the domestic area. Ann handed a block (representing his lunch bucket) to Simon and told him to go to work. He did so. Shortly she called to him and told him it was time to come home. Dutifully he returned only to have her throw her arms around him and say, "Oh, darling, I'm so glad you're home." Startled, Simon dropped the block and said, "Let me out of here!" With that, he ran to another area. This may have been a familiar scene to Ann, but it was foreign to Simon.

Appropriate pictures placed in the domestic area add the stimulation some children need, but positioning a mirror so the child actually sees his participation, not just think it, is magnetic. Listening to what transpires is refreshing and revealing. In a wholesome atmosphere, the children fully enjoy dramatic play.

On occasion something can be made to encourage later dramatic play. For example, airplanes can be fashioned at the woodworking table for use after a trip to the airport; musical instruments can be made and used at music time. A discarded box from a new appliance can be sawed, painted, and decorated to become a house, store, bus, airplane, or whatever the children imagine.

Dramatic play adds new life to the children and to the program. With appropriate props, the children can dramatize home life, camping, vacations, and visits. They also should try occupational settings such as bakery, airline, barber shop, beauty salon, medical office or hospital, construction site, school, library, pet store, restaurant, or gas station. They can be vehicle drivers, garbage collectors, bankers, firemen, dancers, members of an orchestra, and many more.

Teaching Suggestions

- Add variety to the dramatic play area by using only part of the equipment at a time, by rearranging the equipment, or adding something special.
- Provide the following items:
  - Stove, refrigerator, cupboard (either purchased, homemade, or constructed from boards, boxes, or blocks), ironing board, and iron
  - Dolls, doll clothes, crib, buggy, bed, high chair
  - Dishes, pots and pans, silverware, measuring cups and spoons

Dress-ups are used for imaginative play.

- Dress-up clothing (masculine, feminine, occupational) such as hats, scarves, gloves, purses, wallets, ties, vests, belts, bandanas, shoes of all varieties, large pieces of colored fabric, ribbons, lace, girdles, jewelry, eyeglass frames, rubber boots, jackets, caps
- Special props such as doctor's and nurse's bags, stethoscopes, firemen equipment, Indian jewelry and headdresses, suitcases, trunks
- For water opportunities: dishes, cleaning materials, clothes for washing, pouring and measuring utensils, a large tub, buckets, porous and nonporous materials, sponges
- Cans, cartons, plastic bottles
- Foodstuffs (occasionally)
- Mirrors
- Telephones

- Cover an easel with flannel or felt and provide fabric of different colors, shapes, or figures for exploration and dramatic play.
- Provide a magnetic board with magnetic objects or a flannel board with story characters.
- Occasionally in this area prepare food for lunch or snack.
- Put emphasis on self-discovery. Include both imaginative play with dress-ups and props and real experiences. Visit a hospital and have followup play at school so that the children are no longer afraid of the equipment or experience. Have a mother bathe her baby or the children wash dolls—a change from being on the receiving end of the experience. Have wash day—with real materials and tasks.
- Provide two or more of the same object (telephone, doll, trunk, tricycle) to encourage interaction.
- Cover the jungle gym or other structure for privacy. Include a flashlight.
- Move the equipment or activity outside.
- Put real flowers on the table.
- Make a portable tent.
- Use participation records (Chapter 5).
- Show pictures and have the children dramatize the situation.
- Have children dramatize a situation and have the other children try to guess what they are doing.

Drawing

Young children spend a lot of time drawing. Whether this is the best experience for them is debatable. Art development has stages, and scribbling is an important beginning. Until children develop eye-hand coordination, muscle control, and the thought process, drawings will be scattered, unrecognizable, and primitive. By examining the drawings of selected children between the ages of 2 and 6 years, progress in ability can be seen. One must remember that each child is unique and that experience also plays an important part.

Many drawing utensils are small, require pressure, or are messy. Adults give pencils, pens, and paper to children to keep them quiet and occupied. Most pencils are inappropriate for small, undeveloped fingers; if the child does use a pencil, a jumbo one with a soft lead is preferred.

Perhaps because of their attractiveness, availability, and inexpensiveness, most children have access to crayons. These come in regular and jumbo sizes, with the jumbo being easier for young children to hold. Pressure needs to be exerted if dark color is desired. Often, the expenditure of energy tires the young hand before the child has had ample opportunity for self-expression. Some suppliers stock plastic crayons, which are less messy than wax crayons, and are very colorful.

Crayons can be used in a number of different ways.

Drawings of similar objects done by children ages 3, 5, and 6 years.

Crayon twist. Lay the crayon on its side and rotate it.

Shavings. Grate crayons. Place between two sheets of waxed paper and press with a warm iron.

Crayon melt. Heat a frying pan or griddle to "warm." Place a piece of aluminum foil in the bottom. Have the child make a picture with crayon on the foil. Then apply a piece of newsprint or construction paper over the drawing and press gently. The paper will absorb the crayon design. Wipe off any remaining crayon from foil and the next child can make his design.

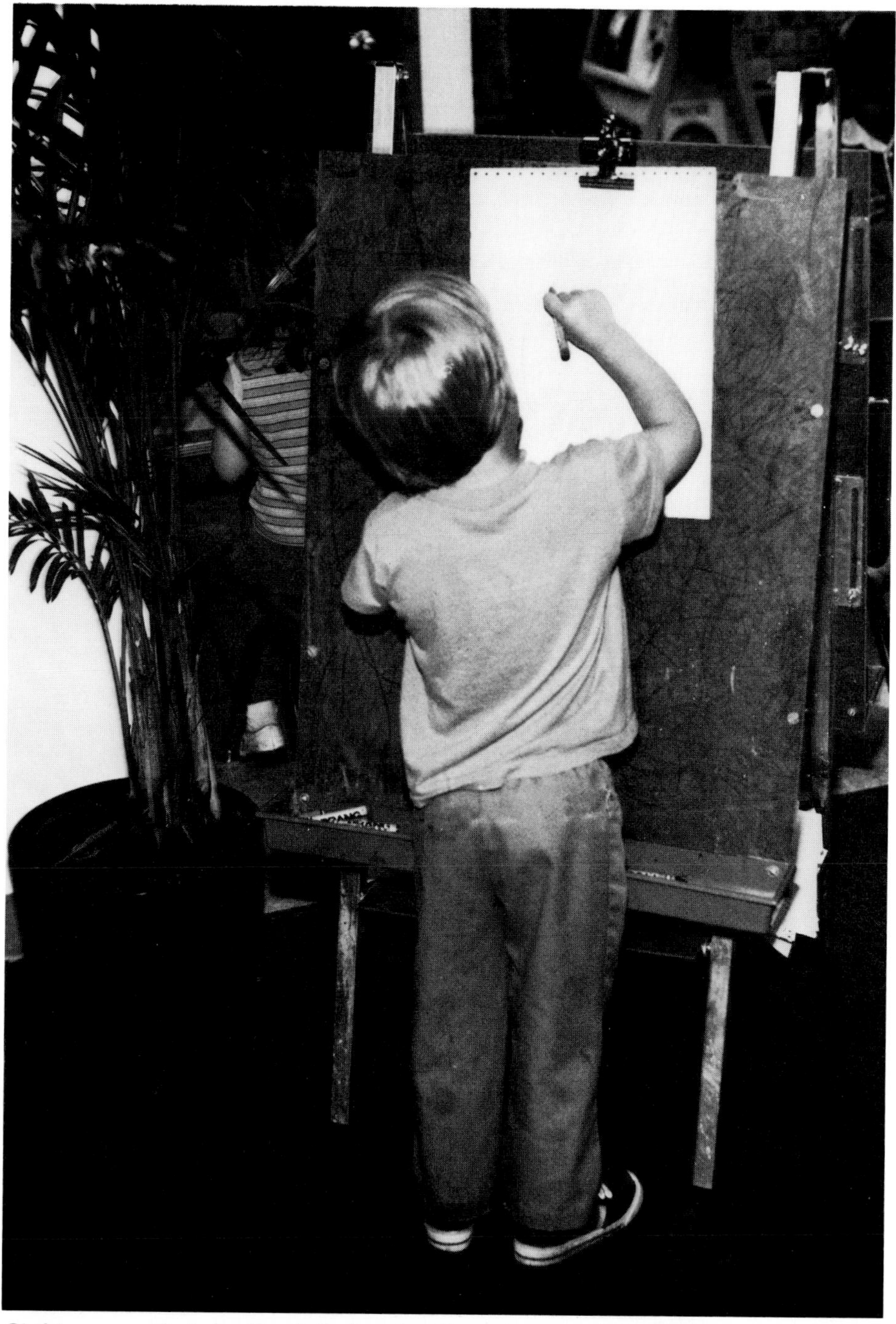

Children use their bodies fully by standing at an easel to draw.

Crayon texture. Place a flat object, such as a leaf, screening, or popsicle stick, under newsprint. Color over it with crayon. Using a crayon directly on sandpaper is another sensory experience.

Large sheets of paper encourage large arm movements. Paint brushes offer a much better experience for young children than do pencils, pens, and crayons. Standing at an easel, children can fully use their bodies.

Chalk provides many of the same experiences as crayons. Because of its dryness, chalk has a tendency to be messy and to rub off. It can be made more permanent if it is dipped into buttermilk or if the paper is rubbed lightly with buttermilk or water before the chalk is applied. Buttermilk brings out the color of the chalk and acts as a fixative. Chalk does not require much pressure but does soil the hands, which some children dislike.

Many adults supply *felt-tip pens* as substitutes for crayons; however, the pens can become messy. They often go into the mouths of children, and they mark anything they touch, such as fabric or bodies. Because such marks may be permanent, pens with ink that washes off hands and out of fabrics would be better for children to use. The pens do have the advantages of requiring less pressure and of being quite brilliant in color.

Children can be given blank sheets of paper or paper formed into a booklet to create their own books. They can make the pictures and dictate the text to an adult. With the child's permission, the book can be used at storytime.

The following materials are suggested:

blackboard and chalk
cardboard (lightweight)
construction paper
fabrics
manila paper
newspaper (want-ad section)
newsprint
oilcloth (use back side)
poster paper
sandpaper
screening
wallpaper
window shades
wood

Painting

Painting can be done in different ways. Therefore, this section will be divided into separate areas: easel painting, finger painting, sponge or block painting, and miscellaneous painting.

Easel Painting

A good easel is of sturdy wood or metal construction, has a place for paint jars and a clip for paper, and is easily cleaned. It should be the correct height for the child. Portability is desirable, so that it can be used outdoors as well as indoors. Indoors, the easel should be out of the traffic pattern, under good lighting, and close to a sink, washroom, and sponges. Side-by-side use encourages children to cooperate and verbalize.

Paint. The children can help prepare the paint. Two to four colors are sufficient. Primary colors are most appealing and educational. Children learn to mix them to create secondary colors. White and black should be offered occasionally.

Dry powder paint and a small amount of water are shaken in a screw-top jar. Red and orange paint mix best in warm water. A small amount of wheat paste or extender is added to thicken the paint. A small amount of liquid detergent in the paint facilitates cleanup of hands, brushes, and clothing, and a pinch of salt keeps the paint from going sour in a warm room. The paint should be stirred well before using.

Children learn to make secondary colors by mixing primary colors of paint. They should be allowed to experiment.

Paint keeps indefinitely if tightly covered and stored in a cool place. Improper storage greatly increases costs.

Jars. The following types of containers are used.

- Half-pint jars with lids for storage
- Baby food jars with lids for storage
- Quart milk cartons washed out and cut down
- Frozen juice cans (6- or 12-oz. size)
- Small food cans, such as those used for tuna and tomato paste
- Muffin tins

Clothing. A cover-up of some kind is always used. A smock, a large T-shirt, a fabric or plastic apron, or an old shirt worn backwards will do. Use of a cover-up is one of the limits for participating in this activity, not because children are messy or infantile, but because it is good policy to protect their clothes.

Materials. The materials useful for painting are many and varied. The following are recommended.

Brushes
bristles ½ to 1 in. wide
good quality
handle approximately 10 to 12 in. long

Paper
butcher paper
cardboard
cartons
construction paper
corrugated paper
finger paint paper
magazines
newspaper
newsprint
paper sacks
paper towels
wallpaper

Fabrics
burlap
cotton
leather
nylon
oilcloth
plastic
vinyl

Other Surfaces or Materials
clay
metal
rocks
seashells
wood (boxes, branches, scraps)

Techniques. The following recommendations are helpful:

- Using one brush for each color keeps colors true but does not provide much opportunity for the child to explore. Occasionally time should be allowed for experimentation.
- Before applying the brush to paper, the end should be wiped on the top of the jar.
- If easels are unavailable, paper can be placed on a large table or on the floor out of the traffic pattern. Paint is put in muffin tins and flat containers.
- A place nearby should be provided for hanging pictures to dry.

Cleanup. Children should be encouraged to cover unused paint and wash out brushes and empty jars. They should hang their pictures to dry. If space is limited, a large, portable, wooden clothes-drying frame can be used, or newspapers can be placed on the floor out of the traffic pattern. Spills on tray, easel, and floor should be wiped up. A tarp, plastic sheet, or newspapers placed on the floor before painting aids in cleanup.

Finger Painting

Finger painting is a good emotional release. Children can express many moods, such as joy, concern, interest, curiosity, and sorrow. They can show fear, for example, and then quickly wipe it away.

Finger painting provides an excellent sensory experience. Adding different substances to the paint—sand, glitter, rice, or paper—can change the experience. To color the paint, powder paint is added to dry ingredients or food coloring to wet ingredients. (*Note:* Food coloring stains some surfaces. It can usually be removed from plastic surfaces by putting full-strength liquid detergent on the spot, leaving it a few minutes, then wiping it off with a damp sponge or cloth.)

Materials. Recipes for finger paint are found in Appendix D. A number of surfaces can be used, including paper (butcher, shelf, hard-surfaced wrapping), oilcloth, tabletops, wood, wallpaper, cardboard, glass, plastic, or vinyl. Sponges are provided to dampen paper or tabletop and for cleanup, and racks are needed for drying the paintings. The children wear cover-ups.

Procedure. The following suggestions will ensure a pleasant finger painting session:

- Define limits for children and teachers.
- Dampen table or paper with sponge so paper adheres to surface.
- Spread paper smoothly on table.
- Put a heaping tablespoon of finger paint on the paper. (Colorless paint may be used; the teacher can sprinkle powdered tempera on paper. If children sprinkle tempera, cans become messy and hard to hold.)

- Play several types of music during the activity.
- Mention that the children can also make designs with their fists, knuckles, palms, and fingernails.
- Encourage children to clean up. Have sponges and water ready.

Finger painting can also be done directly on tabletops. When this is done, a design can be "lifted" onto paper.

Sponge or Block Painting

Sponge or block painting is done by dipping a sponge or other object into thick paint and then making a print on paper. The procedure is repeated in different positions and colors to make designs.

Sponges are cut into small pieces. A spring clothespin makes an excellent handle. Other objects include cork, pieces of wood, spools, potatoes, string, potato mashers, sink stoppers, and plastic forks. Designs can be carved in potatoes or other firm vegetables or fruits, such as carrots, turnips, lemons, or apples. A leaf or other object can be painted and then printed on paper.

Paints should be quite thick. A small amount of wheat paste is used as a thickener. The paint is placed in staggered cups of a muffin tin or small aluminum pie pans.

The best paper for printing is butcher paper or cardboard. Absorbent paper can also be used.

Miscellaneous Painting

Brush painting. Different kinds of brushes can be used for painting. Some unusual ones include toothbrushes, bottle brushes, hairbrushes, food brushes, and straws from a broom.

Bubble painting. For bubble painting, liquid soap and water are put in a bowl that is about 8 in. across the top and coloring is added. The children are given straws and encouraged to blow many bubbles in the bowl. When bubbles rise over the top, a piece of absorbent paper is placed over the bowl. The paper breaks the bubbles, and the design is printed on the paper with the top of the bowl as the border. (This activity is appropriate for children who can blow into a straw. Young children may suck on the straw and get the soap mixture into their mouths.)

Crayon and paint. The child makes a design on paper with crayons and then paints over it. The wax resists the paint.

Doily painting. A paper or plastic doily is placed on a piece of butcher paper. Paint is brushed over the doily. When the doily is lifted a design is left. The doily can be used to print onto another piece of paper, too.

Dry powder painting. Wads of dry cotton can be dipped into dry powder paint and applied to damp paper.

Ink blots. For ink blots, paper is folded in half and reopened. A few drops of paint are placed on one side of the paper. The paper is then refolded and pressed firmly. This creates a symmetrical design. Newsprint is best for this experience.

Marble painting. To prepare for marble painting, paper is cut to fit the bottom of a shoe box. Marbles are dipped in thick paint, put in the box, and rolled around. Marbles or Ping Pong balls can also be dipped in paint and rolled on paper.

Murals. For murals, children are provided with a long sheet of butcher paper, paint, brushes, and encouragement. They will do the rest.

Painting on different materials. A number of materials give experience in texture. These include cloth, paper towels, smooth paper, sponge, glass, plastic, leather, linoleum, egg cartons, aluminum foil, cone-shaped spools, corrugated paper, mailing tubes, paper bags, pleated muffin cups, waxed paper, tissue paper, metal, stone, rocks, and wallpaper.

Painting with water. Children can paint with water on boards, sidewalks, and other large surfaces that water will not damage. They should be given small pans of water and large brushes.

Roll-on deodorant bottles with removable balls can be used for painting.

Snow painting. For snow painting, the child "paints" over a picture (greeting cards are good) with a mixture of 1 part Epsom salts to 1 part boiling water—cooled before painting. Evaporation leaves crystals.

Splash painting. Dripping paint on a sheet of paper creates a splash painting. The design is duplicated by covering the paper with another sheet and rolling it with a rolling pin.

Roll-on painting. Some roll-on deodorant containers have a removable ball. This can be taken out and replaced after filling the container with paint. The children can then roll on the paint.

Spool painting. To do spool painting, the edges of a spool are nicked for design. A wire is inserted through the spool and twisted to make a handle. The spool is then dipped into thick paint and rolled on the paper.

Straw painting. For straw painting, a drinking straw is dipped into paint and sucked to get a small amount of paint into the straw. The paint is then gently blown onto the paper. This is inappropriate for children who suck rather than blow through the straw.

String painting. A long piece of string is dipped into paint and arranged on one half of a piece of paper. The other half is folded over the string and pressed. The string is pulled out, and the design appears on both halves of the sheet. Different strings and colors of paint can be used.

Tempera wash. For a tempera wash, glue or paraffin wax is dripped on paper and allowed to dry overnight. A wash with tempera paint is done over the design.

Towel painting. A design is painted on a plastic tabletop or similar hard surface, and a paper towel is pressed on the painted surface. The towel is then removed and allowed to dry. This can also be done over a finger painting.

A paper towel can be painted directly with brush and easel paint.

Vinyl painting. Vinyl is applied to a wall or rolled out on the floor. Children paint on it and then wipe it off.

Sand

Most young children are delighted to play in sand. They run their hands through it, smooth out roads, construct tunnels and ditches, and make cakes. They socialize in sand; discussing, sharing ideas and materials, participating in collective monologue, and learning to cooperate.

Whether sand is used in a large area on the playground or in a sandbox matters little as long as space is sufficient for exploring. Props such as trucks, shovels, buckets, sifters, measuring spoons and cups, and containers stimulate the imagination of young children. Seashells make an interesting and lifelike addition.

Definite limits are set up so the children know how the sand is to be used. These

Sand and water in a large outdoor area stimulate creativity.

are expressed as follows: "Keep the sand in the sand area." "Shovels, hoes, and rakes stay close to the ground." "Sand is for building, not throwing."

During the winter, a sandbox can be used inside the school; however, some floors are easily scratched and require extra maintenance. For these reasons, some schools prohibit sand use in the classroom. Canvas, plastic, or newspapers can be spread to protect the floors.

Water changes the consistency of sand and makes it easier to manipulate. In summer, a hose stimulates creativity for children. Sand is dampened for pretend cooking and molding. A board nearby is convenient for dumping cakes and products or for children to sit on if the whole area is damp.

Sand toys are best stored near the sand area, separating them from other toys. Trucks, cars, measuring cups, sifters, gelatin molds, and so on are placed on low shelves; buckets and shovels are hung on low hooks or nails. A messy storage area discourages children from using the equipment and may cause accidents.

Stringing

Stringing objects encourages the use of small muscles and eye-hand coordination. Some children lack the control and concentration necessary to make the experience pleasurable; others enjoy it.

Helpful Hints

- Allow plenty of time for children to experiment.
- Make sure needles are large enough for the children to grasp, have blunt ends, and have an object tied on the end to keep objects from sliding off. Use a double thread so needle will not become unthreaded. Yarn may be better to use.

Stringing encourages eye-hand coordination.

- If needles are not used, make ends of string or yarn firm by covering with transparent or masking tape, or by dipping in paste or wax and allowing to dry. A shoelace makes an excellent string because of the hard tip.
- Color dry macaroni with water and food coloring rather than with wood alcohol, which colors well and dries rapidly but may cause gastrointestinal upset. When using food coloring, place small amounts of water and coloring in a small bowl and let the macaroni stand in the solution until the desired shade. Remove with a fork and place on paper towels until the excess moisture is absorbed. Spread individual pieces of macaroni on sheets of waxed paper and let dry overnight. If not separated, the macaroni will dry in clusters.

Suggested Materials

aluminum foil
beads (clay, see recipe in Appendix D)
beads (large, wooden)
breakfast cereals
cranberries
foam packing material
Lifesavers
macaroni (plain or colored)
paper
popcorn (may be difficult)
small spools
straws (½-in. lengths)
Styrofoam packing

Water

Children need to have water experiences. Water has a soothing effect. It gives way to the motion of one's hands. At school, basins and sinks are generally low and available to the children. Water can be used daily or just for special occasions.

Water encourages action, as do props. When children participate in this activity, wearing a cover-up is a prerequisite. Sponges, towels, mops, and buckets should be close at hand and used by the children for spills and cleanup. The number of children at this activity is limited by providing only a set number of cover-ups.

If water is not desired in certain areas of the classroom, these areas should be separated by as much distance as possible and the rationale explained to the children. "Water in the book area could ruin our books." They should be told where and when water can be used.

One preschool teacher had difficulty accepting water play. She felt water was for drinking and washing only. In her particular preschool group were several children who never passed the water to play in the other areas. As children measured, spilled, poured, wiped, and experimented with water, the teacher's dislike for it intensified. After a considerable length of time (and admitting she could not eliminate water from the room), she

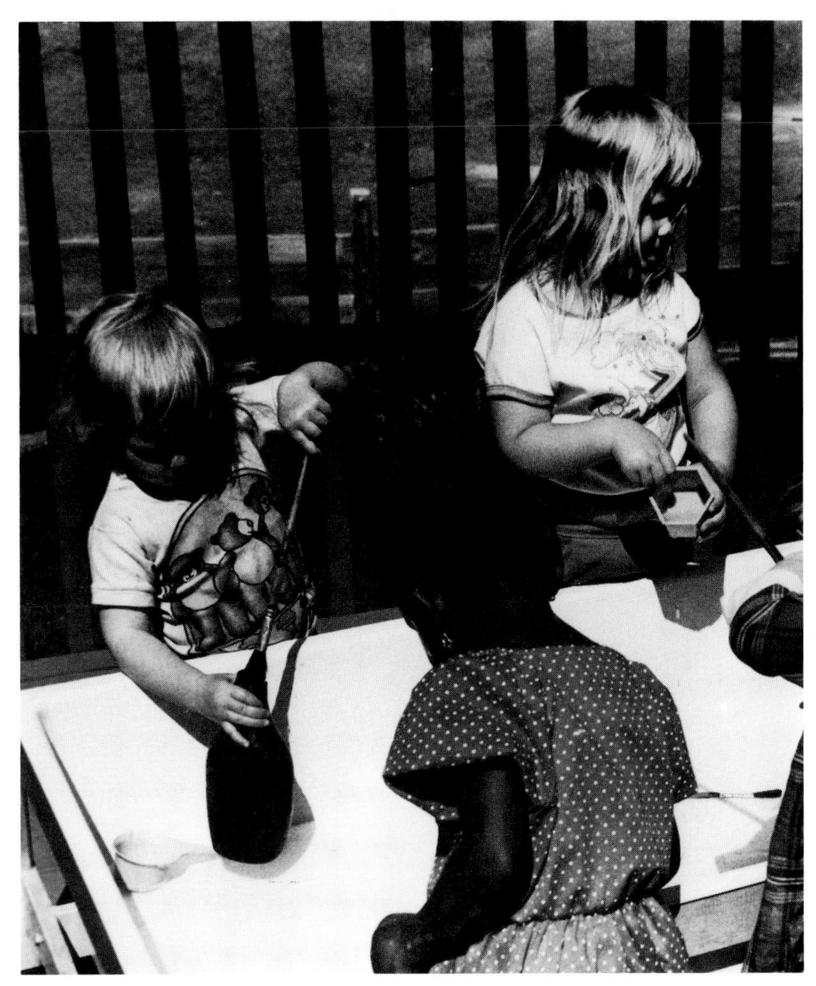

Water painting is a good activity for outdoors.

realized that the experience had a therapeutic effect upon the children, and she began to recognize other values as well. Perhaps instead of fighting the presence of water, she should have joined the activity!

Teachers may consider the following suggestions for water use:

- Give children a bucket of clear water and a large brush and let them "paint" anything outdoors that water will not damage.
- Make a concentrated soap solution and provide straws for the children. Coloring may be added. Give each child some solution in a small bowl or fill a water table for group experience.
- Get a plastic container with a squeeze handle similar to that used with window cleaner. Let the children squirt at waterproof targets such as a fence or tree.
- Let the children bathe dolls or wash doll clothes.
- Have a box of water toys readily available for use in the water table.
- Provide containers, water, and food coloring. Children can make and mix colors. Eyedroppers and plastic egg cartons are easy to use and clean.
- Encourage water play in the domestic area.
- During the summer, have a hose running in sand area.
- Have a wading pool during summer months.
- If other sources of water play are not available, cut a tire in half and fill each half with water. Or use a Thermos jug, a large tub, or large 5-gal plastic jug with a spout.

- Encourage children to help water a garden, plants, or animals.
- Talk about the characteristics of water and evaporation.
- Talk about weather, which involves rain, snow, and ice.
- Involve the children in cleanup using sponges and water.
- Provide containers and spouts for measuring and exploring water.
- Introduce new terms and characteristics of water (recycling, buoyancy, volume, weight, leveling).

Chapter 6 also contains a section on water.

Woodworking

Very young children enjoy pounding and banging; preschool children obtain satisfaction from using tools and wood. Their first experiences are exploratory. They like to build simple structures and should be permitted to use their imaginations. The names they select for their objects should be accepted without comments indicating they look like something else, need some additions or changes, or are poorly done. To them, the objects are real. Patterning, as in other areas, has no place in woodworking.

An excellent experience for both girls and boys, woodworking requires close supervision. Precise limits must be set and maintained for obvious reasons. For example, a group of children enjoyed working with the wood and tools; however, when they left the work table, the tools were left out. Later, a distressed youngster picked up a hammer and threw it through a large panel of glass. This would not have happened if the tools had been returned to their proper storage.

Woodworking is not used each day. Despite its many values and interests, the activity also has drawbacks—a limited number of children participate at a time, constant, careful

Woodworking is an excellent experience for both girls and boys.

supervision is necessary, some children take a long time to finish a project, tools and materials are expensive, and children are easily injured.

Inexpensive substitutes for woodworking are use of fiberboard, Cellotex, acoustical tile, or a log of soft wood. The children can hammer small nails into them.

Equipment

Workbench. A workbench can be purchased or made by cutting the legs off a wooden kitchen table. The correct height is a little shorter than half the child's height. Sawhorses with a sturdy plank may also be used.

Hammer. A claw hammer, the most practical for general use, should be well balanced, have a broad head, and weigh 7 to 13 oz. It should be made with the same careful workmanship and durable materials as regular carpenter tools. A toy hammer is *not* acceptable.

Saw. Both rip and cross-cut saws should be provided, and the teacher should know the use of each. An eight- to ten-point cross-cut saw, 12 to 20 in. in length, is desirable.

A saw is held gently and used with long, even downward strokes. A groove that makes sawing easier is initiated by drawing the saw toward one on the first stroke.

Nails. A variety of nails creates interest. Roofing nails are useful because of the large heads; however, they may split the wood. Four-penny, six-penny, eight-penny, and ten-penny nails, $1\frac{1}{4}$ or $1\frac{1}{2}$ in. in length, are good.

Wood. A local lumberyard or carpenter will usually provide pieces of scrap wood. Softwoods, such as yellow or white pine or poplar, are easier for children to use. Wood of various sizes and shapes stimulates imagination. Wheels or dowels may be used as smokestacks, handles, and so on.

Plane. Many types and sizes of planes are available. The block plane is best for

Tools for woodworking should be of the same quality as regular carpenter tools.

young children. They should be taught always to plane in an uphill direction and with the grain.

Vise. A vise mounted on the workbench holds the wood securely and allows the child to use both hands in sawing or hammering. Several vises may be mounted on the workbench.

Brace and bit. Children may need help in using a brace and bit. A 6-in. sweep is desirable for young children. Several different bits may be purchased. Recommended sizes are nos. 3, 4, 8, 12, and 16.

Sandpaper. Sandpaper can be used in a variety of sizes: fine 2/0, medium 1/0, and coarse 2 and 3. Sandpaper mounted on a wood block is easier for children to use.

Other general tools and materials. The following are useful for woodworking:

brushes
cans
carpenter's pencil
fabrics
glue
clamps (4 or 6 in.)
leather
paint
paper
pliers
rasp
rubber
ruler
safety visor
screwdriver (4- to 6-in. handle, ¼-in. blade)
spools
square
string
tongue depressors
wire
yarn

Miscellaneous Sensory Experiences

Feel or Texture

- In a table used for water or sand, use substances such as flour, cornmeal, rice, beans, or wheat.
- Place items of various texture on a table and let children feel them. Try wool, silk, cotton, corduroy, velvet, oilcloth, felt, screening, paper, sawdust, shavings, and fur.
- Dip colored yarn into a thick wheat paste mixture. Shape it on waxed paper and let it dry to make interesting designs.
- Place various objects in a box or paper sack. Let the children feel them and try to identify them before seeing them.
- Ask the children to walk around the room and touch objects that are similar (e.g., those made of wood or metal, those that are smooth or cold).
- Put cornstarch in a bowl and add enough water so that the cornstarch is semiliquid or runny. The mixture, sometimes called "ooblick," feels both moist and dry. It "runs" through the fingers but becomes hard when the hand is clenched.
- Have a small picture and a replica of same object, such as a dog. Put a number of replicas in "feel box." Have the child look at the pictures and try to locate replicas by feeling in the box.
- Show replicas or pictures of objects and ask children to describe how they would feel. Then provide real objects, if possible, and feel them.
- Make a mixture using equal parts of liquid glue and cornstarch (try 1 cup of each). The substance has an unusual feel and can be molded and rolled. It is called "glarch" or "glurch" (glue and starch).

Smell

- In small containers, place small amounts of common liquids that have odors (e.g., perfume, extracts, vinegar, household commodities). Let the children smell them and try to identify them. Be sure to avoid harmful odors!

- Show children pictures of things and ask them to describe what they think they would smell like.
- Ask children to name their favorite smells and tell why they like them.
- Talk about how smell helps us (e.g., smell of smoke means danger).

Taste

- In small bowls, place staple items that look alike but have different tastes (white sugar, salt, flour, powdered sugar, soap flakes, tapioca, coconut). Taste them and talk about the differences.
- In small bowls, place staple items that have the same name but have different characteristics (white sugar, brown sugar, raw sugar, powdered sugar, sugar cane, sugar cubes, and others). Taste them and talk about the differences.
- Have plates of vegetables or fruits. Ask the children to taste and compare them (juicy, crunchy, sweet, sour).
- Have the same fruit or vegetable prepared in different ways (raw, cooked, peeled, unpeeled, or as juice). Taste and compare.
- Have new foods as a snack or at lunch.
- Talk about vegetables that are generally eaten raw (lettuce) and those that can be eaten raw or cooked. Serve some of them at snack.

Sound

- Fill containers with different items. Have the children shake them and try to guess what is inside.
- Have a group of duplicate containers with invisible contents. See if the children can correctly match them by shaking them.
- Play a record or tape and see if the children can identify the sounds. Pictures or replicas can go with the sounds. See if the children can match them.
- Make "telephones" with two empty juice cans and a string 10 to 20 ft long. Poke a hole in the bottom of a can, put string through bottom, and tie a knot inside the can. Hold string taut. Let the children talk and listen to each other.
- Borrow telephones from the telephone company (if available) to teach telephone courtesy and proper use.
- Record children's voices on tape. Play it back and see if they can identify the child who is speaking.
- Encourage the children to make poems or rhyming words.
- Have one child imitate a sound, such as an animal or vehicle, and another guess what it is.
- Behind a screen make sounds of common household items. See if the children can identify them.
- Tell a story of a child's day and have the children make the appropriate sounds (brushing teeth, turning on water, car starting, horns on way to school, pet sounds).
- Have the children tell how they feel when they hear certain sounds, such as a dog, siren, band, familiar voice, or bell.
- Make the sound of an animal and have the children pretend to be that animal.

Sight

- Have the children look at various objects. Ask them to describe how the objects would feel before they touched them (hard, smooth, cold, and so on).
- Have the children look at a picture. Ask them to "act out" the scene.
- Have the children act out their favorite game or activity. See if the other children can guess it.
- Have the children put crayon shavings, things of nature (e.g., flower petals, seeds, leaves), or small objects between two pieces of waxed paper and then press with a warm iron.

Earphones make sound an interesting sensory experience.

- Talk about the differences between opaque and clear things.
- Ask the children how they tell if something is hot just by looking at it.
- Have the children watch you complete a task and then model it.
- Show four to six objects. Have the children close their eyes while you remove one object. Have them name the missing object.
- From a variety of objects, have the children group items that are alike in color, size, or composition. Can the objects be grouped in other ways such as by shape or use?
- From a group of objects, have the children select the things that would be used by a certain family member (father, mother, baby).
- Show a suitcase full of clothes. Have the children decide what articles are needed for different occasions or seasons.

- Show a flower. Point to and name the different parts. Hand the flower to different children and ask each to name and point to one part.

Miscellaneous Ideas for Small-Muscle Development

- Pegboards
- Small, colored cubes
- Snap blocks
- Small plastic blocks representing bricks
- Puzzles (commercial or handmade)
- Tinkertoys
- Assorted table toys (small vehicles, people, animals)

Many activities afford opportunities for exchange of ideas.

Spool knitting aids small-muscle development.

- Geoboards. Use a piece of wood of any size but preferably about 4 by 6 in. or 5 by 8 in. Hammer small nails into it about ½ in. apart. Give the child some small colored rubber bands and let him create his own design by stretching the bands over the nails.
- Picture lotto or card games
- Mobiles. Use a coat hanger, string or yarn, and a variety of either purchased or handmade objects.
- Spool knitting
- Sorting buttons by size, shape, color, composition, and so on.
- Sewing cards (purchased or handmade)
- Sewing on burlap or rubberized burlap
- Plastic objects that fit together (Multi-fits, Knoppers, Bristle Blocks)
- Creative arts (cutting, pasting, stringing, painting)
- Holder for dried flowers, pencils, and so on. Take a small jar of interesting shape. Let the child tear small pieces of masking tape, ½ to 1 in. long, and stick on bottle. Lightly rub wax shoe polish over tape, making interesting design.
- Pipe cleaners. Let child make interesting shapes.
- Manipulation (zippers, buttons, snaps)

DEVELOPMENTAL EXAMPLES

Some activities discussed in this chapter require almost the same materials for children of any age (blocks, clay, domestic area, and sand, for example). Children participate with raw materials in a manner consistent with their interest and skills. The intensity and duration of any activity differ with age; younger children most often play alone and immaturely, older ones cooperatively and in more complex ways.

Planning for some of the other activities (collage, cutting and pasting, drawing, painting, stringing, and woodworking) varies with age level, as shown in the following examples.

Cutting and Pasting

Age 2 Cutting is minimal part of the activity. Use of scissors needs careful supervision. Lines to be cut must be simple. Children are more interested in squeezing the glue or brushing on the paste. The picture has few objects pasted on.

Age 3 Some children attempt to cut. Again, use of scissors needs careful supervision, and lines to be cut must be simple. Pasting is still fascinating, but most children still have few objects on their picture. Color, form, and balance are informal.

Age 4 Many children pick up scissors first. Cutting is often crude, but child attempts it. Lines can be varied; child may prefer to cut pictures from magazines. Applying paste is minimal part of project. Picture begins to have form and balance.

Age 5 Most children are adept at using scissors and can follow a pattern when cutting. Activity seems to balance between use of the scissors and applying paste to make an aesthetic picture. Child may begin with preconceived notion of what he wants the picture to look like.

Stringing

Age 2 The child is not too interested in the activity. He may attempt to poke the string through a hole while the object is lying on table but does not try to steady the object or string (the other hand may not even be involved in activity). If an adult offers help, the child may turn away from the activity entirely, or after accepting help, may pull the object off and turn away.

Age 3 The child may observe activity with caution or attempt to string one or two objects. Large holes and objects are preferred. If string becomes limp, the child becomes discouraged. He may accept help from adult and watch as he is shown how to hold tip of string close to hole and how to hold object, but usually loses interest quickly.

Age 4 The child usually knows the relationship between holding the object and string and can string wooden beads easily. He now prefers a little challenge, such as a smaller hole or object, and may stay with the activity long enough to make a necklace or bracelet.

Age 5 The child enjoys stringing things and may ask for the activity or stay longer when it is provided. He introduces originality into the pattern and use of the finished string.

Woodworking

Proper use of woodworking tools is much more difficult for young hands than scissors, paste, or string. The children need the coordination of eyes and hands and strength in fingers, hands, and arms. Saws, hammers, and other tools can cause immediate and serious injury to the yielder or receiver of the tool. The younger the "carpenter," the more simple the experience. Young children need help to get the feel of a hammer or saw or the motion of using sandpaper attached to a block. With age, experience, and supervision, children can begin to take more responsibility for the use of tools. They'll want to make more complex projects and may even want to paint them.

CUMULATIVE LESSON PLAN

- Paint large boxes
- Glue small boxes together
- Play in large appliance boxes
- Make rhythm instruments

See Appendix C.

ESPECIALLY FOR PARENTS

A child does not have to attend a preschool group in order to express himself through the use of materials. You can provide such experiences at home, either by interacting personally with your child, inviting peers in, or supplying materials for his enjoyment. (For parents who desire further information on how to promote healthy growth in young children, see Taylor reference at end of chapter.)

If parents take interest and pride in their child's accomplishments, he will also. For example, let the child decorate a clean, empty gallon (or larger) ice cream container as a wastebasket or toy box for his room. When a child has boxes he has decorated and perhaps labeled with an appropriate picture, he is encouraged to take more responsibility and pride in his room.

Parents need to look at creative activities with an artistic and appreciative eye. The child should not be chastised for messiness, imperfect products, or lack of skills. The child learns many things through expressing himself creatively and should be encouraged in his pursuit.

You may not have a lot of time, money, or materials, but many artistic activities are relatively inexpensive and readily available. Go back through the activities presented earlier in this chapter and find a few ways you can use them in your home. The values, techniques, and goals are similar at the center or at home. The child's work needs to be appreciated and displayed in both places. Help him to feel that his creations are valued.

Blocks

Most commercial blocks are quite expensive; however, small sets can be purchased or made. Many lumberyards or carpenters will cut them for you if you do not have the equipment and skills at home. Your child can help sand and finish the blocks. Not only will you have blocks, but you will have involved other creative experiences as well—woodworking and finishing.

Cardboard boxes, empty metal cans, spools, and other items can be used for building purposes. Look around your house and see how many ideas you can come up with. (How about letting your child help arrange food cans on shelves?) To add a challenge, try a combination of things, such as boxes, blocks, dishes, and toys.

Clay

Clay provides many possibilities and lasts a long time when properly stored. Commercial clay is available, but any of the recipes in Appendix D could be made easily by parents and the child.

Many artistic activities are relatively inexpensive.

The child can have his own bag of clay, his own utensils, and his own place to work. This stimulates verbalization even if not related to the clay experience. If the child has had many food experiences (rolling cookies, kneading bread, making pie crust), dough-clay may be less interesting to him.

Collage, Cutting and Pasting

Many parents have a work cupboard or drawer where children have access to paper, scissors, and other materials. If the parents and the child agree that he can use whatever is in the drawer (within established limits), he may spend many hours with these materials.

He needs good tools (scissors that actually cut, glue that comes out of the tube and sticks), time to work, and a place where he will be undisturbed.

For a gift or special occasions, he can decorate a can or bottle. He can make something for a family gathering, such as place mats or decoration, or he can cut pictures related to a certain topic from magazines or catalogs. Save greeting and birthday cards for the child to cut and paste.

Together with your child, design a holder for gadgets, shoes, clothes, or toys for his room, possibly made out of plastic, burlap, or other fabric. Let the child cut and paste pictures or fabric designs to help him remember what goes in each pocket.

Many 2- and 3-year-olds are fascinated with scissors and often cut their hair, curtains, or other valuable things. They are not deliberately seeking things of value or beauty to cut. Experiences with scissors in the home need to be provided under favorable circumstances so that the child has an opportunity to use them within safe limits.

Dramatic Play

Many children do not have small-sized play equipment at home, but they do have real family experiences. They may play with mother's pots and pans, stand on a stool to help with the dishes, or play with water in the tub or washbasin. This is their way of learning various roles; they see and need to try them.

With little or no cost, dress-up clothes can be available. Clothes that older brothers or sisters have outgrown are better for young children than discarded adult clothes.

On a boring or rainy day, try covering a card table with a sheet or blanket for renewed interest. A flashlight or perhaps even a little treat brightens up the day for almost any youngster.

If the family has a baby, let the child help you take care of it, or let him do similar activities with a doll.

Involve the child in food preparation and other household chores, such as setting the table, using the vacuum, or watering plants.

Take your child on errands with you and then provide props and ideas for him to reenact at home. He will learn about his world and so will you.

Drawing

Small portable or wall-hung chalkboards are inexpensive and can be adjusted to the height of the child. He will have many hours of enjoyment. The boards may also be used for family purposes, such as leaving notes or playing games. The child can be responsible for keeping the board and eraser clean.

Chalk can be used on paper or other materials, but because of its small size and limited qualities, the child may find this medium less satisfying than others.

Wax crayons have some characteristics in common with chalk. Jumbo crayons are easier for small fingers to hold. Ask about the availability of plastic crayons. Get a large pad of plain paper so your child can create his own designs, use his large muscles, and draw to his heart's content. At this age, don't stifle his creativity by providing coloring books.

For dinner, or for some special occasion, let the child draw original designs on paper napkins or paper towels for place mats. These have different textures than drawing paper and should be fun. Do not demand perfection or require the child to stay for a long period of time. Let him be the artist.

Felt-tip pens, wide or fine, are generally easy to hold, come in bright colors, and mark easily. There are precautions to take: keep them out of mouths, use water-based pens, and keep other items away from the drawing area.

Easel Painting

Many homes do not have an easel. A chalkboard or heavy cardboard can be covered for painting. A child seems to have better control when standing or working on the floor rather than on a tabletop, which is generally so high that he has to kneel on a chair. In good weather, heavy cardboard can be hung on a fence outside.

Some parents dislike having a child paint at home. Covering the floor, giving the child a protective covering, and establishing limits often eliminate many of the difficulties. However, it may be easier and may fulfill the same purpose if you give the child a brush and a bucket of water and turn him loose outside.

Finger Painting

Finger painting is another experience that many parents avoid. They do not know how to make the necessary preparations for the child to have a satisfying experience and to keep themselves calm. One mother makes finger paint out of soap, puts her children in the bathtub, and lets them go to it. When they are through, she washes off the children and rinses out the tub, and everybody is happy.

Finger paint can be obtained commercially or can be made from any of the recipes in Appendix D. It provides a satisfying experience that many other activities do not give. Because some paints stain, be sure to protect surfaces.

An activity your child can do at home is to finger-paint on a large sheet of paper, let it dry, and use if for wrapping gifts. He can also finger-paint on a hard surface and blot the design onto absorbent paper. When the painting is dry, make a colored frame for it and hang it in his room.

Sponge or Block Painting

Paint for block printing can be purchased or a child can help mix it. For this activity the paint has to be thicker than regular easel paint (use wheat paste, extender, or less water). An old muffin tin works well for dipping.

Cut small pieces of a sponge and attach them to spring clothespins, Popsicle sticks, small wooden dowels, or old handles. Sponges are easily cleaned.

Look for things that make interesting designs. Cut some block designs from wood, potatoes, or corks. Invite the whole family to participate.

Sponge or block painting is an enjoyable activity, and designs can be used for greeting cards, decorative hangings, table decorations, or gift paper.

Miscellaneous Painting

Many activities, including those listed earlier in this chapter, can be used equally well in the home as in the school. Help the child to know where and on what he can paint. Set the limits with him before he does something that offends you.

Sand

Sand is a soothing medium that should be provided for children. If possible, have a sand area outside that is large enough for the child to move around in or substitute a large tub or box. Find a way to cover and protect the sand from animals and debris. Occasionally add water and props such as cars, measuring cups and spoons, and molds.

Many parks and playgrounds have sand areas. If you take your child there, he may have an opportunity to interact with other children. For some reason, sand stimulates interaction and cooperation.

Stringing

At times stringing is tedious for young fingers. Give the child some chances to develop his small muscles and eye-hand coordination, but be flexible and understanding.

The child can be given opportunities to lace shoes or wind laces around hooks on boots, string tools or washers on wire for Dad, or make a necklace using different kinds of beads, breakfast cereal, Lifesavers, straws, or spools. With a needle and thread, the child can string buttons, and, using heavy twine or a clothes hanger bent into a curve, he can string jar rings (this keeps the rings neat and is a worthy task). You can also check with a paint store or interior decorator for paint chips, fabric samples, or plastic samples that can be strung on a chain.

Sand is a soothing medium that delights most young children.

If you have access to some old tires or tubes, the child can string them on rope. This involves use of large muscles and of the whole body.

Water

Most parents do not have to look far for water experiences for their children as the latter are attracted to water. In addition to household uses, such as washing people, animals, dishes, cars, and clothes, watering plants and lawns, and preparing food, some of the following ideas can be considered:

- Demonstrate the use of steam for cooking and pressing.
- Point out and make use of community resources, such as lake, river, pond, or fountain.
- Observe activities relying on water, such as fishing, logging, or boating.
- Relate water to weather and seasons.
- Explain words pertaining to water (e.g., evaporate, buoyancy, recycling).
- Note how some clothing is related to water, such as seasonal wear or waterproofed items.
- Tell how plumbing works and what repairs are needed.
- Go swimming or wading.
- Go through a car wash or let the child help wash the car.
- Take a trip to the fire station and have the fireman explain how water helps put out fires, how hoses are used, and so on.
- Explain or observe irrigation of crops.
- Visit a shipyard or dock or learn about them through use of books, pictures, and replicas.
- Watch the water wagon as it washes the streets.

Children need and enjoy water experiences.

Woodworking

If you do not have a place at home for woodworking, you can often visit community centers, hobby shops, or schools. Young children may be restricted from using the equipment and materials, however.

Children should have good quality tools. Poor imitations are a waste of money, do not work, do not last, and often do not even resemble real tools. (See pages 78–80.)

As in a school setting, children need to be supervised when using potentially dangerous tools. Go over the limits with your child; be sure that he fully understands what they are and why he must abide by them. Stay with your child whenever the tools are being used. Help him put them away immediately after finishing the activity.

A child may assist with woodworking at home by

- Helping to repair something (e.g., a handle, chair, toy)
- Helping to make some blocks for his own use
- Having his own tools and kit
- Making simple objects such as a toy boat or airplane
- Learning the names and uses of different tools (saw, hammer, brace and bit, pliers)
- Working on a project with an adult
- Making holes in lids for insect jars
- Sorting nails into jars for future use
- Learning how to care for and replace tools

Miscellaneous Ideas for Small-Muscle Development

Parents may consider trying the following suggestions to encourage small-muscle development:

- Use commercial or handmade puppets.
- Make card lotto games by using gummed stickers of animals, flowers, and other objects.
- From pre-made pictures, let the child match a person's occupation to the place he works (e.g., nurse to hospital, baker to bakery, letter carrier to post office or mail box, player to sports arena).
- Let the child nest small boxes or food storage containers.
- Provide felt objects (animals, food, clothing) and let the child manipulate them on a flannel board.
- Paste a picture or greeting card on lightweight cardboard. Cut it into puzzle pieces for the child to assemble.

APPLICATION OF PRINCIPLES

1. Briefly discuss the values of providing creative experiences for young children. Include some personal experiences.
2. What role does the teacher play in helping young children express themselves through creative activities?
3. In what activities in your center do the children express their creativity most?
4. What creative materials can young children help prepare and clean up? Initiate some of these opportunities.
5. Explain how you would set up an activity differently for:
   a. 2-year-olds and painting
      4-year-olds and painting
   b. 2-year-olds and sand
      5-year-olds and sand
   c. 3-year-olds and cutting
      5-year-olds and cutting
   d. 4-year-olds and woodworking
      5-year-olds and woodworking
   e. 2-year-olds and water
      3-year-olds and water

6. Plan and use two different sensory experiences with children between the ages of 2 and 5.
7. Role play with a partner. One be a teacher who firmly believes in using art experiences in the classroom and one be a teacher who firmly believes that art has no place in the classroom. After three minutes, switch roles. Discuss feelings in both roles.

References

Gotz, Ignacio L. "On Children and TV." In *Reading in Early Childhood Education 78/79.* Guilford, Conn.: Dushkin, 1978.

Green, Marjorie, and Elizabeth Woods. *A Nursery School Handbook.* Sierra Madre, Calif.: Sierra Madre Community Nursery School Association, 1963.

Hoover, Francis L. *Art Activities for the Very Young.* Worcester, Mass.: Davis, 1967.

Lieberman, J. "Playfulness and Divergent Thinking: An Investigation of Their Relationship at the Kindergarten Level." *Journal of Genetic Psychology* 107(1965): 219–224.

Taylor, Barbara J. *When I Do, I Learn.* Provo, Utah: Brigham Young University Press, 1974.

Sarah

4

Language Arts

Hey! diddle, diddle, the cat and the fiddle
The cow jumped over the moon.
The little boy laughed to see such sport
And the dish ran away with the spoon!

MAIN PRINCIPLES

1. The teacher plays a major role in the development and use of language in young children.
2. Language arts consists of four distinct but interrelated areas: listening, speaking, writing, and reading.
3. Children of different ages use language differently.
4. Parents can enhance their child's experiences with language.

By design and because of its importance, this chapter on language arts follows the chapter on creative, artistic, and sensory expression. Besides being enjoyable, many basics in art activities lay the foundation for language arts. Considerable verbalization takes place as children practice questioning, explaining, interacting, and listening skills. Use of small muscles in art projects is practice for holding writing implements. Young children usually spend a fair amount of time in artwork. This increase in the interest span is important for reading. Pictures express ideas, can be identified and labeled, and are symbolistic. Puzzles demand careful attention to detail, shape, and spatial relationships, as does reading. Blocks can be made into various configurations, so too can lines for letters and numbers.

The goal in language arts is to help children develop and improve their ability to communicate. Language is oral, auditory, and visual and may be used to express personal or social ideas. One depends on it to clarify norms, to inform, and to transmit needs, feelings, and desires. Inability to communicate with another, whether due to language barrier or sensory impairment, impresses one with how much language is taken for granted and how much we depend on it in our daily lives.

This chapter is designed to emphasize the importance of the four areas of language (listening, speaking, writing, reading) and their interdependence especially for children between the ages of 2 and 6. Not within the scope of this book are: details about language acquisition, problems related to each of the areas of development, possible referrals for diagnosis and treatment, specific approaches to teaching and reading, or ways of dealing with bilingual children.

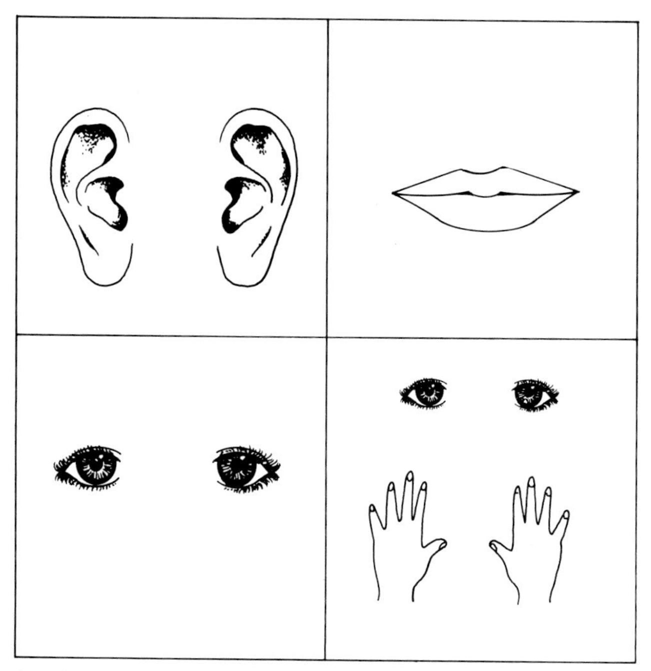

Symbols of the four areas of language: listening, speaking, reading, and writing.

ROLE OF THE TEACHER

If the teacher wants to encourage language use and development in young children, she must be a good listener, a good model, and an interested and caring person. She must also provide for individual needs of the children. The teacher plans wisely so that language is an integral part of each day and each area of the curriculum. To say "Now, it's language time" would be foolish and inaccurate. Language time is all the time. Nonverbal or body language is often better understood than verbal language. One can easily tell from a facial expression, movement of the body, or breathing whether the sender is pleased or displeased.

Hendrick (1980) lists seven basic ways to foster language development: (1) listen to the children, (2) give them something real to talk about, (3) encourage conversation and dialogue, (4) use questions to generate and develop language, (5) provide auditory training, (6) seek professional assistance promptly, when necessary, and (7) become acquainted with and draw on research-based language development programs.

A review of additional references indicates that generally desired components for language development include favorable socioeconomic background, enriching experiences, sensory practice, respect for the child, interaction with other children, quality adult model, same language used at home and school, attentive listeners for the child, noncritical attitude toward the child's language skills, flexibility in the child's life, and time to enjoy speaking and listening experiences.

If language is so much a part of living, why is it important to provide specific opportunities for children to just talk or listen? Consider these values of language:

1. It enriches or supplements firsthand experiences.
2. It enhances self-image and builds self-control.
3. It portrays identifiable sex roles.
4. It helps establishment of social relations through sharing.
5. It facilitates accurate conceptualization, clarifies ideas and stimulates new ones, and presents information.

6. It fosters aesthetic appreciation and stimulates creativity.
7. It provides literary experiences.
8. It acquaints children with another way of learning about their environment.
9. It provides auditory experiences and practice.
10. It provides opportunities for a change of pace and enjoyment of materials and people.

Thorough planning by the teacher is crucial if she is to utilize the many opportunities to foster language and identify and meet the needs of children individually and collectively.

LISTENING

Too often, adults do not listen to young children, even though they learn much about them and their concerns merely by doing so. Adults who expect children to listen need to model good listening. A child can be complimented by saying: "What a good idea!" "You thought of a different way to do it!" "I like your idea!" Such approval tells the child that the adult can listen, too.

Because research reveals that auditory discrimination correlates positively with reading achievement, good listening experiences must be planned and executed often. Children learn to be selective by giving attention to others or the task at hand (when important) rather than attending to the fly, other children outside, or thoughts within his head.

Listening experiences help the child to increase his vocabulary, learn the structure of spoken language, add concepts and ideas, increase his speech accuracy, and interact with others. They also stimulate his imagination.

Some periods are natural for language development. One is during group time when

Group time often provides a listening experience that helps the child increase his vocabulary.

stories, poetry, finger plays, and songs are used; another is during free play with friends and props.

Stories and Storytime

The response of children to stories varies greatly. Some sit quietly during storytime, some make frequent comments, some do neither. Usually children who are read to often will ask for stories, sit quietly, and add comments or questions. Some children introduce interesting and somewhat original ideas or trains of thought during the experience. Encouraging children to make comments during the story may or may not be appropriate, depending upon the size of the group, the interest of the children, and the number of interruptions. If one child is disturbing the children, the teacher can say, "After we finish the story, I'd like to hear more about that. Could you tell me later?" She must then follow through and let him tell what he was thinking. The time lapse may or may not dampen his desire to talk. While not wanting to stifle one child's interest or imagination, the teacher must also consider the rest of the children.

Books and stories provide a worthwhile experience for children. Books attractively displayed on a rack or table beckon children. A small space, a cluttered area, too many books, or a reading area located in a traffic pattern can have a discouraging effect. The teacher should provide large blocks of time for various activities, including looking at books. Children like to sit quietly, undisturbed, while they look at books or have a story read to them individually or in a small, intimate group. A variety of books should be provided, some favorites, some new.

The teacher can be aware of the interests of the children and encourage them to spend time with books. One child may be fascinated with spiders, another with boats, another with weather. The teacher should point out to the individual child that he can learn more about his interests through looking at the books. The teacher might select one or more of these "special" books to use during group storytime.

Books displayed on a rack attract children.

Looking through a book can be a casual pastime.

The attitude and feelings of the teacher herself will greatly influence the children's interest in the story. One teacher felt sure the children would not enjoy the story she had prepared. She was right; they picked up her attitude about it. On another day the same teacher was very excited about the story she had prepared. She was surprised when the children responded to her enthusiasm.

When a teacher wants to introduce a new topic, she may select a story or book as the means to do it. When she provides a book with excellent pictures and factual text, she encourages the children to develop new interests. She should make sure that the children understand the words and meaning.

Storytime should be relaxed and leisurely, with the length depending on the children. They should be comfortably seated on the floor. If they get restless but need to stay in the group, some activities can be started to involve them, such as a finger play or a song. The children should be watched and not the clock! If the teacher explains why they need to stay, rather than just demanding that they do so, cooperation will be better.

Thorough preparation of the story (whether it includes use of visual aids or just reading) will add interest for the children and flexibility for the teacher. When necessary, the teacher should be able to lengthen or shorten the story.

A child's attention may be regained by mentioning his name. When necessary to separate two children, the teacher can move in casually but confidently and say, "I would like to sit by Denise and Michael today." She can then sit down and attend to the story. A teacher can often reinterest a child merely by putting her hand on his shoulder or hand. If a particular child has an extremely difficult time enjoying storytime, it may be better for him to sit quietly in another area, not as punishment, but as preparation. He is given the option of entering the group when he is ready.

Storytime is when the two-teacher model works well. The lead teacher can begin and conduct the storytime while the support teacher assists with slow children, those who need quieting, or other interruptions.

Books are helpful to children who need time to assimilate the many facts thrown at them. Casually looking through a book may help children develop some concrete ideas pertaining to their world. Occasionally they should be encouraged to act out a story.

Teachers should take advantage of teachable moments. One day, after a heavy snow storm, the teacher told the children about the many things she had observed on the way to school. It sounded like a story! One child said: "Tell it again, teacher."

Criteria for Selecting Books and Stories

Realistic, Accurate Material

The materials should be realistic and reported accurately. Factuality helps children develop validity of concepts and to form mental pictures for future use. Young children have difficulty distinguishing between what is real and what is fantasy. The younger the child, the more he needs realistic stories. Most children can more appropriately deal with abstract concepts after their fifth birthday. Human characteristics (talking, dressing, feeling) given to animals, objects, or things confuse young children. Some children handle abstract or inconsistent ideas younger than other children. Fantasy stories should be used in small proportion to such realistic stories as here-and-now experiences until the children can better distinguish real from unreal.

The question of telling fairy tales to young children always arises. During the preoperational stage of development, young children are unable to understand fairy tales. Many fairy tales produce fear, deal with advanced concepts, or contain morals. They are better left until the school years (Arbuthnot 1972; Kohlberg 1966; Leeper 1979; Read 1971; Spock 1976; Taylor 1973).

In a recent publication, Griffin (1982) discusses animal disguises, animals smaller than children who need protection and security, animation of machines, competitive themes, extravagantly unreal happenings, bizarre creatures, imagination, hidden emotional problems, morals, and folk and fairy tales. It is recommended to teachers of young children.

Another avenue of inquiry concerns the use of Mother Goose rhymes. These are often accepted because of the rhyme and rhythm, the humor, the suspense, and the repetition, but they should be used discriminately. Mother Goose rhymes, originally written as adult political satire, are usually enjoyed by young children.

Support of Firsthand Experiences

Books promote learning by supporting firsthand experiences. A book may be used to introduce a new idea, especially when followed by a direct experience, such as a field trip, a visitor, replicas, or other personal involvement.

Books help children clarify concepts about their environment. Books may also be used to stimulate dramatic play, give role models, define behavior, or encourage curiosity. Books often put into words and pictures things the children want to know about but lack skills to ask.

Young children like to hear stories about familiar things that they can also do, such as participating with the family, caring for a pet, visiting the community, developing new skills, or learning new information.

Literary Value

Literature should have value for the reader or listener of any age. For young children, the following are important:

- A definite plot (ability to discern author's purpose and fulfillment)
- Interesting sounds or plays on words (catch phrases, repetition of incidents or ideas)
- A light element of surprise or suspense
- Language that is clear, descriptive, and understandable
- Direct conversation that adds interest and helps children develop respect for language
- An uplifting effect (a book that contains familiar elements and helps to promote sound concepts is generally appropriate. Elements that produce fear, nightmares, poor social relationships, or emotional upsets should be used with caution. Some excellent books depict children conquering fears or potentially upsetting situations. These help children learn to deal with normal experiences.)
- Accurate portrayal of sex, ethnic, and social models

- Interest for age of children, reflecting their point of view in timeliness, problem solving, creativity, and so on
- A positive influence on language art experiences in listening, speaking, writing, and reading
- The ability to stimulate the imagination

Each year the John Newberry Award is given for the best literary contribution to children's literature; however, it is not limited to books for preschool children. Librarians know the Newberry Award winners and should be able to help determine their appropriateness for a specific group.

Good Illustrations

Young children like visuals that are clear and fairly large and clarify the text. Books should have an appropriate art style and be aesthetically appealing. Abstract illustrations are generally confusing and annoying to young children.

Most adults prefer color in picture books and so do most children; however, some favorite picture books are in black and white, sepia and white, or only two colors. Children consider clarity more important than color. The pictures should be uncluttered, yet contain some supportive detail. Children enjoy discovering a ladybug or butterfly in the grass, but when the text calls for a brown and white cow and the picture is of a black one, the children are confused by the inconsistency.

Action in the picture gives further clarification, especially when the visual adds an element of information not generally known (instead of a goat just standing in the field, he might be eating a tin can or pulling a small cart, for example).

Photographs are interesting for children because they often give space relationships that may not be obvious in an artist's drawing. Photographs also give a mental picture to correlate with firsthand experiences.

Another annual award, given for the outstanding picture book, is the Caldecott Award. Libraries often have a display of these books. The teacher can look through them for ones appropriate for her group of children. All of the winners are not of interest to preschool children.

Group Storytime

When planning a group storytime, several factors are considered:

- Appropriateness of the story. The teacher should know the children well enough to plan according to their needs, interests, abilities, interest span, and maturity level.
- Variety. Children are more willing to attend the group experience if it is interesting and challenging. They like some repetition but also some variety.
- Length of time the children are expected to sit. This depends on the children. Usually a 3-year-old sits quietly a shorter period than a 4-year-old, but there can be differences among children, from day to day, or as weather changes. If the children grow restless, they can be allowed to participate more in the story; the teacher can also eliminate parts of the story or add interesting elements to it.
- Visual aids. Often these add interest, but should be used wisely.
- Preparation of the teacher. The teacher should be well prepared and have all of her materials before the story begins. Often, if a teacher leaves to get something, the children want to leave, too. The teacher should evaluate her personal actions, such as how often she reads instead of tells a story, her voice, her eye contact, and other techniques that add to the appeal of this experience for the children.

To create extra interest in storytime, whether the group is large or small, methods of presentation should vary. Some examples:

1. Use the book.
2. Tell the story, with or without aids.

Good illustrations are large and clear.

3. Use flannel board aids.
4. Use only one picture and display it at appropriate time.
5. Use flip cards.
6. Use real objects or replicas.

Group storytime is planned according to the interests and needs of the children.

A flannel board is used to enhance a story.

7. Have the children dramatize the story after it is read or discussed.
8. Act it out as you tell it.
9. Use your own creative methods.

Sources of Books for Young Children

If at all possible, the purchaser of books for young children should read the books before buying or checking them out of a library. Some publishers mail an annotated catalog with an age guide, but some books listed as appropriate for preschoolers may be too advanced or too simple or may cover too broad an age range for a particular group of children.

Listed in Appendix E are some publishers of children's books and also some appropriate books for young children.

In addition to using stories and books as good listening experiences for young children, the value of poetry, finger plays, and Mother Goose should be taken into consideration (Chapter 7).

Items in the following list are used to increase listening ability:

- Poetry
- Finger plays
- Mother Goose rhymes
- Musical bottles (all the same size but with different amounts of water in each)
- Sound boxes, tubes, and cans
- Tape recordings (commercial or classroom). Listen to a taped story. Play it again. Stop it at various places and ask what will happen next. Make a tape of children's voices and familiar sounds and have them guess who or what it is.
- Record player and records
- Listening walk
- Letter sounds
- Rhyming words and nonrhyming words
- Repetition in stories
- Rhythm. The teacher beats and the children repeat.
- Simple directions
- Objects dropped onto soft or hard surfaces. Use such objects as a pillow, block, feather, rock, scarf, or nail.
- Heartbeat of person or animal
- Sounds in the classroom. Have children imitate them.
- Sounds in the environment, such as those from a household, playground, or transportation. Use sounds with and without pictures.
- Puppets. Have children listen and then repeat words or actions.
- Games
  - "Simon Says"
  - Teacher says, "I am thinking about an animal and its name sounds like 'how'." Children guess.
  - "Mother-Baby." One child pretends to be a mother animal, makes the appropriate sound, then closes eyes. Another child pretending to be the baby animal hides and also makes the appropriate sound. The mother finds the baby.
  - "Head, Shoulders, Knees, and Toes"
- Commands, such as "Ready, set, go!"
- Telephones (answering, dialing, etiquette)
- Stories. Have children listen and then dramatize.
- Field trips. Tell children what to expect; dramatize later.
- Whispering times (*Shhhhhh Bang,* by Margaret Wise Brown)
- Foreign words. Teach certain words or how to count to 10.

- Etiquette (simple rules for meals, manners, interaction)
- Talk about interesting times and things.
- Objects. Provide children with box or bag of objects. Describe an object and have each child find it in his bag.
- Prepositions. Give directions ("Sit on the chair," "Roll under the table," "Stand beside the box,") and have children respond using their bodies. When children are thoroughly familiar with the prepositions, continue the game at a future time by using a toy ("Put the car under the rug," "Put it between the blocks," "Put it beside the truck," and so on).

SPEAKING

Oral language is used to share, exchange, or test ideas; to express feelings; to gain new knowledge; to develop auditory acuity; to build relationships; to practice words and grammar; and to provide enjoyment. The younger the children, the less they verbalize; rather, they use physical methods for egocentric purposes. They take things, walk over others, bite, cry, kick, and scream. As children mature, they progressively use more verbalization.

Helping young children increase their speaking skills is desirable, but adults may do the opposite. When children receive too much attention, they do not need to speak; they can point, grunt, or cry. Children may use behavior below their developmental level just because it "pays off." Adults may carry on their own two-way conversation by commenting and responding to themselves rather than giving the children a chance to respond. An adult may offer a choice to a child and when the child hesitates (or when the adult knows what he expects), the adult may respond as if making a democratic choice for the child.

Young children need attractive environments that are conducive to play, promote cooperation and enjoyment, and encourage verbal interaction. When they have thoughts, they want and need to express them. In some classrooms, however, teachers are known to talk 75 to 90% of the time. Of course, they need to give instructions, keep order, and teach the children, but when teachers use language mainly to command, to stop or change behavior, or to maintain order, children speak infrequently. Frequent use of positive support comments decreases the need for disciplinary or negative statements and commands. In one study done by Serbin and O'Leary (1975), nursery school teachers were found to react more to good or bad behavior of boys than girls. Teachers were rewarding boys for aggression and girls for passivity. In other words, they were "teaching girls to shut up!"

The teacher can verbally interact with each child many times during the day (when the child enters; during free play; in problem solving; while offering suggestions, introducing new vocabulary, promoting cooperation, or initiating new activities; or when called upon) *but the teacher must refrain from taking over or monopolizing the children and their activities.* She should use a soft but reassuring tone and talk *with* but not *down* to or *at* them. Each child should be told frequently how special he is to her.

The teacher must learn how to establish rapport and a spontaneous flow of communication that provides comfort and security for each child. When a teacher talks with children about interesting things, she gets a rewarding response. The teacher can also help the shy child to verbalize by providing a variety of experiences, such as stories, songs, finger plays, new encounters, and friendly companions. Seefeldt (1980) suggests that teachers be as "precise as possible, using many concept words, descriptions and abstractions that relate to the experience of the child. . . . Adults should act as resources for children's language."

The teacher who shows sincere interest by getting down on the level of the children, by listening attentively, and by making appropriate comments, can expect other "talking

A teacher establishes rapport with children by using a soft, reassuring tone of voice and talking with and not at them.

times" with them. The teacher further encourages language by expanding conversations ("Yes, I see your new shoes," when a child says, "New shoes") and by elaborating on what children say without controlling the whole conversation ("Your new shoes have two straps and two buckles"). The teacher may also need to assist very young children who are trying to use words and verbs that are irregular in forming plurals or past tenses.

> As children grow older, interactive dialogues and eventually small group discussions are a key means to development of language. Such activity includes vocabulary development, an important base for learning to read. Teachers can develop the ability and desire of children to speak interactively (with one another) by providing learning experiences having to do with (1) room arrangement, (2) use of equipment, (3) scheduling, and (4) activities. (Lundsteen and Tarrow 1981)

Physical and cognitive factors influence ability to produce speech sounds. The lower face, including the mouth and jaw, develops later in head growth. It grows considerably during late preschool and early middle childhood and again during adolescence. Eruption, loss, and replacement of teeth affect the child's ability to produce sounds (Stone and Church 1973).

By getting down on the level of the children, the teacher shows sincere interest and encourages "talking time."

Several authors discuss two popular myths about learning language: (1) that children learn by imitation and (2) that children learn by being corrected. Imitation by itself is insufficient, and correction does not occur with enough frequency to change verbal patterns. Something more than imitation and correction is involved. "All theories of language development agree that experience, conceptualization, and communication continuously influence the way children develop language" (Swartz and Robison 1982).

Items on the following list are used to increase speaking ability:

- Poetry
- Finger plays
- Mother Goose rhymes
- Puppets (stick, sack, felt, cone, sock, glove, finger). A puppet stage is also useful. Remind the children that the puppets are kind and gentle, thus avoiding aggressive and loud behavior.
- Telephone (for courtesy and conversation)
- "Just talking" about things that are of interest to the children, such as stimulating objects and activities. Setting aside time to talk and being a willing listener are important. Encourage verbal expression during art and other times; ask children what they would do under different conditions; ask them to describe things in a basket or box (fruit, toys, first aid items); ask them to tell about things they like.
- Props. Put on various articles of clothing and ask the children to guess who you are or what your occupation is. Have a sack or box with hats for various occupations (firefighter, sports figure, doctor, skier, mail carrier, construction worker, nurse, baker, soldier). Have a child pull out a hat and describe the occupation or have a child match a hat to a picture. Stress that occupations can be for either males or females.
- Objects. Show different objects and ask the children how many different names they can think of for them (e.g., a stuffed dog could be called a dog, animal, toy, pet, friend, or stuffed; a knife could be called a tool, metal, plastic, or "cutter").

Puppets encourage verbalization.

- Recordings. Record original poems or songs and what the children say about their activities.
- Stories. Discuss a story; let the children retell a story using visual aids; use a wordless book and let the children supply the story; tell a group story (each child tells part of it); have the children tell stories to each other.
- Television. Make a large cardboard TV set. Slip different pictures into its "window" and ask the children to tell about them. Provide a large box and let the children pretend they are actors and actresses.
- Naming (especially for younger children). Teacher points to a body part, and the children name it; teacher shows an object or picture, and the children name it, a good way to show differences between similar sounds and to detect pronunciation problems (e.g., *th* in thread and thimble; *sp* in spool and spinner; *g* in garage and girl); teacher paints each cup in an egg carton a different color and asks the children to name each color.
- Field trip. Discuss preparations and behavior with children, such as what they should ask, what they think they will see, and how they should act. Go to interesting places (construction sites, garbage dump, road repair area, airport) so the children will be stimulated. Provide dramatic play as a follow-up.
- Boxes. Put a number of textured objects in a box and small holes for the children to reach in to feel and describe objects. Place something in a box and ask the children what they think is in it. Answer some of their questions about the contents.
- Songs
- Questions. Ask open-ended questions that require thought and verbalization rather than yes, no, or one word answers; propose questions (why, what, where, when, how) and assist the children to find out the answers.
- Tape recorder. Speak into it and play it back.
- Videotape. Tape happenings in the classroom. Let the children view the tape and supply the dialogue.

- Definitions. Introduce new terms and provide opportunity for the children to practice their meanings.
- Food experiences. Let children help shop for, prepare, and eat different foods. Encourage conversation at snack time.
- Dramatic play. Provide an area in the classroom where the children can reenact such community themes as firefighting, hair styling, camping, traveling, eating at a restaurant, or visiting a park.
- Lessons in cause and effect. Dramatize, show pictures, or discuss certain situations. Propose the question, What would happen if—? See how many solutions the children can find.
- "Show and Tell." This may be less effective with younger children. Also, some children feel compelled to have something every time, so you may need a schedule. This is a time for children—not teachers—to talk.
- Invitation. Toss a bean bag or roll a ball to each child and ask him to answer a certain question (e.g., "What is your name?" or "In the story, what did the dog do?"). Arrange a "special day" for each child. Ask the parents to send photos and treasures to school. Invite family members to attend also (babies are fun, mothers might bring treats the child helped prepare, fathers have interesting hobbies or occupations, siblings might play an instrument).
- "Spotlight." Have a place in your room where you display interesting science things. Rotate display but give the children enough time to enjoy and investigate. Use this area to stimulate curiosity and conversation.
- Microphone. Encourage the children to pretend they are talking through a microphone (use a small can, tube, or fist).

WRITING

To think that children under 6 years of age can maneuver writing implements with accuracy and precision or that they have mental organizational skills sophisticated enough to compose a short story indicates total ignorance as to how young children develop and learn. More realistic is the image of a young child crudely holding writing tools, making indistinguishable strokes at scattered locations on the page, giving first one description of his marks and then another, and combining unrelated ideas. Children do pretend to make up, write, and read stories of their own. They see adults do it, so why can't they?

Handwriting has several aspects: physical ability, organizational skills and idea presentation, and language skills (vocabulary, syntax, grammar).

Physical ability includes good use of hands and fingers. Writing requires more than whole-hand grasp and uncontrolled large gross movements. The fingers need to have a good grasp of the utensil, and the arm needs to rest comfortably on a tabletop. The physical prerequisites are often lacking in 4- and 5-year-olds. Their control generally is still imprecise and awkward. Practice and some instruction are needed.

> As in most areas of learning, learning to form letters takes time. It is a lengthy process for several reasons. First, the movements are not easy to make. Second, there are many letters. Third, some letters are very similar to other letters, making it easy to confuse one with another. Fourth, the child must learn that with these special two-dimensional symbols, orientation is a significant attribute. It is not just the configuration of the lines that makes one letter different from the other, but the left-right or up-down orientation as well. . . . If allowed to proceed at their own pace and in their own way, without pressure and fanfare, children will often approach learning to write letters with mastery behavior similar to that used when working puzzles or building with blocks." (Schickedanz 1977)

The second aspect of writing, **organizational skills and idea presentation,** is difficult for young children, who are still in the egocentric stage and have difficulty expressing ideas or seeing things from another's viewpoint. They think others can see into their minds and know their thoughts and that others have the same view as they do. Expressing simple, often unrelated, ideas is the extent of their ability.

The third aspect of writing, **language skills,** is also difficult for young children. They know nothing about the use of capital letters, punctuation, placement of elements in the sentence, spelling, or the use of descriptive words. It will be some years before these attributes are developed.

Beginning writing experiences include the use of jumbo crayons and pencils, large sheets of paper, something interesting to draw, and motivation. When utensils and materials are readily available, the children are encouraged to use them.

Young children should learn manuscript letters (printing) before cursive ones for two reasons. First, when children have had extensive experience with drawing and painting, they may have already mastered basic strokes required in handwriting. Second, as children begin their initial reading, manuscript letters more nearly resemble the print.

When a child expresses interest in writing, parents generally teach the capital letters only. When this occurs, the child must learn two different ways of writing. As a beginner, it is easier for the child to learn capital and lowercase letters in simple words such as his name and familiar objects and terms. Again, this type of writing looks like the type in books. Teachers in the classroom should write names on artwork and possessions by starting in the upper left-hand corner and by using upper- and lowercase letters. The adult should sit down by the children and make the letters neatly as a good model for the children to follow. Writing from across the table or in an awkward position distorts the letters. Children are proud of their work and deserve to have their names neatly written on it.

Help is given with writing as each child expresses an interest.

Use of small muscles in play is practice for holding writing implements.

Writing is not generally one of the regular curriculum areas for young children, but most preschools give help with writing as each child indicates interest. Individually, the experience can be one of joy and success. In some kindergartens, writing practice is one of the regular curriculum areas. Generally, teachers have a specific way of presenting the different letters that is not necessarily consecutive. Many preschool children memorize the alphabet before it has actual meaning to them. Rote memorization of the alphabet may seem important to adults but has little value to the preschool child.

The following activities are recommended to increase writing ability:

- Practice in using and strengthening small muscles (pegboards, cutting, puzzles, stringing, lacing, zipping, drawing, painting)
- Body movement. This helps children to observe, gives them a sense of high, low, and other directions, and teaches them shape and line. (For example, they can be told to swing arms in circle or to hold legs straight). The teacher can also ask the children to make their bodies in shapes shown on cards (Chapter 7).
- Practice in right-left concept ("Hokey-Pokey"; body movement; streamer of paper or bell tied onto one arm or leg)
- Use of manipulative toys (Tinkertoys, snap blocks, magnetic boards, blocks)
- Games (Twister; Do As I'm Doing; circle games such as mulberry bush or ring-around-a-rosy); spinner games, commercial or handmade
- Practice with letters. Each child is given an envelope containing the letters of his name, so he can put them together like a puzzle. Felt letters and numbers are available to use on the flannel board or magnetic ones to use with magnets. Wood, plastic, paper, sandpaper, or fabric letters are provided to manipulate or trace.
- Naming objects. The teacher lines up objects from left to right or top to bottom and asks children to point to and name object in order of placement.
- Drawing. (1) Partly completed designs are finished by the children. (2) The children

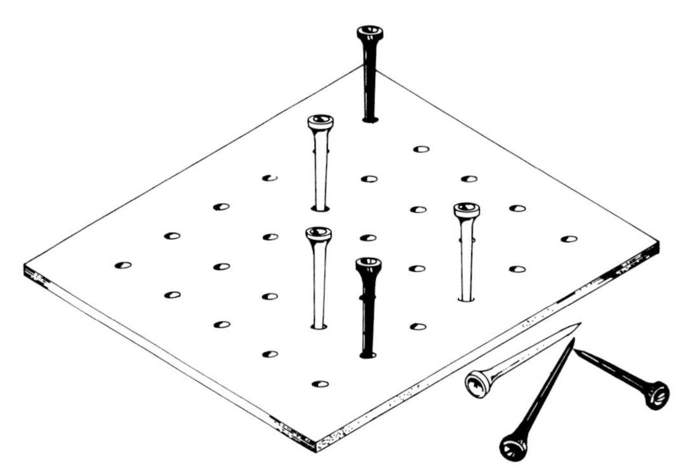

Sticking golf tees into Styrofoam helps increase abilities needed for writing.

reproduce designs using an implement, noting left to right and top to bottom. (3) With crayons, the children follow patterns, making slanted, straight, and curved lines (tepees, boxes, and a road). (4) The children make designs and letters in the air. (5) The children draw a line to match items (mother and baby animals, two shoes, go-togethers).

- Labeling. Each child wears label with his name that he can put into a chart to indicate an area he will play in, put into a "helper" chart, or use as a model when writing his name.
- Art. The children can write in finger paint or sand; paste a variety of shapes to make letters and designs; weave paper, fabric, or yarn mats; stick golf tees in Styrofoam; and hammer small nails into fiberboard.
- Sewing cards (commercial or handmade)

READING

Ivan, a happy 5-year-old, sat looking at the *Wall Street Journal.* His mother had called him several times to prepare for dinner. Still he sat and looked. Finally, mother became exasperated. "Ivan, if you don't come to dinner right this minute, I'll give your food to the dog!" Reluctantly, Ivan laid down the paper and strolled to the table. Still in deep thought, he finally said, "Mom, I just can't figure out why Dad likes that paper so much. It doesn't have any pictures, and it is all the same color!" Ivan was trying to equate his own reading experiences with those of his father. Ivan liked pictures, action, and color.

When young children are read to frequently and when parents are good models of reading, children begin their reading careers early. As Ivan and a parent sat down to read together, Ivan talked about the pictures, asked questions, and added new dialogue. He turned the pages when he was ready. Sometimes he or his parent made additions to the text and sometimes deletions. He memorized his favorite books and could tell when a word was misused or omitted. He figured out that the marks on the pages had something to do with the pictures, an important discovery in developing reading skill and comprehension. He also noticed that when he asked questions that his parents or teachers could not answer, they went to books, so, when he had questions, he looked at books. He did not always find what he wanted, but he knew the procedure followed by adults.

Reading = written symbols + experience + meaning. If children do not have the repertoire of ideas to make sense out of something, the reading makes no sense, either.

Factors that influence the child's ability to learn to read are age, vision, visual perception, eye-hand coordination, visual recall, hearing, emotional-social factors, language development, mental and intellectual factors, and attention span (Leeper et al. 1979). Researchers note a positive relationship between auditory discrimination, motor control, and reading readiness; auditory development is more important than visual development in early reading. Physicians identify 6½ years as the age by which most children have developed sufficient visual power to read printed symbols (Broman 1982).

Wilson and Hall (1972) identified the components of reading readiness as: **physical** (general health, sex, hearing, vision, age); **perceptual** (auditory, visual, and directional); **cognitive** (mental age); **linguistic** (oral language facility, speaking, and listening); **psychological** (attitude toward self and others, school, and process of reading); and **environmental** (home and experiential background). Lundsteen and Tarrow (1981) classify reading as a "thinking process that depends on concepts and operations." Their classification is based heavily on Piaget's concepts of spatial relationships, seriation, whole-part

Individual maturation is an important factor in a child's ability to read.

relationships, multiple and simultaneous classification, reversibility, and conservation combined with visual perception, eye-hand and hand-hand coordination, language background, auditory discrimination, autonomous problem solving, and the ability to accept discipline. Elkind (1978) lists four requirements for successful beginning reading: (1) a language-rich environment, (2) attachment to adults who model and reward reading behavior, (3) attainment of concrete operations, and (4) an instructional program. However the components are labeled, they point to individual maturation of the child, his past experiences, motivation, and opportunities.

Should reading be taught before first grade? Several early childhood educators say yes *and* no (Durkin 1978; Elkind 1978; Hymes 1981; Ramsey 1980; Schickedanz 1977). In general, here are their responses combined with those of this author:

YES, if

1. there is an internal desire to learn to read;
2. the methods fit the child under 6 years of age and the child fits the methods;
3. it further extends language arts;
4. the individual child is "ready;"
5. the child has had enriching experiences;
6. teachers create an interest and awareness in words and books;
7. expectations are individualized;
8. firsthand experiences support reading and vice versa;
9. provision is made for frequent talking, questioning, answering, and problem-solving on the part of the child;
10. parents are involved in knowing how to help without pressuring their children.

A

B

<u>KAGOME KAGOME</u>	〈かごめ かごめ〉
KAGOME KAGOME	かごめ かごめ
KAGONO NAKANO TORIWA	かごの 中の 鳥は
ITSU ITSU DEAU	いついつ であう
YOAKENO BANNI	夜明けの 晩に
TSURUTO KAMEGA SUBETTA	鶴と 亀が すべった
USHIRONO SYOMEN DARE	後の 正面 だーれ?

For adults only. Identify the individual words and meaning of the shorthand (A) and the Japanese (B).

NO, if

1. instruction is given through workbooks, rote memorization, dittoed material, or routine exercises;
2. every child is considered to have the same experiences and abilities and is expected to perform uniformly;
3. a premium is put on quietness;
4. a stigma is attached to the child's reading group;
5. other areas of curriculum or personal development are excluded or it robs legitimate curriculum from later school experiences;
6. the child has had limited or no contact with reading materials in the home;
7. the teacher is merely giving in to parent pressure;
8. it is used only as an ego-builder for the teacher;
9. teachers are untrained in teaching reading.

Throughout this text, activities are suggested to increase skills and abilities in children. The samples of shorthand and Japanese on page 114 and the music below are symbol-reading exercises just for adults.

As you approached each of these exercises, you probably looked for familiar signs. If you felt comfortable with one option more than the other two, you probably concentrated there. If none of the three exercises gave you any clues, you probably became frustrated and moved on to the next paragraph. Young children learning to read look for familiar symbols in their environment (names, road signs, designs) and then try to match them to symbols in written material. You just went through a similar experience.

The following elements help to increase reading ability:

- Games where sound and listening are important
- A cozy place to read (loft or tent with pillows)
- A variety of good books appropriate for the child
- A discussion about the care of books
- Enrichment of the child's vocabulary
- Displayed pictures. Talk about the artist's meaning. Add information the children might not notice. Note detail and color. Display children's artwork. Rotate pictures. Include famous paintings.

Hum the music and identify the two songs (do not use a piano or other musical instrument).

- Uninterrupted time
- Visual discrimination. Using an eye chart, have each child point in the direction the letter faces. From sets of pictures, have the children select those that are similar and those that are different. Have the children look at pictures and tell what part is missing (nose, hair, leaves, and so on). Have the children compare properties of objects (small, large; smallest, largest). Using animal shapes, have the children make appropriate sounds.
- Seriation. Have the children accurately line up sequence pictures, such as size, variation in color, or stacking of shoes, socks, sticks, cups, jars, ribbons, and so on. Have the children help measure other children and line them up according to height.
- Classification. Have the children put objects into appropriate groups and then look for other ways of grouping.
- Card games (bingo and picture variations; "Old Maid"; "Fish"; matching pictures of shapes, sizes, and colors; combining two properties such as size and shape; large cards with numbers and letters the children can arrange)
- Poster or chart. Use a helper chart where child's name is placed by a picture with word for activity or an assignment. Have a chart on which the child places his name beside the activity he wishes to participate in. Make a word dictionary as children learn new words (include pictures).
- Food. Make a list, go to the grocery store, buy food for lunch or snack (observe labels). Make something using a recipe.
- Typewriter or computer
- Curriculum areas. (1) Have a pattern for blocks that go in certain places. (2) Provide puzzles and rubber stamps of objects, letters, and numbers. (3) Have toys placed in right box or area. (4) Supply sewing cards. (5) Cover light cardboard with sandpaper, plastic, fabric, or wood and cut into puzzle pieces. (6) Have children reproduce designs with pegs, beads, or blocks.
- Symbols. (1) Place a sticker or design on each child's locker. (2) Wear name tags daily. (3) Write each child's name on his artwork. (4) Use one picture of only boys, one of only girls, and one of both boys and girls; hold up one picture and have those children respond to actions or questions (no verbalization is used).
- Artwork. Ask children to tell about their artwork. Write down what they say and read it back to them.
- Community. (1) Take a trip to the local library. (2) Observe safety and speed signs. (3) Go to some interesting places and observe signs. Write a thank you note.
- Decentering. Help children focus on more than one aspect at a time (they will need to recognize parts and whole if they are to learn to read—individual letters make whole words; whole words make ideas; ideas make stories).
- Practice. Give the children opportunities to practice concepts of conservation, reversibility, seriation, whole-part relationships, multiple and simultaneous classification. (Some examples are listed above and in Chapter 11.)

DEVELOPMENTAL CHARACTERISTICS

Listening

Age 2 Understands most simple words and sentences. Likes to hear commercial "jingles" and catchy tunes. Listens to simple stories. Likes nursery rhymes.

Age 3 Likes to hear familiar sounds (animals, transportation, household). Likes one-on-one reading experiences. Has rather short but attentive listening span.

Age 4 Listens longer to stories. Still likes one-on-one experiences. May bring favorite stories to be read. Can follow simple directions.

Age 5 Seems content to listen for period of time. Enjoys stories, songs, finger plays, and rhymes. Can follow more directions.

Speaking

Age 2 Has a favorite word: "No!" Tries to say simple words; may use short sentences and carry on simple conversation. Names simple objects (body parts, pictures). Likes short responses.

Age 3 Can carry on a conversation. Uses simple words and short sentences (3 to 4 words). May carry on a monologue. Asks "why" to gain adult attention.

Age 4 Is quick to pick up new words. Learns words for ideas, actions, and feelings. Combines more words. Is integrating rules of grammar; may have difficulty with irregular past tense or plurals. Is boastful and quarrelsome. May carry on a monologue. Talks about imaginary companion. Experiments with language. Asks "why" for knowledge.

Age 5 Has highly socialized speech. Is a continual talker. Uses "because" sentences. Has wide vocabulary, uses six- to eight-word sentences. Can verbally compare two or more objects.

Writing

Age 2 Scribbles; repeats radial or circular pattern. Uses whole-hand grasp, whole-arm movement. Fills whole page. Is fascinated by markings.

Age 3 Prints large, single, capital letters anywhere on page. Likes to draw and paint (images are large, simple, and incomplete).

Age 4 May recognize a few letters including own name. May write name or a few capital letters (large and irregular). Likes to draw and paint. Human figures are "stick," drawings crude. Draws circles and squares.

Age 5 Prints first name (large, irregular letters increasing in size). Frequently reverses letters and numbers or writes from right to left. Prints numbers (uneven and medium-sized). Can write some upper-case and lower-case letters. Has better grasp on writing utensils. Likes to draw and paint. Pictures are more complex and complete. Combines squares and circles. Likes to copy a model. May ask about spelling.

Reading

Age 2 May recognize objects, turn pages in books, point to or name objects.

Ages 3, 4, 5 May learn to read simple words (some memorize or remember). May identify words that look alike or different. Recognize a few words (own name, signs, TV words, food containers).

"It is just too difficult for them [4- and 5-year-olds] to master from a rule-and-analysis point of view" in learning decoding skills. "It is that the thinking of preprimary and kindergarten children is not governed by rules. Though they can learn many of the specifics that go into rules and operate with these on an intuitive basis, they cannot integrate the specifics into an organized system" (Schickedanz 1977).

Some children under 6 years of age do learn to read. Elkind (1978) conducted two studies on early readers. In both studies, he found that "early reading children were superior to non-early-reading children on Piagetian measures of conservation. They were also better on certain psycholinguistic measure, such as sound blending." In interviews of parents of the subject children Elkind found a "rich background of early experience with spoken and written language provided by homes where books and magazines are plentiful and where parents frequently read to the children." Social motivation and wanting to please significant adults were also necessary factors.

CUMULATIVE LESSON PLAN

- Look at and talk about the composition and construction of boxes (wood, cardboard, plastic-covered, and so on.)
- Have a variety of objects and boxes to talk about and match.
- Read *The Box with Red Wheels* by Petersham.

ESPECIALLY FOR PARENTS

Language arts are more than books; they include listening, speaking, writing, and reading. Language is developed through meaningful activities, time to mature, stimulating things to think about, opportunities to solve problems, observation, and, mostly, encouragement of loving parents. It is worth your time to read over the information and suggested activities for listening, speaking, writing, and reading that have been directed to teachers in this chapter.

Parents do see their child in circumstances different from the teacher and do spend more time with the child over the years. Parents are responsible for the total well-being of the child; the teacher is mainly concerned with his education. While a teacher has certain privileges and responsibilities for the child's education, the parents are the real teachers of their children. Parents may say, "Oh, I wouldn't know how to teach my child!" But like it or not, parents *are* teachers of their children.

One of the best ways for you to assist in the language development of your child is to be a good model—listen to your child, give him opportunities to ask and answer questions and to talk, provide art experiences that allow him to practice prereading and prewriting skills, and show him that you read for enjoyment.

Here are a few additional parent-child activities to foster the development of language arts:

Listening

- Be an attentive listener.
- Take time to talk with, not to, your child. Plan some interesting and exciting things that encourage questions and increase knowledge.
- Help him select good television programs. View them with him so you can understand his concerns. (When the average American child graduates from high school, he has spent more time watching television than attending school.)
- Provide some appropriate listening experiences (records, tapes). Be aware of loudness to prevent hearing problems.
- Read to your child often. Use a variety of topics but don't get too concerned if he asks for favorites. Find a cozy place and time without interruption. Closeness (on your lap or next to you) increases the pleasure.
- Tell (instead of read) often. You may have a family tradition or "continued" series.
- Play the "position" game with your child (learn about prepositions).

Speaking

- Be an attentive listener.
- Give honest praise frequently.
- Speak clearly; be positive, joyful.
- Avoid baby talk or "talking down."
- Help your child make up some games so he can take part in establishing rules.
- Let him participate in a family gathering with a poem, a song, or an idea.
- Play a game with him, such as "What would happen if . . ."

- Write down descriptions of his pictures, novel sayings, and poems.
- Talk about rhyming words.
- Assign a family member to record the family conversation at dinner one night and learn who talks the most, whether members share in the discussion or talk only about personal interests, and how much time is spent in pleasant conversation.
- Increase your child's vocabulary by introducing and defining appropriate words and terms. Allow firsthand opportunities to understand the new terms.
- While you are doing household tasks, errands, or activities, briefly explain what is happening.
- Make your verbal and nonverbal language (gestures, actions) compatible. How would you expect a child to respond if you said, "Have some of this delicious broccoli," while you had a sick look on your face?

Writing

- Do your correspondence with a positive attitude.
- Give your child some sheets of paper (or a booklet) and let him draw a story while you write down his comments.
- Help him write a letter to someone.
- Provide good writing tools—his own, if possible.
- Appreciate his attempts at writing.
- Show him how to write his name and other words as he indicates interest (use upper- and lowercase letters).

Reading

- Provide your child quality listening experiences.
- Take him to the library often.
- Purchase some good books for him.
- Help him to find out things by using books.
- When he is interested and ready, have some alphabet or number cards for his exploration.
- Let him have some magazines of his own so he can look through them, cut out pictures, and write in them.
- Point out pictures and ideas in magazines.
- Talk about the care of books.
- Provide a quiet, comfortable, well-lighted place to read, away from distractions.
- When reading to and with the child, give him time to look at the pictures, let him turn the pages; frequently let him choose the books.
- Have books arranged but available for use.
- Choose books that are physically appropriate to child's stage (e.g., cardboard for 2-year-olds; also note the size and shape).

A closing, informative quote: "Either consciously or unconsciously, parents *do* identify and define the reading process for their children and they *do* model behavior that either supports or negates the value of reading. Because of the importance of modeling and the impact of the home environment, there is a need for parents to serve as *informed* guides for their children" (Simmons and Lawrence 1981).

For children's books, see Appendix E.

APPLICATION OF PRINCIPLES

1. Briefly describe the four distinct but interrelated areas of language as they pertain to young children.

2. Using a storybook for visuals, tell the story to a group of children. What do you need to remember about your voice? Your eye contact? Interruptions from children?
3. Give some criteria for books for young children. How often should you use fairy tales? Why?
4. Write and illustrate an original story for young children. Use it with a small group of children. Discuss the experience with another teacher.
5. Engage three to five children in a spontaneous conversation. Talk about *their* interests.
6. During creative time, note how children of different ages hold writing implements. Should you encourage a child who is using his left hand to change to his right hand?
7. Display some meaningful words around the room such as name tags for the children, labels on furniture, and words under pictures. Note which children comment, show interest, or attempt to write their own name on pictures.
8. Use games, toys, or other ways to help children discriminate and describe colors, shapes, and sizes.
9. Observe the differences in interest span in children of the same or different ages.

References

Arbuthnot, May H. *Children and Books.* Chicago: Scott, Foresman, 1972.

Broman, Betty L. *The Early Years in Childhood Education.* 2d ed. Boston: Houghton Mifflin, 1982.

Durkin, Dolores. "Pre-first Grade Starts in Reading: Where Do We Stand?" *Educational Leadership* 38(1978): 174–177.

Elkind, David. "We Can Teach Reading Better." In *Readings in Early Childhood Education 78/79.* Guilford, Conn.: Dushkin, 1978, pp. 244–246.

Griffin, Elinor F. *Island of Childhood: Education in the Special World of Nursery School.* New York: Teachers College Press, Columbia University, 1982.

Hendrick, Joanne. *The Whole Child.* 2d ed. St. Louis: C. V. Mosby, 1980.

Hymes, James L., Jr. *Teaching the Child Under Six.* Columbus, Ohio: Charles E. Merrill, 1981.

Kohlberg, Lawrence. "Cognitive Stages of Preschool Education." *Human Development* 9, nos. 1 and 2, 1966.

Leeper, Sarah H., Ruth J. Dales, Dora S. Skipper, and Ralph L. Witherspoon. *Good Schools for Young Children.* New York: Macmillan, 1979.

Lundsteen, S., and N. Tarrow. *Guiding Young Children's Learning.* New York: McGraw-Hill, 1981.

Ramsey, Marjorie E., and Kathleen M. Bayless. *Kindergarten: Programs and Practices.* St. Louis: C. V. Mosby, 1980.

Read, Katherine. *The Nursery School.* Philadelphia: W. B. Saunders, 1971.

Schickedanz, Judith A., Mary E. York, Ida S. Stewart, and Doris White. *Strategies for Teaching Young Children.* Englewood Cliffs, N.J.: Prentice-Hall, 1977.

Seefeldt, Carol. *A Curriculum for Preschools.* Columbus, Ohio: Charles E. Merrill, 1980.

Serbin, Lisa A., and K. Daniel O'Leary. "How Nursery Schools Teach Girls to Shut Up." *Psychology Today,* December 1975.

Simmons, Barbara, and Paula S. Lawrence. "Beginning Reading: Welcome Parents." *Childhood Education* 57(January/February 1981): 156–160.

Spock, Benjamin. "Are Fairy Tales Good for Children?" *Redbook* June 1976, 136–138.

Stone, L. Joseph, and Joseph Church. *Childhood and Adolescence.* New York: Random House, 1973.

Swartz, Sydney L., and Helen F. Robison. *Designing Curriculum for Early Childhood.* Boston: Allyn & Bacon, 1982.

Taylor, Barbara J. "The Ability of Three-, Four-, and Five-Year-Old Children to Distinguish Fantasy from Reality." *Journal of Genetic Psychology* 122 (1973): 315–318.

Wilson, R., and M. A. Hall. *Reading and the Elementary School Child: Theory and Practice for Teachers.* New York: Van Nostrand, Reinhold, 1972.

5

Music and Movement Education

Jack and Jill went up the hill
to get a pail of water,
Jack fell down and broke his crown
And Jill came tumbling after.

MAIN PRINCIPLES

1. Music is an enjoyable art form that aids self-expression.
2. Movement education is a viable curriculum area because of its enjoyment and value for children.
3. Alert teachers and parents bring many spontaneous and planned music and movement opportunities into the lives of young children.

How about a new version of the above nursery rhyme:

A whistling Jack and a singing Jill
went skipping merrily up the hill.
They filled their pail clear to the top
and started home without a stop.
They both were quick, they both were
agile;
Their bodies had developed so they were
no longer fragile.
They sang and played the whole day through;
they liked themselves, and others, too.

The feeling one has about his body and his abilities is very important in the development of a good self-image. One likes to feel confident in trying things, in interacting with others, and in exploring the environment.

From the time a baby is old enough to be aware of sounds, he attends to those that are rhythmic and melodious. Some of his first games are pat-a-cake, bye-bye, and peek-a-boo. Toddlers and young preschoolers readily sing and perform to catchy commercials on the radio or television, while 4- and 5-year-olds enjoy songs, finger plays, and activities that have rhythm or repetition. Music has a definite effect upon the way one feels and moves.

MUSIC

For the past decade, there have been increased emphasis and research on brain development and the functions of each half of the brain—the left for verbal and analytic thought, the right for intuition and for understanding patterns. The verbal-analytic half is extremely important in dealing with the object world and in learning spoken language as well as reading and writing. The right hemisphere is used to perceive and express novel and complex visual, spatial, and musical patterns. Both brain halves are specialized and complementary, but may be in conflict. The left hemisphere tends to be dominant (Galin 1976). Therefore, specific experiences must be provided to exercise the right hemisphere. Creativity is one way, whether through music, art, science, or other means.

Each person needs to find acceptable ways of expressing himself openly without fear of ridicule or embarrassment. Music or movement is more comfortable than verbalization for some individuals.

In his six-year study, Petzold (1969) reported that "children's musical development will be seriously limited if they do not acquire an aural (listening) understanding of the elements of music while they are young." Young children often listen acutely, consciously or subconsciously respond to environmental sounds, and then participate before any audience. Later on, they may not be willing to do these things.

Young children are not good at keeping quiet; their minds, bodies, and mouths seem to be in perpetual motion. They need a balance of activities for their physical, social, emotional, and intellectual development. Many opportunities are offered through music. They receive encouragement for talent, develop language, practice auditory discrimination, explore, learn about culture and ethnic groups, express individuality, feel success, and learn musical concepts such as rhythm (steady and melodic pattern), tempo (fast, slow), pitch (high, low), timbre (tone quality of different instruments), dynamics (loud, soft), and melody and its related words, phrasing, accent, and mood (Swartz and Robison 1982). Margolin (1976) states that "children must be exposed to listening with intent to identify sounds, rhythms, intensities, pitch. . . . It is one aspect of a child's musical development to hear sounds; it is quite another to know how to identify them within some sort of conceptual framework related to a subject matter area." Music can, and should, help develop good listening skills.

A child's acceptance or rejection of music depends on his "chronological age, previous musical experiences, and cultural background" (McCall 1971). Younger children and those from homes and backgrounds where music is prevalent seem to be more accepting and appreciative of opportunities to interact in a musical setting.

The role of the adult in structuring an environment that fosters and facilitates music and language growth in young children is identified by Bayless and Ramsey (1982) as:

1. Increasing their own awareness of the range of musical opportunities
2. Providing a wealth of music experiences
3. Making music an integral part of the day
4. Building a strong and varied repertoire of rhythms, finger plays, poetry, and movement exercises
5. Fostering a sharing, verbal atmosphere surrounding young children
6. Recognizing the individual differences reflected in each child's musical preferences
7. Delighting in music with young children

8. Interacting with children as they sing or speak
9. Helping young children put their own nonsense, rhymes, riddles, and verses to music
10. Using music to expand memory
11. Playing a supportive role as young children experiment and discover music

A wise teacher discovers the developmental stage of each child and then plans beneficial experiences, avoiding activities that are too complex or frustrating. She provides some type of music every day; she encourages spontaneous expression both indoors and outdoors, using a variety of methods and activities. She picks up and encourages the rhythmic movements of the children. She values individuality and plans accordingly. If she is not musically inclined herself, she arranges for another person to assist her, uses records and tapes, or invites a guest rather than eliminate music from the daily curriculum. She provides experiences that help the children release their feelings constructively, whether the feelings are of anger and hostility or of joy and excitement. She may even need to provide props to encourage creative expression, such as long, full skirts, crepe paper streamers, scarves, or yarn balls. In sum, an experienced teacher knows the many values of music.

Music should occur spontaneously. Some experiences, however, must be structured— not to the exclusion of creative thinking or moving, but to the extent that a specific time or activity is planned. When the experience is for group activity, more planning is required than if it is to be incidental. And, of course, a teacher sets up and maintains necessary limits in teaching music as well as in other curriculum areas.

Children develop a lifelong appreciation for music as a result of a pleasant introduction. Many children are observant enough to pick up rhythmic sounds around them; for example, the dripping sound that is annoying to an adult may be incorporated into play by a child.

Music is often an individual, spontaneous event.

Teaching Songs

Young children learn songs best through repetition. They do not read, their experience is limited, and they cannot remember new long sentences and phrases. The songs should be easy to sing and have familiar ideas, repetition, a distinct rhythm, and a limited range of notes (middle C through G above, according to Lundsteen and Tarrow 1981; Middle C to 8 tones above, according to Bayless and Ramsey 1982 and Ramsey and Bayless 1980).

The teacher sings the song slowly and clearly, repeating it several times. Then she invites the children: "Sing along with me when you are ready." She may use visual aids to help clarify ideas or sequence. Most of all, she is enthusiastic. Just as careful thought goes into the selection of the songs (the children's interests, their abilities, their stage of development) as for any other item in her schedule. Children especially like using their own names, things they can do, holidays, birthdays, nature, weather, fun and nonsense, feelings, home activities, families, pets, body parts, and abilities.

Songs should be short (no more than two phrases of words) and written in a 5-tone scale. Children like question-and-answer, folk, patriotic, and seasonal songs (Bayless and Ramsey 1982). Sheehy (1968) states: "Songs are to be sung, not to be talked about." Pitcher et al. (1974) remind us as follows:

> The teacher should not expect a response on the first day or the second. It takes time for a young child to understand and remember the words and longer still to gain a clear conception of a melody. . . . Encourage him to sing, even if he isn't singing your tune. Vocal chords need exercise, and he needs vocal expression. Drill on either words or music is harmful for preschool children. Sing the song, straight through, and let him catch what he can, even if it is only the last note. Pitch will come on the wave of rhythm. (P. 47)

Introducing Rhythm Instruments

Because of frustrating experiences with rhythm instruments, some teachers include this experience infrequently or never in their curriculum. Suppose someone placed in front of you a very exciting and new object—and told you not to touch it! Wouldn't that be frustrating? Now, also suppose that you knew what to do with the object and your body was saying, "Pick it up and see what you can do with it!" and somebody kept saying, "I'll show or tell you how to do it." The minute you got the "go ahead," wouldn't you do as much, as fast, and as loud as you could? Does it make sense to place something like a rhythm instrument in front of a child and then tell him not to touch it?

The teacher may want to introduce one kind of instrument at a time. She should try to have enough of the same kind so that each child can explore it on the same day. When first introducing the instrument, she may want to talk about its properties or use. Then she should identify a signal of when to start and when to stop playing and let the children try it. If the number of instruments is limited, the children take turns so that each child knows he will get a chance. On other days, different instruments are introduced. After the children are exposed to several kinds, the instruments are combined for a more advanced experience. Each child should have an opportunity to use all the instruments—even if for a short time.

On return use of the instruments, the children are allowed to select the instruments they want to play, with the understanding there will be trading. The children can be responsible for passing out and gathering in the instruments.

Activities to Increase Music Abilities

Music is often limited to singing songs. Singing is fun and a good musical activity but is only one of many possibilities. Suggested activities in other chapters could be enhanced or varied with the addition of music. The following ideas are submitted as being useful; however, it is hoped that the reader will be creative when planning music experiences for young children.

- Use finger plays, chants, and poems.
- Provide experiences with a variety of musical instruments.
- Make and use rhythm instruments.
- Play a variety of records, tapes, and music—classical, contemporary, instrumental, rhythmical, tempo, participation, listening, and so on.
- Teach the children how to use tape recorders. Tapes with songs, instrumentation, and stories can be checked out from many libraries. They make great individual or group listening opportunities. They last better than records; they don't scratch as easily and can be used in the car or outdoors.
- Sing songs (with and without aids, with and without actions).
- Sing scale songs ("I Love Little Pussy," "Do, Re, Mi").
- Encourage children to sing while they play.
- Often, let the children choose songs to sing.
- For children who are reluctant to suggest songs, make a large cube with a picture for a song on each side. Roll the cube like a die and sing the song that comes up on top. Or make a "singing tree." Pick a leaf off the tree. Turn it over for the song title. Or make a flower out of construction paper. Print the name of a song on it. Attach it to a straw and "plant" it in a clay pot of dirt. Let a child select a flower and then sing that song. Or place objects in a basket that represent certain songs. A child selects an object to sing about.
- Invite guests who sing, dance, or play musical instruments.
- Plan an activity around high-low, fast-slow, or loud-soft music.
- Identify natural rhythm in the classroom or play yard, such as clocks, squeaks, drips, bouncing balls, and swaying trees.
- Go on a walking field trip to hear and identify rhythm.
- Go places where music can be heard (band or orchestra practice, parade, sporting event, stores, television studio, dance studio).
- During each season, go for a walk and listen to different sounds (e.g., crunch of ice

Tape recorders can be used in groups or individually for good listening experiences.

and snow, snap of a twig, rustle of leaves, pattern of rain, blowing of wind, stepping on stones or in puddles).

- Combine experiences so the children can listen, create, sing, move, and experiment with sounds (based on the developmental level of the children).

A piano is used as an activity in itself or as accompaniment to other activities.

- Use music with other curriculum areas (art and science) and activities (free play and snack).
- Be constantly aware of opportunities for spontaneous music.
- Have some specific listening experiences. Make sounds and then have the children repeat and identify them.
- Clap rhythm patterns to names, poems, and nursery rhymes and have the children repeat them or do them with you.
- Use body actions to music ("Head, Shoulders, Knees, and Toes").
- Exercise to music (aerobics are popular with children).
- Provide props that encourage rhythm and music (blocks, sticks, coconut shells, shakers, bells).
- Use a piano often, if available. You can vary the tempo and rhythm for exciting activities.
- Obtain an autoharp, an excellent instrument to use with children (available in different sizes and prices).
- Fill matching film cans for identifying sounds.
- Use visual aids to create interest in music (objects, posters, charts, pictures, movie boxes, transparencies, costumes, flip charts, drawing on a chalkboard).
- Play circle games ("Mulberry Bush," "Ring Around-a-Rosy," "Hokey-Pokey," "This is the way we . . .").
- Practice body sounds (hum, click teeth, snap fingers, blink eyes, clap, slap, rub, tap, shake).
- Use music outdoors often.
- Provide guidelines so children will know what is expected of them in various activities. Can they play the autoharp, or is it just for teachers? How about the new dancing drum? Do the instruments stay in a certain area? Who can operate the record player and tape recorder?
- Provide opportunities to support musical concepts such as rhythm, tempo, timbre, dynamics, and melody.
- Over a period of time, teach about three groups of instruments: woodwind, percussion, and string.

See the activities under "Listening" in Chapter 4.

MOVEMENT EDUCATION

Young children are doers, talkers, and movers. Their bodies are not naturally still; however, movement should be encouraged in the right places and in the right ways, with time, space, ideas, and props.

When children discover the great potential in their body movements, they want to explore the possibilities. They test, try to understand and accept their bodies, and begin to feel confident and to lose self-consciousness. They feel joy and pleasure in free movement. "Many times, movement exploration may lead directly into a creative dance experience or may form the basis for a folk dance. As such, it is the process, the solving of a problem, and the discovering of a new way, rather than an end product, that are important" (Clark 1969).

Movement may take place in a quiet and solitary setting or in an active group. Moha, a quiet 3-year-old, sat listening to a record. Then he commented: "It goes around and around!" His head began going around and around, then his arms, and finally his whole body. He was transferring the motion from the record to his body and finding it to be a delightful experience.

Movement is a viable and important part of the daily curriculum—not an add-on. It can easily be integrated as an expression medium. It is natural, essential, and valuable for physical and mental health and can also enhance academic learning; it aids in problem solving, exploration, and success. It helps to encourage inquisitiveness and creativity in children, who have an innate drive to master their environment through sensorimotor activities. Through space exploration, they can develop body control, ease and confidence in movement, motor skills of coordination, strength, flexibility, balance, laterality, and directionality. Their bodies move in time (fast, medium, sudden, or sustained), in force (strong or light), in flow (bound, free, or a combination), in tension-relaxation, and in such relationships as near and far, front and back, over and under, lead and follow, or unison and contrast (Day 1983).

According to Lundsteen and Tarrow (1981), factors that affect movement are: (1) body awareness and actions (what is moved), (2) space (where one moves), (3) effort, or quality, of movement (how), and (4) relationship (with whom or what). Appropriate experiences can be provided so children can practice and become more proficient in the use of their bodies. Competition, such as pitting boys against girls or children against each other, is avoided. Rather each child tries to improve his own physical skills and abilities.

Children who are restricted or forbidden to explore are at a definite disadvantage. One young child was given an ample number of playthings and good physical care and attention, but was restricted in space. She soon became listless, subject to illness, overweight, and insecure. Becoming concerned, her mother sought professional help, only to be encouraged to "open up the child's world." The child soon returned to her usual happy self when she was allowed more freedom to explore, find toys of her interest, interact with other children, and become more independent.

Body movement can be classified into two different categories: (1) locomotor (propelling the body through space as in running, jumping, and leaping) and (2) nonlocomotor (stationary activities, such as stretching, twisting, and bending). Both kinds are necessary to develop good body skills.

Items in the following list are recommended to increase movement skills:

- Place a series of footprints on the floor. Ask the children to walk or skip on them, jump from one to another, roll over them, and so on. Have footprints spaced at varying intervals.
- Provide a balance beam. For beginners, have it close to the floor. Raise it as the children develop skill.
- Encourage the children to act out their feelings (stamp, pound, yell, glide, skip, dance).
- Tell them to act out movement in nature (sway, bend, tap).
- Encourage each child to move in his own way.
- Give mental images and have the children imitate them (rowing a boat, walking in wind, flying like a bird, walking with a broken leg, pulling a heavy load, carrying a vase on the head, and so on).
- Use records or tapes that encourage gross movement, listening, interpreting, and moving. (Hap Palmer records are good; see record sources in Appendix E.)
- Provide props that encourage movement, such as scarves, balls, clothes, and streamers.
- Make obstacle courses both indoors and outdoors. Verbally tell the children what is expected or have indicators for over this, around that, under this, between those, and so on.
- Encourage the children to explore space by running, rolling, jumping, swinging arms, and so on. At times have them confined to a small area, at other times let them move as far as they desire.
- Provide a mat for tumbling, jumping, and rolling.
- Do activities using various body parts (touch your elbow, touch your elbow to your toe; put your hand on your knee; put your nose on your knee).
- Encourage the children to make their bodies tall, small, straight, or crooked.

Children release their feelings through rhythmic movements.

- Provide many opportunities to practice locomotor skills (walking, crawling, hopping, jumping, running, leaping, skipping, galloping, rolling, climbing, sliding).
- Provide many opportunities to practice nonlocomotor skills (bending, swaying, rocking, stretching, turning, pulling, pushing, twisting, curling, standing, sitting, kneeling, reaching).
- Go on a walk; jump over cracks, straddle a rock, balance on a curb, skip around fountain, and so on.
- Play the sponge game. Each child has a sponge (approximately 4 by 6 in.). The children follow the directions of a teacher or another child: "Put your sponge on your head." "Walk without letting it fall off." "Put it on your shoulder, your arm, your shoe." "Crawl with it on your back." "Jump over it." "Sit on it." "Roll on it." Length of this activity is determined by the interest of the children.
- Dramatize stories or activities.
- Sing songs that encourage actions (e.g., "Wiggle Song," "Head, Shoulders, Knees, and Toes," "Do As I'm Doing," "The Bus Song").
- Ask the children to go to various parts of the room "without using their feet," "like a ball," backwards, and so on.
- Have the children pretend to be Raggedy Ann and Raggedy Andy (no bones).
- Use body cards and have the children model poses.
- Plan activities during which the children use their bodies to learn about location (especially good for learning about prepositions).

- Make and use equipment (hula hoops out of plastic tubing, scoops out of plastic bleach bottles, and balls from yarn).
- Use hula hoop. Move inside of the hoop, roll it, jump into it, crawl through it, or share it with a friend.
- Combine activities using a rope, hula hoop, beanbag, and ball.
- Play games such as "Twister," "Mother, May I?," "What Can You Do?," and tag.
- Make body shadows.
- Pretend to jump across a stream, narrow at first then wider and wider.
- Follow a rhythm chart. Picture of a hand indicates when to clap, picture of a foot indicates when to stamp.
- Practice ball handling as the children develop such skills as rolling, catching, throwing, bouncing, and kicking.
- Use beanbags to throw at a target (bucket, box), kick them, or balance them on the head or back.
- Provide rope experiences. Rope can be made into shapes, jumped over, crawled under, or used to circumscribe space.
- Get a small parachute (tablecloth or sheet may also work) and have children try the activities in the following list. Original activities are also encouraged.

  Marshmallow: Hold parachute waist high. On signal, throw arms and parachute as high as possible. Let parachute float down softly.
  Waves: Gently wave parachute up and down and observe rippling motion.
  Cover-up: Hold parachute waist high. On signal, extend arms upward and while still holding onto parachute turn around and squat on ground. Chute covers participants.
  Bouncers: Place two yarn or other small balls in center of parachute. Try to keep them bouncing by shaking parachute up and down.
  Catchers: Space teachers and children around the outside of parachute. Slowly move parachute up and down. On count of "three," the teacher calls either "boys" or "girls." The called group runs under parachute, and others try to catch them.

- Show pictures of animals and have children imitate their movements, such as sliding like a snake, jumping like a kangaroo, flying like a bird, and hopping like a bunny.
- Have an animal walk. Imitate a bear, seal, crab, frog, duck, or monkey.
- Take a field trip to a gymnasium, sports area, or dance studio.
- Have the children move as they would in different occupations (sanitation worker, engineer, baker, mountain climber, forest ranger, and so on). Note that occupations can be for both sexes.
- Tell each child to form a circle with his body; then add a partner to form a circle; continue to add more children to form still larger circles. Do the same with other shapes such as a line, square, or triangle.
- Show pictures of a circus. Have the children pretend to be dancing bears, prancing horses, stalking tigers, trunk-and-tail-holding elephants, and performing lions.
- Let the children practice coordination skills by walking first on a piece of string or yarn placed on the floor, then on the wide side of a balance beam placed on the floor, then on the narrow side of the beam. Begin to raise the beam slightly from the floor as skills develop.
- Make a number of pictures of animals and tape to the floor. Bunnies mean to hop; frogs to jump; and ducks to sway. Start with a series of the same animal; later mix up the pictures so the actions will vary as the child moves around.
- Demonstrate flexibility and stretching to children by using a large rubber band. Ask the children to use their bodies in the same way—stretching and flexing in various ways.
- Take a make-believe ride in an elevator, stretching high, higher, highest as the elevator goes up and low, lower, lowest as it comes down.

- Pantomime different activities.
- Help children see movement in everyday things such as animals, people, or objects (clocks, faucets, cars, trains).
- Suggest ideas to children and let them express their individuality (colors, moods, holidays).

DEVELOPMENTAL CHARACTERISTICS

Age 2: Enjoys listening to sounds; jabbers. Loves action songs and finger plays. Sings spontaneously with or without an adult but matches few tones correctly. May sing phrases of songs or hum parts. Experiments with rhythm. Walks on tiptoe. Pushes and pulls toys. Actively explores his environment. Climbs stairs with both feet on each step. Stands on balance beam. Jumps immaturely (two-foot take-off). Throws small ball a short distance with no control. Walks sidewards and backwards.

Age 3: May or may not sing, but likes songs and rhythm. Walks a 10-ft line, heel to toe. Hops two to three steps. Walks on balance beam for short distance. Throws ball about 10 ft. Climbs stairs alternating feet. Rides tricycle.

Age 4: Creates own rhythm. Keeps rhythm somewhat. Enjoys singing, especially action songs. Is more observant of sound and rhythm around him. Runs well, jumps, and walks on a balance beam. Walks easily up and down stairs. Likes to be independent; resists many directions. Feels quite confident about body skills; notes abilities of other children. Has good balance; likes to carry liquids without spilling them. Can throw objects at a target. Enjoys climbing and obstacle courses. Begins to kick large balls.

Age 5: Enjoys singing; has large repertoire of songs. Likes rhythm instruments; can keep time. Participates to records and tapes; is coordinated. Has interest in musical instruments; enjoys guests. Learns to skip. Has boundless energy; wiggles. Runs, hops, jumps, and climbs with proficiency. Attempts roller-skating, rope jumping, stilt walking, and swing "pumping." Is more coordinated at throwing and catching. Plays games with simple rules; enjoys company. Broad jumps 2 to 3 ft. Rides a two-wheel bike.

The above information was compiled from Althouse 1981; Arnheim and Sinclair 1979; Bayless and Ramsey 1982; Cratty 1970; and Maxim 1980.

CUMULATIVE LESSON PLAN

- Use instruments made earlier as a rhythm experience.
- Have several boxes. Ask the children to show what they can do with each box (e.g., *small box:* put toys in, carry a treat, hold a treasure; *apple or orange box:* use as a boat, hat, turtle shell, house for a pet; *large box:* play in, make a house or car, saw, paint).
- Let the children tell a story and use the box as a prop (e.g., television screen, cave, or airplane).

ESPECIALLY FOR PARENTS

Children whose parents appreciate music and have musical talents are indeed fortunate, because parents share things they enjoy. A father who sings will sing with his children. A mother who plays the piano will play it with her children. Some families form their own musical groups—either singing or instrumental—and spend many delightful hours together. They also attend concerts and share their talents with others.

But what of the child who does not have musical parents or opportunities to hear good music? Some parents have had negative early musical experiences, resent not having financial resources to participate in music, resent the amount of commitment required to master musical skills, or have no desire to get involved with music. Possibly none of these parents sees the real value in music as either enjoyment or physical or emotional release. These parents and their children can learn to enjoy music together.

Here are some suggestions to try with your child (select those that best suit you or design more appropriate ones):

- If possible, have a record player (one that your child can use) and a variety of records (classical, popular, contemporary, ethnic). Help the child learn proper care of the player and the records. Also help him identify the records by name.
- If no record player is available, turn on the radio during musical programs. Watch concerts on television.
- Take your child to the library where he can listen to records or check some out for home listening.
- Purchase, rent, or check out a tape recorder from the library. Get some appropriate tapes for the child; use them outside or in the car.
- Help your child make some simple musical instruments: oatmeal boxes for drums; cans or paper tubes with various objects in them (rice, rocks) for shakers; waxed paper over a comb, or rhythm sticks.
- Listen to sounds and ask your child to reproduce them.
- Encourage him to move like things in nature (trees, animals).
- Clap various rhythms and see if he can reproduce them.
- Take him to a band concert in the park (it is easier for a child to sit and listen there than at a formal concert).
- Make sounds and have him do the actions, then change roles.
- Make a game. Show him a picture of an instrument and have him imitate the way it is played. Then you imitate the instrument and have him find the picture of it.
- Learn some simple, fun song with him.
- Dance with him, using a variety of rhythms.
- Imitate household sounds such as dripping water, motors, or clocks.
- Record the child's voice. Play it for him and the family.
- Take your child to the local music store and ask the clerk to demonstrate some of the instruments.
- Ask a friend, neighbor, or relative to play their instrument for the child.
- Take him to a school band or orchestra rehearsal.
- Go for a walk and listen for the many different sounds.
- Visit a dance studio.
- Use suggestions made earlier in this chapter.

Parents are also encouraged to provide many opportunities for the child to move about in space, to gain control of his body, and to develop new skills. Parents are discouraged from enrolling preschool children in a rigorous gymnastic or competitive athletic program.

Many of the activities suggested for teachers of young children earlier in this chapter are also appropriate for parents to use. Be aware of the abilities and characteristics of children this age—do not push the child faster than he is ready or beyond his endurance; do provide activities that are challenging and likely to be successful.

You may think you do not have appropriate equipment for your child. Many pieces of equipment can be easily made or used at the local park. In addition, you may take your child on field trips within the community, such as a hike on a nearby hill or observation at a local spa, a track meet, or an athletic event (e.g., weight lifting, marathon, tennis match). The locality generally has places for swimming, boating, and running. Remember, you are trying to encourage the child to develop his body, not compete for the Olympic team.

The home may have a number of climbing opportunities: a tree, a hill, stairs, a pole, or a ladder. Chances may be available for jumping on an inner tube or on an old mattress or for broad jumps or high jumps. Be sure your child is in a safe environment—remove obstacles, talk about precautions and limitations, and encourage him to see that activities are safe.

When possible, participate with your child. Remind him how much better he can do things now that he is older and stronger. Take music outside; enjoy it while you play games, do chores such as gardening or washing the car, and appreciate nature.

Books for children on music and movement education are listed in Appendix E.

APPLICATION OF PRINCIPLES

1. Make an effort to use more music with young children. Sing, hum, or move to music outdoors as well as indoors.
2. Encourage the children to use their large muscles by imitating animals, feelings, objects, or people, sometimes with and sometimes without musical accompaniment.
3. Over a period of a few weeks, learn and teach three new songs to young children. Use visual aids for one of the songs.
4. Use rhythm instruments, first without accompaniment and later with a record or piano, using a steady beat.
5. Invite a guest who has musical talents. What suggestions would you offer to that person?
6. Originate an outdoor game that involves the use of a ball, a parachute or small sheet, or obstacle course.
7. Make a list of five records and five song books you would like to own personally.

References

Althouse, Rosemary. *The Young Child: Learning with Understanding.* New York: Teachers College Press, Columbia University, 1981.

Arnheim, D. D., and W. A. Sinclair. *The Clumsy Child.* 2d ed. St. Louis: C. V. Mosby, 1979.

Bayless, Kathleen M., and Marjorie E. Ramsey. *Music: A Way of Life for the Young Child.* St. Louis: C. V. Mosby, 1982.

Clark, Carol E. *Rhythmic Activities.* Dansville, N.Y.: Instructor, 1969.

Cratty, Bryant J. *Perceptual and Motor Development in Infants and Children.* London: Macmillan, 1970.

Day, Barbara. *Early Childhood Education: Creative Learning Activities.* 2d ed. New York: Macmillan, 1983.

Galin, D. "Educating Both Halves of the Brain." *Childhood Education* 53(October 1976):17–20.

Lundsteen, S., and N. Tarrow. *Guiding Young Children's Learning.* New York: McGraw-Hill, 1981.

Margolin, Edythe. Chapter 9 in *Young Children: Their Curriculum and Learning Processes.* New York: Macmillan, 1976.

Maxim, George. *The Very Young.* Belmont, Calif.: Wadsworth, 1980.

McCall, Adeline. *This Is Music for Today—Kindergarten and Nursery School.* Boston: Allyn & Bacon, 1971.

Petzold, R. "Auditory Perception by Children." *Journal of Research in Music Education* 17(1969): 82–87.

Pitcher, Evelyn G., M. B. Lasher, S. G. Feinburg, and L. A. Braun. *Helping Young Children Learn.* 2d ed. Columbus, Ohio: Charles E. Merrill, 1974.

Ramsey, Marjorie E., and Kathleen M. Bayless. *Kindergarten: Programs and Practices.* St. Louis: C. V. Mosby, 1980.

Sheehy, Emma D. *Children Discover Music and Dance.* New York: Teachers College Press, Columbia University, 1968, 1974.

Swartz, S. L., and H. F. Robison. *Designing Curriculum for Early Childhood.* Boston: Allyn & Bacon, 1982.

6
Science

Mary, Mary, quite contrary,
How does your garden grow?
With silver bells and cockle shells
And pretty maids all in a row.

MAIN PRINCIPLES

1. Young children want to learn about themselves and others.
2. They need multisensory opportunities to learn about their environment.
3. Their natural curiosity can be enhanced.
4. Children have different interests and abilities to absorb knowledge at different ages.
5. Teachers and parents can encourage exploration and interests in young children.

In one sentence, Carson (1956) sums up the essence of science with young children:

> If I had influence with the good fairy who is supposed to preside over the christening of all children, I should ask that her gift to each child in the world be a sense of wonder so indestructible that it would last throughout life, as an unfailing antidote against the boredom and disenchantments of later life, the sterile preoccupation with things that are artificial, the alienation from the sources of our strength.

Science is a part of our daily lives. It is of vital importance to each and every one of us—through natural resources, through medicine, through production and consumption of goods and services, through life itself. If it is so much a part of us, why do some parents and teachers find the subject one that is intimidating, frustrating, and to be avoided? Young children are interested and excited about their environment. They need to keep that curiosity alive.

Science is the process of inquiry. Young children are natural scientists with spontaneous and ingenious ideas. They are, at this stage, egocentric. They see no reasons for things except for their benefit (mothers make cookies because children are hungry, or the sun comes out so they can play). As they grow and have experiences, they become less egocentric; they look for physical, magical, or psychological reasons as causes for events. While in the preoperational stage, they live in the here-and-now. They believe all they see. "It's true! I saw it on television," is a common response. Then children try to duplicate some feats, only to end up injured or disappointed. Young children have limited ability to understand causality, reason logically, or predict consequences.

Regardless of the age of the "scientist," most approach the solution to their problem with a combination of the following: observing, identifying, inferring, classifying, hypothesizing, predicting, testing, generalizing, reaching conclusions, readjusting, retesting, interpreting, and concluding. In the process of finding out, they ask skillful questions, infer new ideas, and make further experiments. Here's an example: Ingrid is playing house. She is having difficulty getting ready to go shopping with the other mothers. Her doll is still in the water table. Hurrying to get it dressed, she spills water on the floor. She notices that the other mothers are ready to leave. She takes the doll dress, uses it to wipe up the floor, and then cannot get it on the doll because the moisture makes it stick to the doll's body. Still trying to hurry, she drops the dress on the floor, runs to the drawer, and gets another dress. This time it goes on easier but is much too large for the doll. She wraps the excess dress about the doll, jumps into her high heels and runs behind the others, yelling, "My baby is so bad today. She wouldn't get dressed, but she's ready now." Ingrid went through several of the steps of the scientist, making adjustments when needed. That's what science is, a "way of doing things and solving problems. It is a style which leads a person to wonder, to seek, to discover, to know, and then to wonder anew. It is a style in which good feelings of joy, excitement, and beauty accompany these active interactions with one's world. Not only children, but adults can experience science. It's a way of life!" (Holt 1977)

Young children often have misconceptions about their world; these need to be clarified and revised. By listening to or watching young children, adults receive clues as to when they need to offer a first-hand experience to get the child thinking in the right direction. For example, a teacher demonstrated the principle of rain at the center. No questions were asked by the children so the teacher thought they had learned the concepts as she had planned them. The next day, a mother asked the teacher if she would be interested in her daughter's comments about the science experience. The teacher said she surely would. The child had said, "Mother, God doesn't make the rain; I learned how to make it at school." Without this vital feedback, the teacher would have assumed that the children had gained correct concepts. Instead, she was back to the drawing board for another attempt to teach about rain.

ROLE OF THE TEACHER

In order for the teacher to stimulate children to explore, investigate, and question, the teacher herself needs an inquiring mind. She must have a positive attitude toward curiosity and questioning. She must be knowledgeable and able to communicate on the level of the children. She need not feel uninformed or put down by questions; however, she does need to find answers to questions, either with the children when possible or by herself. She should then discuss her findings with the children.

The process of finding out, often for himself, is important to the young child.

> When planning science programs for young children, one should consider that science includes both the process of inquiry and the products which result from inquiry. Though it is important for some scientifically obtained information to be passed on for the sake of practicality and safety, it is important for teachers to understand that if children are really to understand science, they must be permitted to *abstract* knowledge on their own, or at least be permitted to *verify* for themselves much of the information they are given. (Schickedanz et al. 1977)

Along with the importance of process and children constructing their own knowledge, Lundsteen and Tarrow (1981) caution not to underestimate children, but "remember to 'think big' about young children when setting goals and planning learning activities. . . . What we cannot forgive ourselves for is 'thinking small' about children, lacking respect for them."

In scientific discovery, teachers need to encourage the use of language in predicting, discussing, experimenting, and evaluating. In doing so, they must consider the child's level of maturity, his past experiences, his interests, and his misconceptions. The activities should be directed toward building upon his present and familiar concepts; they should be accurate, concrete, relevant, explained simply, and repeated (Watrin 1978).

Science is not a matter of teaching facts. It should include multisensory, firsthand, spontaneous, integrated, and repeated activities that involve both appropriate materials and processes. "When we present science experiences in the early childhood years, we are not introducing new activities to children. We are merely defining a process they began at birth: making sense out of their world with the intellectual processes currently available to them" (Harlan 1976).

Howe (1978) has identified two important areas in building scientific concepts: (1) experiences that promote the growth of logical thinking and (2) experiences with things of the natural world. She continues:

> Researchers are convinced that growing up is not in itself enough to cause children to give up contact with adults and peers who will question and challenge their ideas. They also need much experience with living things: animals, insects, trees; and with non-living things: rocks, running water, sunshine, the wind. . . . Science is not a set of skills and behaviors nor a group of processes. It is knowledge and a way of knowing, knowledge of the universe, of the earth, of living organisms. It is the belief that the world is knowable and worth knowing, and that we can, by our actions, attain some knowledge of it.

The teacher is responsible for providing science experiences in the curriculum. Besides having a positive attitude, encouraging exploration, supplying accurate information, avoiding harmful and dangerous things, and permitting time and materials for the child to discover for himself, she needs to determine what limits are necessary, set them, and then let the children explore within these guidelines. She provides a wide variety of experiences but takes cues from the children. Their interests are vital. From participating with and listening to young children, she increases her own observation powers. She takes the opportunity to encourage spontaneous scientific experiences, but also provides some planned ones, taking every possible opportunity to help children get clear, basic concepts. She involves the children in the experiences as they take place; firsthand experience has no substitute. Many children are reluctant to enter into the activity, but with the assistance of an understanding teacher, they gain confidence in themselves and in their exploration. (Note that these opportunities are called "experiences" and not "experiments." The former connotes involvement, the latter observation.)

Values for Children

Following are some of the main benefits children derive from science experiences:

1. Building confidence in themselves and in their environment.
2. Gaining necessary firsthand experiences
3. Developing basic concepts
4. Increasing observation skills
5. Receiving opportunities to use tools, equipment, and familiar materials
6. Receiving aid in problem solving
7. Stimulating their curiosity for exploration and discovery while increasing their basic knowledge
8. Developing sensory, physical, emotional, intellectual, spiritual, and social attributes
9. Developing language through increased vocabulary and an opportunity to ask and answer questions

General Format

Teaching about the various areas of science is similar and includes the preceding information. The activity sections will be divided into three areas: social, biological, and physical science, each with a sample miniplan. Do not be discouraged about the use of academic terms to classify activities. After all, that is what this chapter is all about: science.

ACTIVITIES TO INCREASE AWARENESS OF SOCIAL SCIENCE

The study of social science includes anthropology, ecology, economics, current events, geography, history, political science, psychology, sociology, and other related fields. Some of these fields are more appropriate than others for teaching young children. A few ideas will be given here; the teacher can develop activities of interest and value to the children she teaches.

SAMPLE MINIPLAN INVOLVING SOCIAL SCIENCE

Theme

A park

Ideas to Emphasize

1. Areas are set aside in a park for different activities, such as games, eating, and playing.
2. Each person can help take good care of the park.
3. Parks are provided for beauty and enjoyment.

Learning Activities

1. If possible, take the children to a nearby park. Let them play in the various areas and on the equipment. Take a snack or picnic lunch to eat there. Walk around the park, noting the trees, shrubs, buildings, and other things. Have a story under one of the trees. Discuss the importance of keeping the park clean and beautiful.
2. If unable to visit a park, discuss parks in general, using visual aids, such as pictures and books. Ask the children how many have ever visited a park, what they did at the park, and how they should care for them. Role play (playing, picknicking) and then eat outside. At least take a walk around the school playground and notice things that are also seen at parks such as landscaping and areas set off for different activities.

- Experiences with **ecology.** Talk about such natural resources as water and energy. Talk about the care of the center and the community. Have a general cleanup.
- Experiences with **economics.** Provide activities that teach the children the principle of supply and demand (number and amount of creative materials, for example, and who will use them; care of unused materials). Give the children weekly or daily opportunities to help with center responsibilities. Teach care and respect for property and rules for behavior, such as sharing, replacing all toys and parts in proper places, and cooperating in play and ideas.
- Experiences with **current events.** Know what is going on locally, nationally, and personally within families. Help children to verbalize happenings and the impact on them.

- Experiences with **geography.** Give the children experiences with various maps (e.g., road, community, center, play yard). Have a fabric or plastic printed community with props, a farm with animals and equipment, a doll house and furniture, or a floor plan of a room or outdoor area and ask for the children's help in rearrangement. Talk about concepts of direction, location, distance. Talk about Earth (land, sea, air; the solar system). Talk about geographic features in the community such as rocks, rivers, and mountains. Walk or ride on field trips around the school or community, noting routes, buildings, and landmarks. Make a mural showing important landmarks in the community such as homes of children, churches, stores, and parks.
- Experiences with **history.** Talk about the changes in the children. What are they able to do that they could not do earlier? (Use book, *The Growing Story,* by Ruth Krauss.) Talk about families and holidays.
- Experiences with **sociology.** Provide opportunities for children to participate in group living and learn cooperation, responsibility, courtesy, and sharing. Discuss ways people help each other. Help the children accept and appreciate peers who are of a different race, culture, size, or sex, those who have a handicap, and those with diverse beliefs and ideas. Include nonsexist curriculum experiences. Provide props for dramatic play about families and careers. Ask the children what they want to be when they grow up; provide props (clothes, books, and games) for practice. Provide artistic materials for each child to make a picture about his family (he can draw, paint, or cut and paste pictures). Invite resource persons to tell stories, share hobbies and interests, demonstrate skills, and bring objects from past. Talk about behavioral guidelines. Let the children help establish and enforce necessary rules of safety, protection, and responsibility for the classroom, field trips, care of animals, and so on. Invite a safety guard or policeman to tell how he helps the children and the community. Make and post a "helper" chart for snacktime, cleanup, and watering plants. Provide opportunities for children to select playmates, materials, and activities and allow time to enjoy them. Invite a community helper to the center. Invite parents to come and share their occupations.

ACTIVITIES TO INCREASE AWARENESS OF BIOLOGICAL SCIENCE

Biological science is the study of plant and animal life. In this chapter, for ease in planning, the activities are divided into four areas: animals (broad definition), people, plants, and food. Examples of these four areas will also be found in other chapters as they relate to different curriculum topics. Emphasis is placed on making experiences meaningful and appropriate for the children who participate.

Animals

- Have a small box with pictures of animals and also a duplicate of each cut into a silhouette from black paper. Children match the animal with its "shadow."
- Make animal shadow pictures on a screen using a strong light and imagination.
- Sing "Over in the Meadow."
- Make or purchase an ant farm or observe ants in their natural setting.
- Have animals in the classroom often. Teach about the care and characteristics of each. Some good classroom pets are: ants, butterflies, caterpillars, earthworms, frogs, gerbils, goldfish, guinea pigs, hamsters, and hermit crabs. On special occasions hatch eggs and bring in baby animals (a goat, lamb, rabbit, or other available animals).
- Build an insect collection in boxes or jars.
- Collect ants, ladybugs, caterpillars, earthworms, and butterflies from the play yard.
- Make self-correcting card games: (1) the same animals on two different cards for

Guinea pigs make good classroom pets.

matching; (2) pictures of animal and its habitat for matching; and (3) classification of animals, such as those that fly or have four legs.

- Make a net out of nylon stocking. Go bug catching.
- Borrow a pet from a family, a farm, or a pet store. Make sure the animal is tame and free of disease. (A pet show of animals from home may be inadvisable, because some animals do not get along!)
- Observe or discuss the characteristic movement of animals (some swim, some fly, some hop, and so on).
- Observe or discuss physical characteristics of various animals (e.g., flipper, wing, web-foot, claws, or number of legs).
- Observe or discuss the diet of various animals (e.g., hay, grain, milk, carrots, or nuts).
- Observe and discuss birth, nutrition, and habits of animals or insects.
- Observe frogs in various stages from egg to tadpole to frog.
- Observe and discuss various housing for animals such as a nest, hole, house, or cage.
- Observe animals with their young (care and feeding).
- Imitate animal sounds.
- Learn the names of adult male and female animals and babies.
- Discuss how animals protect themselves through camouflage, hibernation, claws, odor, horns, or stinger.
- If possible, feel the covering of various animals (e.g., shell, fur, wool, skin, feathers).
- Observe animals at work (mule, bee, ant, spider, beaver, squirrel, or horse).
- Care for animals at the center or home by cleaning cages, feeding, and watering

(this increases self-reliance). Discuss ways animals are cared for and limits in handling them.

- Using heavy paper, make a series of pictures about an animal, with each picture emphasizing a different part of the animal, such as the head, ears, or feet. Make identical pictures on cards for the children to match, to chart, or to form a puzzle.
- Observe wild animals at a park or zoo, if possible.
- Visit a ranch or farm to see poultry, sheep, cattle, dairy animals, or mink.
- Rather than discussing general characteristics of animals, such as habitat, coverings,

A bird's nest shows the child one type of wildlife housing.

and diet, discuss many characteristics about one animal at a time (e.g., where a cow lives, information about its calf, uses of its hide, and sounds it makes).

- Make feeding places for birds in your play yard.
- Bring in a variety of bird nests.
- Catch a caterpillar, then watch it spin a cocoon and eventually emerge as a butterfly.

SAMPLE MINIPLAN INVOLVING ANIMALS

Theme

Covering of animals

Ideas to Emphasize

1. Animals have specific body coverings.
2. Each type of covering feels different when touched.
3. These coverings help the animal.

Learning Activities

If possible, take the children to a nearby farm to observe animals. If this is not possible, bring several caged animals to school. Talk about different coverings: hair on a horse or dog, fur on a rabbit, feathers on a chicken or other bird, wool on a lamb, shell on a turtle, and scales on fish. (If animals are not available, be sure to have some good samples of these coverings for the children to feel and examine.) Use the number of coverings you feel are appropriate for the children you are teaching—you can use this theme for several days. Discuss each type of covering, its color, how it helps the animal, how it feels, how it differs from other coverings, where the animal lives, uses of coverings to man, and other facts. Give the children time to ask and answer questions and make comments. At the end of the discussion, have pictures of animals with both similar and dissimilar coverings. Let the children group the pictures according to similar coverings.

People

- Focus on helping the children increase their self-image: draw an outline around each child's body and let him color or finish it; let the children make a "me" puppet; provide a place to make a mural of handprints and footprints; let the children participate in a group experience, such as holding visual aids for a story or song, introducing a toy, or choosing an activity).
- Discuss things the children can do now that they could not do when younger or smaller.
- Make a chart and show how the body works.
- Display photographs of the children at their eye level.
- Have at least one full-length mirror.
- Weigh and measure each child. Post the chart.
- Observe different characteristics of people (e.g., hair, eye, and skin coloring; height, weight, sex). Talk about "special" characteristics of each child.

- Use a real skeleton or a replica to talk about bones.
- Learn about such different parts of the body as the digestive tract, heart, tongue, hair, and eyes.
- Stimulate the five senses (Chapter 3).
- Visit a local health center, doctor's office, or hospital.
- Invite a resource person, such as a doctor or nurse.
- Visit or invite community helpers to your classroom.
- Discuss the different places people live, such as apartments, houses, trailers, and dormitories, and then visit some of them.
- Discuss ways to stay healthy (e.g., proper nutrition, clothing, rest).
- Observe someone with a cast on. Discuss the healing process.
- Observe a mother bathing, feeding, or dressing a baby.
- Discuss and enact roles of various family members.
- Make a family portrait by cutting pictures from magazines and pasting them on construction paper or paper plate.
- Throughout the day, assist children to solve problems through verbalization, cooperation, and sharing.
- Involve the children in establishing guidelines for behavior.
- Talk about common emotions. "How did it make you feel?" "How did it make someone

SAMPLE MINIPLAN INVOLVING PEOPLE

Theme

Sounds around us

Ideas to Emphasize

1. We hear through our ears.
2. Sounds are all around us.
3. Sounds help us identify people and things.

Learning Activities

1. Have the children place their hands over their eyes. Talk to them. Ask them if they can hear you. Ask them to put their hands over their mouths. Can they hear you? Have them put their hands over their ears. Can they still hear you? Discuss the use of ears.
2. Play a tape of familiar sounds while the children listen. Include sounds that are normal in the home, such as an alarm clock; brushing teeth; going downstairs; preparing breakfast; running water; beating or mixing; setting table; crying baby; pet noises; radio or television; ringing telephone or doorbell; opening and closing door; running car; typing; and so on. Arrange the sounds in logical sequence so they can easily be used as part of a story. The second time the tape is played, stop it after each sound while the children discuss it. Be accepting of their ideas. Encourage them to make sounds they heard earlier in the day and let the other children guess what the sound represents. Also talk about how certain sounds protect us, such as those from smoke alarms, horns, sirens, or bells.
3. Play a game making and identifying the sounds of animals, transportation, occupations, and so on.

else feel?" "What can we do to help someone feel happy?" "What should we do when someone is unhappy?"

- Use a large hand mirror for the children to see their facial expressions for different emotions.
- Talk about the importance of good mental hygiene.

Plants

- Talk about using plants for food, clothing, protection, beauty, and health.
- Talk about different ways to start plants from bulbs, seeds, sets, slips, or parts of the produce (potato).
- Observe and discuss trees and shrubs during different parts of the year.
- Prepare soil and plant a garden. Seeds for beans, melons, pumpkins, grass, and radishes germinate easily.
- If outdoor space is unavailable, plant a garden inside the classroom in a water table, pots, milk cartons, cans, jars, egg cartons, or paper cups.
- When possible, harvest, prepare, and use produce grown at school.
- Use *The Carrot Seed,* story and record by Ruth Krauss.
- Soak bean seeds overnight. Open and examine them with a magnifying glass. Plant some beans against a glass container. Watch them grow, roots down, stem up.
- Observe how plants grow from seeds inside fruit (avocado, orange, apple). Note that they require light and water and grow toward source of light. Also observe how some seeds grow faster than others. Sprout seeds for snacks, such as alfalfa, mung beans, soybeans, and wheat.
- Gather weeds and flowers. Dry them. Make decorations. (Watch for allergies in children.)

Magnifying natural items broadens the child's perspective.

- Seal seeds and a picture of the produce in a small plastic bag. Have a second bag of the same seeds and picture separately. Have the children match them.
- Prepare a nature table using plants and produce. Change often, or use produce for snacks or lunch.
- Gather different kinds of seeds (fruit, vegetable, weed).
- Observe changes in nature during different seasons.
- Discuss the cycle of a tree and its uses for lumber and paper.
- Plant and observe growth of seeds in a terrarium.
- Have plants in the classroom. Let the children help care for them.
- Talk about and eat the different parts of the plant, such as seeds (peas, beans, corn, peanuts), roots (carrots, radishes, beets, onions, potatoes), stems (celery, asparagus, rhubarb), leaves (lettuce, cabbage, spinach), blossoms (broccoli, cauliflower), and fruit (apples, berries, grapes).
- Observe the growth of plants in water (tops of carrots or turnips; bird seed on a damp sponge; sweet or white potato in a jar).
- With heavy paper or tag board make a series of pictures about a plant, each picture emphasizing a different part (blossom, root, leaf, or stem). Place pictures on a chart, and make individual cards identical to those on the chart. Children match card to chart or form a puzzle.
- Go on a nature walk often. Take a sack for gathering treasures to make a collage.
- Visit a plant nursery or greenhouse.
- Provide a variety of nuts. Let the children sort them by kinds and learn their names. Help them crack and taste the different kinds of nuts. Some may need to be roasted.

Children can help care for plants in the classroom.

SAMPLE MINIPLAN INVOLVING PLANTS

Theme

Beans

Ideas to Emphasize

1. Bean seeds are usually larger than other seeds.
2. Beans grow on a vine or stem.
3. Beans are prepared for eating in different ways. Sprouts are eaten fresh, while green beans are usually cooked. Dried beans need to be soaked and cooked before eating.

Learning Activities

Bean seeds, along with a variety of other seeds, such as beet, radish, carrot, and tomato, are placed on the science table. The teacher points out characteristics of the various seeds, and the children look at the seeds through a magnifying glass. During art, the seeds are used in a collage. An appropriate bean dish (e.g., chili or string or lima beans) is served for lunch, and sprouts or bean salad for a snack. Bean seeds for sprouting and planting are soaked overnight. The children plant the beans in a terrarium or in paper cups to take home. Seeds for sprouting are placed in wire or plastic containers. The children care for the plants, noting daily changes.

Food

- Discuss the different tastes of food, such as sour, sweet, bitter, and salty. Show a picture or replica of the tongue and point out where these different tastes are located.
- Discuss different ways food grows—fish, shrimp, crab, oysters, and rice in water, apples and pears on trees, potatoes, carrots, and peanuts under ground, and tomatoes and corn above ground. (See section on plants.)
- Let the children help prepare fruits and vegetables for lunch or a snack.
- Observe differences in fruits and vegetables (color, taste, peeling, texture, and moisture).
- Taste fruits and vegetables in various forms (raw, cooked, or as juice).
- Experiment with coconut (husk, shell, liquid, chunks, shredded, toasted).
- Prepare food using dairy products (ice cream, butter, pudding, cottage cheese, cheese).
- Bake cookies, bread, and pies.
- Use water to make soup and gelatin and to boil corn.
- Observe a raw egg and see the difference when eggs are soft-boiled, hard boiled, or fried.
- Pop popcorn. Discuss how heat makes the kernel expand.
- Make something for lunch or a snack (applesauce, spaghetti, sandwiches, fruit or vegetable plate).
- Provide empty food containers to stimulate interest in the domestic area.
- Use the basic four food chart to discuss nutrition.
- Provide a certain food commodity in various forms, such as sugar (raw, refined, brown, powdered) or wheat (grains, cracked, flour).
- Examine food in various stages (e.g., potato as seed, potato for eating, potato sprouting).

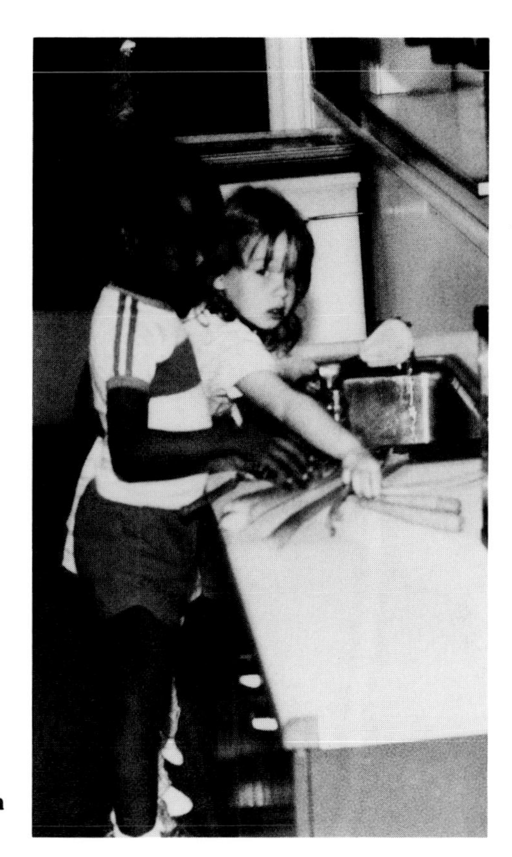

Children can help prepare food for lunch or snack.

SAMPLE MINIPLAN INVOLVING FOOD

Theme

Apples

Ideas to Emphasize

1. Apples are prepared for eating in different ways.
2. Apples are green, yellow, or red.
3. Apples grow on trees.
4. An apple has different parts.

Learning Activities

Pictures of apples in different forms are placed on the bulletin board. A low table nearby, washed and covered with butcher paper, contains apples of different colors and sizes. With the children, the teacher discusses how apples are grown, their various colors, different ways they are eaten, and the kind of covering. Children wash their hands. Under careful supervision, the teacher and children peel, core, and cut the apples. The apples are placed in an electric saucepan, cooked, and served for a snack.

- Involve the five senses with food (smell different fruits and vegetables both raw and cooked; touch the various peelings; touch the food after it has been cooked; taste food as ingredients, and then cooked; sample foods that look alike but taste different such as apple, pear, onion, turnip, radish, and white potato; compare peelings and meat of fruit and vegetables).
- Use household tools (grinder, peeler, beater, mixer).

See Chapter 10 for further information on food.

ACTIVITIES TO INCREASE AWARENESS OF PHYSICAL SCIENCE

Physical science is the study of material things and their properties and reactions when they are changed or combined. It includes areas such as astronomy, chemistry, engineering, geology, physics, and other related fields. These subjects are difficult to teach to young children because they are more abstract than other sciences; nevertheless, children should be exposed to physical science. Children are natural explorers and are curious about many things. It is appropriate for the teacher to utilize the scientific method: observe the children, provide experiences to which they can relate, help them ask and answer questions, encourage their exploration, help them come up with alternate solutions, introduce good terms and help the children practice them. Be excited yourself!

Here are some suggested activities. Use, modify, or discard them as you feel appropriate for your children.

Astronomy and Meteorology

Astronomy is especially difficult to teach at school because most observable activity occurs at night; however, you may want to discuss the warmth and light from the sun and encourage the children to notice sunsets and the stars and moon at night.

A visit to a planetarium is not the best for young children. They often are fearful when lights are turned off in an unfamiliar place. However, they may be interested in watching television reports about space preparation and exploration.

Cloud formations can be discussed and observed.

Chemistry

- Have the children mix things together and see the results. Even sand and water is of interest to them.
- Provide experiences to see how heat affects cooking, wearing apparel, and activities.
- Observe how light changes things (growth, warmth, appearance).
- Discuss use of light (flashlight, lamp, sun, candle, sun dial, shadows).
- Talk about the seasons and how people and animals prepare for them; note how the landscape changes.
- Observe the difference in temperature in the shade and in the sun, or during different seasons of the year.
- Perform simple experiments such as dissolving sugar and salt in water.
- Investigate water. It evaporates, cleans, changes things (rocks, sand), comes in different forms (liquid, gas, solid), is used for many purposes (mixing paint, drinking, play), and can be an excellent emotional release. Following are some suggested uses.
  - Siphon from one container to another.
  - Float objects (soap, toys, wood, metals); show effects of size and weight.
  - Observe reflections.
  - Blow bubbles (air and water).
  - Wash and dry doll clothes (evaporation).

Blowing bubbles demonstrates a relationship between air and water.

- Build dams and canals.
- Feel the force as water comes from tap.
- Observe evaporation by marking the water level in a pan and checking it daily.
- Build a snowman; make snow angels.
- Freeze ice, watch it melt; use ice to set gelatin.
- Stretch various materials (fabrics, plastic, paper, rubber) over can and pour water over it. Show that water goes through some things easier than others.
- Introduce terms *porous* and *nonporous*. Allow experimentation.
- Water plants.
- Discuss wearing apparel for water (boots, umbrella, cover-ups).
- Clean with water. Talk about absorption.
- Observe moisture on glass of ice water on hot day.
- Boil water to produce steam.
- Pour water through funnel or from one container to another.
- Prepare creative materials.
- Drink water.

- Prepare food and cook it.
- Change the consistency of materials by changing the amount of water.
- Play in water (sail boats, wash self or toys).
- Talk about conservation, pollution, recycling.
- Mix colors. Observe the changes.
- Using different sized cups or containers, have children pour water back and forth for experience in varying volume.
- With different amounts of water in glasses or jars, have a child gently tap the glass with a spoon for different musical tones.
- Have the children determine objects that would sink or float.

■ Make crystals (see Miniplan).

■ Prepare a mineral garden. Mix 8 tsp of salt, 8 tsp of water, and 2 tsp of household ammonia in a pint of water. Pour into a shallow pan. Paint a clinker a variety of colors with water paint; put it into the mixture. Watch it grow. As the water evaporates, the salt crystals are left behind.

SAMPLE MINIPLAN INVOLVING PHYSICAL SCIENCE

Theme

Crystals

Ideas to Emphasize

1. Crystals are clear and angular in shape.
2. Crystals are found in the earth or can be made (jewelry, candy).

Learning Activities

1. The teacher shows the children different crystals and rocks. She explains what a crystal is and what things are crystals (sand, sugar, salt). Then she shows some crystals previously made. The children examine the crystals using a magnifying glass and then are given materials for making crystals to take home.
2. On another table are many objects. Some are crystals, some are not. The teacher helps the children identify the crystals.

Two Methods for Making Crystals

Method 1. Mix ½ cup each of salt, liquid bluing, and water and 1 tb of ammonia. Pour over crumpled paper towels. Crystals begin to form in one hour, reaching a peak in about four hours and lasting a couple of days.

Method 2. Break a brick or warm charcoal briquette into small pieces (warmth makes crystals form faster). Place several pieces in the center of a bowl. Mix ¼ cup salt, ¼ cup liquid bluing, ¼ cup water, and 1 tb ammonia. Pour solution over the pieces of coal or brick. Fill a medicine dropper with food coloring and drop small amounts over the brick pile. Let the crystals grow. They will crumble easily. Watch and note when first crystals appear and how fast they develop. Crystals are formed because water is drawn into the brick, leaving the solids. The ammonia, bluing, and salt form a complex crystal. Use a hand lens to observe the crystals. (Challand and Brandt 1963)

- Prepare a clinker or coal garden. This garden grows in a hurry. Wash four or five small pieces of coal or clinkers and arrange them in a pan or bowl. Mix together: 1 cup water, 6 tb table salt, and 4 tsp liquid bluing. Slowly pour solution over each clinker or piece of coal. Set the pan in the sunlight. If color is desired, drop one drop of any color of food coloring on each piece. Crystals will form in a few hours, but the larger ones will take several days to grow.
  WARNING: If a chemical garden is made by using water glass (sodium silicate) and metallic crystals, EXTREME CAUTION must be exercised. Some of the crystals are poisonous!
- Make a discovery chart. As children are exposed to chemistry, they will "discover" different things about it. Help them make and post a chart of their new findings. Use their ideas in a group setting.

Geology

- Discuss various kinds of rocks.
- Discuss various fuels and methods of heating (coal, oil, gas, electricity, steam, solar).
- Provide a museum or nature shelf with rocks, shells, and cones.
- On a science table, provide different kinds of soil, such as sand, clay, and volcanic ash. Place a magnifying glass nearby.
- Bring in a collection of rocks. Note how the rock changes color when it is wet.
- Examine pieces of coal with a magnifying glass.
- Point out and discuss the topography of your area (hills, mountains, valleys).
- Take field trips to local geological sites.
- Examine the properties of sand (varying volume, consistency with and without use of water).
- Notice the different surfaces of the play yard (sand, dirt, grass, asphalt, concrete). Discuss their uses.
- Make a discovery chart. As children are exposed to geology, they will "discover" different things about it. Help them make and post a chart of their new findings. Also use the chart in a group setting.

Physics

- Observe machines at work (dump truck, street sweeper, steamroller, garbage truck, derrick, steam shovel, farm, home).
- Familiarize children with gravity by placing a car on an inclined board or a wagon on a slope. Talk about roads.
- Talk about balance through use of blocks, teeter-totter, and weights. Let children use their bodies in balancing.
- Discuss and have children participate in activities involving friction.
- Use a magnifying glass to examine various materials and objects.
- With the children discover the use of a magnet and show things that are attracted and things that are not. Introduce, define, and experiment with new terms, such as *attract* and *repel*. Sprinkle pepper or lightweight visible material over water and watch it float. Dip small pieces of soap into the water, and watch the material go away from (be repelled by) the soap. Sprinkle sugar into the water, and watch the material float to (be attracted by) the sugar.
- Explore the uses of household tools and appliances (vacuum, eggbeater, mixer).
- Talk about various methods of communication (telephone, telegraph, radio, television, newspaper, magazine, letter).
- Make a game. Have the child focus on one dimension (color). When he knows this, add another dimension (shape). When he understands these, look for something that contains both the shape and color. Add another dimension, such as density (thick,

Exploring the use of an eggbeater can be a lesson in physics.

thin). Have the child look for something that includes all three. Then add another (size), and look for all four. ("Look for something that is red, square, thin, and large.") Use only when the child is ready to combine dimensions.

- Observe shapes (round, square, oblong, triangular, hexagonal, octagonal, free-form); look for objects that are these shapes.
- Use a lever (e.g., claw hammer).
- Use wheels. Show how they aid in work, play, and in the home (motors, pulleys, roller skates, toys, sewing machine, clocks).
- Provide substances and their opposites (wet and dry, long and short, hard and soft, hot and cold, sweet and sour, rough and smooth).
- Explore the weather (seasons, time of day, changes, temperature).
- Discuss how weather is influenced by sun, clouds, and wind.
- Observe and discuss fog (watch it move, lift); mist; rain (moisture it provides, appearance of sky, temperature); sun (warmth, light); frost; hail; snow. Talk about appropriate wearing apparel for different types of weather.
- Dress dolls or flannel board characters of children for different types of weather.
- Investigate the characteristics of snow (taste, feel, appearance).
- Make a simple chart that shows snow, rain, sun, and wind. An arrow can be turned to indicate the current weather.
- Discuss wind. Use kites, pinwheels, or balloons (with caution). Watch smoke. Observe dry leaves when wind blows. Watch a weather vane or wind sock. Discuss strength of wind.
- Explore air (movement made by fan, how it occupies space but is unseen). Use paper bag, balloon (with caution), pinwheel, whistle, parachute, weather vane, tire pump, and bubbles.
- Use woodworking tools and materials.

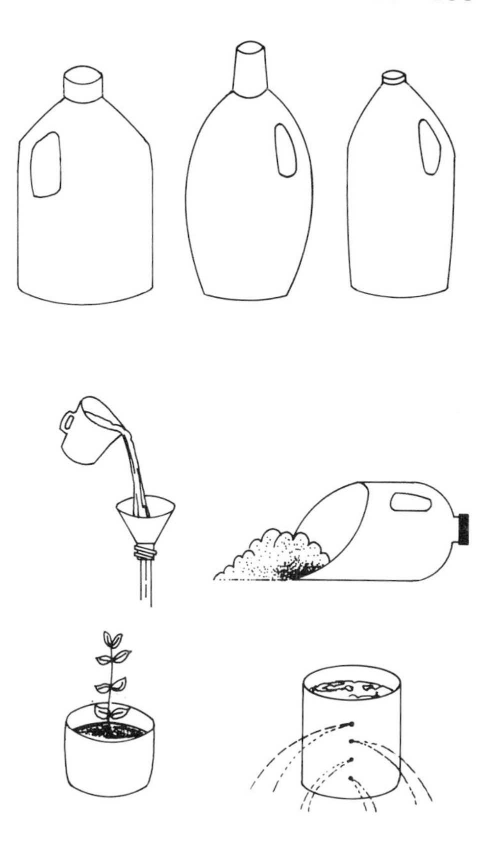

Empty plastic gallon bottles can be cut for funnels, scoops, pots, or sieves.

- Discuss occupational tools and their uses.
- Bring in a camera (a box camera is good). Take pictures of the children. Talk about how the camera works.
- Bring in and explore lenses (magnifying glass, old box-type camera, binoculars, eye-glasses, telescope, jar with water in it).
- Investigate how water or air can cause pressure, as in a balloon, bottle, can, or parachute.
- Use a straw or medicine dropper to illustrate a vacuum being created as air is removed and another substance rushes in to fill space.
- Introduce vibration by using rubber bands, strings on piano or other instrument, tuning fork.
- Provide scales, thermometers, prisms, and color paddles.
- Have an outdoor science area with boards and boxes, levers, wheels and axles, pendulums, and pulley (clotheslines).
- Provide windup toys and objects (clocks) so that children can explore their workings.
- Assist the children to work with batteries, switches, bells, and lights.
- Provide gears and springs for exploration (alarm clock, gear-driven toys, music boxes).
- Acquire empty plastic gallon containers. Cut and use them as funnels, scoops, pots, vases or other containers, sieves, bug catchers, and so on.
- Make a discovery chart. Through exposure, children will "discover" different things about physics. Help them make and post a chart of their new findings. Use the chart in a group setting.

DEVELOPMENTAL CHARACTERISTICS

The amount of intellectual development in children is often difficult to determine. Their lack of language and the adult's inability to determine precisely what and how to measure are both limiting factors.

Essentially, young children participate in many scientific activities. They may stay for long or short periods of time and feel joy or frustration. They are self-centered, seeing their own point of view, and center on only one aspect at a time. They are limited in their ability to handle abstract ideas.

Young children play alone, or alongside another child. Eventually they join a small group; later they enjoy the companionship and ideas of others. They tend to judge others by their own acts. Not until later are they able to consider motives behind actions.

Intellectually, children begin by repeated experimentation with objects. They believe that natural phenomena are created by human beings and that inanimate objects have life and human characteristics.

To make science exciting and meaningful for young children, activities are based on familiar ideas. The children are encouraged to explore and discover; however, adults should be willing and able to assist when appropriate.

For a more detailed breakdown of the child's abilities related to science, see Althouse (1981) or Good (1977).

CUMULATIVE LESSON PLAN

- In one section of the room, make a grocery store out of large boxes (appliance boxes work well). Provide many empty boxes that originally contained food products.
- Use a box for a cash register; make or purchase money.
- Include labeled cans, plastic fruit and vegetables, some toys, doll clothes, and paper sacks.

ESPECIALLY FOR PARENTS

As parents, you must be observant of things happening in your own home and community. Children learn many things about science if experiences and time for exploration are provided for them. You, too, may learn some very interesting facts. As you read the chapters of this book, look at the ideas to see how practical or feasible they are for you and your child. If they are good, use them. If they are inappropriate, substitute better ones. These are suggestions to help you become more aware of the environment and see how it relates to your child.

Almost everything we do is a part of science—whether it is called social, biological, or physical—and young children are interested in what is going on around them. Because you are with your child more than a teacher, you have many more opportunities to help him understand the fascination of science. For example, do you know why salt is used in freezing ice cream? What makes popcorn pop? Do you know the principle of gravity? How can heavy airplanes stay up in the air, or heavy boats float? If you do not know answers, take the child to the library (or to a book) and find out together. *Keep the information simple and on his level of understanding.* Complicated lectures will discourage him from asking questions in the future. There are many good resources for accurate information: a knowledgeable friend, a school teacher, a college student, or the bibliography at the end of this chapter. In Appendix E are science-oriented books for children.

Ideas abound for discovering things with your child (depending on where you live); therefore, only a few suggestions for the social, biological, and physical sciences will be given here.

Do not make science too hard or negative. Enjoy science *with* your child. It's a fascinating world!

Social Science

- Take a tour around the community. Point out interesting and important landmarks and various people who assist us.
- Take a trip to the fire station, police station, post office, or hospital.
- Take your child to a doctor and a dentist for a checkup.
- As you do daily errands, briefly tell the child how the people you see can help us (service station attendant, cleaner, baker, banker, grocer).
- Assist the child in doing something nice for a neighbor, relative, or friend (a visit, a treat, an errand).
- Discuss family occupations with the child.
- Talk about your extended family (grandparents, aunts and uncles, cousins) and visit them.
- Ask your child to tell you things that make him happy and how he can make others happy. Discuss good social techniques.
- Invite friends or guests into your home and let the child help entertain them.
- Take a picnic to the park.
- Take your child to church.
- Take your child to appropriate community affairs, including athletic events.
- If possible, visit a local radio or television station.
- Go swimming at a community pool.

Biological Science

Animals

- Get your child a pet and teach him how to care for it.
- Take him to a zoo, a pet shop, or an animal farm.
- Visit someone who has an unusual pet or who raises animals.
- Discuss local insects with him (bees, mosquitoes, fleas).
- Discuss how and where various animals live. Visit some of them, if possible.
- Take him to a local poultry, dairy, or other farm.
- Take a walk and look for birds, insects, and animals common to your community.
- Visit a fish hatchery or go fishing.
- Make a house or bath for birds.

People

- Help your child learn how and why we keep our bodies clean (washing, brushing hair and teeth).
- Discuss how eating good food and getting proper rest helps build strong bodies.
- Help him learn about his body and skills. Encourage development of a positive attitude toward himself.
- Give him some enjoyable, stimulating sensory experiences.
- Help him to recognize and appreciate different physical characteristics of people.
- Visit a friend or neighbor who has several children.
- Play a game with your child. "If you wanted to find out about something, what would you do?" (ask, use senses, look in book, and so on).
- Give him some quality experiences with older people (e.g., grandparents, community workers, neighbors).

Plants and Food

- Plant a garden. Provide a special area for the child.
- Go on a nature walk. Gather leaves, cones, other things.
- Sprout seeds in your kitchen (use screen or plastic tray or flower pots).

Children profit from quality experiences with older people.

- Get seed tapes from variety or grocery store and plant them indoors.
- Grow herbs or seasonings in a hanging pot in the house.
- Grow vegetables in water (carrot or turnip tops, sweet potato, others).
- Plant seeds indoors in empty milk carton cut lengthwise, egg cartons, or ice cream container.
- Make a bottle garden or terrarium.
- Get some house plants (African violets, ferns, ornamental fruit trees). Let the child help care for and water them.
- Plant some bulbs in glass jar. Put some bulbs in with heads pointed upward and some pointed downward. Observe how stem always grows upward.
- At Christmastime, purchase a tree with needles (in large can) that can be decorated and then planted outside in the spring.
- At special times of year, have appropriate plants (e.g., poinsettia, cactus, or amaryllis at Christmas, lily at Easter).
- Plant strawberries in wooden or clay barrel. Grow and eat them.
- Make some hanging baskets for your porch, patio, or window.
- Make some duplicate leaf or blossom cards; then play a game similar to "Old Maid."
- Put a stalk of celery in a bottle containing water and food coloring. Observe how the water is carried to the leaves.
- Purchase some fresh cobs of popcorn. Let dry; then pop.
- Purchase and observe Indian corn.
- Visit a seed store, plant nursery, local orchard, commercial garden, berry patch, or greenhouse.
- Go to a park.
- Observe the landscaping around your home and area.
- Let the child assist in grocery shopping, especially produce buying.

- Visit a local cannery.
- Purchase (or grow) squash or pumpkin. Eat the produce, but save the seeds. Dry, roast, and eat some; plant some.
- Assist your child in pressing flowers and leaves.
- Let him arrange a vase of flowers.
- Gather a variety of weeds and make an arrangement.
- Purchase some raw peanuts. Shell and roast them. Then make peanut butter by grinding the peanuts.
- Show your child how you prepare food for refrigerating, shelving, canning, bottling, drying, or freezing.
- Let him assist in food preparation.
- Show him how heat changes food.
- Have a chart and show what constitutes a good diet. Let him check off the things he eats each day.
- Make a drying frame and dry some fruit. Make fruit leather.

Physical Science

- Take your child to a local museum, planetarium, aquarium, or rock show. Know that he may tire quickly.
- Discuss recycling of water and resources.
- Visit a local water source (dam, lake, fountain, storage).
- Give your child many water experiences.
- Discuss the daily and seasonal weather with him.
- Observe the stars and moon at night.
- Show how wheels help you daily.
- Explain about machines you use (e.g., sewing machine, lawn mower).
- Tell your child how you heat and cool your home and cook food, and discuss other related conveniences.
- Tell him some of the techniques you use in your work or at home (safety factors, efficient use of time and energy).
- Make a game. Get a piece of cardboard about 12 in. square. Divide it into four squares and color each square one of the following colors: red, yellow, blue, and white. Have your child help you cut out pictures of flowers that are each of the above colors. Paste each on individual cards. Make a spinner with the four colors plus two more colors, such as green and black. Flip the spinner. If it lands on one of the four main colors, take one flower of that color. If it lands on green or black, that turn is forfeited. Play until all flowers have been "won."

For appropriate books for children related to science, see Appendix E.

APPLICATION OF PRINCIPLES

1. What is your attitude toward using science with young children? How has it changed since reading the chapter and being with young children? How comfortable do you feel in providing science experiences for young children? Where can you get some help if you need it?
2. Think back over your classroom activities during the past week. List four to seven ways they have been involved with science. Which activities were spontaneous? Which were planned?
3. List as many values as you can that young children gain from participating in science experiences.
4. Give some suggestions as to how you can provide social, biological, and physical sciences in your group.

5. What are the advantages and disadvantages of having pets in the classroom?
6. How could you use plants in your classroom? How could the children be involved?
7. List some local field trips that would increase the science knowledge of the children in your group.

References

Althouse, R. *The Young Child: Learning With Understanding.* New York: Teachers College Press, Columbia University, 1981.

Carson, R. *The Sense of Wonder.* New York: Harper & Row, 1956.

Challand, Helen, and Elizabeth Brandt. *Science Activities from A to Z.* Chicago: Children's Press, 1963.

Good, Ronald G. *How Children Learn Science.* New York: Macmillan, 1977.

Harlan, J. D. *Science Experiences for the Early Childhood Years.* 2d ed. Columbus, Ohio: Charles E. Merrill, 1976, 1980.

Holt, Bess-Gene. *Science With Young Children.* Washington, D.C.: National Association for the Education of Young Children, 1977.

Howe, Ann C. "Childhood Experiences in Science." In *Readings in Early Childhood Education 78/79.* Guilford, Conn.: Dushkin, 1978.

Lundsteen, S., and N. Tarrow. *Guiding Young Children's Learning.* New York: McGraw-Hill, 1981.

Schickedanz, Judith A., Mary E. York, Ida S. Stewart, and Doris White. *Strategies for Teaching Young Children.* Englewood Cliffs, N.J.: Prentice-Hall, 1977.

Watrin, R., and P. H. Furfey. *Learning Activities for the Young Preschool Child.* New York: D. Van Nostrand, 1978.

Book

7 Transition Activities

Wee Willie Winkie, runs through the town,
In his silver slippers and his nightgown,
Rapping at each window, calling at each lock:
"Are the children all in bed for it's eight o'clock!"

MAIN PRINCIPLES

1. Periods between activities require careful planning, variety, and cooperation.
2. Good transition periods
   a. Provide good learning opportunities for children and adults
   b. Reduce random and disruptive behavior
   c. Promote self-confidence and independence in children
   d. Meet individual and group needs of children
   e. Increase participation
   f. Add variety to the curriculum

If a teacher of young children is asked what part of the day is the most troublesome or frustrating, the answer is generally, "When we're changing from one activity to another!" This is especially true with an inexperienced teacher. A bit of organization and planning, however, can change a dreaded period to one of pleasure and reward.

Webster's Ninth New Collegiate Dictionary defines transition as "a passage from one state, stage, subject, or place to another." When one works with young children, transitions occur frequently, from the time they enter the door until they leave for home. It is not like a formal high school or college class where students enter at a specified time, hear a lecture on a designated topic, and then leave at the sound of a bell. Young children can be interested in an activity for a long period of time—in fact, they sometimes need to be reminded that it will soon "be time for another activity."

In an effort to find ways to reduce random behavior during transition from one activity to another, the teachers should review the plan for the day before the children arrive. A few extra minutes spent on transition activities will be well worth the effort. During the meeting, a song can be reviewed, any activities using props readied, and specifics discussed with other teachers if their assistance is needed. A few extra activities should be ready to use when needed. Preparation before children arrive pays off while they are there.

A few extra activities should be planned for use when needed during transition times.

How can children be encouraged to clean up their toys and materials before moving on to the next activity? Possibly by observing when they begin to lose interest and then stepping in to suggest that the blocks be put on the shelf or to assist in clearing up the art materials and putting things away. Possibly by giving a few minutes' warning. Possibly by having something of interest planned and started before the children begin random or running behavior. What happens at transition times really depends on the teacher. If she stops to clean up or get involved with a single child, or is not ready for the next activity, the children usually go right on past her. Then she has difficulty regaining her lead.

Several studies have focused on the amount of time teachers and children spend in transitions. Berk (1976) found that for children under the age of 6 years, transitions were the most prominent activity in all schools studied, ranging from 20 percent of the time in the community day care center to 30 to 35 percent in all settings, including a Head Start and a Montessori preschool. That is a lot of time when children may not know what is expected of them and can increase aggression, class disruption, or deviant behavior (Kounin 1970). Reporting on the behavior of passive and aggressive children who were not provided with positive transitions, Wolfgang (1977) observed that the passive child (1) remains stationary, showing no response to commands, (2) withdraws to some quiet place, or (3) silently does what he or she is told. Meanwhile, the aggressive child responds by (1) destroying materials, (2) throwing objects, (3) becoming verbally aggressive, or (4) running and forcing the teacher to chase him or her.

In the daily activities, most teachers plan for curriculum areas, such as art, free play, and music, but neglect transition times—and then wonder why they are so difficult to manage. When teachers do not know what to expect, how can the children know? Teachers who write into their lesson plan the specific activities to be used at transition times find control of the children much easier. Teachers should also try to delay unnatural breaks in classroom activity, minimize interruption of activities, and, when possible, allow completion of an activity before introducing another (Borg 1975).

Transition times are not merely time-consumers; they can be very valuable teaching times. Much learning and feedback comes at times when the group is small and time is available for informal conversation. Transition can be a time of relationship building or a time for relaxation or emotional or physical release.

GOOD TRANSITION ACTIVITIES

A good transition activity will accomplish one or more of the following: Enable the child to see the conclusion or completion of an activity, allow for child involvement and independence, set the mood for the next activity, reinforce ideas already learned, preassess the present knowledge of the child, be used as a valuable teaching time in all areas of development, help the child build good relationships with others, and add interest and variety to the daily schedule. Thus, the activity should:

1. Provide a variety of experiences. Using the same finger play or song day after day may discourage children from coming. Make it so exciting that the children will be there in order not to miss something!
2. Encourage self-control. When moving from one room or location to another, try putting something on the floor for the children to follow (yarn or paper objects such as footprints) or give them a particular way to go (e.g., jumping like a frog) *until* they have established the routine. *Then* try saying that all those wearing shoes (or green, or stripes) can go to the next activity or place. Still later on, just tell them what is expected ("We're going to lunch, now"), and let them take responsibility for getting there. It removes the external control and helps them build internal control, independence, and self-confidence—very important steps. To reiterate this point: At first give the children a specific idea of how to go and where they are expected to go; then move to verbalization and independence building. Teachers who must always tell children how and what to do do not have confidence in the children or themselves.
3. Prepare the children for what is to follow (snack, story, going outside). A transition period may be used as specific preparation for an activity or as a quieting time for the children.
4. Meet the needs, interests, and developmental abilities of the children. Transition time should encourage participation, provide some learning, and be enjoyable and flexible. The teacher should watch the children for clues as to length, type of activity, and expectations.
5. Be started by the teacher when the first children arrive in the area. Other children will finish their activities and join the group. If a teacher waits until all the children are there before she begins, there is no incentive for the children to get there. "Why hurry so you can wait?"

TEACHING SUGGESTIONS

Following are some suggestions that could be used as transition activities. Use only those that are appropriate for your group of children, and add other ideas of your own.

Animal

Have an animal concealed until group time. Then bring it into the group or take the children to the animal, whichever is more appropriate. Discuss, touch, and enjoy the animal.

Ball Toss

As each child (e.g., John) comes to the group, the teacher says, "John is ready." Toss or roll a soft ball to the child, who returns it. Repeat as each child arrives.

Body Cards

The teacher shows large cards on which have been drawn different positions. The children use their bodies to represent the symbols.

Another way to use body cards is to have silhouette figures cut out of tag board. The teacher holds up an example, and the children form that position with their bodies.

Body cards with stick figures representing different positions that children can imitate.

Body cards with silhouette figures that children can imitate.

Chalkboard

With the teacher drawing stick figures, the children supply a story. It is surprising how rapidly the story content changes. Some children who do not ordinarily express themselves become verbal in such a setting. Accept the children's ideas and let the story flow freely. If children are able, have them draw some of the story on the chalkboard.

Children's Original Stories

Without Props or Aids

One day a group of children was waiting for story time before the teacher was ready. One child volunteered, "I'll tell you a story." The other children agreed; so Dell moved to the place usually occupied by the teacher and told his story. It was short and to the point: "Once there was a dog." Then he returned to his place in the group. Other children wanted a turn. Some of the stories were familiar ones, some were "make-believe." The children thoroughly enjoyed participating. Children who wanted to tell a story were given the chance, but those who did not were not forced to do so.

With Props or Aids

Paste pictures into an old book (e.g., a dress pattern book) with a stiff back and heavy pages. (Children or teachers may do this.) At story time, show the pictures and let the children make up a story. This can be used over and over.

Children enjoy active participation in a transition activity.

Provide the children with flannel board cutouts and let them make up a story, or let them use visuals that teachers have previously used. The stories may be traditional or original.

Cognitive Concepts

Suppose you want to see how children respond to certain situations. "I want to buy some oranges. Where do I go to get them?" "Where can I get a new collar for my dog?" This gives the children an opportunity to think. Before you respond, "No, you can't buy it there," ask for further clarification. The child may be perfectly correct!

Teach about prepositions by using an object in relationship to another object. "Where is the spoon?" (Over, under, beside, on, or in the box.) Then give the child a chance to place the object and tell its relationship. A better activity would be for the child to use his body in relationship to an object; however, space may be a limitation.

Enforcing Themes

Example 1. When a theme concerns air, use a canister vacuum with hose attached to blow rather than suck air. Place the opening directly up, put a Ping-Pong ball on opening, and turn on vacuum. Ball bounces up and down.

Example 2. For theme on magnets, tell story, *Mickey's Magnet,* by Franklyn M.

Branley and Eleanor K. Vaughan (New York: Scholastic Book Services, 1956). Demonstrate how Mickey kept spilling and picking up pins. Then divide children into groups and give them objects and magnets. Let them determine which objects are attracted by the magnet.

Exercises

Exercises such as "Head, Shoulders, Knees, and Toes" help to reduce some of the tensions and physical needs of children. Many exercises can be used.

With children sitting on the floor, legs outstretched, have them touch the opposite knee with their fingers. Try it with an elbow, then the nose.

Have the children pretend they are rag dolls. Help them relax by first hanging their heads, then moving their arms limply, then their legs, and so on until they are on the floor.

Have the children walk around the room as they think animals would walk, using their own creative imaginations without patterning from teachers.

Use some of the suggested movement activities in Chapter 5.

When stimulating activity occurs just before a quiet period, it is important to provide an activity immediately after it to relax the children. Some of the finger plays on this and following pages work nicely for this purpose.

Feel Box

Take a small cardboard box (about 16 by 8 by 8 in. or a size that can be easily handled by a child) and cut out one side. On each end make holes large enough for the child's hands. He puts his hands in the ends and holds the open side away from himself so that he cannot see inside the box, but the other children can. The child closes his eyes while the teacher places an object through the open side into the box. The child feels the object and tries to guess what it is.

Films

Films should never take the place of actual experience, but can be used infrequently as supplements to firsthand experiences. Carefully evaluate each film as to length, concepts taught (including vocabulary), interest for the children, and value to be gained from the film. Consider also whether **this is the best way to teach a particular topic.**

Finger Plays

Children enjoy "doing" as well as "seeing." Finger plays should be short and of interest to the children; some help teach number concepts. Teachers should know the finger plays well before attempting to teach them to the children; make sure all teachers with the group do the finger plays the same way. Following are some favorites (some by authors unknown, some used by permission) along with some body actions for children.

One Little Body

Two little hands go clap, clap, clap! (*Do actions as mentioned.*)
Two little feet go tap, tap, tap!
Two little hands go thump, thump, thump!
Two little feet go jump, jump, jump!
One little body turns around;
One little body sits quietly down.

Hands

On my head my hands I place,
On my shoulders, on my face.
On my waist, and by my side;
Quickly at my back they hide.

I can wave them way up high,
Like the little birdies fly.
I can clap them: one, two, three.
Now see how quiet they can be.

Little Hands

Open, shut them; open, shut them;
Give a little clap.
Open, shut them; open, shut them;
Lay them in your lap.

Creep them, creep them slowly upward
To the rosy cheek;
Open wide the shining eyes,
Through the fingers peek.

Open, shut them; open, shut them;
To the shoulders fly;
Let them like the birdies flutter,
Flutter to the sky.

Falling, falling slowly downward,
Nearly to the ground;
Quickly raise them, all the fingers
Twirling round and round.

Open, shut them; open, shut them;
Give a little clap.
Open, shut them; open, shut them;
Lay them in your lap.

Creep them; creep them; creep them
Right up to your chin;
Open wide your little mouth,
But do not let them in!

I Have Two Eyes to See With

I have two eyes to see with, I have two feet to run.
I have two hands to feel with, and a nose, I have but one.
I have two ears to hear with, and a tongue to say "Good day."
And two red cheeks for you to kiss before I go to play.

Ten Little Fingers

Ten little fingers, and they all belong to me.
I can make them do things, would you like to see?
I can shut them up tight, or open them wide.
I can put them together, or make them all hide.
I can make them jump high. I can make them jump low.
I can fold them quietly, and hold them just so!

Who Feels Happy?

Who feels happy, who feels gay?
All who do, snap your fingers this way.
Who feels happy, who feels gay?
All who do, stamp your feet this way.
(*Let the children suggest different actions.*)

Where Is Thumpkin?

Where is Thumpkin? Where is Thumpkin?	*(Hide hands behind back.)*
Here am I. Here am I.	*(Show one thumb then other.)*
How are you today, sir?	
Very well, I thank you.	
Run away, run away.	*(Return each hand to back.)*
Repeat song using "Pointer" (index finger); "Tall Man" (middle finger); "Ring Man" (ring finger); "Baby" (little finger); and "All the Men" (all fingers at once).	*(Repeat actions showing appropriate finger, then return hands to back.)*

Night and Morning

This little boy is going to bed;
(Place first finger of right hand on palm of left hand.)
Down on the pillow he lays his head;
(Thumb of left hand is pillow.)
Pulls the covers up round him tight,
(Fingers of left hand close.)
And this is the way he sleeps all night!
Morning comes, he opens his eyes;
(Open and blink eyes.)
Back with a toss the cover flies;
(Fingers of left hand open quickly.)
Up he jumps, is dressed and away.
(Right index finger is up and hopping away.)
Ready for frolic and play all day.

Going to Sleep

Some things go to sleep in such a funny way—
Little birds stand on one leg and tuck their heads away.
(Do actions.)
Little chickens do the same, a-sitting on their perch;
Little mice lie soft and still, as if they were in church.
(Crouch down quietly.)
Little kittens all curl up in such a funny ball.
(Curl up.)
Sleepy children all stretch out
So they'll grow straight and tall.
(Stretch arms, legs, body.)

Bunny Song

Here is my bunny with ears so funny,
And here is his hole in the ground.
When a noise he hears,
He pricks up his ears
And jumps in his hole with a bound.
(Right fist forms bunny, and two
fingers the ears. Left hand is
closed to make a "hole.")

Five Little Kittens

There were five little kittens.	*(Hold left hand up;*
One little kitten went to sleep.	*with right hand fold*
Two little kittens went to sleep.	*the left-hand*
Three little kittens went to sleep.	*fingers into the*
Four little kittens went to sleep.	*palm, one by one,*
Five little kittens went to sleep.	*starting with the*
All the kittens were fast asleep.	*little finger.)*

My Little Kitten

My little kitten ran up a tree. (Fingers run up arms.)
And sat on a limb to look at me. (Hands are placed on opposite shoulders.)
I said, "Come, kitty," and down he ran, (Fingers run down arms.)
And drank all the milk (Hand is cupped, opposite hand drinks.)
I poured in his pan.

The Turtle

The turtle crawls on the ground
And makes a little rustling sound.
He carries his house wherever he goes,
And when he is scared,
He pulls in his nose and covers his toes.

Quacking Ducks

Five little ducks went out to play,	*(Hold up five fingers.)*
Over the hills and far away.	*(Fingers run away.)*
When the Mother duck said,	*(Make quacking motion*
"Quack, quack, quack."	*with both hands.)*
Four little ducks came waddling back.	*(Four fingers return.)*
Four little ducks went out to play,	*(Four fingers run away.)*
Continue words and motions until . . .	
No little ducks came waddling back.	
BUT, when the Mother duck said,	*(Make deliberate*
"QUACK, QUACK, QUACK!"	*quacking motion.)*
Five little ducks came waddling back!	*(All fingers return.)*

Five Little Squirrels

Five little squirrels sitting on a tree.	*(Hold up hand.)*
The first one said, "What do I see?"	*(Shield eyes with hand.)*
The second one said, "A man with a gun."	*(Take aim.)*
The third one said, "Oh! Let's run!"	*(Hands run away.)*
The fourth one said, "Let's hide in the shade."	
The fifth one said, "I'm not afraid!"	*(Thumbs under armpits.)*
When "BANG!" went the gun	*(Clap hands loudly.)*
And away they all run.	*(Hands go behind back.)*

The Beehive

Here is the beehive	*(Close fist, thumb inside.)*
Where are the bees?	
Hidden away where nobody sees.	
Soon they'll come creeping out of the hive;	
One, two, three, four, five	*(Bring out finger with each number.)*
BZZZZZZZ, BZZZZZZZZZ.	*(Fingers and hands fly around.)*

Eensy, Weensy Spider

Eensy, weensy spider	*(Opposite thumbs and index fingers*
Climbed up the water spout.	*climb up each other.)*
Down came the rain	*(Quickly lower hands and arms.)*
And washed the spider out.	
Out came the sun	*(Make circle of arms around head.)*
And dried up all the rain.	
So eensy, weensy spider	
Climbed up the spout again.	*(Repeat thumbs and finger motion.)*

Little Jenny Wren

As little Jenny Wren	
Was sitting by her shed,	*(Hold arms at back, like wings.)*
She waggled with her tail	*(Shake hips.)*
And she nodded with her head	*(Nod head.)*
She waggled with her tail	*(Repeat above.)*
And she nodded with her head	
As little Jenny Wren	
Was sitting by her shed.	

Pig

I had a little pig,	*(Make a fist with thumb up.)*
And I fed it in a trough.	*(Make cup of left hand.)*
He go so big and fat,	*(Make circle with arms.)*
That his tail popped off!	*(Clap hands to knees.)*
So, I got me a hammer	*(Use one hand as hammer.)*
And I got me a nail,	*(Hammer on thumb of other hand.)*
And I made the pig	*(Continue hammering motion.)*
A wooden tail!	

Frogs

Five little frogs standing in a row,	*(Hold up five fingers.)*
This little frog stubbed his toe;	*(Point to each finger in*
This little frog cried, "Oh, Oh, Oh."	*turn.)*
This little frog laughed and was glad;	
This little frog cried and was sad;	
This little frog did just what he should—	
He ran for the doctor as fast as he could.	

Here Is a Ball

A little ball,	*(Make ball with fingers.)*
A bigger ball,	*(Make ball with both hands.)*
A great big ball I see.	*(Make ball with both arms.)*
Now let's count the balls we've made.	
One, two, three!	*(Repeat previous 3 circles.)*

My Dolly

This is how my dolly walks,	*(Walk around a circle stiff-*
This is how she walks, you see.	*legged and arms raised.)*
This is how my dolly runs,	*(Run stiff-legged.)*
This is how she runs, you see.	
This is how my dolly talks,	*(Bend over, say, "Mama,*
This is how she talks, you see.	*Mama.")*

The Fruit Tree

Way up high in the apple tree,	*(Extend arms up high.)*
Two little apples smiled down on me.	*(Put hands around eyes.)*
I shook that tree as hard as I could,	*(Pretend to shake tree.)*
And down came the apples:	*(Arms move to ground.)*
M-m-m-m, were they good!	*(Rub stomach.)*

Repeat poem and motions using different kinds of fruit: pears, peach, banana, orange, cherry, and so on.
For last verse, use a lemon tree. Last action is pulling a sour face and saying "U-u-u-uh! They were sour!"

The House

This is the roof of the house so good	*(Raise arms above head,*
There are the walls all made of wood.	*fingers touching.)*
These are the windows to let in the light.	*(Arms encircle head.)*
This is the door that shuts so tight.	*(Clap hands together.)*
This is the chimney so straight and tall.	*(Raise arms straight.)*
What a good house for us, one and all!	

Five Little Astronauts

Five little astronauts	*(Hold up five fingers.)*
Ready for outer space.	
The first one said,	*(Hold up one finger.)*
"Let's have a race."	
The second one said,	*(Hold up two fingers.)*
"The weather's too rough."	
The third one said,	*(Hold up three fingers.)*
"Oh, don't be so gruff."	
The fourth one said,	*(Hold up four fingers.)*
"I'm ready enough."	
The fifth one said,	*(Hold up five fingers.)*
"Let's blast off!"	
10, 9, 8, 7, 6, 5, 4, 3, 2, 1	*(Hold up 10 fingers. Lower one finger with each number.)*
BLAST OFF!!!	*(Clap loudly, say "Blast Off.")*

The Soldiers

Five little soldiers	*(Hold up five fingers on one hand.)*
Standing in a row;	
Three stood straight	*(Hold three up straight and tall.)*
And two just so,	*(Bend two fingers.)*
Along came the captain	*(Hold up index finger of opposite hand.)*
And what do you think?	
They all stood straight,	*(Hold five fingers straight and tall.)*
As quick as a wink.	

Jack-in-the-Box

Jack-in-the-Box, all shut up tight,
(Close fist with thumb inside and cover with palm of other hand, or curl up body on floor with arms around head.)
Not a breath of air or a bit of light,
How tired he must be, all folded up.

Let's open the lid.
And up he'll jump.
(*Thumbs pop out of fist, or child jumps up, extending arms.*)

For more information on finger plays, see Appendix E.

Guessing Games

Say: "I am thinking of something that ______ (give a couple of clues). Can you guess what it is?" (Use animals or transportation vehicles; describe a child.) Children can also take a turn giving clues.

Guests

Often bringing a guest into the school is easier than taking children on a particular field trip. By bringing the guest to school, the children can enjoy the experience in a familiar setting. This is often helpful.

A doctor, father of one child in the center, came to the school with his black bag. Rexene backed off, saying, "But I don't want a shot today." She was assured by the teachers and the doctor that he had not come to give shots that day. This particular doctor was a bone specialist. After showing the children all the things he carried in his bag, he asked, "Have any of you ever known someone who had broken a bone?" Some did, and some did not. He went on to explain how he helped people when they had a broken bone. He applied a cast to a teacher's arm for demonstration—none of the children would be his patient! How real the experience was to the children! They expressed sympathy to the teacher, as if she really had a broken arm. After the cast was dry, the doctor removed it. Many of the children were concerned, thinking he would cut off the teacher's arm with the cast. He took care to explain away all their fears and questions. After the cast was removed, the children said how glad they were that the teacher's arm was better. The children examined the cast, tried it on, and explored it in every way. This was an excellent experience for them because the doctor could communicate with them on their level. One child commented, "My dog has a broken leg, but he doesn't have a cast on." Shortly after this classroom experience, the teacher's own young son broke his arm, and she had information to make the experience less frightening for him.

A carpenter also paid a visit to a group of preschool children. The visit had been prearranged and well planned. Through his conversation, he helped the children to understand his occupation better. He brought a small door that was nearly completed and let the children finish it by putting screws in predrilled holes. He explained the use of all his tools, and, upon departing, gave each child a carpenter's pencil. How busy the woodworking bench was that day!

A musician invited as a guest should be asked to explain about the instrument briefly and then play tunes that are familiar to the children. The children can listen to some selections, but they also enjoy participating. If the children are not allowed to touch or use the instrument, they may be able to sing or dance with the music. Although a guest may be very talented and want to display his or her skills, young children are easily bored and may walk out on the guest. The experience should be kept simple, therefore, with the length of the presentation varied according to the interests of the children.

Mirror Image

The teacher shows a mirror, and the children see how it reflects their movements and expressions. The mirror is removed and the teacher or a child makes movements for the others to reflect.

Musical Experiences

Children enjoy expressing themselves—verbally or physically—through music. Free, spontaneous movement should be encouraged. Occasional honest praise helps to motivate the quiet child.

A number of records and tapes encourage children to participate. When selecting this material, see that they give ideas but do not restrict freedom to interpret actions. A list of record sources is found in Appendix E.

Use the piano from time to time, sometimes to accompany songs, sometimes to teach specific concepts (high and low, loud and soft, fast and slow); sometimes encourage child participation (marching, moving to various rhythms).

Some of the ideas under "Exercises" could be used with the addition of music. For other specific suggestions, see activities listed at the end of Chapter 5.

Number Experiences

With the aid of a flannel board, chalkboard, bulletin board, finger plays, games, songs, and other methods, provide some relaxed and enjoyable but meaningful experiences with numbers. Many preschool children can do rote counting but still do not understand number symbols. For example, when interrupted in counting, they must return to the beginning—they cannot continue where they left off.

For some specific ideas, see finger plays listed previously that include numbers, see Chapter 11, or try some of the following. (*Note:* It is generally easier for young children to count forward than backward.)

This Old Man

This old man, he played one,
He played knick-knack on his thumb;
With a knick-knack waddy-wack, give my dog a bone,
This old man came rolling home.

This old man, he played two (shoe); three (knee); four (door);
five (hive); six (sticks); seven (up to heaven); eight (gate);
nine (vine); ten (hen).

One Red Valentine

One red valentine, two red valentines,
Three red valentines, four;
I'll snip and cut and color and paste
And then make twenty more.

Over in the Meadow*

(Southern Appalachian Folk Song)

Over in the meadow in the sand in the sun
Lived an old mother turtle and her little baby one.
"Swim," said the mother; "I swim," said the one
And he swam and was happy in the sand in the sun.

Over in the hollow in a pool in the bogs
Lived an old mother froggie and her two polliwogs.
"Kick," said the mother, "We kick," said the wogs,
Then they kicked and kicked into little green frogs.

* Song has ten verses. For another version, see *Over in the Meadow* by John Langstaff (New York: Brace and World, 1957).

Over in the meadow in a nest in the tree
Lived an old mother birdie and her little babies three.
"Sing," said the mother, "We sing," said the three
And they sang and were happy in the nest in the tree.

Ten Little Indians

One little, two little, three little Indians,
Four little, five little, six little Indians,
Seven little, eight little, nine little Indians,
Ten little Indian boys.

One Elephant

(Chilean folk song)

One elephant went out to play,
All on a spider's web one day.
He had such enormous fun,
He called on another elephant to come.

(Children extend arms down, clasp own hands, pretend to walk like an elephant.)

Continue counting as "elephants" (children) are added to group. Two elephants went out to play . . . Three elephants . . . Four elephants, and so on.)

Three Blue Pigeons

(American folk song)

Three blue pigeons, sitting on the wall,
Three blue pigeons, sitting on the wall.
One flew away. Whee-ee-ee-ee!
Two blue pigeons, sitting on the wall,
Two blue pigeons, sitting on the wall.
One flew away. Whee-ee-ee-ee!

(Repeat, using one blue pigeon, then no blue pigeons.)

Five Fat Turkeys Are We

Five fat turkeys are we, we slept all night in a tree,
When the cook came around we couldn't be found,
And that is why we're here, you see!

(Repeat, using four, three, two, one, and no fat turkeys.)

Five Little Buns

(Traditional English song)

Five little buns in a baker's shop,
Nice and round with sugar on the top,
Along came a little boy (girl) with a penny to pay,
And bought a sugar bun and took it right away.

(Repeat, using four, three, two, one, and no little buns.)

Five Little Chickadees

(Old counting song)

Five little chick-a-dees peeping at the door,
One flew away and then there were four.

Refrain:
Chick-a-dee, chick-a-dee, happy and gay,
Chick-a-dee, chick-a-dee, fly away.

Four little chick-a-dees sitting on a tree (*refrain*).
Three little chick-a-dees looking at you (*refrain*).
Two little chick-a-dees sitting in the sun (*refrain*).
One little chick-a-dee left all alone,
He flew away and then there were none (*refrain*).

Nursery Rhymes

Young children enjoy the play on words, repetition, and nonsense that are incorporated in nursery rhymes. Pictures add to the enjoyment. Through repetition they learn the rhymes without formal training. Nursery rhymes should be selected by the same criteria used for books.

Following are some nursery rhymes familiar to most young children:

Curly Locks
Deedle, Deedle Dumpling
Hickory, Dickory, Dock!
Humpty Dumpty
Jack Be Nimble, Jack Be Quick
Little Bo-Peep
Little Boy Blue
Little Jack Horner
Little Miss Muffett
Simple Simon
To Market, To Market
Lucy Locket
Mary Had a Little Lamb
Mary, Mary, Quite Contrary
Old King Cole
Pease Porridge Hot
Peter, Peter, Pumpkin Eater
Rock-a-Bye, Baby
Rub-a-Dub-Dub
Seesaw, Margery Daw
Twinkle, Twinkle Little Star
Wee Willie Winkie

See Appendix E for references on Mother Goose Rhymes.

Original Stories from Adults

Perhaps you have written a story, or would like to, and are interested in the reactions of the children. You do not want to use it as your main story, but you do want to try it. Use it as the children are assembling for a group time. (Maybe a parent, a friend, or someone else has written a story and would like response from a group of young children. Try it for them, if you think it would be appropriate.)

Writing for young children is challenging. You need to know their interests, needs, and some of their growth characteristics. Your story should be short, simple, and realistic. Writing in poetry form is stimulating and exciting. (*See* Chapter 3.)

Pantomime

Read a favorite story to the children. Briefly talk about it with the children. Help them identify some key concepts or characteristics. Encourage them to act it out. Sometimes they are better at pantomiming than at reciting.

A flannel board is a valuable aid to transition activities.

Paper Bag

Give each child a paper sack and tell him to go around the room, putting into his sack objects of a certain color or shape (or other description). Examine the contents with the group.

Have two sacks or boxes with identical contents. Have a child "feel" in his sack and name an object in it. The second sack is handed to another child, who is requested to find the same object. Sacks are passed around until all the children have had a turn (Harlan 1973).

Give each child a paper sack. Go into the play yard or on a walk and ask them to either pick up garbage or bring back some things for making a picture. At group time, examine the contents and then proceed with the appropriate activity (keeping the community clean or appreciating things of beauty in nature).

Show a paper bag. Ask the children how many ways the bag can be used. Brainstorm. Try some of the ideas.

Pictures

Select with care the pictures you use with young children. Avoid confusion and distraction.

A teacher can show an interesting picture and start talking about it—the children will generally join in—or a teacher can hold up a picture and stimulate verbal responses by asking questions such as, "What do you think these children are doing?" "Would you like to do what they are doing?" "What time of year is shown in the picture?"

A bulletin board with selected pictures can also be very effective for discussion.

Do not hesitate to get quality (perhaps, famous) artwork from the local library or other available sources. Help the children appreciate aesthetic values.

Poetry

Listen to the conversation of children; it is truly poetic! The play on words, the fun sounds, and the humor are delightful. Too often adults think that poetry has no place in the lives of young children. How wrong they are! An excellent introduction to poetry when a child is young is a priceless experience that will add greatly to his future enjoyment of it.

Young children thoroughly enjoy the rhythmic quality of poetry (nursery rhymes included). They can often be heard reciting a line, phrase, or entire poem as they play. It encourages them to sharpen their hearing perception. They begin to discriminate between similar sounds, they enjoy the sense and nonsense of poetry, and they learn new things.

Poetry should be a part of the teacher's repertoire. When appropriate, she can recite it, expressing her enjoyment of the verse and also showing the children that she values it.

Select poetry as carefully as you do other language experiences. Use it in a similar way: for a transition, to support areas of curriculum, to create interest, and to verbalize with the children. You can dramatize it or use it spontaneously or as a planned activity, with or without visual aids. If the children seem interested, use more verses; if they become restless, only a first verse or the first and last verses may be sufficient.

The teacher's attitude toward poetry will be influential. A teacher who enjoys and appreciates it will select and share it enthusiastically and will use different types: poems related to children's everyday experiences, nonsense verses for fun, poems that bring melody and rhythm to the ear, poems with special meaning, and poems that stimulate and encourage verbal exploration. Through repetition, not through rigid memorization, children learn and enjoy poetry.

As you can tell, using poetry with young children is a great favorite of this author. When I was required to use poetry as a student in a children's literature class, the experience started off on a reluctant note. The children responded so well, my timidity vanished, and now it is impossible to get along without using it often in the classroom. If you cannot find a poem on a specific topic, you might even try writing your own.

Among the many excellent sources of poetry for young children are favorite authors such as Dorothy Aldis, Dorothy Baruch, Polly Chase Boyden, Marchette Chute, Rachel Field, Rose Fyleman, Josette Frank, Kate Greenaway, A. A. Milne, Elizabeth Madox Roberts, Carl Sandburg, Robert Louis Stevenson, and James S. Tippett. Other poetry references appear in Appendix E.

Preparation for a Field Trip

Tell the children about an excursion just before you go. Help them to understand why you are going and what you will see and do. Set up the guidelines, and make necessary stops at the bathroom and water fountain before leaving the center.

After a field trip, use transition time to discuss what happened, to ask and answer questions, or to draw or write a story of the group's experience.

For additional information about field trips, see Chapter 8.

Puppets

Several kinds of puppets are available and add interest to activities. Sack, finger, hand, sock, tube, clothespin, and stick puppets can be easily made and used by either children or teachers. Making something for later use (perhaps at group time) adds an element of anticipation for the children.

Make sure the puppets are realistically represented and that correct concepts are taught. This should be a learning experience as well as a fun one.

Some shy children who do not respond to a person will to a puppet. Use this experience to encourage verbalization, or have the puppet give instructions for the children to follow: "Lester, please hold a picture while we sing." "Mindy, please put the cow on the flannel board." "All hop like bunnies."

Set the guidelines for puppet use before the children become loud or aggressive.

A hand puppet is easily made from a paper sack.

Merely saying, "These are friendly puppets who have come to help us today" may deter any problems.

Rhyming Games

Read a poem, show objects, or tell the children certain words. Ask them to think of words that rhyme. Some of their responses will be very interesting.

Rhythms

For suggestions, see music and movement activities at the end of Chapter 5.

Role Playing

Encourage a child or children to act out a story or activity. Let others guess what it is. Give a turn to all who want one.

Science

If you are interested in having all the children participate in a science experience, this is an excellent time. Sometimes have the whole group together, and sometimes use small groups for discussion and participation.

For suggested activities, see Chapter 6.

Songs

Most children enjoy singing simple songs. Songs that use the names of the individual children tend to have magical power. (*See* "Mary Wore Her Red Dress" in *American Folk Songs for Children* by Ruth Seeger. Moiselle Renstrom has some delightful songs in her books, *Merrily We Sing, Rhythm Fun,* and *Tune Time.* An excellent variety of songs is also found in books by Kathleen M. Bayless and Marjorie E. Ramsey or by P. F. Nielsen, F. Sucher, and C. Carmen.

A review of Chapter 5, including how to teach a song to young children, might be appropriate at this stage.

Stories with Action

Have you ever been on an action walk with children? This activity brings out an element of suspense that delights each child.

The children and teachers sit on the floor, using their hands to make the sound effects: clapping for walking; rubbing the hands together for going through tall grass; gently pounding on the chest for going over a bridge; fists pounding on the legs for running. Use your own imagination and comments from the children to carry you through an enjoyable experience.

Several versions of an animal "hunt" are available. Ramsey and Bayless (1980) take a bear hunt; Curtis (1982) takes a tiger hunt; still others take a cougar hunt. Here is an original example of how such an activity could be used.

Let's Go Camping

Everyone sits down. The teacher begins; the children repeat what the teacher says and does and participate through entire activity.

"Let's go camping." (Children repeat.) "We'll need our sleeping bags, food, ______, ______." (Children repeat.) Pretend to gather and pack items. "We have walked a long way." (Children repeat.) "I'm getting hungry." (Children repeat.) Pretend to fix and eat meal. "I'm getting so sleepy!" (Children repeat.) Yawn, stretch, and pretend to prepare sleeping bag and self for bed. "Let's crawl into our sleeping bags." (Children repeat.) Wiggle as if getting in and going to sleep. "Somebody is snoring!" (Children repeat.) Snore and blow out air. "Somebody is snoring louder than anyone else!" (Children repeat.) Snore and blow out air. ______ (use child's name) isn't sleepy; so he goes for a walk in the woods. As he is walking (slap hands rhythmically on the legs), he goes over some cobble rocks (make click with tongue in mouth); then he goes over a bridge (pound fists on legs); then he goes over some dry dirt (rub hands together). And do you know what he sees when he gets there? He sees a fire in the forest, and the wind is blowing the fire (put arms up in the air and wave back and forth, saying "Whoo-oo-oo, whoo-oo-oo!").

When he sees the fire, he runs back over the dry dirt (action), over the bridge (action), and over the cobble rocks (action) to the camp. He wakes everyone up and tells of the fire. All get up and run to the fire, first over the cobble rocks (action), then the bridge (action), and last over the dry dirt (action). They see the fire with the wind blowing it (action) and decide to go back and get some water (go back through actions). They get some buckets and pour water into them (say "shh-hhh-hh-pt") and go back to the fire (with actions). They pour the water on the fire that the wind is blowing ("whoo-oo-oo," slow down), and the fire goes out.

Now we're very tired; so we go back to the camp across the dry dirt, bridge, and rocks (very slow actions), crawl into our sleeping bags, and all start to snore (action). And guess who snores the loudest of all?

If this activity seems too long for the children, delete parts of it. Usually they respond, "Oh, let's do it again!"

Storybooks

Select an appropriate book, other than one to be used at actual story time. Show the pictures to the children and stimulate their conversation.

A child may select a book he would like you to read for story time. Use it while the children are gathering, but use the book you had already prepared for the entire group.

Surprise Box

Occasionally a teacher or a child can bring a "surprise" or gather up familiar things from the room. Teacher or child feels the object in a box and describes it. Others try to guess its identity.

Talking Time for Children

Many opportunities should be provided for the young child to express himself and his ideas as well as to listen to others. Following are some ideas which have been tried and found to be effective:

- Ask which children in the group are absent that day. This helps the children to become more aware of each child.
- Talk about the weather. Has there been a recent change? What kinds of wearing apparel are appropriate for today?
- If you know a child has done or is about to do something exciting, let him share it with the group.
- Casually, get feedback from the children on certain concepts so that you will know if more time and information are needed.
- Talk about things the children have been doing during the morning. How did the finger paint feel? Was it fun to climb on the jungle gym? See other ideas presented in Chapter 4.

"Think" Box

Designate a good-sized box as the "think" box. Use it as often as the value dictates. The teacher brings the box to group time and encourages verbal expression from the children. "What do you think is in the box today?" As the children guess, the teacher

Transition times are good for feedback and informal conversation.

may add clues. For example, one day the box may include gloves—baseball glove, ski glove, boxing glove, lady's dress glove, and child's winter glove. The teacher says to the children, "What does a glove look like?" "How many kinds of gloves do you know about?" As the children name some that are in the box, she takes them out. The teacher may give added clues: "It's a kind of glove you play a game with," or "You wear it in the winter."

Another use of the "think" box is to have parents and children, the day before you use the box, to bring things (something soft, something your favorite color, something about an animal, or a picture of something in your house). The enthusiasm of parents and children is usually high. On the teaching day have the child place his object in the box, unseen by others. At the appropriate time the child shows and tells about his object. The setting is very informal so that even the shy child participates. To prevent boredom, select a few different children to bring objects each time the box is used.

Television

Make a television screen by cutting a hole in a large box. Let the children take turns being the actors and actresses. You may want to encourage the children to use props.

Another idea is to use a box that is large enough to cut a screen that is visible to the group. Make a continuous story on butcher paper. Roll the story on a dowel and attach the other end of the story to another dowel. As you tell the story, unroll the pictures from one dowel to the other, showing the pictures through the "screen."

CUMULATIVE LESSON PLAN

- "Think" box
- "Jack-in-the-Box." Use the one on page 174, or another version in *Singing Fun,* by Lucille Wood and Louise B. Scott (Bowmar, 1954). Also see *Music: A Way of Life for the Young Child,* by Kathleen M. Bayless and Marjorie E. Ramsey (St. Louis: Mosby, 1982).

For sources of different activities, see Appendix E.

APPLICATION OF PRINCIPLES

1. For one week, note the different activities which are used for transitions. Which ones do the children respond to best?
2. Be particularly aware of the children's actions, voices, and involvement during transitions. How does the tempo in the room change? Are teachers more concerned with "things" (cleanup, getting next activity ready) or "people"? Use examples.
3. Plan and use a new transition activity. Begin it as the first child or children assemble. How do things change as more children join the activity?
4. Learn and use four new finger plays in the next month.
5. Memorize and use four poems. Stimulate children to use rhyming words and to write their own poems.
6. Make and use a plan that will use transition periods as learning experiences for children and teachers.

References

Berk, Laura. "How Well Do Classroom Practices Reflect Teacher Goals?" *Young Children* 32(November 1976): 64–81.

Borg, Walter, Philip Langer, and Jeanette Wilson. "Teacher Classroom Management Skills and Pupil Behavior." *Journal of Experimental Education* 44(1975): 2.

Harlan, Jean. "The Paper Bag Principle." *Young Children* 28(August 1973): 355–357.

Kounin, Jacob S. *Discipline and Group Management in Classrooms.* New York: Holt, Rinehart & Winston, 1970.

Wolfgang, Charles. *Helping Aggressive and Passive Preschoolers Through Play.* Columbus, Ohio: Charles E. Merrill, 1977.

8
Field Trips

Ride a cock horse to Banbury Cross
To see a fine lady upon a white horse;
Rings on her fingers, and bells on her toes,
She shall have music wherever she goes!

MAIN PRINCIPLES

1. Children learn about their environment and its people through firsthand visits.
2. Adults must plan well to make a field trip meaningful to young children.

The children must always come first! Stop and consider why a field trip is important. New children might need to adjust to their new environment and friends before venturing away from the classroom. Would it be best to visit a site, or could the experience be just as valuable if a resource person came to the center? Many questions need to be answered before deciding on an appropriate place and time for an excursion.

Field trips are an extension of social studies. Instead of having to learn about roles and careers from miniature experiences, the child is given an opportunity to see things as they are. The child begins to tie maps, locations, occupations, and so on into a more meaningful world. Unconsciously, he attempts to try out the scientist's method of exploration: gaining information, observing, and concluding.

Children can observe and study in the natural setting when trips outside of the familiar classroom meet their needs and interests. However, the frequency of the trips needs careful consideration; some children enjoy going often while others need the security of the classroom. Rather than continually going to new and different places, the teacher might well consider returning to a successful and well-liked location, particularly during a different season or when activities are different.

VALUES FOR CHILDREN

The following are considered worthwhile reasons for taking young children on field trips:

1. To gain firsthand experiences on their developmental level
2. To see career models
3. To increase and clarify concepts
4. To increase language skills by learning and associating new words with experiences

Field trips give children a chance to see things as they really are.

5. To increase their frame of reference and sense of observation
6. To develop initiative and creativeness in dramatic play
7. To help build good relationships with other children and adults through a group experience

8. To give parents an opportunity to participate
9. To have fun

ESSENTIALS FOR FIELD TRIPS

Taking young children on a field trip is not the easiest or most profitable way to teach. Some inexperienced teachers feel that a field trip requires little planning and are surprised at the failure of the trip or the endless details.

The teacher needs to consider the following questions carefully:

1. Where will we go?
2. Why should we go to this particular place?
3. How will we travel? How can we prepare the children and reinforce the experience upon our return?
4. What are the interests of the children? What will we see? What are the costs?
5. When shall we go (time of year, day)?
6. Who will supervise? Who is contact person at destination?

A checklist assists the teacher in making and carrying out plans for a successful trip.

Planning

In order to avoid unpleasant consequences, teachers should plan to make the most of time, money, and energy when planning a field trip. One teacher, upon hearing that sheep were to be sheared not too far away, arranged to take the children. When they arrived, the man was roughly shearing the sheep. Some were cut and bleeding. The children became upset and wanted to get bandages to cover the wounds. They soon turned to other, more pleasant things.

Field trips should always be planned with the needs, interests, and ages of the children in mind. What would be appropriate for one age may be inappropriate for another.

The route to be used on a field trip should avoid construction, delays, and dangerous areas but include interesting points. Every aspect of safety must be considered.

On a walk, an empty sack or two is always taken to bring back the many objects that are found. These objects are used in future planning on a science table or for artistic projects.

Wonderful spontaneous occurrences should never be overlooked—perhaps someone is changing a flat tire, or repair equipment is being used just through the fence. An observant teacher discovers many exciting things very close to the center.

Destination

The teacher should be aware of places of interest in the community. Listening to the comments and watching the play of the children could give an indication of their interests. Parents also may be asked for suggestions. The decision for a field trip must be carefully made; perhaps the children have been some places many times; in other places, danger, loud noise, or unexpected activity may be encountered. There are also places that parents want the privilege of taking their own children.

Proposed Purposes

In selecting a site, the purpose of the trip must be kept in mind. It may well be appropriate or inappropriate. Can the same thing be accomplished another way?

CHECKLIST FOR FIELD TRIP

1. Destination ______________________________
2. Proposed purpose ______________________________
3. Preplanning (check and record information)
   a. School policies ______________________________
   b. Readiness of children ______________________________
   c. Previsit ______________________________
      1. Person who conducts visit ______________________________
      2. Safety ______________________________
      3. Restrooms/fountains ______________________________
   d. Mode of travel ______________________________
   e. Supervision ______________________________
   f. Permission of center official ______________________________
4. Actual trip
   a. Time of departure and return ______________________________
   b. Supervision (list persons) ______________________________
   c. Parental permission (check for each child) ______________________________
   d. Transportation (list mode) ______________________________
   e. Preparation of children (list ways) ______________________________
   f. Assignment of children (give specifics) ______________________________
5. Follow-up (informal discussion, art, food, dramatic play, pictures, classroom project, and so on)
   a. ______________________________
   b. ______________________________
   c. ______________________________
6. Evaluation after trip
   a. What went well on the trip?
   b. How did the children respond to the experience and follow-up activities?
   c. How were problems solved?
   d. What changes are recommended for a future visit? (e.g., preparation of children, follow-up, time)

Preplanning

School Policies

Before planning an outing, the policies of the center must be checked and observed. Every precaution for the safety of the children must be taken.

Readiness of Children

A field trip can be either beneficial or detrimental to the children. If they are taken on an excursion before they feel comfortable in the center, the experience may produce fear and anxiety. For example, a group of 4-year-olds was taken for a walk on the university campus of which their center was a part. One child kept repeating, "But my daddy won't know where I am." The teacher tried to assure him that they were close to the school and would return before it was time to go home. This was no consolation; the child kept repeating the same concern. He felt uncomfortable the entire walk. Upon his return, he heaved a sigh of relief and began exploring the play area.

Some hesitant children can be encouraged to participate in a field trip. A teacher had planned a bus ride for her 3-year-olds. The children had been prepared earlier, and the preparation continued as they walked a short distance to the bus stop. As the bus pulled into sight, Melinda began to cry and to withdraw from the group. She said, "I'm not getting on that bus. You can't make me!" The teacher tried to calm her, telling her that if she didn't want to go on the bus, the two would return to the school. As the other children and teachers boarded the bus, Melinda stood very close to one teacher. When all were on the bus except the two of them, the teacher asked if Melinda would like to look into the bus. She quickly poked her head in and then drew back. The teacher began to explain about the bus until Melinda decided she would like to sit in it. She entered the bus, and the bus driver asked the teacher, "Shall I drive off?" The teacher asked him to wait, which he did. Melinda pondered for a moment and then said, "I think I will ride down to the corner." When she was offered the choice of getting off the bus or continuing her ride as they approached the corner, she decided to continue. Because she was not forced to take the ride, she became more comfortable, taking several minutes to adjust. Throughout the ride she sat close to the teacher, clutching her hand. After the ride she talked freely about it and seemed to have enjoyed it. She had not been ready for the experience when it began, but by the time it was over, she felt quite comfortable.

When possible, arrange for a field trip with a small group of children. This provides an opportunity for each child to be able to hear, see, and participate.

Previsit

One of the prerequisites of a successful field trip is a visit to the location in advance. Many a field trip has ended in failure because the person conducting it directed the information to the teachers rather than to the children. A successful field trip is one that involves the children and stimulates them to learn more about the particular subject.

At the previsit, the teacher should insist on discussing the visit with the person who will conduct it when the children come. She should not accept the statement that, "Anybody who is here can take you through." It just does not work. The teacher needs to explain about the interests and abilities of the children—an informed person should meet the children.

During the previsit, the teacher should inquire about bathrooms, drinking fountains, and any other things that may be important to or distract from the excursion (e.g., change of shift, everybody out to lunch, special clothing to be worn, limits).

Other Items

In the early stages, decisions are made regarding method of travel (bus, car, foot), cost, and how much supervision is required. Written permission is obtained from the school official. Unattended details can prevent a trip at the last minute.

Actual Trip

Time

Time is an element deserving much consideration. A student who was planning a walk across campus to a botany lab was asked how long the walk would take. She replied, "I can make it in five minutes." She was then asked, "But how long does the walk take on a 4-year-old level?" Children like to explore, investigate, and enjoy details as they walk. Plenty of time is allotted, because sometimes getting there is more impressive than the actual visit. An otherwise successful experience can be ruined by hurrying. Too much time is better than too little.

A field trip is often more successful when taken near the beginning of the day when children are less likely to be fatigued or involved in another activity and when roads and people are not so busy.

Field trips should be avoided near holidays. At these times, the children are either overly stimulated or too fatigued. Also, their interest is not always as keen.

Supervision

Before leaving on a field trip, enough adult help must be assured. At least two adults are needed, regardless of how few children. Also, a few tissues, Band-Aids, and other necessities should be tucked into a pocket. When going by car, two adults are required per car, one to concentrate on the driving, and the other sitting in the back seat to supervise the children and to see that each child is comfortably **seated.** When walking, an adult for every three to five children, depending upon the ages and activeness of the children and the distance, should be sufficient. In addition, an adult is needed to stay behind at the school or in the car in case a child decides he does not want to participate. Planning ahead for this possibility saves confusion and time.

If a sufficient number of staff members is not available, a parent can be asked to participate, preferably one whose child is secure in the group setting. An insecure or aggressive child may cause concern to both teachers and parent during the trip.

Parental Permission

Written permission is obtained from parents in advance. Consideration should be given to the parents' wishes; some prefer to take their own children on some trips, while others are appreciative if a teacher does it. Some parents want their children to remain in the safety of the classroom. Plans must be made for the children who cannot go on the field trip and the parents notified.

One preschool has found the following form satisfactory:

Dear Parent:

We are conducting a field trip for the children. We will be visiting ______

______ (place) ______ on ______ (date) ______.

We will go by ______ (foot, car, bus) ______.

If you give permission for your child to go, please sign below.

______
(Child's name)

______ (Date) ______ (Signature of Parent or Guardian)

This form is used with *each* field trip. In this way, parents are informed of the details. If a form granting permission for events of the entire year is signed by parents ahead of time, they may not be aware of the child's current activities and thus lose some of the value of the experience.

Transportation

When arranging transportation for field trips, precautions are taken to see that the drivers have valid licenses, carry adequate insurance, and are capable of the task and that their cars are in good running condition. Serious concern should be given to this responsibility. Some states now have a new seat belt or car seat law. This should be checked very carefully!

A parent who is asked to help transport the children should be an asset to the group. If she has to bring along other children, for example, her value may be decreased. Needs and expectations should be clearly stated to parent volunteers.

In some instances, school buses or public transportation are available. Time schedules should be checked in advance to avoid confusion and worry.

Preparation of Children

Children should be prepared as near to the time of the field trip as possible. If they are told in advance, they become upset if plans go awry. Perhaps not enough adults are available on the appointed day or a storm prevents the trip. Charles, for example, had been told of a field trip for Wednesday. He came to school, but because he was ill, his mother was asked to take him home. Resisting, he climbed under the desk and held on with all his might. He did not want to miss that trip! His mother finally removed him, but he screamed and cried all the way out the door. It would have been better if Charles had been unaware of the trip.

The children are given a general idea of what will occur on the trip. One group of children was taken to the local fire station on a wintry day. The doors were closed because of cold weather. When a well-meaning fireman stepped to the fire truck and turned on the siren, several children became frightened by the noise. Their fright could have lessened by proper preparation.

Taking a group picnic or individual sack lunch adds to the excursion. Eating seems to reinforce the experience.

As often as possible, a walking excursion is planned with stops along the way to examine things of interest. The child will find many things ordinarily overlooked by fast-paced, tall adults!

Assignment of Children

Several ways are available for assigning children to adults or small groups. One way is to let them go with the adult of their choice. Another way is to assign the children. Still another way is to have colored name tags—"All children with a blue tag go with Miss ______, who also has a blue tag"—and so on. This way each teacher is assured of not getting too many children who are difficult to supervise, she knows for which children she is responsible, and each child feels he is going with someone special.

Limits for the trip should be clearly defined. Both children and adults must understand why these limits must be observed.

Follow-Up

Bring to the children's attention some activities you held in preparation for the field trip. Now expand their "geography" into the real world.

Many methods increase and stimulate knowledge of a field trip. A bulletin board, for example, with pictures and materials conveys information before the visit and reinforces it afterwards.

Dramatic play clarifies and increases concepts. One teacher provided small cots and bandages and placed doctor and nurse kits strategically throughout the classroom. Many of the children wandered about aimlessly, paying no attention to them. That morning the class toured a nearby health center. When the children returned to school, there was much activity. They now had firsthand ideas about nurses, doctors, and a hospital. It was fascinating to see how their ideas had increased.

Because dramatic play after a field trip is important, the children should have sufficient time and props to work through their ideas. For example, large blocks can be used to make a bus after a bus ride, instruments can be played after a parade, or a cooking experience can be provided after a trip to the grocery store or bakery.

Stories, pictures, songs, and creative materials add to the learning experience of a trip. Children need more than one exposure if they are to develop correct concepts and a sound foundation. Relaxed talk about the trip elicits information from the children, but they should not be expected to "spit back" specific or detailed information.

The children are invited to help prepare a "thank-you" note and picture for the privilege of visiting a certain place. This will help the children express appreciation and also use some of their artistic and language skills.

Evaluation

As soon after the field trip as possible, the experience should be evaluated. What were the strong points? What were the weak ones? What concepts were learned by the children? Was the experience of interest to them? How could the trip have been improved or planned differently? What teaching aids could be employed to increase the children's knowledge and understanding? When could the topic be used again to the children's advantage?

SUGGESTED PLAN FOR A FIELD TRIP

Destination

Nearby construction site

Proposed Purposes

1. To increase sand play, cooperation, and language
2. To build concepts of work safety
3. To help Sam clarify some misconceptions about his father's occupation

Preassessment

Several days before excursion, take these steps to see how much present knowledge the children have:

- Encourage the children to look at and identify construction vehicles from replicas or pictures.
- Ask the children what construction they have seen, if they know someone who works on construction, and other pertinent questions.
- Around the room, place pictures of buildings in various stages of construction. Also put samples of building materials on the science table.
- Use sand with miniature construction vehicles, or use the woodworking bench and tools.

Ideas to Emphasize

1. Heavy equipment helps in construction.
   a. Backhoes dig rapidly.
   b. Trucks haul off the dirt.
   c. Bulldozers smooth the dirt.
2. Workers operate the equipment and do other jobs (pour cement, read plans, hammer, make forms, place steel).
3. Different materials are used for making buildings.
4. Workers must obey safety rules.

Planning

- The bulletin board contains pictures of equipment at work.
- The children have been in the center long enough to be ready for a nearby field trip.
- The teacher makes a previsit to the site to determine the best route and also the best place for the children to observe.
- The following times are allotted: 10 min to walk over, 15 min to observe, and 10 min to return. The trip takes place as soon as all the children arrive at school.
- Each adult supervises five children. (Parents are invited, if needed.) The children help decide which adults they accompany.
- Written permission is secured from the parents. Notify parents if any special clothing is needed for children (e.g., walking shoes, warm coat).
- Because the construction is nearby, the children walk; transportation is not involved.
- The school policies have been checked. The trip is approved by an official.

Involvement of the Children

- The children hear the story, *Mike Mulligan and the Steam Shovel,* by Virginia Lee Burton. Discussion follows, and the children are told of the field trip.
- Limits are clearly defined with the children's help.
- At the site, the teachers point out various jobs of the workmen and the different materials used. Discussion follows.
- The teacher points out safety practices of workers (hard hats, appropriate clothing, warning devices on equipment).
- After the field trip, trucks and steam shovels are placed in the sand area for role playing. Teachers listen and observe carefully.
- During evaluation, teachers discuss the strengths and weaknesses of the experience.

SUGGESTED FIELD TRIPS

You do not have to leave your classroom to have a field trip! Consider having self-contained experiences such as (1) a sensory trip (look for things that stimulate each of the senses, preferably one at a time, or have some children look for "smell" things and others look for "feel" things), (2) a shape trip, (3) a color trip, (4) things made of similar materials (wood, for example), or (5) a "living" trip (plants, animals).

Keep in mind that a field trip should be on the **developmental level** of the children involved and should be **fairly close** to the school. Some places may be familiar to some children and unfamiliar to others. For example, Juan's parents operate a restaurant, and he spends a great deal of time there. He may have a special interest in visiting a restaurant or may be totally disinterested.

A previsit by a teacher to a construction site determines the best place for children to observe.

Know your community and special attractions. You might consider some of the following:

airport terminal	aquarium	athletic field or building
apartment house	artist's studio	bakery

bank
beach or seashore
bird-watching
boat ride
body paint shop
bus depot
bus ride
car dealer
car wash
collector (rock, insect, coin)
community specialties (cave, livestock show, cheese factory)
construction site and equipment
dairy
dance studio
dentist's office
department store
dock
doctor's office (also eye doctor)
dog kennel
dormitory
elevator
escalator
factory (food, clothing, furniture, toy, other)
farm
fire station
fish hatchery
fish market
flower garden or show, florist, or greenhouse
foundry
grocery store
hair stylist
harbor
hobby shop
hospital
house
junkyard
laundry
library
livestock show or auction
lumberyard
lunchroom
manufacturer (car, household)
marching band
museum
music department or rehearsal
newspaper
nursing home
orchard
office
park
pet shop
photo studio
planetarium
police station or car
post office
pottery factory
poultry farm
recreation areas (bowling alley, gym, hobby display, skating rink, swimming pool)
repair shop (bike, car, shoes, watch)
restaurant
road construction
road equipment building
school
seed store
service station
sewage disposal plant
stable
streetcar ride or station
subway
television, radio, or recording studio
trailer park
train depot
truck terminal
upholstery shop
water (dam, lock, lake, stream, river)
woods
zoo

CUMULATIVE LESSON PLAN

- Visit a box factory.
- Go to a fruit-packing shed.
- Visit a commercial establishment where they box merchandise.

ESPECIALLY FOR PARENTS

Field trips for parents and children are for two main purposes: (1) to build good relationships with each other, and (2) to increase the child's knowledge as he indicates interest and readiness.
(CAUTION: Avoid too many experiences too fast.)

Preceding and following are listed some possible trips for parents and child. Some of them may be impossible or inappropriate; look for those that are feasible. These are merely suggestions to help you look around your community and discover places of interest for your child now and in future years.

airplane ride
air show
amusement park
animal shelter
animal show
assembly line
athletic event
aviary
beehive
boat races
bottling plant
brick plant

bridge
butcher shop
camping
chandler
candy factory
car manufacturer
carnival or circus
carpenter
carpet weaver
church
clock maker
coal mine
concert
cotton plantation
doll hospital
drive-in (food, theatre, bank)
fair (state, local)
family reunion
festival
fishing
frozen food plant
fruit-packing shed
fur breeder
garbage dump
glass factory
gravel pit
hiking
holiday celebration
hunting
ice cream store
Indian reservation
map maker
meat processing plant
mountains, canyons
musical instrument factory (piano, other)
nut farm
oil drilling
paint factory
painter
paper mill
parade
peanut plantation
perfume factory
piano tuner
picnic
power plant
printer
recycling plant
rock and mineral show
rock hunting
rodeo
shopping center
vacation
veterinarian
visit to relatives
warehouse
weaver

Parents may consider some of the above ideas more in the category of necessities than pleasures. Whenever you can, take your child along with you and explain what is occurring—not in a complicated, lecture fashion, but in understandable, interesting terms the child can handle.

SUMMARY

Field trips can support many areas of learning. The trips can be initiated by either parents or teachers and sometimes by both. Because of time, expense, liability, and availability, however, parents are more likely to take their children to certain places than are teachers.

While a field trip is necessary to learn about certain locations or occupations, never underestimate the value of bringing a guest into the school. The principles for planning are similar for both.

APPLICATION OF PRINCIPLES

1. Make a list of appropriate field trips near your center.
2. With another adult, select and plan a field trip. Fill out the checklist on page 190. If possible, take the trip, being sure to evaluate it properly upon your return.
3. Why is it important to make a previsit before taking a field trip? What are the value of follow-up activities?
4. Devise a method of advising the parents of field trips and getting parental permission.
5. How appropriate are the center's present field trip policies for children, parents, and staff? Make constructive suggestions.
6. Evaluate the legal and moral responsibilities related to taking children on field trips. Have local, state, or federal laws been passed related to field trips (e.g., liability, seat belts) that apply to your center?

9
Special Occasions

I asked my Mother for fifty cents
To see the elephant jump the fence.
He jumped so high that he touched the sky
And never came down until the 4th of July!

MAIN PRINCIPLES

1. Children enjoy celebrations; however, they do not always understand their rationale or significance.
2. Teachers and parents must be selective in introducing young children to different occasions.

The celebration of special occasions or activities should be planned with discretion, depending upon the children, their developmental level, the extent of their involvement, and the philosophy of parents and center.

Holiday celebrations can be of national, cultural, or local interest. Throughout the country, one can find celebrations in common (patriotic holidays and some religious days). Asian children celebrate the Chinese New Year and Children's Day. Children in New Orleans probably know much about and look forward to Mardi Gras. Some families have specific celebrations and ways to conduct them. The teacher should learn about the families of the young children in their classrooms. She could also provide enriching experiences for other children by inviting families to share their beliefs and traditions.

The celebration should be as close to the actual day as possible and reveal as much of the true meaning as the children can comprehend. Teachers and parents who start on the next holiday the day after a current one often diminish the value of each holiday.

Special occasions are a means of informing children about the past and its importance. Because children have so much to learn about their world, celebrations are taken slowly. Oftimes the children enjoy the activities but make no specific connection with a holiday or tradition. In time, there will be better integration.

> Holiday celebrations with young children can be pure fun and relaxation, and, at the same time, they can impart historical knowledge in an accurate and authentic manner. On the other hand, when poorly planned, they can become disasters and serve to perpetuate myths. Urging a realistic approach to the celebration of holidays, Parker and Temple suggest that it would be a mistake to attempt to explain the historical significance of the holiday, because young children could not understand it; rather, they believe that the social significance of

the day can be realized by associating it with the activities and experiences of the children. (Seefeldt 1977)

In other words, the holiday is integrated into the regular routine, the focus is kept simple and low-key, and a few appropriate concepts are selected. Parents can be involved when additional adult help is needed.

Special occasions need not always be grandiose. Attention can be centered on a special child, a visitor, or even on a fire drill. Children need to know how to handle a variety of situations. Experience in the center reduces fear and frustration in future happenings.

Teachers should have the following goals:

1. To teach true concepts about the occasion
2. To support or give firsthand experiences on the developmental level of the children
3. To increase understanding about one's own world
4. To build social relationships with others who have similar or different values
5. To inform about other customs and practices (family, religious, cultural, national, community)

VALUES FOR CHILDREN

Children benefit from such experiences if they are planned for the individual child as well as for the total group. The following criteria are considered:

1. Total developmental level of the children, including interest, attention span, and skills
2. Possibility of increasing existing knowledge or of clarifying concepts
3. Activities that are child-centered but adult-initiated
4. Possibility of increasing independence
5. Use of food, which should be child-prepared, simple, nutritional, and in small quantities
6. Opportunity to increase understanding about and relationships with others

BIRTHDAYS

Ideas to Emphasize

1. Birthdays are fun.
2. A birthday can be shared with others.
3. With each birthday, one becomes a year older.
4. People celebrate birthdays in different ways.

The most special of special occasions is a child's own birthday. It indicates that the child is growing up—something that seems to give him some sort of magical power. He deserves, and should get, some recognition on his day. Next to his own birthday, a child most enjoys sharing the birthday of others.

Some centers formulate a policy with regard to a child's birthday. Some parents like to send a simple treat. Often the occasion seems more special if the children at school prepare something.

When a luncheon or snack is served in the center, the child having the birthday can stand while others sing "Happy Birthday" to him; then he can pass out a treat prepared either at home or school. In this way he is sharing his birthday with others—a concept that should be cultivated.

Teaching Suggestions

- Make and decorate cookies or cupcakes.
- Make gelatin or pudding.

A birthday seems more special if the children at school prepare something for the occasion.

- Pop corn.
- Freeze ice cream.
- Make a nutritious snack of fruit, vegetables, and nuts.
- Display pictures of the child as he has been growing up.
- Make a birthday hat.
- Let the child be a "special helper."
- Make a birthday card or picture for the child.
- Talk about different ways people celebrate their birthdays.

See other suggestions in chapters 3 and 10 and under "Books for Children" in Appendix E.

HALLOWEEN

Ideas to Emphasize

1. Halloween is a time to have fun.
2. Halloween is a make-believe time.
3. Halloween comes in the fall.

This occasion creates fear if witches, goblins, and masks are emphasized. Costumes often frighten young children and add confusion and discomfort by inhibiting the child's activities; masks limit vision and cause accidents. This is an appropriate time to talk about safety (e.g., crossing streets and unobstructed vision).

A 4-year-old boy watched his older brother put on a grotesque mask. The younger boy, even though he had seen his brother put on the mask, became frightened and began to cry. To him, his brother actually became that vicious monster by putting on the mask. To a 4-year-old it's a here-and-now world.

Teaching Suggestions

- Cut a face on a pumpkin and hollow it out. The seeds can be saved for a spring planting experience or toasted for a snack. The children can talk about the slickness of the inside of the pumpkin and how it feels to cut with a knife. The group should be kept small so that each child can participate.
- Make Halloween cookies.
- Serve a pumpkin dessert for snack or lunch.
- Make and serve orange gelatin for snack or lunch.
- Visit a cider mill or make apple cider.
- Provide a collage of materials to make trick-or-treat bags.
- Use orange and black materials for art projects.
- Make paper plate masks attached to a tongue depressor.
- Make puppets for dramatic play.
- Use appropriate Halloween stories, songs, and pictures.
- Encourage the children to draw pictures about Halloween.
- Encourage the children to talk about Halloween.
- Take a field trip to a nearby pumpkin field or a store.

THANKSGIVING

Ideas to Emphasize

1. Thanksgiving is a day to be thankful for many things including families, homes, and food.
2. Families get together at Thanksgiving, usually for a big dinner.
3. Thanksgiving comes when crops have been harvested. (Explain.)
4. Some people do not celebrate Thanksgiving.

A young child's understanding of this holiday is rather limited and sometimes surprising. For this reason, simplicity is best. Ideas about the Pilgrims are too abstract for

At Halloween, a pumpkin dessert is appropriate for snack or lunch.

most preschoolers; they better handle ideas of sharing, planting and harvesting food, conservation of resources, and food preparation.

Teaching Suggestions

- Encourage the children to draw pictures about Thanksgiving.
- In a relaxed atmosphere, ask the children to tell things for which they are thankful.
- Obtain ideas from children's suggestions.
- Plan for individual children. One teacher provided apples and let the children stick colored toothpicks into them to look like tail feathers on turkeys. Many of the children were sticking toothpicks into apples but they had no concept of what the teacher had intended.
- Use appropriate stories, songs, and pictures.
- Encourage the children to talk about Thanksgiving.
- Make and eat a traditional Thanksgiving food.
- Visit a turkey farm, if possible.
- Make art projects using seeds, grasses, twigs, and feathers.
- Cut pictures of food from magazines and paste them on paper plates.

See chapters 3 and 10 for applicable ideas.

HANUKKAH*

Ideas to Emphasize

1. Hanukkah is a festival of lights.
2. Hanukkah celebrations involve some item using oil and some dairy foods. These come from stories related to the holiday.
3. Special foods are eaten on this holiday.
4. Hanukkah comes in winter in the United States.
5. Children in Israel celebrate Hanukkah as a national as well as a religious holiday.

Teaching Suggestions

Ask a family in your center, a staff member, or a representative of a local synagogue to let you borrow a **Chanukiah** (Hanukkah menorah or candalabrum). Show the children that it has nine places that can be lit. Some Chanukiahs use candles of many colors and some use oil. When candles are used, one is lit each day for eight days. The ninth candle, called a **shamash,** is lit first and then used to light the other eight candles.

Two major traditional foods are eaten during the eight days of Hanukkah. Potato **latkes,** or pancakes with applesauce, are fried in oil, which is related to the historical story of Hanukkah. Dairy foods, such as **blintzes** (cheese crepes), cheesecake, or noodles and cheese are eaten in honor of Judith.

Three special customs relating to children are part of this holiday. First, children are given money, called **Hanukkah gelt.** Second, in some families, children up to the age of 12 or 13 (the age of Bar or Bat Mitzvah) are given a small gift each of the eight nights. Third is the custom of playing games of **dreidel.** The dreidel is a small, four-sided top with a Hebrew letter on each side. The letters are: *nun, gimel, he,* and *shin.* They stand for the Hebrew words *neis, gadol, hayah,* and *sham,* which mean, "A great miracle happened there." Dreidels all over the world, except in Israel, say that.

* Information for this section was prepared by Dr. Blythe F. Hinitz of the Child Study Center, Trenton State College, Trenton, NJ 08625.

In Israel, the dreidels read *nun, gimmel, he,* and *pe,* which stand for neis, gadol, hayah, po, "A great miracle happened here."

CHRISTMAS

Ideas to Emphasize

1. Christmas is a time for fun.
2. Love for others is expressed through giving.
3. Christmas comes in the winter.
4. Special things are made at Christmas time (e.g., gifts, cookies, tree decorations, and cards).
5. Christmas is Jesus' birthday (may or may not be appropriate).
6. Some people do not celebrate Christmas but have other celebrations around this time of year, such as Hanukkah and the Chinese New Year (Flemming 1977).

Because of the commercialism at Christmas, children get many confusing ideas. Parents should be free to convey their personal ideas to their children—religious or commercial. A safe policy for the center staff is to take a "middle of the road" approach, neither encouraging nor discouraging Jesus Christ or Santa Claus.

Some centers dismiss for the Christmas holidays in advance of the special day. For this reason, it is wise to refrain from overstimulating the children. Suggested guidelines would be to devote no more than two or three days and as close to Christmas as possible.

The ideas of giving and sharing can include animals as well as people: a feeder for birds, nuts for squirrels, a new collar for a dog, or a pet for the school.

Teaching Suggestions

- Learn some Christmas songs; go caroling nearby; play Christmas music.
- Make and decorate Christmas cookies or cupcakes.
- Make ornaments for a tree:
  - Cut egg cartons into individual sections; paint with easel paint and hang by pipe cleaners.
  - Cut colored construction paper into strips; make chains.
  - Decorate small metal pie containers; hang with yarn.
  - Decorate jar lids with pictures from wrapping paper or old Christmas cards. Punch hole in one end; hang with pipe cleaner.
  - Make aluminum foil decorations.
  - Use cornstarch dough (see Appendix D) and Christmas cookie cutters.
  - Paint pine cones and apply glitter.
- Make mobiles using wire, paper, spools, fabrics, yarn, and so on.
- Draw pictures about Christmas.
- Use red and green colors in art projects, food, and so on.
- Paste with cotton (resembling snow).
- Make Christmas cards or wrapping paper from old Christmas cards, magazines, wrapping paper, glitter, and paint.
- Use appropriate stories, finger plays, and songs.
- If children make gifts for home, keep them simple and child-oriented. Objects made of clay or plaster of paris may be easier for their small hands.
- Decorate a 9-in. nonwaxed paper plate with small macaroni products (noodles, macaroni, shellroni). Teacher can spray with gold paint. Place a snapshot or silhouette of the child in the center and make a hanger out of yarn.

- Make simple gifts for center staff members (janitor, cook),
- Talk about and make things appropriate for non-Christian believers.
- Invite a guest in to show how Christmas is celebrated in different families or cultures.
- Provide a variety of different bells (e.g., sleigh, dinner, cow, ship's). Sing with and listen to the bells and then discuss differences.
- Increase language by using terms usually associated with this holiday.

See other suggestions in chapters 3 and 10.

VALENTINE'S DAY

Ideas to Emphasize

1. Valentine's Day is a time for fun.
2. Love is shown by giving valentines.
3. Valentine colors are red and white.

Young children can relate to Valentine's Day because the idea of love and friendship is familiar and important to them.

Teaching Suggestions

- Draw pictures about Valentine's Day.
- Use red and white colors in art projects.
- Provide varied heart-shaped stencils for tracing and cutting.
- Make valentines from lace, paper doilies, construction paper, pictures, ribbon, and fabrics.
- Make heart-shaped cookies.
- Make red gelatin; cut in heart shape.
- Use appropriate stories, songs, and pictures.
- Talk about this holiday.
- Mail valentines.
- Talk about the postal system; make a trip to the post office.

NOTE: Discourage parents from sending valentines from home. They get lost or mixed up; some children bring them and some do not. Instead, plan to make valentines or play a postman game where each child receives a valentine.

EASTER

Ideas to Emphasize

1. Easter comes in the spring.
2. New growth begins in the spring.
3. Easter is a time for fun.
4. Some people do not celebrate Easter.

Because of the religious significance of this holiday, this is another time when parents prefer to inform their children.

This occasion is obscure to young children, because their ability to think in abstract or complex terms is just beginning. Renewal of life is shown by planting and observing the changes in the outdoor environment and life around them.

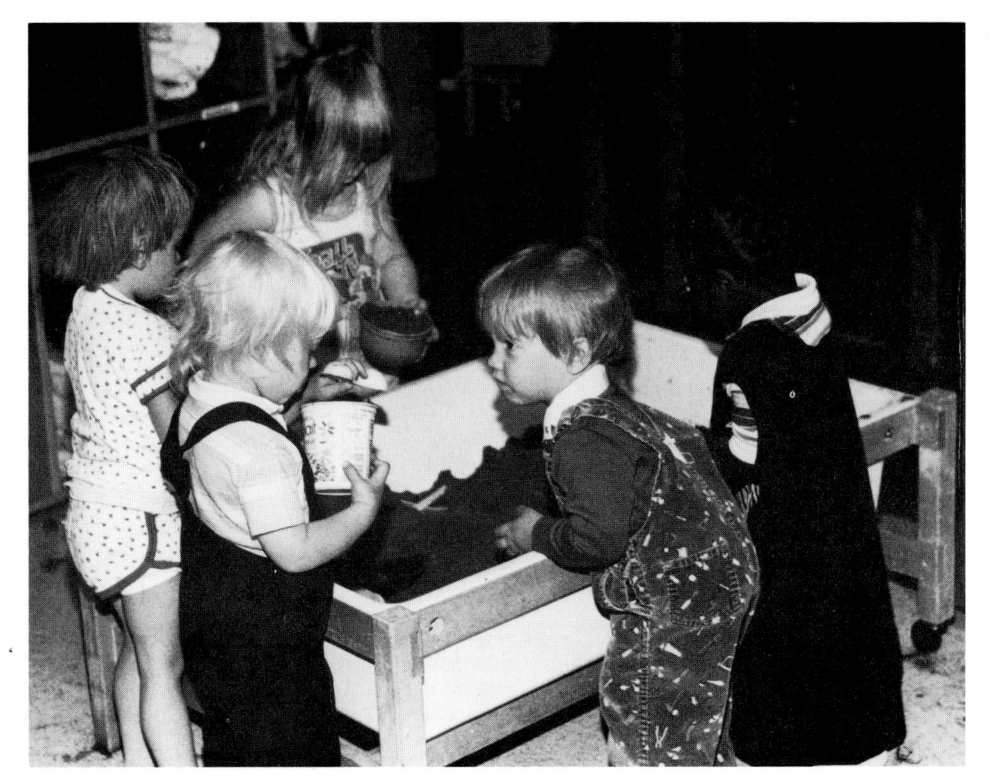

Seeds or bulbs can be planted around Eastertime.

Teaching Suggestions

- Talk about the changes in nature that occur in the spring.
- Explore the new growth in the play yard. Take a walk.
- Plant bulbs and seeds indoors or outdoors.
- Acquire an incubator and hatch chicken or duck eggs.
- Add a new pet to the center family.
- Color eggs.
- Make Easter baskets from egg cartons, cottage cheese cartons, or small boxes. Paint them (if nonwaxed), fill them with artificial grass, and make handles from ribbons or pipe cleaners.
- Use appropriate stories, poems, and finger plays.
- Sing spring songs (e.g., "Popcorn Popping on the Apricot Tree").
- Discuss the fact that only some people celebrate Easter.
- Modify some art (Chapter 3) or food activities (Chapter 10).

FOURTH OF JULY

Ideas to Emphasize

1. The Fourth of July is the birthday of our country.
2. Our country's name is the United States of America.
3. The flag is the symbol of our country.
4. The colors of our flag are red, white, and blue.
5. The Fourth of July comes in summertime and is a time for fun.

Easter baskets can be made of egg cartons and pipe cleaners.

Teaching Suggestions

- Ask the children how they will celebrate the Fourth.
- Talk about the name of our country.
- Show a globe or map. Indicate our country and your state.
- Take the children to see a flag and tell them about it briefly.
- Show the children how to respect the flag.
- Have a parade. Use flags, musical instruments, and marching music (piano, record, tape).
- Tell the children how they can respect and protect our country (patriotism, conserving resources).
- Have a pasting experience using red, white, and blue.
- Make three-cornered hats out of newspaper or newsprint.
- Let the children decorate wagons, tricycles, and boxes for a parade.
- Use appropriate stories, finger plays, songs, and poems.

EXERCISE FOR TEACHERS

Write or plan for some special occasions appropriate for your children and locality. In some sections of our country, a religion, culture, or foreign population predominates. Help all of the children in your center to understand and appreciate the ways and values of others. If you lack the knowledge or aids to properly teach these concepts, invite a parent or guest in to assist you.

Hendrick (1980) states: "We must realize that the basic purpose of providing multicultural experiences is *not* to teach the children facts about Puerto Rico or Japan, or to prove to the community that the teacher is not prejudiced. *The purpose of multicultural curriculum is to attach positive feelings to multicultural experiences so that each child will feel included and valued, and will also feel friendly and respectful toward people from other ethnic and cultural groups.*"

Many holidays are inappropriate to use as special occasions with young children. Be selective so the children gain from each experience provided and not be bombarded with every holiday that comes along. Some holidays are left until the children are older and better able to understand and appreciate their significance. Methods of teaching must also be selective to avoid confusion and incorrect concepts.

CUMULATIVE LESSON PLAN

- Decorate a box for a special event.
- Make a box.

ESPECIALLY FOR PARENTS

Celebrating special occasions gives parents an opportunity to take the lead in teaching the values they want their children to have. A teacher may be limited in the information she imparts or the activities she plans because of national or local restrictions. However, information in this chapter is easily applied in either a home or school setting.

Parents reminisce about religious and other special occasions and have certain customs or ideas they want to pass on to their children. Because schools are not in session during most holidays, the actual celebration may be with parents or the family, but preparation for a holiday may or may not begin at school. Sometimes events are planned so far in advance that all the excitement is gone by the time they arrive. It is difficult for young children to wait, even for a short period of time.

Because special occasions are such personal matters, only a few suggestions will be given for each. Custom or tradition will be determining factors in each household.

Birthday

- Let your child help make a traditional birthday food.
- Give him several possible activities and let him decide how to celebrate.
- Keep formal parties simple in number of children, activities, and food.
- Encourage your child to share the day with others.
- Help the child pick out several acceptable toys or articles of clothing at a store; let him select one for his present.
- Give him special privileges (within reason).
- Do something special with your child alone.
- Start a birthday tradition (musical cake plate, activity).
- Help him record events of the day in a book or journal.
- Take pictures.

Halloween

- Make decorations.
- Go to a field or store and get a pumpkin.
- Carve a pumpkin.
- Prepare a meal using fall foods.
- Start a family tradition.

Thanksgiving

- Make it a family time.
- Begin a family tradition.

- Observe crops being harvested.
- Visit a turkey farm.
- Make decorations.
- Prepare food.
- Prepare to be a guest or have guests.
- Discuss things for which you are thankful.
- Show appreciation through attitude and action.
- Share something with others.

Hanukkah

Plan this to meet your own particular needs. Seek information or individuals in your community who can help you and the child understand the values and traditions of others. See discussion earlier in this chapter.

Christmas

The following suggestions should be modified to fit your circumstances.

- Make gifts.
- Show love by doing good deeds for others.
- Go Christmas shopping.
- Make food for holidays.
- Decorate tree and house.
- Make decorative wrapping paper and wrap presents.
- Begin a family tradition.
- Share something with others.
- Teach own values, whether religious, cultural, or commercial.
- Visit someone who celebrates Christmas differently than you do.
- Visit someone who is ill or lonely.

Valentine's Day

- Make and deliver valentines.
- Make a treat for the family.
- Express love verbally.
- Do good deeds for others.
- Make decorations.
- Begin a family tradition.

Easter

Again, the suggestions here can be modified fo fit your own circumstances.

- Select and purchase new clothes.
- Observe new life in plants and animals.
- Get a new pet.
- Plant bulbs.
- Plant a garden.
- Hatch eggs.
- Color eggs.
- Go on an egg hunt.
- Go on a hike or walk.
- Make decorations.
- Begin a family tradition.
- Teach your own values (religious, cultural, or commercial).

Fourth of July

- Attend special community activities such as a parade or program.
- Display the flag with respect. Discuss patriotism.
- Briefly explain why we celebrate the Fourth of July.
- Make decorations.
- Begin a family tradition.

Other Special Occasions

Parents are encouraged to promote special family, religious, national, or local holidays whether they have been passed from generation to generation or have originated within the nuclear family. Each child should know and be proud of his heritage.

For some appropriate books for children that are related to special occasions, see Appendix E.

APPLICATION OF PRINCIPLES

1. List some holidays celebrated in your community. Which ones can be adapted for young children? How would you do it? Which ones are too adult-centered?
2. Are there some ethnic, religious, or cultural occasions that would be of value or interest to the children in your center? If so, select one and make plans to implement it. List some people and activities that could help the children gain a better understanding of the occasion.
3. Explain how special occasions can be overemphasized.
4. How would you handle a situation when parents object to the celebration of a particular holiday at school (e.g., Christmas, Easter, Hanukkah, Halloween, Chinese New Year)?

References

Flemming, B., D. S. Hamilton, and J. D. Hicks. *Resources for Creative Teaching in Early Childhood Education.* New York: Harcourt Brace Jovanovich, 1977.

Hendrick, Joanne. *The Whole Child: New Trends in Early Education.* St. Louis: C. V. Mosby, 1980.

Seefeldt, Carol. *Social Studies for the Preschool-Primary Child.* Columbus, Ohio: Charles E. Merrill, 1977, pp. 115–124.

10
Food: Nutrition, Preparation, and Enjoyment

Little Miss Muffett sat on her tuffett
Eating her curds and whey.
Along came a spider and sat down beside her
And frightened Miss Muffett away!

MAIN PRINCIPLES

1. Well-nourished children feel, act, and learn better than undernourished children.
2. Through food experiences, young children learn about their world, their environment, and themselves.
3. Young children enjoy participating in food experiences.
4. The adult is responsible for teaching children about proper nutrition and food preparation.

Some children do not have opportunities to participate in food preparation because some adults feel time pressure, do not understand the abilities of children, or are unwilling to involve them. Nevertheless, this area offers additional experiences in becoming independent, in learning about nutrition, in feeling accomplishment and satisfaction, and in contributing a service.

This chapter is intended to: (1) give an overview of nutrition and its importance to young children, (2) discuss the involvement of children in food preparation, and (3) give suggestions as to how to make eating more enjoyable for children. Further reading is encouraged in the area of nutrition, especially as it applies to the growth and development of the young child. At the end of this chapter and in Appendix E are many references, or the local library or state department of welfare or social services can be contacted.

NUTRITION

When malnourished children are mentioned, one commonly pictures children from low income homes. Some of these children do come from such homes; some parents with limited food budgets lack good spending knowledge. But, some children of the affluent are also malnourished; some of these parents also lack knowledge as to effective use of their money—they spend freely on junk foods, do not consider nutritional value, or fail to plan well-balanced meals. Powers and Presley (1978) report: "The volume of research over the past several decades should be sufficient to establish the importance of diet. To quote Drs. Emanuel Cheraskin and W. Marshall Ringsdorf, Jr., 'The evidence suggests that *malnutrition* because of poor food choices is very likely a bigger problem than undernutrition.' "

Basic nutrients to be included in the daily diet are carbohydrates, fats, protein, minerals, vitamins, and water. Amounts vary according to a person's age. Most nutrition books give proper amounts, as well as height and weight charts based on body structure. Following are the nutrients and good sources:

Calcium — cheese, collards, cream soups, greens, kale, milk, mustard greens, yogurt

Carbohydrate — bread, cereal, corn, dried beans, fruit, milk, potatoes, sugar, vegetables

Fat — butter, cheese, margarine, oils, salad dressing and oil, whole milk

Iron — clams, dried beans, dried fruit, dried peas, heart, liver, meat, nuts, oysters, prune juice, raisins, red meat, spinach

Niacin — bread (whole grain and enriched), cereals (fortified), fish, legumes, liver, meat, nuts, peanut butter, poultry, wheat germ

Protein — beef, cheese, dried beans and peas, eggs, fish, lamb, milk, nuts, oats (rolled), pork, poultry, rice (unpolished), soybeans, veal, wheat germ

Riboflavin (vitamin B_2) — cottage cheese, eggs, fish, green leafy vegetables, liver, meat, milk, wheat germ, yogurt

Thiamine (vitamin B_1) — asparagus, bread (whole grain and enriched), cereals (fortified), eggs, fresh greens, lean pork, legumes, liver, milk, nuts, potatoes, wheat germ

Vitamin A — cabbage, cantaloupe, carrots, eggs, greens, liver, papaya, spinach, sweet potatoes

Vitamin C — broccoli, cabbage, grapefruit, green pepper, mango, oranges, spinach, strawberries, tomatoes

Water — "Many people do not even think of water as a nutrient, and yet death will occur in a matter of only a few days if water is not available. The importance of water is suggested by the fact that the normal body is 55 to 65% water by weight" (McWilliams 1975).

A more familiar way of identifying daily food requirements is the Basic Four Food Plan:

1. **Milk and dairy products.** Can be used for drinking, eating, and cooking. Recommended amount depends on individual's age.
2. **Meat and meat products.** Include animal protein foods (fish, meat, and poultry) and eggs, nuts, and dried beans as alternatives. Recommended amount is two or more servings per day.
3. **Fruits and vegetables.** Recommended amount is four or more servings per day—one citrus; one dark green, leafy, or yellow vegetable; and two others.

4. **Bread and cereals.** Include whole grain or enriched breads and cereal products, crackers, rice, and pasta. Recommended amount is four or more servings per day.

Some children have a group experience for four or less hours per day during which they likely have a snack. Children in all-day care should have two snacks and a meal, appropriately spaced. In the latter case, the center would undoubtedly come under local, state, or federal regulations. Caution must be exercised to see that the children receive at least part of their daily nutritional requirements.

Too often when children are involved in the preparation and serving of food, the content of the food is high in carbohydrates (sugar and starch). Children can help in many areas of food preparation, not just in the dessert. As they become more involved, they learn about the importance of including nutritious foods in their diets and reducing or eliminating junk foods.

By the time a child enters a group experience, he has had many prior experiences with food. In regard to nutrition, Powers and Presley state: "The most important time of life for the child, nutritionally, is before birth . . . during his prenatal life. . . . The next most important time of the baby's life, nutritionally speaking, is immediately following birth. The first 'growth spurt' comes during early infancy, until around the child's first birthday." During this period, adults (generally parents) have decided what, how much, and when the child will eat. They are disturbed when his appetite diminishes or he eats erratically. "Following this period of explosive growth in the first year of life, he reaches a 'plateau' stage [from ages 1 to around 5] and growth is more gradual and almost unnoticed. *What* he eats is far more important than *how much* he eats. This especially applies to milk during preschool years" (Powers and Presley 1978). Even though they seem to be burning up considerable energy in their daily routines, children do not require large quantities of food until they begin another growth spurt.

Children can receive part of their daily nutritional requirement at the care center.

Some signs of dietary deficiencies include irritability, poor sleep habits, fatigue, lack of concentration, loss of interest, frequent illnesses with prolonged recovery, and craving of sweets.

Influences on Children

Young children lack in literacy, worldliness, and experience. As a result, their eating habits and preferences are influenced by those around them (mainly through parental purchases and attitudes toward foods) and other stimulation (television). For years, debates have concerned the use of young children as agents in selling food products—children want what they see, and they believe what they hear.

Adults must be careful to purchase nourishing foods, because children pick up food purchasing and eating habits from adults. To tell a child to eat or not eat a certain food while the adult does the opposite is poor and ineffectual teaching.

An estimate of the number of hours children watch television per week has been set at 26.3 for those of preschool age and 25 for those between 6 and 16 years of age. "Kindergarten children often are unable to separate commercials from the program and frequently explain them as part of the program. Younger school-age children (5 to 10 years) attend more closely to commercials than do older children (11 to 12 years)" (Pipes 1977).

A child should learn to include nutritious foods in his diet.

Many groups have tried to curtail the number and intensity of food commercials aimed at young children.

> Joan Gussow, a nutrition writer who testified before a Senate sub-committee in 1972, spelled out some of the objectional aspects of television promotion of food products to children. She and others monitored 388 network commercials during a week of viewing children's TV programs and learned that 82 percent of the commercials involved food, drink, and vitamin pill ads directed at children. . . . They urge children to eat the worst type of food and swallow the worst type of drinks. Children are being lured into wanting the worst cereals that man has designed. Anything that is "fun, sweet, sparkly, gay, colorful, thick, and chocolately, magicky, or crunchily delicious" will eventually parade before the youngsters' eyes on the living room screen. Even vitamins become a vehicle for implanting the belief that if a child doesn't eat right it won't much matter—if he takes his vitamins. The major thrust, with the unstated thesis that only sweetened products are good, leaves a total impact. . . . This sweet pitch "sets up a conflict between the parent and child and, in fact, between the child and any number of authority figures—doctors, dentists, and teachers as well as parents. . . . They conclude on a warning note that unless the trend is changed, "we can expect a continued growth of heart disease, hypertension, and poor dental health—the diseases that result from poor eating habits established in childhood which cripple and kill in adulthood." (Powers and Presley 1978)

Harmful Ingredients

Sugar

Fortified cereals are frequently listed as important elements in the daily diet. On many cereal packages, however, sugar is listed as the first ingredient, indicating that the product contains more sugar than any other ingredient.

Sugar can be harmful in a child's diet, causing cavities, dulling the appetite for good food, and giving a false sense of "being full." It is suspect in behavioral problems and causes the body to react in unnatural ways. "Refined sugar and refined starches are mood-changing foods to which many growing children are especially sensitive. Usually the impact can be ascertained by comparing the child's diet with his behavior" (Powers and Presley 1978).

Two substances have been identified as possible causes of inappropriate behavior: sugar and caffeine.

> Hyperkinesis manifests itself in various ways. The child may be extremely restless, impulsive and even destructive at times. He may resent all attempts at restriction or restraint and all corrective measures. He is often emotionally disturbed, shows a lack of tolerance to stress and anxiety and is easily excited. He may have a short attention span, at first evidencing an interest, then without warning, flying off on a tangent. He may be quarrelsome, and a small child may have difficulty in muscular coordination. He may rock, knock his head against the floor or wall, and in other ways exhibit unpredictable behavior. As he becomes older, he will almost surely have difficulty with schooling. He is not only a problem to himself but to all those around him. (Thurston 1979)

A hyperactive child is undoubtedly under a great deal of stress. In working with such children, pediatricians report that improved nutrition (mainly the elimination of sugar and caffeine) can help change behavior. (It is thought that these two substances keep the child "hyped up" and then let him down.) Especially near holidays teachers see children becoming irritable, aggressive, listless, or defiant, possibly due to increased intake of sugar.

Growth of the human brain is essentially complete by the child's second birthday; however, its development is closely related to nutrition. The brain uses carbohydrates, in the form of glucose, more than any other tissue or organ, requiring "stable blood sugar to ensure a reliable, smooth supply of energy. If there is not enough, the mind falters. If there is a sudden rush of glucose, as might happen with a caffeinated or sweetened drink is ingested, the brain becomes overcharged. Either way, there is stress on the brain which affects the rest of the body. This is why a major emphasis should be placed upon carbohydrate control and the stabilization of blood sugar in a child. Sugar abuses directly affect the operation of the child's brain, which in turn influences how well he is to learn and how he will behave. These are the readily seen results, but deterioration of the child's general health is a slower, less dramatic process that often goes unrecognized" (Powers and Presley 1978).

Besides affecting the brain, sugar causes the phagocytes to function improperly. "The phagocytes (specialized leukocytes or 'white cells') in the blood perform two essential functions: they ingest bacteria and, as scavengers, ingest dead tissue and degenerated cells. In other words, healthy phagocytes are not only useful, they are crucial to our resistance to disease" (Powers and Presley 1978).

Because the sugars in fruit juices are similar to those in purer form, gram for gram, "if juices are used they should be accompanied by solid, preferably protein food and should be assessed carefully for their effects upon the child" (Powers and Presley 1978.)

Rather than use refined sugar or artificial sweeteners, brown sugar, honey, or molasses is recommended in some texts (i.e., Endres and Rockwell 1980), while others urge use of little or no sugars in the diets of young children.

Caffeine

As mentioned earlier, caffeine is also suspected of causing or increasing hyperactivity. Caffeinated drinks are readily available, well advertised, and addictive. If adults realized the harmfulness of these drinks, they would restrict children and themselves from drinking them. In the preceding section, phagocytes were mentioned. Powers and Presley (1978) continue:

> Added to the sugar effects upon the phagocytic index is the fact that many sugared drinks, especially all colas such as Coca-Cola and Pepsi, also contain caffein. Beverages that are not always recognized as containing caffein include Dr. Pepper, Tab, and all diet colas. The caffein raises, then lowers, a child's blood sugar in much the same way as sugar. The mechanism involves drawing stored sugar from the liver, which accounts for the pickup, then the let-down, as the sugar is dispersed through many very complex metabolic pathways in the body. Many parents do not realize that there is the caffein equivalent of a half-cup of coffee (40–54 milligrams) in every diet cola, whether it be Diet Dr. Pepper, Diet Pepsi, or Tab.

Powers and Presley describe the following effects of ingesting caffeine:

> Auditory perception and hand-eye coordination are significantly impaired. These conditions are accompanied by mental confusion and poor concentration and only add to those problems the hyperactive-learning disabled child is already struggling with. . . . Not only does caffein tamper with the steady flow of blood sugar to the brain, but the side effects of that result may be expressed in a number of unexpected ways—nervousness, fatigue, and anxiety may increase.

Teachers who have children who habitually exhibit these symptoms should check with the parents to see how much sugar and caffeine the children are consuming.

Chocolate

Chocolate should be considered with caffeine but because of its popularity is singled out for emphasis. Thurston (1978) warns: "The use of chocolate should be avoided at all costs. Chocolate interferes with calcium metabolism and also places a great burden on the liver. . . . Cocoa and chocolate drinks are unacceptable, as the cacao bean, from which they are made, contains a chemical (an alkaloid) very similar to the one in coffee and just as stimulating. Most authorities on the subject claim that cocoa and chocolate can adversely affect the liver. . . ." Pure chocolate contains 20 mg of caffeine per ounce. (Carob, a substitute available in health food stores, is very similar to chocolate but is devoid of theobromine and other objectionable features of the cacao bean.)

Additives

Among those doing research on the influence of additives on young children is Dr. Ben F. Feingold, chief emeritus of the department of allergy at Kaiser-Permanente Medical Center, San Francisco. He has found that some hyperactive children are especially sensitive to artificial food flavorings and colorings. (A friend's preschooler stayed with us for a few days while the parents went on a short trip. As a special treat, we made our favorite almond cookies. The child was allergic to the flavoring, became ill, and didn't much care for his visit!) Red food coloring has especially been suspect of increasing hyperactivity and causing learning problems in some children. Upon removal of foods containing these additives, behavior changes have been seen, some within two or three weeks—even in children who have been on drugs for many years. Thurston (1979) wonders "if the improvement noted in these children was due not only to the elimination of the chemicals, but also to the elimination of the basic ingredients (white flour or sugar, or both) of the foods containing the colors and flavors."

Salt has been linked with hypertension. Some researchers have successfully reduced blood pressure in hypertensive patients by using a low-sodium rice diet. Others feel that reduced sodium intakes may or may not be beneficial to children, but suggest the salt shaker not be placed on the table (Endres and Rockwell 1980). Children generally do not like their food seasoned as much as adults do. However, when salt is used, iodized salt is highly recommended.

Lead pollution is also believed to cause hyperactivity, a symptom seen in persons with acute lead poisoning. Other environmental factors, such as noise (both audible and inaudible), fumes (including odorless), and light (natural and artificial) have been shown to cause hyperactivity in some children and adults (Thurston 1979).

Summary

Parents and teachers can get young children off to a good nutritional start: no commercial baby foods, sweets, or juices in infancy. Reward the preschooler with good food, not "goodies" and soft drinks; limit treats to "high holidays" only; never permit caffeine in any form (tea, coffee, colas, some root beer, or chocolate); and eliminate refined sugar as completely as possible (Powers and Presley 1978).

If allergies are not listed on the intake form, the teacher should ask the parent if a child has allergies, and if so, what they are, how the child reacts, and how the situation should be handled if the child has an allergic reaction at the center.

PREPARATION

Through participation in the preparation of food, young children learn much about their world, their environment, and themselves. They have **psychomotor** experiences (coordinating eyes and hands and in spatial relationships), **cognitive** experiences (planning, sequencing, discriminating, deciding), and **affective** experiences (working and sharing with others, being persistent, feeling satisfaction). They develop and increase **language** skills through asking, answering, and listening. Academic opportunities lie in **reading** (interpreting the symbols of measurement and ingredients), in **science** (seeing how ingredients react to heat, moisture, and so on), in **math** (combining the right amounts of ingredients), in **motor skills** (stirring, beating, rolling, chopping), and in **social skills** (taking turns, verbalizing, eating, and sharing cultural experiences).

Food is not a separate or infrequently used topic and is included in all areas of the curriculum. Food of some type is prepared every day in the center and is a vital part of the children's activities. At snack time, food is used for nourishment as well as a socializer. The children have an opportunity to prepare and serve food and learn proper etiquette. Food is used as a science experience, in growing, harvesting, preparing, or eating. It is used in an art activity. It is used successfully and interestingly in math. It is used in a social study theme or a movement activity. It is frequently used as the topic of music, stories, or spontaneous conversation. Thinking and speaking are a part of each of the above activities, thereby stimulating verbal expression.

The greatest benefit from experience with food appears to be the change in the attitudes of children toward themselves. After preparing, cooking, and eating applesauce at nursery school one day, Pia asked her mother if she would buy a bushel of apples so that Pia could make more applesauce that afternoon. After another cooking experience, Joseph informed his mother, "I am going to make spaghetti for Dad for dinner tonight because I learned how to do it at school today." Still another child, Val, pleaded, "If you'd just let us make doughnuts at school, I'd show you how."

As with any activity, certain precautions are taken. When children use sharp knives, for example, the teacher must instruct and supervise. When they use cords, utensils, and other apparatuses, the teacher indicates precautions or limits to encourage safety.

Some children have frequent opportunities at home to help with food preparation and cooking and find different ways of doing things. For example, some mothers mix bread with their hands, others with an electric mixer, and others with a hand-turned mixer. Some children aid in the process of bread baking from grinding the wheat through tasting the warm, fragrant product. But even these experiences take on new dimensions when done with a group of peers.

In food preparation, new terms and definitions are added to the vocabulary of the children and opportunities provided for practicing them. Consider some of these terms—**measure, ingredients, recipe, beat, stir, fold**—or these processes—**dipping, scrubbing, shaking, spreading, rolling, peeling, cracking, juicing, cutting, grinding, blending, grating,** and **scraping.**

Different products have different characteristics: some are soft, others hard; some smooth, others textured; some crunchy, others "quiet." In bread, gluten is desired, so it is mixed a long time; in muffins, gluten is not desired, so the dry ingredients are stirred in quickly.

To aid children in independence and learning, a picture recipe can be prepared (Figure 10.1) and the children assisted in following it. If the cups, spoons, and so on are depicted actual size, the children hold them up to the recipe to "measure" whether they have the right cup or spoon. Pictures from labels of the ingredients (when available) also aid the children in getting the correct amount of the right ingredient. Making and eating the product takes on significance because of personal involvement.

All children are allowed to participate, even though several may have to be involved at a time or the process repeated several times. The group is divided into two parts with the lead teacher working with one half and the support teacher working with the other half, or a parent can be invited in to assist. Each child should have as many opportunities as possible.

At the time of actual preparation, health and safety are emphasized by (1) making sure each child washes and dries his hands thoroughly and puts on a cover-up and (2) washing all surfaces and utensils that will be used. Then:

1. Show the recipe, utensils, and ingredients.
2. Explain why the recipe is read in its entirety before beginning to measure.
3. Talk with the children about what they can do and the sequence that will be used.
4. Be perceptive to the questions and feelings of each child. Be an observer and facilitator as much as possible. Be sure to mention when the food is to be eaten! They'll want to know!
5. Upon completion, involve the children in cleaning up the table and area as a normal part of the experience.

While assisting the children in food preparation, the teacher makes the experience calm and comfortable. She avoids hovering over the children and giving them too many

Mix cheese and garlic. Then add it to softened butter. Sift baking powder, salt, and flour together. Add to cheese mix. Make balls and mash with fork. Bake at 350° for 20 minutes.

Picture recipe for children to follow in preparing cookies.

strict instructions. A relaxed atmosphere, with the teacher entering into the action and verbalization when necessary, provides an enjoyable interaction. Encourage the children to use their senses, when appropriate: "Smell that aroma." "You can taste ______." "Did you see how he cracked the egg?"

Some special preparations are needed, depending upon the type of food experience (washing fruit or vegetables, supervising dangerous tools such as knives and graters, getting proper equipment and ingredients). The recipe should have been tried beforehand,

Before taking part in food preparation, each child washes his hands thoroughly.

With proper supervision, children can try out equipment needed for food preparation.

all tools should work properly, and all necessary equipment and ingredients should be available. A negative experience is avoided by being well prepared in advance.

The teacher can be adventurous but secure in what is planned. When proper supervision is available, some different kinds of equipment and methods of preparation can be tried; children need and want some safe opportunities to try knives, for example. They should be helped to cut, spread, and slice. Grinders, choppers, peelers, graters, blenders, and other available appliances can be used, but with constant promotion of safety and proper use of tools.

CHECKLIST FOR A FOOD EXPERIENCE

Food experience (name) ______________________________

Date to be used ______________________________

Approval (if necessary) ______________________________

Materials needed (list each ingredient) ______________________________

____

____

Equipment needed and preparation ______________________________

____

____

Responsibility of adults ______________________________

____

Participation of children ______________________________

____

Any possible problems ______________________________

____

Disposition of food product ______________________________

____

Evaluation of experience ______________________________

____

____

Discussion of Checklist

1. Decide on the specific experience.
2. Record the date. Avoid conflicts with holidays, other curriculum plans, or other teachers.
3. If necessary, discuss the experience with the appropriate person and get approval.
4. List all materials needed. Check to see that all supplies are fresh and available. Order necessary supplies, bring them from home, or have children bring them, if necessary.
5. List all equipment needed, including the equipment inside the classroom, such as tables, chairs, and cover-ups. Kitchen equipment might include bowls, appliances, pans, tools, hot pads, and cleaning supplies. Check all equipment for usability and safety.
6. Double check both the list of materials and equipment needed. Failure of the experience could be attributed to poor planning.
7. Write down how you expect the adult to contribute to the experience (crack the eggs, encourage children to participate, get cover-ups, actually cook food). Discuss this with the adult.
8. List the specific participation of the child (cracking eggs, putting on cover-up, measuring ingredients, cooking food).
9. Anticipate problems. Discuss possibilities with both adults and children so problems can be reduced or eliminated. Unexpected problems may still arise.
10. Check children's health records to be sure no one is allergic to the ingredients or end product.
11. Inform the children when the product will be eaten. Is it for snack time today or a picnic tomorrow? Can they take it home? Is it all right for them to taste during the experience? Eating the product is the highlight of the experience!
12. Be sure to evaluate the total experience, and record your thoughts and feelings. Then you will have a foundation for planning similar experiences. Do not be discouraged if the experience had some drawbacks or did not go the way you planned.

Snack Suggestions From Basic Four Food Groups

Milk and Dairy Products
butter for crackers and bread
cheese chunks
cottage cheese
kabobs (cheese and lunch meat)
milk (whole, powdered, canned)
puddings
yogurt

Meat and Meat Products
beef jerky
creamed meat sauces (chicken, tuna)
eggs
fish sticks
lunch meat
meatballs
meat loaf
meat sandwich fillings
nuts and nut butters
poultry
wieners (sparingly)

Fruits and Vegetables
applesauce
dried fruit (or fruit leather)
fresh fruit (apples, apricots, bananas, cherries, coconut, dates, grapes, melons, peaches, pears, pineapple, plums, strawberries, and the important citrus, including grapefruit, lemons, oranges, and tangerines)
fruit or vegetable salad
juice (fruit or vegetable, low in sugar content)
kabobs
popcorn
Popsicles made from fruit (low in sugar content)
potatoes (raw, frozen, baked)
raisins
soup or stew with vegetables
sprouts

tomatoes (cooked or fresh)
vegetables (cooked or fresh, including asparagus, beans, beets, broccoli, cabbage, cauliflower, celery, corn, cucumber, lettuce, okra, onions, peas, peppers, radishes, spinach, squash, turnip and greens, and zucchini)

Breads and Cereals

bread (preferably whole wheat or Boston brown; bran muffins; enriched white; occasionally biscuits, bread sticks, melba toast, fruit, nut)
cereal (enriched, cooked or prepared)
Chinese noodles
cookies (low in sugar and fat)
crackers (preferably whole wheat or grain)
granola
macaroni, noodles, spaghetti, other pasta
pancakes (occasionally)
rice (unpolished)
sandwiches (made with enriched bread)
waffles (occasionally)

Combinations

apple wedges spread with cream cheese, peanut butter, or other spreads
bacon and eggs
baked potato with melted or cream cheese
cabbage with corned beef and steamed rice
carrot, raisin, apple, and pineapple salad
celery stuffed with cottage cheese, peanut butter, cream cheese, fruit, raisins
cheese and fruit cube kabobs
cheese melted on wheat crackers or on wheat or enriched bread
chicken with dumplings, noodles, or vegetables
cottage cheese with fruit or vegetables
creamed meat sauce on enriched bread
creamed peas and new potatoes
creamed tuna over rice or enriched toast
custard, with or without fruit
dairy dip (cottage cheese, sour cream, seasoning)
eggnog (made with milk, eggs, honey, and flavoring)
macaroni and cheese
meat and vegetable soup or stew
meatballs and spaghetti
milk shake (made with fruit or peanut butter and fruit)
peanut butter on crackers
pocket sandwiches
raw vegetables and cottage cheese dip
rice pudding (with or without raisins)
salad nest (mayonnaise and Chinese noddles, peas for eggs)
salads
spaghetti with meat sauce
sweet potatoes baked with apple slices
tapioca pudding
trail mix (nuts, seeds, dried fruit)
tuna casserole
yogurt Popsicles (orange juice concentrate and yogurt)

Uncooked Food

butter (Appendix D)
fruit salads (e.g., Waldorf)
instant puddings
no-bake cookies (Appendix D)
nut butters
sandwich fillings
vegetable plates and salads (coleslaw, green bean, three-bean)

Cooked Foods

(The following may be prepared using a hot plate, an electric saucepan, or an electric frying pan. For recipes, see book accompanying appliance.)
apples (baked or made into sauce)
cottage cheese (Appendix D)
dumplings
doughnuts
eggs
fritters
fruit
grilled sandwiches
meat
pancakes
pizzas
popcorn
potatoes (baked, fried)
puddings
scones
soup
spaghetti and sauce
stewed fruit or vegetables
tacos
toast (French or regular)
vegetables
white sauce
yogurt (Appendix D)

Some food recipes are in Appendix D, or some of your favorite nutritional ones can be used. Endres and Rockwell (1980) have an excellent section on ethnic recipes and discussion on cultural foods.

ENJOYMENT

Good nutrition is equally important for both sexes. Food preparation is fun for boys and girls; therefore, it follows that good health and the making of tasty cuisine result in its enjoyment. Good health and safety habits begin early in the child's life; however, adults must provide information and supervision.

Food and eating habits may be heavily laden with emotion. If the child is to utilize the food he eats, he must do so in a loving atmosphere. Force, anger, hostility, and other unpleasantness should be absent from meals.

Here are some techniques to promote good attitudes toward food and eating:

1. Food

Understand the background of the child with regard to his culture and personal food preferences.

Introduce new foods slowly, always in the presence of a known, and preferably liked, food. Even if the child only asks about it, fingers it, or ignores it, the food will be more familiar another time. Encourage him to taste, but do not force him to eat it.

Use family style as appropriate. Children often eat more when they serve themselves; however, some take more than they can or want to eat.

Encourage small portions. Letting children ask for more gives them a sense of satisfaction rather than of failure for not being able to eat all their food.

Serve finger foods and expect children to be more adept with fingers than utensils.

Be sure a liquid is available to drink when dry foods are served, if only water. Dry foods are hard for young children to swallow.

Serve food separately rather than in casseroles, stew, and mixtures.

Serve the food in bite-sized pieces.

Vary the consistency of food served at each meal (soft, crisp, and chewy).

When possible, let the children choose (e.g., between two fruits or two vegetables).

Help the children to enjoy a wide variety of foods.

Children are encouraged to drink water frequently.

Use peer influence in a positive way. Encourage children to bring their favorite fruit or vegetable. Let the group prepare them all, cut into bite-sized pieces, and have a "tasting" snack session.

Be aware of the nutritional value of each food served.

Provide opportunities to taste food at times other than snack or lunch (tasting table, science).

Serve foods that are mild and natural in flavor; strong flavors are rejected by young children. Dilute strongly flavored juices (grapefruit, grape, pineapple) with water.

Encourage the children to drink water frequently.

Most young children prefer food served at room temperature; hot food may frighten them, and they often stir hard ice cream until it becomes liquid.

Never use food as a weapon, such as refusing dessert until after all other food is eaten. A nourishing dessert should be as important as other foods.

2. Environment

Precede all eating situations with a calm, quiet activity. Excited or overstimulated children do not enjoy their food as much as tranquil children.

Require children to wash and dry their hands before eating or working with food.

Let the children serve themselves when possible. Use child-sized pitchers, glasses, and utensils.

Make sure the children are comfortably seated with feet touching the floor.

Let children assist in setting the tables.

Make the area attractive and peaceful.

See that the food is attractively presented in color, variety, and consistency. (Popular food colors for young children include green, orange, yellow, pink.)

Meet their social needs by providing time and association with peers.

Help the children use this experience in an educational way. Make it a time to learn about, identify, and talk about the food.

Before eating, all the children wash and dry their hands.

Assist the children in developing and using good table manners and etiquette.

Help build a bridge between home and center in behavior during eating and in promoting and understanding about food habits in different ethnic groups.

Help the children to become more conscious of nutrition and eating proper foods.

Be patient and understanding about the different rates at which young children eat. Often eating takes less priority than socialization and exploration.

Handle table accidents calmly and reassuringly (have sponges close at hand). Let the children resolve the situation as much as possible.

If a child refuses to eat, invite him to the table to enjoy the conversation rather than going to another activity.

CUMULATIVE LESSON PLAN

- Let the children prepare a box lunch for a picnic.
- Use empty food product boxes in dramatic play.

ESPECIALLY FOR PARENTS

The food preferences of preschool children are reported by parents to be meat, cereal grains, baked products, fruit, and sweets. Children frequently ask for dairy products, cereal, and snack foods, such as cookies, crackers, fruit juice, and dry beverage mixes. They obviously prefer carbohydrate-rich foods, those that are easy to chew, and cereals, breads, and crackers over meat and other protein-rich foods. Cheese and yogurt are becoming more popular with young children (Pipes 1977). Your child may or may not share these preferences.

Some parents say: "My child just won't eat nourishing foods. She only wants potato chips or sugar-coated cereal." Such parents must recognize that they do the buying and have two choices: going "cold turkey," that is, no more buying of junk foods, or gradually but firmly replacing junk food with nourishing foods. If parents buy or give in, children will persist in nagging for junk food. Parents need to set a goal of providing well-balanced and nourishing food for all family members—starting today!

Because the child has more meals and snacks in the home than in the school, he also has more opportunities for participation. Start with some simple opportunities; as he shows interest and ability, increase the selection in kind and complexity.

Things other than food preparation make mealtimes pleasant. Decorations, setting the table, eating in a different location (outside, for instance), soothing music, or a guest also add interest. Mealtimes should be happy affairs, with discussions of interesting topics and everyone having a chance to hear and be heard. Unpleasantries can be handled at another time.

To involve your child further in meal planning, let him help check home supplies, make a list, and go shopping with you.

If you have a garden, let your child help plant, care for, and harvest the crops. This will give him an understanding about produce that he would never get by just purchasing it. If you have no garden, take your child with you to the market. Show him how to select various fruits and vegetables. Talk with him about quantity, quality, and cost. Discuss different ways to prepare and store food. This is not to be a formal lecture, but done as if you were talking to yourself out loud. On your return home, let your child assist in putting the groceries in their proper places, thereby learning about different methods of storage (refrigerator, shelf, freezer). When you are ready to use these items, he can get them. He will also learn how to store similar things together and how to make some orderly arrangements.

Interestingly, a thin child usually becomes a thin adult while a chubby child usually becomes a chubby adult. Avoid weight problems later in life by helping your child develop good food and eating habits while young. Talk about the importance of good nutrition. Help him to understand why we need to eat certain foods and either avoid or limit others. The eating habits and attitudes he forms early in life are very important in his later health. Perhaps posting a chart of the basic four food groups, including a column for your child to record his daily intake through pictures, would be enjoyable and beneficial. (Be sure to read through this entire chapter, especially about nutrition. The aids for teachers can also be used by parents.)

Make food preparation fun rather than dull. Occasional suggestions from your child as to a dish or a menu will increase his interest. On more than one occasion, my own two sons (at preschool age) said, "Mother, why don't you go to a meeting so we can make something for supper?" or "I can do that for supper." And they said it with confidence.

Encourage your child to eat a variety of foods. Introduce new foods, one at a time, in small quantities with the suggestion, "Just try it." Forcing a child to eat a certain food often creates a dislike that could have been avoided. Each time you serve it, encourage him to eat a little. "Taste it, and if you want more, you can have it." Deal in the positive. Compliment him when he does taste it. I have used this technique many times in the classroom. One time a child said, "Well, aren't you going to say you're glad I tasted it?" when I forgot to complete my part.

Serve finger foods to young children, and expect them to use their fingers on other foods as well. Manipulating silverware may be difficult for them at first, but they soon develop the skills and the desire to use it. One caution: when a child is mature enough, encourage him to use the utensils when appropriate and his fingers when appropriate.

Children can help clear the tables—especially their own dishes—and many want to help wash and dry the dishes. Rotate the jobs—washing dishes, wiping dishes, taking out the garbage, sweeping up crumbs, clearing the table—so that the routine does not become monotonous but remains an opportunity to help and learn.

As a tie to the center, ask your child what food he helped prepare or what he ate at school that day. You may want to ask his teacher to share a recipe, or you may be willing to share a family recipe or food experience (religious, cultural, personal) with the group, remembering to use nutritious foods.

A child can help prepare food at home in a number of ways. He can:

Brush vegetables (e.g., potatoes, carrots)
Peel vegetables or fruit (with hand peelers rather than knives)
Shell peas or snip beans
Rinse vegetables (lettuce, tomatoes, radishes)
Whip cream or topping
Make gelatin or instant pudding
Knead bread
Make and bake cookies
Season vegetables
Pour milk, juice, water
Cook meat
Make sandwiches
Make fruit or vegetable salads or plates
Process fruit or vegetables (canning, drying, freezing)
Make fruit drinks
Make Popsicles
Prepare picnic lunch

FOOD-RELATED EXPERIENCES FOR CENTER OR HOME

Field Trips

bakery
berry patch
bottling plant
butcher shop
cannery
cheese factory

cold-storage plant
dairy farm
dairy processing plant
farms (animal, produce)
fields (corn, potato, peanut, pumpkin)
fish hatchery or market
fishing at local lake or river (close supervision mandatory)
flour mill
food processing plant
garden
greenhouse
grain field or mill
grocery or local market
kitchen (restaurant or home of teacher or child)
natural food store
nut store
orchard (seasonal)
picnic
pizza parlor
poultry or turkey ranch
restaurant (specialty, ethnic)

Resource People (with appropriate aids)

baker
beekeeper
butcher
chef
cook at your center or local school
farmer with produce to tell how food is prepared for market and how he sells it (crate, truckload, pound)
fisherman
grocer
milkman
miller
parent to demonstrate preparation and use of products
poultry rancher

Songs

Many good songs concern food. Check your favorite song books. A few examples follow.

From Arlene Dalton, *My Picture Book of Songs* (Chicago: Donahue, 1947):
"Simple Sal"
"Grandpa's Farm"
From Ruth Seeger, *American Folk Songs for Children* (New York: Doubleday, 1948):
"Old Aunt Kate"
"Do, Do, Pity My Case"
From Lucille F. Wood and Louise B. Scott, *Singing Fun* (St. Louis: Webster Publishing, 1954):
"Little Seeds"
"Gathering Eggs"
"I'd Like to Be a Farmer"
"If I Were a Farmer"
"The Singing Farm"
"Ten Yellow Chicks"
"Our Milkman"
"The Bakery Truck"
From Lucille F. Wood and Louise B. Scott, *More Singing Fun* (St. Louis: McGraw-Hill, 1961):
"A Whistling Farm Boy"
"Ice Cream Man"

For a list of books for children related to food experiences, see Appendix E.

APPLICATION OF PRINCIPLES

1. Make a list of food typical of your area, such as fruit, vegetables, meat, and seafood. Tell how you could utilize each of these in your center.
2. Design a lesson plan based on nutrition. Use it in your center.
3. Provide materials and opportunities for your children to practice good sanitary procedures such as washing hands, cleaning nails, and covering clothes.
4. Make a chart of basic nutrients and their sources. Check the information against the food served in your center over the past week. What nutrients need to be included

more often in foods you serve? How often are "harmful" ingredients (sugar, caffeine, chocolate, salt, and other additives) served? Should a specific attempt be made to reduce their use?

5. If possible, provide weekly opportunities in food preparation. Use checklist on page 225.
6. Make a nutritious snack schedule for one month. Also make a quantity and price list. Compare the various menus for food value and cost.
7. Check each child's personal record to see if he has food allergies, dislikes, or cultural restrictions. How do you handle these limitations?

References

Endres, J., and R. Rockwell. *Food, Nutrition and the Young Child.* St. Louis: C. V. Mosby, 1980.

McWilliams, M. *Nutrition for the Growing Years.* New York: Wiley, 1975.

Pipes, P. *Nutrition in Infancy and Childhood.* St. Louis: C. V. Mosby, 1977.

Powers, Hugh, and James Presley. *Food Power: Nutrition and Your Child's Behavior.* New York: St. Martin's Press, 1978.

Thurston, Emory W. *The Parents' Guide to Better Nutrition for Tots to Teens (and Others).* New Canaan, Conn.: Keats, 1979.

11
Mathematics

One, two, buckle my shoe;
Three, four, shut the door.
Five, six, pick up sticks;
Seven, eight, lay them straight!
Nine, ten, a big fat hen.

MAIN PRINCIPLES

1. Mathematics plays an important part in the daily life of young children.
2. The ability to solve mathematical problems depends on the developmental stage of the children.
3. Mathematics provides an opportunity to think, discover, problem solve, and learn.
4. Teachers and parents can provide appropriate learning experiences for young children.
5. In this chapter, mathematics is divided into four categories: sorting and classification, counting, measuring, and exploring space and shapes.

Many adults do not understand (and therefore dislike) mathematics. They have difficulty in balancing their checkbooks, in not having enough money, or in understanding physics and computers, so they want to shield children from math. On the other hand, as soon as children are able, they are expected to tell their age and also hold up the right number of fingers. Adults want children to learn sizes and shapes and to get around easily in their environment. Further, they want children to stack this, compare that, and even recite nursery rhymes or sing songs, many of which deal with numbers. Does this sound as if adults are somewhat inconsistent?

The adults described in the previous paragraph need to look at mathematics in a new light. Good experiences turn one's attitude from negative to positive. Math is all around us; it is vital in our daily lives—to make a phone call, to address correspondence, to locate others, to prepare meals, to use a vehicle, and to do many tasks inside and outside the home. Every aspect of life has mathematics interwoven through it.

STAGE OF DEVELOPMENT

The same question asked about reading could be asked about mathematics. Should it be taught to the young child? The answers would range from absolute yes to emphatic no. The question is rather unfair without defining the term *mathematics.*

Mathematicians disagree as to what mathematics is. The higher the level, the more complex the definition. Suitable definitions come from Schickedanz (1977): "Mathematics provides an agreed-upon system for describing objects, time, and space in terms of quantity or magnitude"; and from Lorton and Walley (1979): "Mathematics is the study of relationships that exist between and among sets of quantity." Payne (1975) says that children should "be assisted toward mathematical understanding by learning how to solve problems, become successful with activities of a mathematical nature, understand the utility of mathematics, and have fun with it." Margolin (1976) states: "The purpose of mathematics for young children is to have them learn to compute with facility. They learn to see how objects in their own environment are placed into a quantitative context." The experience should be of a sensorimotor nature, with the child using his senses and moving himself and objects about in space. As in other areas of curriculum, Piaget advocates teaching mathematics through the **sensorimotor** approach as preparation for logical operations; logic is based on coordination of action even before the development of language.

Piaget's second stage of mental development, **preoperational,** coincides with the ages from 2 through 6—just slightly older than the focus of this text. Broman (1982) says it is "during this stage that children reason and explain through intuition rather than logic. They have difficulty expressing the order of events, explaining relationships, understanding numbers and their relations, understanding what others say accurately, and understanding and remembering rules."

Piaget (1965) stated in his book, *The Child's Conception of Numbers,* that mathematical learning takes place in three stages: (1) coordination within the field of perception; (2) operations that go beyond the field of perception; and (3) transition from perception to deduction, progressive coordination of operations, and gradual development of reversibility. Young children begin stage one and move gradually into stage two. Not until they are in the **concrete operational stage** (ages 7 through 11) of Piaget's stages of mental development do they comprehend concepts of numbers, relationships, and processes.

Young children progress in mathematical knowledge if the activities and expectations match their abilities. In the preoperational stage, young children are very egocentric and generally incapable of seeing a situation from more than one perspective. However, they learn to discriminate color soon after shape and then become "increasingly adept at working with progressively more difficult concepts of size, classification, seriation, and patterning. A child can work with numerals (chanting them, recognizing them, writing them) long before numeration can be comprehended appropriately. The abilities to use numerals in chanting or recognizing situations does not imply that a child can understand numberness. When the child can conserve, he/she moves from the preoperational to the concrete operational stage of the number concept" (Richardson et al. 1980).

Because of the developmental limitations of young children, teachers should be perceptive of opportunities offered. Children depend upon action for learning. They must be able to discover things for themselves through concrete experiences.

Abilities of children of the same chronological age vary greatly. With increasing age and experience, they do more with mathematics. Research indicates that at entrance to kindergarten:

1. Many children can count and find the number of objects to 10, and some are able to count to at least 20;
2. Some can say the number name of 10s in order (that is, 10, 20, 30), but far fewer can say the names when counting by 2s and 5s;
3. Most know the meaning of *first,* and many can identify ordinal positions through *fifth;*
4. Many recognize the numerals from 1 to 10, and some can write them;

5. Most give correct answers to simple addition and subtraction combinations presented verbally either with or without manipulative materials;
6. Most have some knowledge about coins, time, and other measures; about simple fractional concepts; and about geometric shapes (Payne 1975).

LEARNING OPPORTUNITIES

Teachers must have flexible expectations of young children and their mathematical concepts. Teachers should capitalize on spontaneous events to the degree that the experience is meaningful to the children. Many opportunities should be provided for children to see, manipulate, and test ideas in a friendly atmosphere. Children relate objects and activities as a means of putting their world into perspective. Children should be allowed to practice mathematical concepts and then helped to move forward one step at a time.

The child's mathematical concepts should be helped to move forward one step at a time.

Some attainable goals, based on the developmental abilities of individual children in a relaxed atmosphere, would be:

1. To stimulate an interest in numbers and their uses;
2. To show how number concepts can aid in problem solving;
3. To increase worldly knowledge through mathematics;
4. To introduce number symbols and terms as the children indicate readiness.

Addition is the first form of mathematics learned by young children: "We need two more blocks to make this stack as high as that one." This is followed later by subtraction: "If I give you two of my cars, we will both have the same amount!" They can count the number of children and places for snack time and determine if they need to add or remove some chairs. Mathematical terms can be introduced to children as long as these terms are defined and the children have opportunities to practice their meanings. When one wants (or needs) more of something, one adds (gets more). When one wants less (or not as many), one subtracts (or takes away). Some children understand what equal means. This is illustrated by placing the same number of children or objects on one side of a line as on the other.

Maria Montessori devised games, activities, and materials for teaching number concepts to young children. She thought the concept of *zero* (or nothing) was worth special teaching, and she taught numbers in a series of zero to nine just to give special emphasis to zero.

Early in Chapter 4, the importance of auditory skills in learning to read was stated. The best preparation for successful math experiences, however, is visual development. Sight appears to be more important for success in math than in reading (Brophy et al. 1975). If the child is unable to discriminate visually, learning mathematical concepts will be a problem.

Chapter 5 contained a short discussion on the two brain hemispheres: the left for verbal and analytic functioning and the right for intuition and understanding patterns. Piaget says that young children deal with intuition; yet, the child must also be able to

Number symbols are introduced as the child indicates readiness.

analyze if he is to perform mathematical tasks. Both hemispheres are utilized in learning mathematics.

Children need to be in an atmosphere where they can think, discover, solve problems, and learn. They need materials that are safe, malleable, and interesting.

APPROPRIATE MATHEMATICAL EXPERIENCES

Forman and Kuschner (1977) warn that direct teaching cannot build concepts of conservation or of number. These concepts must be developed by the children themselves. "Many teachers have tried to teach conservation and other number concepts to children prior to the age of seven, but most have only failed in these efforts. Although you cannot teach such concepts directly, you can provide the atmosphere and materials that will facilitate the development of concepts of conservation as well as number" (Seefeldt 1980). Instead of planning specific number experiences and expecting the children to learn them, the teacher should plan a variety of opportunities whereby the child can manipulate objects and practice problem solving.

Alberti and Davitt (1974) make the teacher's role very clear: "You, the teacher, hold the key. You must determine the best approach to your class, you should be sensitive to each student's ability and should help him discover a working level high enough to intrigue him but not so high that it will overwhelm him. With new experience you will learn when to introduce new problems, when to dwell longer on one problem, when to review, and when to suggest free play." (P. 96.)

The involvement of mathematics provides excellent vocabulary experiences, with many new words to learn, meanings to explore, descriptions to use, solutions to discuss, and ideas to relate. There are times to contemplate silently and times to seek assistance.

One of the earliest math experiences children have is in counting. They may count as high as 3 (depending on their age); use randomly selected numbers up to 20; or express an astronomically large number, such as 27! The introduction is through the number's cardinal name (how many). Children do not recognize symbols yet, but they have heard their names, so repetition follows, in or out of order. The next step will be in learning each ordinal name (or position, such as first, second, and so on). This often comes from hearing older children select positions or turns. Rote counting has value in repeatedly hearing the names and sequence of numbers; however, when the children are stopped in recitation, they return to the first number. The value of drilling young children in number sequence is questionable, because as yet numbers mean nothing to them. An effective way to teach about positioning is through the use of one's own body. Children learn about standing "beside," "in front of," "near" or other prepositions because they are experiencing the action.

Piaget has outlined the following concepts as appropriate when they correspond to the preschooler's development:

1. Classification (grouping by some common characteristic)
2. Seriation (ordering by a common characteristic)
3. Spatial relationships (distance, movement, and so on)
4. Temporal relationships (time)
5. Conservation (permanence of materials or objects)

Relationship is an important aspect of mathematics. A relationship is necessary to classify, order, and measure space or time, and also in the permanence of things. Relationship between sizes, such as small, smaller, smallest, is one of the more difficult concepts for young children to learn. For example, when given five items of mixed sizes, most young children cannot easily arrange them in appropriate sequence (Copeland 1974). Margolin (1982) states about relationships: "Children's realization of relationships begins to build a form of logic, thinking ahead, anticipating cause and effect. Mathematical concepts require anticipation of possible outcomes. The greater number of experiences of this kind that children have, accompanied by explanations of events by interested adults, the better will foundational skills be developed." Relationships are comparisons, which give children words that symbolize mathematical concepts.

Activities to Increase Mathematical Conceptualization

For convenience, mathematical experiences will be divided into four areas: sorting and classifying, counting, measuring, and exploration of shape and space (also suggested by Seefeldt 1980).

Sorting and Classifying

When children are asked to put things that belong (or go together) in a certain place, they may group them differently than an adult would. Before responding to their appropriateness, or inappropriateness, seek further clarification from the children.

- Ask the children to sort a variety of objects by a common characteristic. Then ask for a different grouping. At first have two or three different possibilities. Use buttons as an example. Sort by color, size, number of holes, composition (wood, glass, plastic, fabric), use (men's, women's, children's), design, and so on. Also useful for this task are animals, cans, clothing, dishes, flowers, food, fruit, jars, leaves, marbles, rocks, seeds, and toys.
- Have objects in sets of four (three belong together, one is different, such as three animals and a pillow or three wheel toys and a shovel). Present the objects to the children and have them select the one that is different. This is an important experience.

A valuable mathematical experience is gained by sorting and classifying objects.

Practice in visual discrimination of size and shape increases mathematical conceptualization.

- Use commercial toys that have different shaped objects to put in corresponding shaped holes.
- Play or sort cards ("Old Maid," "Fish," and so on).
- Have the children place pictures or cards in the proper sequence and tell a story about them.
- Provide many opportunities to develop visual discrimination (e.g., sizes, shapes, similarities, differences, symbols, and designs.)
- Have a display of coins. Discuss characteristics and amounts of each.
- Use math vocabulary: add (more), subtract (less), wide, narrow; large, larger, largest; middle; and so on.
- Have duplicate cards showing certain number of objects or dots on one and a corresponding written symbol on other.
- Make sandpaper shapes and written symbols.

Counting

- Provide many counting-out experiences (number of people for snack, cups for measuring, trikes to ride, and so on.)
- Do number finger plays and nursery rhymes.
- Sing number songs.
- Use books about numbers.
- Recite poems containing numbers.
- Focus on one number at a time (make a book about *four,* that is, talk about animals with four legs, involve four children in an activity, and so on).
- Make and use a daily calendar.
- Count items (number of buttons on a shirt, number of children wearing tie shoes, number of trees in yard, spools, boxes, shovels, instruments).

- Bring in and use a calculator or adding machine.
- Talk about and show objects that have numbers such as bottles, boxes, calendar, cards, cash register, clock, flash cards, license plates, measuring spoons and cups, money, phone, road signs, ruler, scales, speedometer, sports player, tickets, timer, watch, yardstick.
- Make a store. Provide cans, boxes, money, and a cash register. Write number (cost) on articles and amount on money. Make it fun and simple.
- Earn and use tokens.
- Relate numbers to activities: how many times the ball bounced, the clock struck, the teacher clapped.
- Keep attendance records of the children.
- Make a class directory with addresses and phone numbers of the children and teachers. Post it.
- Use counters and containers (e.g., egg carton and poker chips; numbers written on small juice can and Popsicle sticks to go in it).
- Talk with children about the difference between cardinal (1, 2, and 3) and ordinal (first, second, third) numbers.
- Show how grouping helps in counting things.
- Go on a picnic. How much and what will you need to take?
- Play games with number symbol spinners.
- Use a die (dots to represent numbers; numerals can be included on each facet of the die).
- Tell a story and have the children supply number parts (of legs on animals, distance, and so on).
- Count the number of children with certain color clothing, type of shoes, physical characteristics. Count and name the parts of plants or objects.

Snack time can include a counting experience.

- Set the table for a snack or lunch. Decide how many things are needed.
- Have tickets for a snack or lunch.
- Have a variety of clocks (number, digital, modernistic).
- Sell something for a snack or lunch.
- Write numbers on spring clothespins. Hang a clothes line, yarn, or string at the child's level. Have the child take the clothespin from a box and hang it on the line in proper sequence (easily moved around if errors occur).

Measuring

- Provide opportunities for various methods of measurement (length, width, time, size, amount).
- Provide opportunities for linear measurement (use string, stick, measuring tape, yardstick). Introduce the metric system for those who are ready for it. Follow a recipe.
- Weigh each child, measure his height, and post information about him on chart or wall.
- Provide scales for weighing objects (could also be used in a store).
- Introduce a thermometer and have ways for child to use it (hot and cold).
- Introduce the concepts *zero, equal,* and *half* as child is ready.
- Cut an apple. Ask how many pieces are needed to give each person a slice. Ask what the various pieces are called (half, quarter, eighth).
- Pack a sack. Talk about putting heavier things on the bottom.
- Use a compass, barometer, or speedometer.
- Relate measurement to an activity: how long you can stand on one foot, how far you can jump, and so on.
- Talk about center activities that are in the recent past or the near future (yesterday, today, tomorrow).
- Measure ingredients and make an art medium (clay).
- Measure: heel-toe across room, for woodworking, or the amount of space in the block area.

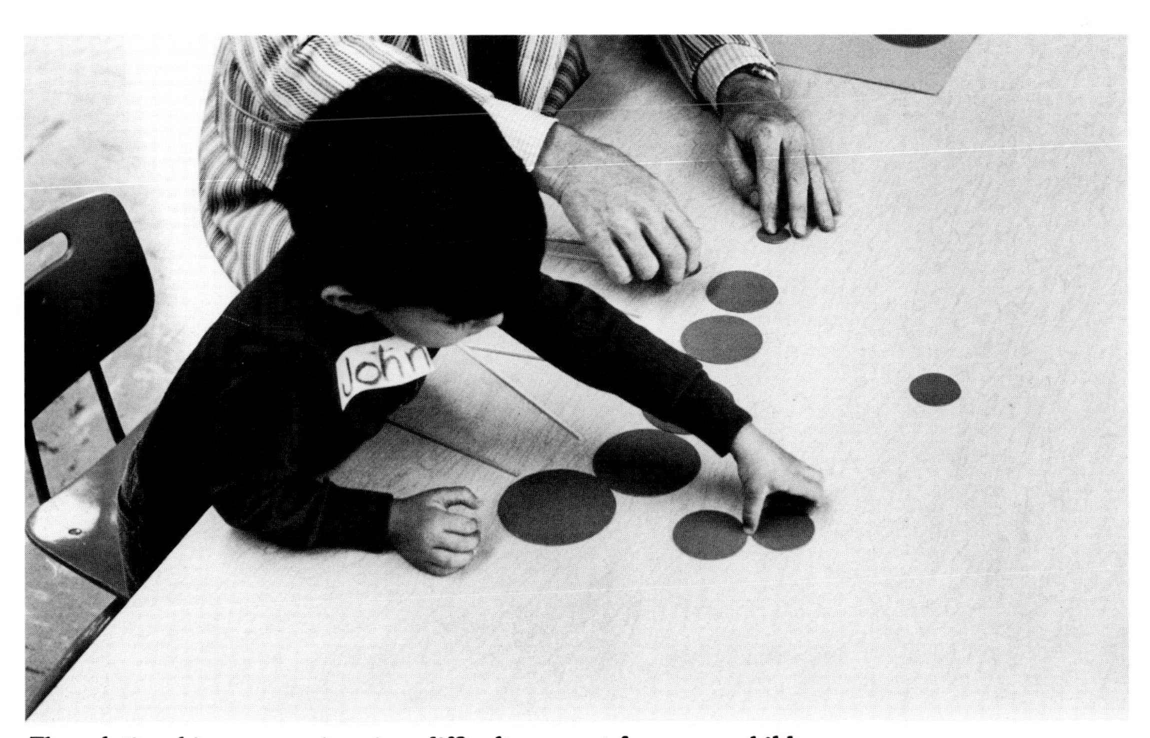

The relationship among sizes is a difficult concept for young children.

- Balance objects in a scale, on a board, or on your head.
- Using measuring cups and spoons, see how many times you need to fill a smaller container to fill a larger one, or how many times a larger one will fill a smaller one.

Exploring Space and Shapes

- Have objects and articles of different sizes and shapes.
- Look around the room and yard for objects of the same shape.
- Take a shoebox and make openings of different shapes. Insert objects through a hole of the same shape.
- Have a discussion in the block area (shapes, sizes, number, relationship to each other).
- Make a poster board with various shapes and designs (keys, objects, people). Put

Children use different length sticks to experiment with geometric shapes.

corresponding objects or shapes and designs in a box. Have children select object and hang it over the appropriate shape.
- Use nesting toys such as cups and dolls.
- Use puzzles.
- Using blocks of different sizes or shapes, ask the children to hand you specific ones or to make certain forms.
- Let the child experiment with geometric shapes.
- Supply dominoes for building or exploring.
- Use magnetic numbers and letters on a magnetic board.
- Toss beanbags into various shaped holes.
- Match objects: bottle with lid, mittens, and so on.
- Have the children reproduce designs with beads, blocks, and so on.
- Play picture or number bingo.
- Using templates of paper, metal, wood, plastic, or cardboard, have the children trace geometric designs.

Books for children related to mathematical experiences are listed in Appendix E.

CUMULATIVE LESSON PLAN

- Measure and weigh boxes.
- Use nesting boxes.
- Match boxes and shapes.

ESPECIALLY FOR PARENTS

Parents need to be aware of their role in helping their children build correct and positive attitudes toward mathematics. True, everyone does not enjoy mathematics, but to influence a child negatively before he has had a chance to try mathematics is unfair. So too is it unfair to push him when he is neither ready nor interested.

From a very young age, your child can have enjoyable counting experiences with you: "One, two, three buttons on your sweater," as you help him fasten them. "One shoe, two shoes." As he grows older, he can have more complex experiences: "Everybody needs a knife, a fork, and a spoon—three things." "Let's bake some potatoes for dinner. How many will we need? One for Daddy, one for Mommy, one for brother, one for sister, and one for you: one, two, three, four, five."

Provide experiences that help rather than hinder concept development. One family had a very modernistic clock in their living room that had a gold ball where each of the twelve numbers should appear. Another family had a clock with Roman numerals, while still another family had a digital clock. Each type of clock presented different opportunities for the children.

Children can be influenced by early experiences with mathematics and by attitudes. Mathematics is too important in everyday living for children to fear or dislike it. What do you think will happen with the proposed change to the metric system? How easy do you think it will be to learn a new system? Will there be a mathematics gap? Can you be supportive and helpful when your children use computers at school? Children and adults need to learn and use methods that are common in the society in which they live.

Some suggested math activities for parents and children follow:

- Provide many opportunities for the child to develop visual discrimination (sizes, shapes, similarities, differences, symbols, designs, sequencing).
- Provide games with dice (or one die) or a number spinner.

- When possible, point out written number symbols and tell the meaning. (Show your child how a road sign reading "55" should correspond with your speedometer.)
- Using a calendar, show how many days until a certain event (for your own sake, limit too much advance warning).
- For a birthday, use candles to represent the person's age.
- When looking at books or pictures, count the number of similar objects.
- Let your child set the table with the proper number of utensils.
- Show him where to look on bottles, cans, and boxes to find numbers (price, quantity).
- Compare prices, quantity, and quality at the store.
- Show your child how much material (fabric, yarn) you would need to make a certain article of clothing or to build an object (fence, birdhouse).
- Ask the shoe salesman to measure your child's feet.
- Give him his own tape measure or metal tape and encourage him to measure and compare different things.
- Hand him an object. Ask him if it is large or small. Then compare it to another object. Ask if it is larger or smaller. Show him how it can be larger than some objects and smaller than others. Size is relative to something.
- Teach the concept of "middle" when your child is ready.
- Ask a cashier to show your child how he knows what numbers to "ring up" and how much money to ask the people for.
- Have your child weigh a certain number of pounds (potatoes).
- Assist him in meaningful counting, not just rote numbers.
- Teach him his phone number and how to dial the telephone.
- Assist him in making something for a meal from a recipe.
- Let him help you prepare a shopping list.
- Buy shoelaces. Count number of eyelets to determine length.
- Show your child your house number and help him learn his address.
- Take him to an athletic event, point out the numbers on each player, and tell him how scoring occurs.
- Let him experiment with measuring spoons and cups.
- Make candy, using a thermometer.
- Make a coin card with coins and values or coin combinations.
- Buy stamps at the post office; look at the numbers.
- Let your child help you fill your car with gas; point out the quantity used and the amount due. Let him pay the cashier.
- Let him observe or participate in bowling (numbered pins and scoring).
- Make a chart showing what amount of money he can earn by doing certain jobs.
- Show him how numbers help us in our everyday life (pencil lead, clothes patterns, recipes, money).
- Make an enjoyable number activity (one button, two spools, three ribbons, and four marshmallows. What can he make with them?).
- Help him to understand ordinal numbers. (First, we get dressed; second, we wash our hands; third, we . . .).
- Get him a transparent savings bank.
- Show him how to locate a radio station or a television channel.
- Provide opportunities to make comparisons: more or less; little, littler, littlest; shapes (number and length of sides); temperature changes.
- Talk about things you do that involve numbers.
- Ask him to put a certain number of objects in certain piles.
- Help him relate a written symbol to objects of same number.
- Help him make a simple picture recipe and then help him make the product.
- Ask stimulating questions. (What shall we do? We only have three oranges and there are five children. Two children want to paint and we have only one brush. How can we find out how tall each child is? How many blocks does it take to make the scale balance?)

- Let the child assist you in sorting clothes for the laundry and in combining things before they are put away (socks in pairs, piles of clothes for each family member).
- Put pictures of objects on low shelves so he knows where his blocks and toys belong.
- On a sheet of paper, draw the outline of objects. Then give the child objects that fit the outline. Let him match them.
- Let the child assist you in record keeping. Determine how much milk is delivered, how many cans you have of a certain food, and so on.
- Obtain boxes of different sizes. Let the child nest them.
- In the grocery store, count how many vegetables or fruits are the same color; count the number of eggs per carton; count bananas in a bunch; count pieces of meat in a carton; count the number of rolls in a package. Compare sizes of similar and different products.

Some nursery rhymes involving number:

"One, Two, Buckle My Shoe"
"This Old Man, He Played One"
"Three Blind Mice"
"The Three Little Kittens"
"Baa, Baa, Black Sheep"
"Sing a Song of Sixpence"

Some favorite songs involving number:

"Hot Cross Buns"
"One Elephant"
"Johnny Works With One Hammer"
"Three Blue Pigeons"
"Five Little Chickadees"
"Over in the Meadow"
"Five Little Buns in the Baker's Shop"
"Roll Over"
"Ten Little Indians"

APPLICATION OF PRINCIPLES

1. Originate an enjoyable method of determining which children in your center can correctly identify number symbols.
2. Using materials in your center, or those suggested in the chapter, provide experiences for children in classification, seriation, and conservation. Observe closely the responses of each child. Which experiences need to be modified or repeated? Why do some of the children have difficulty in understanding some of these concepts?
3. Use at least one mathematical experience each day in your center. Make it fun, stimulating, and desired. Never force a child to participate or to reach a certain level of performance.
4. Use nursery rhymes, songs, food experiences, and stories that mention numbers and number concepts.
5. When appropriate, encourage children to use numbers spontaneously.

References

Alberti, Del, and Robert J. Davitt. *Attribute Games and Problems: Teachers' Guide.* New York: McGraw-Hill, 1974.

Broman, Betty L. *The Early Years in Childhood Education.* Chicago: Rand McNally, 1982, pp. 285–311.

Brophy, Jere E., Thomas L. Good, and Shari E. Nedler. *Teaching in the Preschool.* New York: Harper & Row, 1975.

Copeland, Richard W. *How Children Learn Mathematics: Teaching Implications of Piaget's Research.* 3d ed. London: Collier-Macmillan, 1974, 1979.

Forman, G. E., and Kuschner, D. S. *The Child's Construction of Knowledge: Piaget for Teaching Children.* Belmont, Calif.: Wadsworth, 1977.

Lorton, John, and Bertha Walley. *Introduction to Early Childhood Education.* New York: D. Van Nostrand, 1979.

Margolin, Edythe. *Teaching Young Children at School and Home.* New York: Macmillan, 1982, pp. 249–273.

______. *Young Children: Their Curriculum and Learning Processes.* New York: Macmillan, 1976, pp. 176–205.

Payne, J. N., ed. *Mathematics Learning in Early Childhood.* Reston, Va.: National Council of Teachers of Mathematics, 1975.

Piaget, Jean. *The Child's Conception of Number.* New York: W. W. Norton, 1965.

Richardson, L., K. Goodman, N. Hartman, and H. LePique. *A Mathematics Activity Curriculum for Early Childhood and Special Education.* New York: Macmillan, 1980.

Schickedanz, Judith A. *Strategies for Teaching Young Children.* Englewood Cliffs, N.J.: Prentice-Hall, 1977, pp. 160–208.

Seefeldt, Carol. *A Curriculum for Preschools.* 2d ed. Columbus, Ohio: Charles E. Merrill, 1980, pp. 253–266.

12 Guidance Techniques for Teachers and Parents

There was an old woman who lived in a shoe,
She had so many children, she didn't know what to do.
She gave them some broth without any bread
She whipped them all soundly, and put them to bed.

MAIN PRINCIPLES

1. Children need and want guidelines.
2. Adults and children work cooperatively through some appropriate techniques.

Having given consideration to the curriculum, some workable techniques for child-adult interaction can now be given attention. Adults respond in various ways to children and vice versa. Teachers, for example, are less emotionally involved and therefore often act more objectively than parents do. It is easier to work with the children of others than with one's own. Moreover, parents have more at stake than a teacher because children represent their parents. From the children's viewpoint, some adults are easier to understand than others. Some adults are so insecure and inconsistent that neither children nor adults know what is expected.

For the person who is research oriented or who is a depth seeker, an extensive bibliography has been provided at the end of this chapter and in Appendix E. The person looking for simple techniques that are easy to initiate and that show results should read on or refer to *Dear Mom and Dad* (Taylor 1978), written especially for parents. These techniques are not presented in any particular order after the first one. They just work. As you read through them, pick out one or two that you would like to try. Be persistent. Give each one a fair trial. After you have mastered a few, select others. *Undoubtedly they will mean a change in behavior for both you and the children you teach.*

THE ULTIMATE GOAL: SELF-CONTROL

Parents are large and powerful enough to make children do what the adult wishes; however, a power struggle may ensue. Some adults have a feeling of power knowing they can control someone or something. Children feel the opposite when they are expected to conform with little or no consideration.

For children to survive in this complex world, they must be able to take responsibility for their own actions. If adults are willing to help children practice self-control when they are ready and able, children can develop trust and confidence in their ability to make and carry out decisions. These children will begin to make consistent choices and will be able to adjust to and accept the consequences.

Do not expect too much of young children. They cannot take on situations inappropriate for their age or abilities. Do be patient as they become more able to assume responsibility for their own behavior.

LISTEN TO CHILDREN AND TALK WITH THEM

Have you ever heard a child who was questioned about a certain act reply, "But you said I could!" His response is a result of someone not listening! We often give our undivided attention to another adult but fail to hear the words of children. Sometimes children have to tug and pull at us before we give them even divided attention. Children do have important things to say and ask. We should listen; it is the beginning of understanding.

One way to give children your undivided attention is to stoop or kneel so that you have eye-to-eye contact. Then concentrate on their words. With a limited vocabulary, they may have difficulty conveying complete and desired messages. Interest helps communication.

Besides being poor listeners to children, adults may speak differently to them than to others—talking down in tone or ideas. Listen attentively and speak normally. They want and need information but dislike long, unnecessary lectures. Talk with them about things of their interest and stimulate their thinking. Appreciate and enjoy your conversations with young children. They are refreshing and enlightening.

When children come up with a good suggestion, say: "That's a very good idea. Let's try it!" This indicates that you listened and that you value them and their ideas.

At times it will be important to reflect the children's feelings to them—not by putting ideas or words into their mouths, but by helping them put feelings into words. Griffin (1982) states: "Efforts to comfort, argue a child out of his feelings, point a moral, criticize his attitude, or make up with him if he is angry have no place in this situation and end confidences. The best response communicates both understanding of the feelings and acceptance of them."

PLAN SUCCESSFUL EXPERIENCES

Young children need to have successful experiences at least 80 percent of the time. Everyone like success, but it is especially important to young children. They are just beginning to unravel their world; knowledge and skills are limited. They need encouragement to try new activities and to repeat old ones.

Knowing young children are in the sensorimotor stage of development, adults can plan appropriate experiences with brief explanations, which will assist the children in their actions. Children sense the adult's confidence, which is important in attempting

Children need materials with experiential possibilities to stimulate their curiosity.

something new or difficult. Mastery brings about competence; competence brings about mastery.

Observe each child carefully; then give individual responsibilities and privileges accordingly. Express your honest appreciation and encouragement frequently.

If children only have experiences they can manage easily, they will tend to repeat those and ignore challenging situations. If experiences are always too difficult, they turn away from them. Failure is an unpleasant feeling. Watch the children. See what interests them and how they attack various problems. Help them develop problem-solving abilities by providing toys and materials with endless experiential possibilities to stimulate curiosity; plan time for their exploration. Plan to introduce them to some new experiences to widen their horizons, but make sure these experiences are based on needs, levels of development, and interests. Avoid pushing when children are not ready, but keep curiosity alive when they are ready.

SEND AND RECEIVE CLEAR MESSAGES

When you make a request of children, be sure they understand. If they act unsure then repeat, define, or clarify, but not in a belittling way.

At the center, Rojas would stand near the gate until no one was looking, then run into the parking lot. The teacher showed him how busy the lot was, how fast cars went past the gate, and how difficult it was to see him because of his height. Her words went unheeded, so she warned him that the next time he went out of the gate, she would call his mother to come and take him home. His chance came, and he slipped out of the gate and was gone again. Because of her warning and the presence of real danger, the teacher called his mother, who came and took Rojas home. The next day when he arrived at school, he went to each child and said, "Do you know what happens if you run out of the gate?" and then explained, "Your mother comes and takes you home." He had omitted the reasons, but he was clear on the result.

Requests made of children should be reasonable, clear, and simple. Too many com-

Sympathizing with and helping a child who is hurt sends good messages to all the children.

mands or something that seems unreasonable or complicated causes children to hesitate rather than respond. Think carefully what you are requesting, then be prepared to follow through, as in the case of Rojas. Your hesitancy or inability to follow through adds to the confusion of children.

Speak with confidence, and children respond in the same way. When you end a request with "Okay?", it means you are seeking their agreement to conform. Another familiar phrase is, "You need to . . ." Griffin (1982) defines this as: "the teacher will not change her mind and that she has a good reason for anything she requires." Just use your voice as a teaching tool and expect the children to carry the request through matter-of-factly.

While sending good messages to children, be alert in receiving their messages. Are their words saying what they mean? Are there nonverbal messages? Gestural language often conveys more clues than verbal language. Let children know you understand their feelings by defining them. "I know you are mad because you can't swing. It's Lisa's turn, but when she is through, it will be your turn. Let's find something else to do while you wait." "It really hurts when you fall on the cement. A cool cloth will help your knee feel better."

Be honest in your praise of children and their accomplishments. They will appreciate your sincerity as well as your time to talk and to listen.

REINFORCE ACTIONS YOU WANT REPEATED

It seems much easier to comment on negative than positive behavior. Communication with a particular child may be only to describe his "bad" behavior. To get any recognition at all, he repeats the negative behavior. Is it better to have negative attention than none at all?

Suppose a child picks up his toys and you say, "Thanks for picking up your toys. Your room looks so nice when your toys are on the shelf." By commenting, you are increasing the possibility of his repeating the behavior. But if you say nothing, he may think, "Why should I pick up my toys? Mother (or teacher) doesn't care. She'll just pick them up later." But, how do you show approval for something that has never occurred (the child has never picked up his toys)? You have to watch for the behavior, or even to "catch" the child doing the task. Even if he picked up one toy, say, "That truck looks good on the shelf. Now it won't get stepped on," or "You'll be able to find your truck the next time you want it because it is on the shelf." The next time he may pick up two toys. Again give honest praise. He will probably continue until all the toys are picked up if he gets more recognition for picking them up than for leaving them around. Notice when he is doing good things and acknowledge them.

If you look for good behavior to reinforce, you are likely to find it. If you look for the bad, you are also likely to find it. The more closely a reinforcement (a reward, an approval, a privilege) follows an action, the more likely that action is to be repeated. In fact, if you reinforce a child's action every time he exhibits good behavior, and then begin to taper off to reinforcing less frequently, he will continue to repeat that pattern looking for the approval. Reinforce him occasionally and he'll continue the behavior, wanting the approval but not knowing when it will come.

In reinforcing actions, identify what was appropriate. Rather than saying, "You did a good job," or "I like what you did," say, "You did a good job in sweeping the floor and putting the broom in the closet," or "Thanks for putting the puzzle together. Now the pieces won't get lost." Kind words (thank you, please, excuse me) are important to children and adults.

Two schools of thought deal with inappropriate behavior. One is to ignore the behavior, which will increase in intensity and frequency as the child tries to regain attention. Finding

Good behavior should be encouraged by positive reinforcement.

this behavior unrewarded, the child will discontinue it. The second thought comes from Hendrick (1980):

> While on the subject of reinforcement, I want to comment that I agree with Bettye Caldwell (1977) that it is not effective to "extinguish" aggressive behavior in young children by simply ignoring it. In my experience such behavior does not subside when ignored—apparently because children interpret this laissez-faire attitude as permission (Bandura and Walters 1963). Not only that, one cannot overlook the fact that there are inherent gratifications (pay-offs) in attacking other children; these range from simply seizing what is desired to enjoying hitting someone—if you're angry, hitting somebody feels pretty good. For these reasons, it is important to take more assertive action and stop undesirable behavior rather than let it slip past on the ground that it will go away if no attention is paid to it.

USE A POSITIVE APPROACH

When I tell my college students to be positive rather than negative, some of them rebel. A familiar comment is, "We've had nothing but negative comments all our lives. Now we are expected to adopt a different approach just like that!" It is difficult to see value in and to use an opposing technique at first. But through diligent effort, students see children respond more favorably when positive rather than negative statements are used. The effort pays off.

Occasionally, an adult should analyze how her verbalizations appear to others: "If the teacher thoughtfully considers the words that she uses in speaking to children, she may realize that many of them communicate disapproval, disappointment, criticism, impatience, and other negative attitudes, even though her general attitude toward children is a positive one" (Griffin 1982).

Always telling children what *cannot* be done creates defiance. Turn that around: when children are told what *can* be done, all sorts of possibilities arise, creating a different attitude and encouraging rather than discouraging participation.

Think how you would respond to the following sets of statements:

"Hammer your nail in that wood," or "Don't hammer the table."

"Hang your jacket in your locker," or "Don't throw your jacket on the floor."

"Pour just what you want to drink," or "Don't waste juice!"

If the first of each pair of statements seems too commanding, read them again. Realize that the child is being redirected, that is, given a possible response, an appropriate action. The second statement in each pair leaves him hanging: "Well, what *do* you expect me to do?" He may continue the behavior because no alternative is available.

Positive statements work well with anyone. When a person knows how he is expected to act, the chance of his acting that way is increased. Most people respond better when addressed in a positive way. They feel respected and appreciated. The world of preschoolers is so full of "don'ts," "quits," and "stops," that the children are left with the feeling, "Whatever I do, it is wrong." Using the positive approach opens new avenues for children and their behavior.

In her book, *Guiding Young Children,* Hildebrand (1980) gives some excellent advice. Pay particular attention to chapters 16 and 17 with ways to appreciate positive behavior and ways to cope with troublesome behavior. Chapter 19 lists qualities of a significant adult in the lives of children; Chapter 20 lists ways to involve parents in their children's schooling.

Do not be misled! At times negative statements may be more appropriate than positive ones. When danger is imminent, do or say whatever it takes to stop the action before an injury occurs. Then survey the situation and proceed with positive words and actions.

As a little "homework," keep track of your interaction with a child (or adult) for a

A child's self-respect is enhanced by positive statements.

few days. Mark down every time you respond to that person and see if your positive responses outweigh your negative ones.

PROVIDE GUIDELINES FOR BEHAVIOR

As an undergraduate student, I remember learning in early editions about Katherine Read's three "red flags" in discipline: the child is not allowed to hurt himself, hurt someone else, or destroy property. This good advice has been passed on to my students.

Limits should be considered very carefully and important ones upheld. Unimportant limits should be discarded. Nothing is magical about a set number of limits—have only those that are important for the health and safety of the children and teachers. Help children understand what the limits are and why they are necessary, while giving as much freedom as possible. As children grow and develop, alter the guidelines. Children's increasing reasoning power, skills, and experiences cause them to act more independently. Be consistent, but not inflexible, in enforcing the guidelines. Certain conditions call for altering guidelines, not breaking them or removing them.

If possible, let the children help establish rules. "What do you think we ought to do about . . ." "Can you think of something that would make that situation safer?" "Where should you ride the trike?" Allow for discussions. Establish reasons why or why not a certain thing occurs. Keep stating the reasons (from time to time) until the children understand the rationale. Reasons are important in their learning.

The best time to handle a situation is before it occurs. Watch for trouble spots. Talk about and set up limits before there is an accident. ("When we cross the street on our walk today, we will wait at the corner and all cross together.") With prior admonition, children will know what is to occur and as a consequence will behave acceptably.

Hymes (1981) reports there are classrooms with "sixteen million rules and regulations" and those with only the most general rules: "Be kind to other people," or "Take good care of property." He suggests a three-step method: "Step One, to build understandings: Establish some classroom rules and regulations. Step Two: Don't set up so many that the children gag on them. Step Three calls for great sensitivity. Your classroom rules and regulations must fit your boys and girls. You want reasonable requirements. If you ask more than youngsters can live up to, only evil results." Make sure the established guidelines are within the developmental abilities of the children.

Griffin (1982) captures the feeling of most teachers: "Setting limits is probably the most difficult part of her job for many a teacher. Children need to be prevented from doing some things, and they need to be required to do some things. But in either case, more important than just what limits are set or what is required is recognition of a child's feelings about limits and requirements." Children need to feel that limits are for their health and safety.

When children need to be disciplined for inappropriate behavior, make sure the "punishment fits the crime." Do not be like the old woman in the shoe, who didn't know what to do with all her children, so first she fed them (a common reinforcer) and then she punished them all in the same manner. Were they bad for being children or for being too numerous? Did they misbehave? Will their punishment prevent misbehavior (whatever it was) from happening again? What did they learn from the episode?

In his wisdom and experience, White (1975) recommends child-rearing practices. In his book, *The First Three Years of Life,* he also gives four child-rearing practices he does not recommend: (1) overemphasis on intellectual growth, (2) expensive educational toys, (3) unsupervised play groups, and (4) overindulgence. These items should be given serious consideration.

Whenever a child has been removed from a situation or activity, some legitimate way of returning is extremely important; he must decide when he is ready, and he must have another chance to participate where he misbehaved. Without these two conditions, how can he build self-control?

SHOW RESPECT FOR CHILDREN

When an adult shows respect for children, the children increase in feelings of competence and value, while also improving relationships with peers. Hymes says it is important for children to "develop good feelings about themselves, about their peers and the other humans around them, about the world of reality in which they live" (1981).

Children who are totally immersed in activities that need to be prematurely terminated appreciate a friendly notice. Lee was used to a few minutes' warning before lunch, but he finished his activity early one day. He called, "Mother, aren't you going to tell me it's a few minutes before lunch?" She replied, "Not quite yet." Lee stood silently for several minutes until Mother's warning. Happily, he washed his hands and went to the table.

Another way to show respect for children involves their personal belongings. Encourage them to share as good social etiquette, but never force them. If a child has a personal possession that he doesn't want to share, say to the other child (or children), "This is very special to him. He wants to keep it now, so we'll look for something for you." The child is not made to feel guilty because he does not share; rather, he feels that his rights are respected. Remember that sharing *follows* possessing! At school the problem of sharing may arise infrequently because all the toys belong to everyone; however, one child may be using a particular toy when another wants it. Be fair when handling disagreements between two children. When possible, allow them to settle their own differences. Allow each child to maintain his dignity; avoid forcing guilt feelings upon him.

Children should also be respected for the individuals they are, for what they can do, and for just being themselves. Help them build a good self-image by pointing out assets. "You are able to ride the bike so well." "You have the prettiest blue eyes." "My, but you are strong to help move the table." Show in words and actions that you value them. Avoid comparing abilities, characteristics, activities, and behavior with those of other children. Such comparisons breed dislike and unhappiness.

GUIDE THROUGH LOVE INSTEAD OF FEAR OR GUILT

Sometimes inappropriate behavior must be rebuked. In such a circumstance, make sure the children are aware of the seriousness of the offense. Then let them know you reprimand only their action, that you still love and care for them.

When appropriate, ask them to define the situation. "Do you know why you can't do this?" If they are inaccurate or unclear, explain: "Because it is very dangerous, and you might get hurt (or whatever is the case). I love you, and I would feel very sad if something happened to you." Or, "I care enough about you to stop you when you are doing something that could hurt you or someone else."

Trying to rule through fear or guilt is a growth-stunting procedure. Children never learn to make valid decisions or see true issues. Instead, build a loving and trusting relationship so that you both are able to survive the inevitably rough times when they occur.

BE A GOOD MODEL

The mere fact that we are moving, speaking beings means that we are providing a model for someone. Imitations of good qualities are flattering. But imitations of bad qualities are embarrassing. As parents or teachers we see behavior reflected in the words and actions of children (a comment, a gesture). Sometimes we recognize these behaviors as our own; sometimes, oblivious, we wonder where they could have seen or heard such a thing!

If we have a happy attitude, the children around us are likely to have the same attitude. If we are harsh and critical, so will the children be. Be sure your words and actions say the same thing. If you tell your child to get ready for supper, you get ready, too. If you continue to sit and read the paper while you are telling him to hurry, he becomes confused. If he sits (as you are doing), do not get angry with him for imitating you. He usually follows your action more readily than your words. When your actions and words do not support each other, you are sending a double message.

Keep calm. Be nurturing. Give valid reasons for what you request from the children. An adult who is authoritarian, permissive, or inconsistent does not help the children to form good behavior patterns. If you are unappreciative of the way the children are acting at home or in the classroom, try to analyze what the problem may be. The best way to change someone else's behavior is to change your own; maybe you are expecting too much or not enough; maybe you aren't sure what to expect! Maybe you act defensively, and so do those around you. Try to be more understanding and patient; look for the other person's point of view. Pleasant understanding reduces tension. Evaluate carefully and then make specific plans for improvement.

BE ON GUARD FOR WARNING SIGNALS

When immediate action is called for (a child is about to injure someone or is destroying property), step in unhesitatingly and stop the behavior. If verbal means deter the action, fine ("Put that shovel down," or "Don't hit him with the shovel!"). If that doesn't stop the action, physical means may be necessary ("I'll have to hold onto your arm so you won't hit him with the shovel"). Then discuss the situation with those involved. "When he stepped on your road, it made you want to hit him; but when you hit him, he doesn't know what you want. Tell him with words." Let the child know that you understand his behavior but that there are other, more positive ways of expressing his feelings. Children will not learn the value of property if they are allowed to destroy it. They will not build good interpersonal relationships if they are allowed to harm another individual. Being inquisitive is one thing, but deliberate destruction or injury must not be tolerated.

Being observant can reduce or prevent misbehavior. Children usually give some signals. You can see the tension building in the block area or other places. Children who cannot see at group time will begin subtle physical or verbal actions. Children who need to use the toilet begin to wiggle. The signs are there—learn how to read and respond to them before a problem arises.

A number of authors list causes of misbehavior. Hymes (1952, 1981) says they are: (1) stage of growth, (2) unmet needs, (3) present environment, and (4) not knowing it is inappropriate. According to Dreikurs and Cassel (1972), a child misbehaves (1) to gain attention, (2) to display power, (3) to gain revenge, and (4) to express inadequacy and passivity, that is, to give up. Baruth and Eckstein (1978) and Althouse (1981) add support to Dreikurs and Cassel. To be sure, children misbehave for different reasons. Tommy, a 3-year-old, was brought to a center by his mother. He was new and uncomfortable. As they approached the door, he began to draw back, cry, and hit his mother. She could not understand why he acted this way, but because she was in a hurry, she pushed him in the door. His feet stood firm, and he leaned back against her with all his strength. She tried reasoning, threatening, and then bribing. Still he refused. Even the teacher's invitation was not accepted. Finally the mother bribed him with gum (and who knows what else), and he reluctantly and stubbornly entered the room. He went from toy to toy, kicking or throwing each one. He pushed the other children and took their toys. The teacher's first inclination was to tell him that if he was unable to act friendly, he would not be able to come to the center. That was just what he wanted! Instead, she tried to involve him in interesting activities, one after another. He momentarily became involved—and then remembered to throw the toys and hit the children. It took the entire morning, under the teacher's watchful eye, to help him settle in. His best involvement was in large-muscle, vigorous activity where he could legitimately "let it out."

Osborn and Osborn (1977) discuss three modes of child discipline. The first describes children surrounded by a continuous wall of no's; they cannot break down the wall. Adults make decisions for them, and the children feel that they are bad and unsuccessful. In the second mode, they are allowed to move freely in any direction with no walls or no's. The children become frustrated, insecure, and sometimes hostile. The first mode gives no freedom; the second gives only freedom. The third mode has low walls with doors that can be opened to go in or out. Children are aware of limitations but are free to make choices within the avenues open to them: this is "freedom with control." Through this last mode, children gain the self-control so important in getting along in society.

Adults who approach child guidance through knowledge of child development make the following sound basic assumptions:

1. The development of internal control (self-discipline) is more productive than reliance upon extrinsic control.
2. The causes of or purposes for undesirable behavior should be sought.
3. Knowledge of several guidance approaches or strategies is more effective than reliance on one strategy.
4. "Positive reinforcement is more effective than negative reinforcement" (Hipple 1978).

As teachers and parents, we need to practice our guidance techniques, not at the expense of the children, but in an effort to enhance their self-image and internal control. When misbehavior persists and we have exhausted all avenues, Hendrick (1980) summarizes five steps for helping children learn self-control: (1) warn them, (2) remove them from the activity while keeping them with the teacher, (3) discuss feelings and rules, (4) wait for them to make the decision to return to the activity, and (5) help them return and be more successful. Help them practice these steps until they can control themselves—they'll be happier when they are socially successful, and so will you.

AVOID POWER STRUGGLES

Adults may make a demand or a request of children. When the children do not comply, the adults become angry. They ask or tell the children again. If this still is unsuccessful, adults become defensive, especially if they are questioned or ignored. Do children have the right to question adults? When they are told to do something, they should obey! Or should they? Are the requests reasonable? Do the children understand the nature of the requests? What do adult actions mean to children? Are children being deliberately disobedient? If both adults and children analyze the situation, if adults give rationale for requests, if children verbalize noncompliance, the situation is resolvable. If, on the other hand, each decides stubbornly to win, a power struggle results, and neither wins.

Gordon (1970) suggests a "no-lose" method of resolving conflicts through the following steps of negotiation: (1) identifying and defining the conflict, (2) generating possible alternative solutions, (3) evaluating the alternatives, (4) deciding on the best acceptable solution, and (5) following up to evaluate its success. The adult becomes an active listener, and the children practice problem-solving. This method is superior to having an adult winner who uses authority, power, superior knowledge, and experience or a child who wins because the adult does not want to lose his love, misunderstands about permissiveness, or is too tired or uninterested in negotiating. One winner means one loser, and this brings about resentment, lowered self-image, and breakdown in communication.

OFFER LEGITIMATE CHOICES AND ACCEPT DECISIONS

Choice-making should be a practice developed from early childhood. Choices should be within ability, legitimate, and character building.

Some interesting research from the Gesell Institute of Child Development suggests that ease or difficulty of choice-making is related to age. The average child of 3, 5, 7, or 10 has an easier time deciding between two alternatives because at these ages he is under less "inner stress and strain" than at other ages. He is therefore able to accept choices without too much emotional conflict. Children do not make good decisions at any age when they are ill, fatigued, bombarded, or pressured. Are adults any different?

If a child has a legitimate choice, let him practice decision-making. Bearing in mind that you must be prepared to accept his decision, be careful to form appropriate choices. "You can wear your blue shirt or your green one." "You can play inside or outside." "You can either hear one more story or play a short game before bedtime." If he has no choice, you make a simple outright statement about what is to occur. "Put on your blue shirt." "You will have to stay inside." "It is time for bed now." To offer a child a choice ("Do you want to drink your milk?") and then refuse to accept his answer ("Well, that's too bad; you have to, anyway") increases the negative aspect of his world. Also remember that when a question is worded in such a way that either yes or no can be the answer, the child is most likely to answer in the negative, even if he really wants it to be positive.

Sometimes adults think they are democratic in offering choices to children, when in reality they are weighting the questions in their favor. "Do you want to watch TV, or do you want to help me so we can go and get a treat?" "Do you want to pick up your toys or go to your room?"

If children are going to be able to make good decisions, they need to develop a sound basis upon which to make choices. They need legitimate choices for practice. They also need to be willing and able to handle the consequences of their choices.

ENCOURAGE INDEPENDENCE

Preschool children like to do things themselves. Often, in the interest of time or energy, the parent or teacher assists the children or actually does the task rather than letting children try their skills or problem-solving abilities. Admittedly, some tasks are too difficult for preschoolers to attempt. In such instances, the adult can offer assistance and encouragement. If the task is one the children can handle, let them. It might take longer, but the results are worth the patience.

Encouragement is essential in building independence. "Try, and if you need help, I'll help you" is often enough incentive to get the children started. Then remain nearby. If assistance is needed, help—either through verbal or physical means. Upon completion, give some honest praise: "You did that so well," or "I'm glad you tried. I think you will be able to do it by yourself next time."

Seek long-range goals for children—development of good work habits, initiative, self-direction, and the ability to tackle a job.

PROVIDE ACCEPTABLE AVENUES FOR RELEASE OF FEELINGS

Frustration and anger come easily to preschoolers. They need to express these feelings in such a way that they feel better—not worse. If they are hitting, tell them to hit the clay, the stuffed animal, the punching bag, the pillow, or other suitable objects; but they cannot hit the baby, the television set, or people. Large-muscle activities, such as painting with big strokes, moving to music, riding a stick horse, throwing a ball, or finger painting, are often suitable outlets. At any rate, look for activities that help each child to release his feelings.

The younger the child, the more likely he is to use physical rather than verbal releases. With encouragement, experience, and practice, he will learn acceptable verbal ways of releasing and defining feelings.

HELP CHILDREN LEARN THROUGH PARTICIPATION

Children can learn through observation or lecture, but the most efficient way is through participation. Instead of always telling them, provide opportunities to "experience." Allow plenty of time and materials for exploration.

When asked to perform a task, let children do it their way, unless it is dangerous or harmful. Offer suggestions only if the children need them. With freedom to try ideas, children may find some better ways to do tasks.

ONE FINAL NOTE

As you will recall from Chapter 1, various teaching methods and their effects upon children have been investigated. Repeatedly, research shows that the single most important factor in children's learning is the effectiveness of the teacher. Similarly, in counseling, regardless of the method employed, the counselor makes the difference in the therapy. As adults involved with young children, you are both teachers and counselors. You have the responsibility of seeing that your attitudes and personal attributes are such that they will be more instrumental in helping children reach their potential than if your lives had not crossed theirs.

APPLICATION OF PRINCIPLES

1. Develop good listening skills by not interrupting others when they are talking, by using eye-to-eye contact and being on the speaker's eye level, and by concentrating on the spoken words.
2. Make a chart listing each child in your group. Observe the behavior of each child, and record it on the chart. Note which children need help in social situations. List how you can help each child to control his own behavior.
3. Ask for a set of guidelines or rules for your center. Discuss them with other staff members. Make sure you know and understand what is expected of staff, children, and parents. If you have suggestions or questions, discuss them with your supervisor, teacher, or employer.
4. Carry a piece of paper and a pencil. Note the situation and tally the number of times you or another staff member uses a negative approach ("no, don't, can't, stop") inappropriately. Study your findings. Make an effort to use positive approaches in dealing with children and adults.
5. Practice choice-offering. Is there really a choice? How do you follow through when you have offered an inappropriate choice?
6. If you have a child or parent who needs or wants professional help, where would you refer them in your community? Make a list of agencies in your community that counsel on mental, social, emotional, and physical problems.

References

Althouse, R. *The Young Child: Learning With Understanding.* New York: Teachers College Press, Columbia University, 1981.

Baruth, L. G., and D. G. Eckstein. *The ABC's of Classroom Discipline.* Dubuque, Iowa: Kendall/Hunt, 1978.

Dreikurs, R., and P. Cassel. *Discipline Without Tears.* 2d ed. New York: Hawthorne Books, 1972.

Gordon, Ira. *Parent Effectiveness Training.* New York: Wyden, 1970.

Griffin, Elinor F. *Island of Childhood.* New York: Teachers College Press, Columbia University, 1982.

Hendrick, Joanne. *The Whole Child: New Trends in Early Education.* 2d ed. St. Louis: C. V. Mosby, 1980.

Hildebrand, Verna. *Guiding Young Children.* 2d ed. New York: Macmillan, 1980.

Hipple, Marjorie. "Classroom Discipline Problems? Fifteen Humane Solutions." Childhood Education 54(February 1978): 183–187.

Hymes, James L., Jr. *Understanding Your Child.* Englewood Cliffs, N.J.: Prentice-Hall, 1952.

______. *Teaching the Child Under Six.* 3d ed. Columbus, Ohio: Charles E. Merrill, 1981.

Osborn, D. Keith. "Permissiveness Re-Examined." *Childhood Education* 33(January 1957): 214–217.

Osborn, D. Keith, and J. D. Osborn. *Discipline and Classroom Management.* Athens: University of Georgia, Early Childhood Learning Center, 1977.

Read, Katherine H., and June Patterson. *The Nursery School and Kindergarten.* New York: Holt, Rinehart & Winston, 1980.

Taylor, Barbara J. *Dear Mom and Dad—Parents and the Preschooler.* Provo, Utah: Brigham Young University Press, 1978.

White, Burton L. *The First Three Years of Life.* Englewood Cliffs, N.J.: Prentice-Hall, 1975.

Appendix A
Characteristics of Young Children

THE 2-YEAR-OLD

With People

1. Self
   Imitates activities of others.
   Is domineering; self-assertive; difficult to handle.
   Has tantrums.
   Wants to be independent.
   Is self-involved, curious, full of energy, explorative.
2. Family
   Is dependent and passive in relation to adults, but begins to resist adult influence while striving for independence.
   Depends on family to provide safe, loving environment.
3. Others
   Watches other children; begins parallel play (does own thing near another child).

Development

1. Physical
   Is developing eye-hand coordination.
   Stays with an activity for a period of time, if interested.
   Uses large strokes when painting or drawing. Scribbles randomly, then somewhat organized up-down or circular strokes.
   Stabilizes toilet training but has "accidents."
   Walks, runs, sits in chair without support, climbs stairs (two feet on each stair), builds with blocks.
   Feeds self but is still somewhat messy.
   Learning to dress self but is great at undressing self.
2. Emotional and Social
   Develops feelings of jealousy (continues to age 6).
   May develop fears (real or imagined).
   Is negative: a combination of curiosity, restrictions, and emerging sense of independence.
   Plays alone or may like to be near others even if not playing with them.
   Fairly easily distracted.

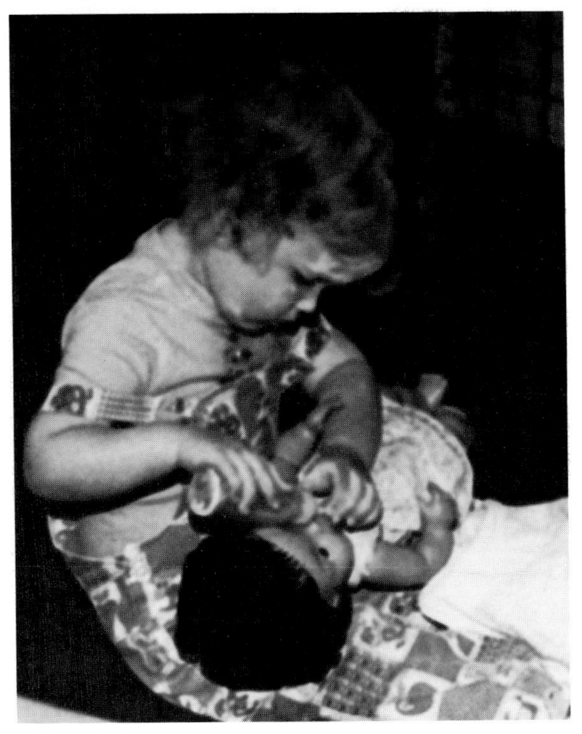

Younger children play alone or parallel to another child.

3. Intellectual and Language
   Responds to own name.
   Follows simple requests.
   Learns mainly through five senses and "doing."
   Learns language rapidly. Understands more than speaks; responds to commands; knows and uses names of people and objects.
   Speaks in short sentences or uses single words to express entire statement or question (early in year).
   Enjoys short, simple, repetitive stories, especially with something he can do, such as feeling texture or poking finger in hole.
4. Moral
   Refuses to share toys.
   Ignores some requests.

THE 3-YEAR-OLD

With People

1. Self
   Still plays alone most of the time.
   Is egocentric (mostly involved with own self).
   Is age of "doing."
2. Family
   Has "we" feeling with mother; is independent of her occasionally.
   Likes to relive babyhood.
   Does small chores about the house.

3. Others
   Begins to accept suggestions.
   Tends to establish social contacts with adults; imitates adult behavior.
   Begins friendships with peers, with discrimination against others in group.
   Friendships are of short duration.

Development

1. Physical
   Coordination is not well developed; small-muscle activities such as cutting, tying, coloring in predrawn lines are difficult. "Draws" crudely. Do not stress activity if child is not ready.
   Tapers off in growth with accompanying decrease in food intake; feeds self (slowly) and dawdles in food.
   Runs, jumps, hops on one foot, climbs stairs (alternating feet).
   Dresses and undresses self somewhat, but still wants or asks for help.
   Walks on balance beam, rides a tricycle.
   Stands on one foot for a short time.
   Enjoys participating in and listening to music.
   Is a great "doer."
2. Emotional and Social
   Gains security in "routines" (same people, same activities, same times).
   May have a short attention span, if uninterested.
   Begins to test limits set by others.
   Learning to make choice between two alternatives.
   Plays with modeling clay, blocks, art materials.
   Likes to dramatize.
   Enjoys finger plays, dramatized songs, moving around and other activities.
3. Intellectual and Language
   Understands language and follows directions more accurately.
   Learns rote counting and some letters.
   Enjoys talking and asks lots of questions; experiments with new words and sounds.
   Enjoys short and simple stories.
   Is able to learn some foreign words.
   Differentiates only slightly between truth and make-believe (reality and fantasy).
4. Moral
   Depends on family to provide sex role models, esteem, sense of security, direction for physical safety, family values and goals, control of aggression.

THE 4-YEAR-OLD

With People

1. Self
   Is assertive, boastful.
   Shows pride in achievement.
   Is energetic to point of adult exhaustion.
   Wants to find out things.
   Is becoming more independent.
2. Family
   Expresses caring behavior toward others; beginning of strong feelings toward family and home.
   Learns family expectations.

3. Others
   Has definite preference for peer mates.
   Plays cooperatively with peers; may need fresh ideas.
   May have preconceived ideas of what or with whom to play.
   Challenges adults by asking questions, needing more supervision, and testing limits.
   Develops qualities of leadership.
   May have an imaginary companion (20 to 50 percent do). (Stone and Church 1973, p. 280)

Development

1. Physical
   Has more highly developed motor skills (can throw a ball, is learning to catch a ball).
   Is highly competitive.
   Runs, jumps, climbs with more confidence; uses eating utensils easily; walks on balance beam with ease.
   Dresses independently when given manageable clothing (zippers, large buttons, elastic waistbands).
   Large- and small-muscle coordination is increasing.
   Has increased physical energy.
   Small muscles are better developed than formerly; likes to print capital letters; uses modeling clay; makes cookies.
2. Emotional and Social
   Tries to gain attention; shows off.
   When disappointed, expresses displeasure loudly or through aggression; can tolerate some frustration.

The 4-year-old likes to play with another child.

May be more fearful now than at earlier age (may fear strange circumstances, aloneness, darkness).
Likes to play with other children in a small group or with another child.
Begins cooperative play; boys and girls play together.
Begins to develop a sense of humor (riddles, jokes, nonsense words).

3. Intellectual and Language
   Increases in language; likes to talk; asks why and how questions and really listens to answers.
   May have an imaginary playmate, either human or animal.
   Visually discriminates some shapes and colors.
   Shows interest in books and printed word. Likes some stories over and over again.
   Learns to take directions and follow rules; is a tattletale.
   Lives in the here-and-now (past and future are somewhat unclear to him).
4. Moral
   Is learning to distinguish between right and wrong.
   Is learning to separate from parents and function independently.

THE 5-YEAR-OLD

With People

1. Self
   Seeks approval; avoids disapproval of adults.
   Is self-assured and conforming.
   Is generally dependable.
2. Family
   Feels rather secure in the family.
   Receives sex role expectancies from parents.
3. Others
   Shows preference for children of his own age and sex.
   Has protective mothering attitude toward younger siblings.
   Enjoys sustained cooperative play.
   Faces new demands upon entering school; admires teacher; is eager to learn.
   May have an imaginary companion.

Development

1. Physical
   Handles self well in bathroom routines.
   Eats well, handles utensils well.
   Has good body control; can throw and catch a ball, climb, jump, skip with good coordination.
   Coordinates movements to music.
   Dresses self; can tie shoes.
   Jumps rope, walks in a straight line, rides a two-wheel bike. Physical skills are important with peers.
   Can draw some simple geometric figures and shapes.
   Has better small-muscle and eye-hand coordination; cuts and pastes but has less difficulty with predrawn lines when cutting or coloring.
2. Emotional and Social
   Tends to be obedient; cooperative; desires to please.
   Friendly, begins to be empathetic.
   Spends more time on projects (painting, building).
   Brags about new accomplishments and skills.

Tends to have frequent but short-lived quarrels.
Expresses feelings freely, often in extreme form (fear, joy, affection, anger, shyness, jealousy).
Likes projects; prefers small group; can play alone; plays selectively.

3. Intellectual and Language
Speaks in full sentences, using clauses and idioms.
Still may have trouble pronouncing a few sounds or letter combinations correctly.
Discriminates beginning sounds, phonic differences and similarities; understands principle of rhyming; enjoys playing with words; asks serious questions and wants honest answers.
Differentiates some between truth and make-believe (reality and fantasy).
Relates past and present events.
Understands more language than is able to use.
May use language aggressively.
Loves stories.
Can remember sequences of numbers, letters, and more than two ideas.
Is an eager learner.
4. Moral
Shares and takes turns.
Is cooperative in cleanup routines if approached in cooperative way.
Is able to give more thought to judgments and decisions.
Is relatively truthful.

References

Association for Supervision and Curriculum Development. "Developmental Characteristics in Children and Youth." 1975. (Reprinted inside cover of Leeper et al., 1979.)
Gesell, Arnold, and Frances Ilg. *Child Development.* New York: 1949.
Gordon, Ira J. *Baby Learning Through Baby Play.* New York: St. Martin's Press, 1970.
Hurlock, Elizabeth B. *Child Development.* New York: McGraw-Hill, 1964.
Maxim, George. *The Very Young.* Belmont, Calif.: Wadsworth Publishing, 1980, p. 116.
O'Brien, Marion, Jan Porterfield, Emily Herbert-Jackson, and Todd R. Risley. *The Toddler Center: A Practical Guide to Day Care for One- and Two-Year-Olds.* Baltimore: University Park Press, 1979.
Rowen, Betty, Joan Byrne, and Lois Winter. *The Learning Match.* Englewood Cliffs, N.J.: Prentice-Hall, 1980, chap. 2.
Stone, L. Joseph, and Joseph Church. *Childhood and Adolescence.* 3d ed. New York: Random House, 1973.
Stott, L. H. *The Longitudinal Study of Individual Development.* Detroit: Merrill-Palmer School, 1955.
"Teaching: No Greater Calling." Salt Lake City: The Church of Jesus Christ of Latter-day Saints, 1978.
White, Burton L. *The First Three Years of Life.* Englewood Cliffs, N.J.: Prentice-Hall, 1975.

Appendix B
Suggested Curriculum Topics

- Care of animals
- Names of young and adult animals
- Names of male and female animals
- Where and how animals live
- How animals help people
- Coverings (shell, fur, feathers)
- Products obtained from animals
- Good pets
- Wild animals
- Circus animals
- Protection (claws, camouflage, hibernation)
- Characteristics of animals

■ Birds
- Names of birds
- Sounds made by birds
- Where birds live
- How birds feed their young
- How birds help people (beauty, sound, eating insects)
- Kinds of nests
- Kinds of eggs birds lay (color, size)
- Characteristics of birds
- Habits of birds (nesting, migration)

■ Categories
- Grouping (vehicles, food, animals, birds, clothing, furniture, persons, buildings, toys, plants, containers, appliances, things to write with, and building, garden, or household tools)
- Multiple classification (things that can be classed in more than one category)
- Ways to help discriminate between categories (senses, experiences)
- Why categories are useful and helpful

■ The Children
- Learning one's own name and worth
- Learning names of other children, teachers, nurse, others
- Where to hang clothing

- Self-confidence
- Good self-image
- Parts of the body
- Complying with requests
- Self-mastery and control

■ Clothing
- Names of garments
- Seasons for wearing different types of clothing
- Sequence for putting on clothing
- Types of fabrics (cotton, wool, leather, plastic)
- Clothing for different occasions (play, party, sleeping)
- Different types of fasteners on clothing (zippers, buttons, snaps)
- Uses of certain pieces of clothing (shoes, hats)
- Color or patterning in clothing (printed, woven)
- Learning to dress and undress dolls

■ Color
- Names of the primary and secondary colors
- How various colors are made
- Shades of same color
- How various colors make you feel
- Uses of colors (red for danger)
- Colors of specific objects (fruits, vehicles, animals)
- How colors are made and actually making some (berries, leaves)
- Tie-dyeing experience

■ Communication
- Physical and verbal communication
- Learning about different languages
- Different forms of communication (radio, television, newspaper, books, telephone)
- Proper names of people, places, and things so that we understand meanings
- How some animals help carry messages (dogs, pigeons)
- Learning to recognize objects from verbal descriptions only
- Telling something interesting about self or activity
- Learning to follow simple directions

■ The Community
- Locations within the community
- Kinds of buildings, industries, parks, highways
- Recognizing community landmarks
- Different communities

■ Community Helpers
- Fireman, policeman, postman, doctor, nurse, dentist, baker, milkman, grocer, merchant, miner, farmer, fisherman (places of work, activities, services)
- How community helpers work together
- Recognizing community helpers by uniforms or clothing

■ Comparatives
- Learning names and relationships by comparing two things (biggest—smallest, hottest—coldest, heaviest—lightest; bigger—smaller, fatter—skinnier, taller—shorter; too loud—too soft, too long—too short, too fat—too skinny)
- Learning names and relationships by comparing more than two things (big, bigger, biggest; short, shorter, shortest; long, longer, longest)
- Learning that one object can be big when compared to some things and small when compared to others

- The concept of "middle"
- Ordinal (first, second, third) and cardinal (1, 2, 3) numbers
- Learning opposites through comparisons (soft, rough)

■ Days of the Week
- Names of the days of the week
- Why days have special names
- Sequence of the days
- Activities for certain days (e.g., Saturday or Sunday)
- Learning about the calendar (days, weeks, months)

■ Environment
- Characteristics of the community (lake, mountains)
- What "pollution" is and how to help prevent it
- Natural resources (coal, gas, oil)
- Conservation of natural resources (forests, water)
- Recycling (water, paper, metal)
- How to respect public property

■ Families
- Learning what a family is
- Learning the immediate family (mother, father, sister, brother, baby)
- Learning the extended family (aunts, uncles, cousins, grandparents)
- What families do together
- Different jobs and responsibilities of family members
- Friends and their names
- Learning about people (physical characteristics, abilities, likes, and so on)
- How to entertain guests
- How to get along with family members
- Good social techniques

■ Food (pages 148–150 and Chapter 10)
- Names of various foods
- Tasting various foods
- Learning about taste (sweet, sour, salty, bitter)
- Preparing food in a variety of ways
- Plant parts used as food (roots, stalk, flower)
- Things that look alike but taste different (salt, sugar, soda)
- Food consumed by animals
- Preparing for and participating in lunch or snack
- Good diet (basic four)
- Where food products come from (animals, farms and gardens, factories)
- Ways of preparing food (raw, boiled, baked)
- Learning when food is green, ripe, and overripe
- Things *not* to be eaten (poisons, medicines)

■ Growing Things (pages 146–148)
- Names of common flowers and plants
- How to care for plants
- Different things that plants grow from (bulb, seed, start)
- Parts of the plant (root, stalk, vine, leaf, flower)
- Parts of plants that are edible (root—carrot, turnip; head—lettuce, cabbage; stalk—celery)
- Sizes and kinds of seeds
- Length of growing time (e.g., rapid for grass and beans; more slowly for corn and squash)

- Fruits grown on trees
- Things needed for growth (sunlight, water, warmth)
- Food that grows above and below the ground
- Growing things that are not edible
- Storing fruit and vegetables
- Why food is washed or cleaned before eating
- Growing things for beauty (shrubs, trees, flowers) and consumption (fruit, vegetables)

■ Health and Cleanliness
- How to clean various body parts (hair, nails, skin, teeth)
- Reasons for keeping clean and healthy
- How to keep healthy (exercise, rest, clothing)
- Proper diet
- Poisonous plants
- Professional people who help us

■ Holidays (Chapter 9)
- Names of holidays
- Activities unique to holidays
- Importance of holidays to children (birthdays, Christmas, Valentine's Day)
- Which holidays come during which seasons
- Family customs for different holidays
- National, religious, cultural, and personal holidays of self and others
- Preparing for and participating in child-centered holiday activities

■ Homes
- Where each child lives
- What a house looks like (inside and out)
- Different types of homes in the community
- Care of homes (inside and out)
- Household equipment and appliances (brushes, mixers, and so on)
- Repair and building tools
- Homes in other countries or areas
- Furnishing rooms
- Building materials
- Visiting a home or apartment
- Performing tasks

■ Identification
- Matching animals (mother and young)
- Categorizing what is sold in specific type of store
- Selecting type of store for a certain item
- Things that belong together (fork and spoon, hat and coat, shoe and sock)
- How to recognize something by one or more of the senses
- How to group objects with similar characteristics (color, material, shape)
- How to discriminate between objects

■ Machines
- Machines for the home or for industry: how they work and what their function is
- Learning to operate machines (mixer, eggbeater, gears)
- How machines make work easier

■ Materials
- Names of different building materials (brick, wood, fiberglass, cement, steel, cinder blocks)
- Names and uses of materials (metal, glass, plaster, paper, cardboard, cloth fabrics, leather, rubber, foil)
- Fabrics (waterproof, resilient, inexpensive)

The curriculum includes learning about different building materials.

- Mathematics (Chapter 11)
  - How to count using familiar things (children, blocks, crackers, clapping)
  - Counting similar and dissimilar objects
  - Recognizing written symbols
  - Learning about parts (fractions) of the whole (e.g., wheel is part of a wagon)
  - Exploring with unit blocks (different shapes and numbers to make other shapes)
  - Making things equal
  - Learning to tell different things by their number (phone, sport participant, house, time)
  - Buying by weight, size, amount
  - Mathematical terms (more—less, how many)
- Music (Chapter 5)
  - Singing songs
  - Playing and listening to records and tapes

- Names and uses of musical instruments
- Ways of making sounds
- Classes of instruments (wind, percussion, string)
- Different ways music makes us feel
- Learning to participate with music
- Discovering rhythm in everyday life (clocks, water dripping, walking)
- Observing different instruments being played
- Imitating music or movement in nature (trees, animals, water)

■ Objects
- Names of parts of an object (e.g., a pencil has a point, lead, shaft, eraser)
- Different materials used to make same or different objects
- Specific uses of different objects (spoon, screwdriver, belt)
- Identifying objects through one or more of the senses
- Naming several objects used for the same purpose (e.g., those that hold water, improve surroundings)

■ Opposites
- Learning opposites (big—little, fat—skinny, loud—soft, hot—cold, long—short, fast—slow, wet—dry, smooth—rough, tall—short, dark—light)
- Combining opposites (big, rough, and dark)
- Discrimination (an object may be big compared to some things and small compared to others)

■ Pattern
- Learning about different patterns (striped, flowered, polka dot, plaid, plain, checked)
- Learning if the pattern is woven into fabric or printed
- Creating own patterns using art materials
- How patterns (shapes) are combined in environment

■ Piagetian Concepts
- Conservation of volume or substance
- Reversibility (water to ice to water)
- Weight of objects (in hand or scale)
- How objects can be grouped in variety of ways (colors, shape, size, material)
- Discovering that learning is enhanced through the senses and movement (sensorimotor)

■ Plurals
- Regular plurals (formed by adding s)
- Irregular plurals (foot—feet, child—children, man—men, tooth—teeth, mouse—mice, sheep—sheep)
- Terms are used for more than one of an object (many, few, group, some)
- When one object is called a "pair" (scissors, glasses, pants)

■ Prepositions
- Names and relationship of various prepositions (in, on, over, under, next to, in front of, in back of, inside, outside, between)
- How to carry out simple commands
- Using one's body in space to learn prepositions (obstacle course)

■ The Preschool
- Labels for materials and objects in the room
- Storage place for toys
- Place for certain activities
- Learning about adults and children
- Limits, responsibilities, and privileges
- Learning routine

- Safety
  - Times and places to be careful (roads, around water)
  - How to prevent accidents
  - Care of injuries
  - Professional people who help us
  - Safety at school and home
  - Reasons for limits under different circumstances
  - Using tools and materials
- Science (Chapter 6)
  - Magnets
  - Magnifying glasses
  - How to measure
  - Heat and how it changes various things
  - Light and prisms
  - Heavy and light objects
  - Liquids, solids, and gases
  - Physical science
  - Social science
  - Producing and preparing food
  - Working with levers
  - Biological science
  - Discovering things about community, nation, and universe
  - How to get along with others
- Seasons
  - Naming the seasons
  - Characteristics of each season
  - What people do during different seasons
  - What people wear during different seasons
  - How seasons affect family, animals, and plants
  - Identifying different seasons from pictures
- Shapes
  - Names of shapes (square, circle, triangle, rectangle, oval, diamond, trapezoid)
  - Uses of different shapes
  - Looking for various shapes in the room
  - Discussing shapes in our daily lives
  - Why certain things are the shapes they are (e.g., wheel)
  - How various shapes are formed (two semicircles make a circle, two triangles a trapezoid)
  - How similar objects (leaves, flowers) are different shapes
  - Making an original design using variety of shapes (could be art project or manipulative experience, for example)
  - Characteristics of various shapes (triangle has three corners, lines in a square are same length)
- Sound (page 145, chapters 5 and 6)
  - Listening for sounds in everyday life
  - Distinguishing things by sound only
  - Differences in sound (high or low, loud or soft)
  - Different ways of making sounds
  - Making sounds of animals
  - Making sounds of transportation vehicles
  - Making sounds that express different emotions
  - Saying rhyming words

- Temperature
  - Terms used with heat (hot—warm, cold—cool, hot—cold)
  - Temperature and the seasons
  - Temperature and heat in cooking
  - How a thermometer registers heat or cold
- Time
  - Learning about the present, past, and future (may be difficult to grasp)
  - Sequence (before and after)
  - Ways to tell time (clock, sun, sundial)
  - Things to do in daylight and dark
- Transportation
  - Names of kinds of transportation (boat, airplane, bus, train, automobile)
  - Ways transportation works
  - What different transports carry and how it feels to ride in each
  - Learning about vehicles
  - Wheels and how they work
  - Transportation in air (airplanes, balloons, helicopters); in water (boats, submarines, ferries); on land (cars, trucks, buses); and underground (subways)
  - Animals used for transportation (horse, camel, elephant)
- Weather and Moisture
  - Precipitation (rain, snow, sleet, hail)
  - Lightning and thunder
  - Visibility (cloudy, foggy, sunny)
  - Labels for different kinds of weather
  - What happens to plants, animals, and people in different weather
  - Water (solids, liquids, gases)
  - Air (evaporation, movement)
  - Wind (windy, breezy, calm)
  - Occupations related to weather (hunting, fishing)
  - How a thermometer indicates temperature
  - How weather is predicted
  - How weather affects the way we feel

Appendix C
Lesson Plans

INFORMATION FOR CUMULATIVE LESSON PLANS

Chapter 2. The Value of Play
- Make a small community out of boxes. Add props as desired.

Chapter 3. Creative, Artistic, and Sensory Expression
- Paint large boxes.
- Glue small boxes together.
- Play in large appliance boxes.
- Make rhythm instruments.

Chapter 4. Language Arts
- Look at and talk about the composition and construction of boxes (wood, cardboard, plastic covered, and so on).
- Have a variety of objects and boxes; talk about and match.
- Read *The Box with Red Wheels* by Petersham.

Chapter 5. Music and Movement Education
- Use instruments made earlier.
- Have several boxes. Ask the children to show what they can do with each box (*small box:* put toys in, carry a treat, hold a treasure; *apple or orange box:* use as a boat, hat, turtle shell, house for a pet; *large box:* play in, make a house or car, saw, paint).
- Let the children tell a story and use the box as a prop (e.g., television, cave, airplane, etc.)

Chapter 6. Science
- In one section of the room, construct a grocery store out of large appliance boxes. Provide many empty boxes which originally contained food products. Use a box for a cash register; use paper or plastic money which has been made or purchased previously. Also include labeled cans, plastic fruit and vegetables, some toys, doll clothes, and paper sacks.

Chapter 7. Transition Activities
- "Think" Box, see page 183.
- "Jack-in-the-Box" on page 174, or another version found in Scott and Wood, *Singing Fun* (Bowmar), or reprinted in Bayless and Ramsey, p. 167)

Chapter 8. Field Trips
- Visit a box factory
- Go to a fruit packing shed.
- Visit a commercial establishment where they box merchandise.

Chapter 9. Special Occasions
- Decorate a box for a special occasion.
- Make a box.

Chapter 10. Food Experiences
Let each child make a box lunch for a picnic.
Use empty food product boxes in dramatic play.

Cumulative Lesson Plan

Daily Planning Outline

Theme: Boxes

Date ____________

Teacher/Planner ________

Preassessment and Findings:

(Teacher: select from these possibilities when working with an individual child or small group of children.)

1. Strategically place boxes of various sizes around the room. Observe if and how they are used by the children.
2. During free play, have numerous toys with many parts. At cleanup time, notice and comment upon the ease of storing toys when they are in proper boxes.
3. During an informal discussion, ask if the children know what boxes are made from and how they are used.
4. Without boxes being present, ask the children to show or tell how they would use different sized boxes.
5. Ask the children to name other kinds of containers (sack, bin, tub, plastic bag, shelf, drawer, and so on).

Ideas to Emphasize

1. Boxes can be used for many things such as carrying and storing.
2. Boxes are made of different materials.
3. It is fun to play with and in boxes.

Schedule of the Day

Approximate Time	Activity Period	Description	Materials Needed	Teacher Responsible
8:30	Opening	Free play	Assortment of small boxes and objects for matching Large appliance boxes Manipulative toys generally stored in boxes (pegs and boards, Tinker-toys, plastic shapes, and so on) Puzzles and books	Carol
		Box lunch	Bread, butter, peanut butter, celery sticks, cookies Knives, bags, small boxes	

Approximate Time	Activity Period	Description	Materials Needed	Teacher Responsible
8:45		Cleanup. Children are reminded to use proper boxes.		
		Transition to gathering time		Dan
8:50	Gathering	"Think" box (teacher has small animal inside box). Children guess; teacher shows.	"Think" box Animal	Dan
		a. Teacher asks children about composition of boxes; shows different kinds.	Wood, plastic, cardboard boxes	
		b. Teacher and children talk about the fun use of boxes during free play.		
		c. From variety of boxes (shapes, kinds, sizes, and composition), children take turns selecting a box and telling how she or he would use it.	Variety of boxes	
9:15	Playtime	Outside activities		Carol
		Jungle gym	Gym is covered.	
		Large boxes	Appliance boxes	
		Sand	Shovels, buckets, and sand toys	
		Selected play	Trikes, wagons	
9:40		Cleanup		Carol
9:45	Gathering	Snack		Dan
		Each child gets his or her box lunch. All eat outside today.	Juice, cups, napkins, box for garbage	
10:00		Cleanup	Box	
		Transition to gathering time: "Jack-in-the Box"		Dan
10:05	Gathering	Story: *The Box with Red Wheels* (Petersham).	Storybook	Dan
		Let children tell a story and use boxes as hat, boat, cave, television screen, and so on.	Boxes	
10:20	Activity	Expressive arts: children glue, paint small boxes; or make	Small boxes, paste, paint, brushes, cardboard	Carol

Approximate Time	Activity Period	Description	Materials Needed	Teacher Responsible
		a "special" box or musical instruments.		
		Make a grocery store. Use empty food produce boxes, box for cash register, box or sack for groceries. This could remain up for days if interest is high.	Large and small sacks Play money	Dan
		(Alternate to store: Make a small community using boxes for buildings. Add props.)	Community outline drawn on plastic, fabric, or card-board Small boxes Props	
10:45		Cleanup	Boxes, sponges, waste basket	Carol
10:50	Closing	Children use musical instruments made from boxes earlier.	Instruments	Dan

Items for Special Attention

Get a good variety of shapes, sizes, kinds, and composition of boxes. Prepare some bases to use as instruments, in grocery store, or in community. Contact furniture store for boxes.

Consider the grocery store or community for creative time, or check on nearby field trips, such as a box factory, a fruit packing shed, or a commercial establishment that boxes merchandise. One of these activities could be used at a later date to support this theme. Make a serious study of the possibilities and then make a selection for the lesson plan. Check to see that the "box" theme is not overdone. Have diversions.

Check to see that food for box lunch is fresh and available.

Evaluation

1. What was the children's response to this theme?
2. Which activities interested them most today? Why?
3. During cleanup, which children saw value in using boxes to store toys rather than just piling them on the shelf?
4. What creative uses of boxes were suggested by the children?
5. What follow-up would be meaningful on this topic?
6. What problems occurred during outdoor snack?
7. How could this plan be modified for use at another time?

Follow-Through for Parents

Learning card:

Today our theme was "Boxes." We provided different sizes, shapes, kinds, and composition of boxes for the children to use. They played in large appliance boxes, made musical instruments, painted boxes, and suggested some appropriate uses of boxes. At a later date, we plan to visit a box factory or watch merchandise being boxed. As an additional exposure to this theme, perhaps you could show your child how you use boxes in your home or work.

Additional Lesson Plan

Daily Planning Outline

Theme: Connectors

Date ____________________

Teacher/Planner __________

Preassessment and Findings:

(Teacher: select from among these possibilities when working with an individual child or small group of children.)

1. Take two pieces of string. Tie them together with a bow or knot.
2. On two different pieces of paper, apply rubber cement and let it dry. Press the cemented pages together.
3. Staple two pieces of paper together.
4. Fasten two pieces of chain together by using a nut and bolt.
5. Show a map of a small community (including houses, stores, and library). Using a small toy car, drive from one place to another.
6. Have some non-examples, such as trying to keep the string, paper, or chain together without an attachment.

Ask the children what attaching two or more things is called. Record their responses on your lesson plan. (**Note:** If the children just restate "tying," "pasting," "stapling," "screwing," or "driving," introduce and demonstrate the word "connector.")

Ideas to Emphasize

1. A connector is something that keeps two or more people or objects together.
2. The *use* of an attachment makes it a connector.
3. Sometimes things are connected and sometimes they are disconnected. Discuss these meanings and show examples.
4. Connectors have different names and are made of different materials.

Schedule of the Day

Approximate Time	Activity Period	Description	Materials Needed	Teacher Responsible
8:30	Opening	Free play	Tinkertoys, rope, bristle blocks, dress-up clothes, belts, zippers, buttons, snaps, puzzles, books	Bess
8:45		Cleanup		Bess
		Transition to gathering time		Ann
8:50	Gathering	Circle game: children hold hands. Song: bone connectors ("head bone is connected to the neck bone," and so on) Teacher uses some preassessment items to see if children		Ann

Approximate Time	Activity Period	Description	Materials Needed	Teacher Responsible
		remember the term "connector."		
		Teacher or child uses additional examples: clothespin, buckle, wire, seat belt, solder, welding, nails, screws, mortar, hands, toys, pipe, sewing, bottle with lid.		
		Teacher asks children to define "connector": something that holds people or things together.		
		Teacher and children connect and disconnect different objects and discuss terms and actions		
9:15	Playtime	Outside activities		Bess
		Woodworking	Wood, saws, hammers, nails.	
		Door latches		
		Selected play	Latch frame: bolt, key and lock, dead bolt, hook, key knob.	
			Trikes, wagons, sand toys.	
9:40		Cleanup		Bess
9:45	Gathering	Snack	Straws,* napkins, knives, glasses	Ann
			Whole wheat bread, butter, honey,* milk	
10:00		Cleanup	Sponges, waste basket, trays	Ann
		Transition to language activity		Bess
10:05	Gathering	Transition: child-selected songs or finger plays	Song "tree"	Bess
			Miscellaneous books	
		Story: *Go Away, Dog* (Nodset)	Flip cards	
10:20	Activity	Creative connecting	Paper, staples, paste, yarn and needles for sewing or stringing	Ann
		Sensory and	Items from first	Bess

* Asterisks indicate connectors. Note that a straw can be a "connector" between the milk and the mouth; that butter and honey can "connect" pieces of bread.

Approximate Time	Activity Period	Description	Materials Needed	Teacher Responsible
		exploration: connectors	gathering time	
10:45		Cleanup	Storage boxes, broom, dustpan	Ann
10:50	Closing	Record: "A Visit to My Little Friend" Variety of finger plays	Record player, record	Bess

Items for Special Attention

Collect and prepare items for gathering time and creative art. Bring in record and see that record player has been repaired. Check to see if there is enough soft wood for woodworking. Call Mrs. Leavitt to see when Peter will have his tonsils out.

Evaluation

1. Which children remembered what a "connector" was? How did their responses influence the other children?
2. Which activities were most interesting to the children today? Why?
3. Which "connectors" were easiest for the children to understand?
4. Which children were unable to grasp the concepts? How did they use the materials supplied?
5. What evidence was there that teaching at a later date on this theme would be meaningful?
6. Identify problems or behavior that needs attention.
7. Express your positive feelings about the day.

Follow-Through for Parents

Learning card:

Today we experimented with and talked about "connectors." Some items of discussion were: clothing (buttons, zippers), art (paste, staples, yarn), household items (nails, wire, nuts, and bolts), and food (butter, honey). As additional experience with this topic, help your child look for a variety of connectors in your environment. Briefly explain their use and value.

Appendix D
Recipes

RECIPES FOR CREATIVE AND ARTISTIC EXPRESSION

Beads

½ c salt
¼ c cornstarch
¼ c water (heated)
Food coloring

Dissolve salt in heated water, stir in cornstarch and food coloring (optional). Knead until smooth. Pinch off small amounts, form into shapes, stick small dowels or pencils through them, and place on waxed paper. When beads are dry, slip off sticks and thread onto yarn.

Salt Beads

Use Salt Ceramic recipe (page 287)
1 tsp food coloring

Roll into balls. Use toothpick or nail to make holes. Let dry, and then string.

Earth Clay

Put desired amount of water in earthen jar. Gradually add clay powder, stirring until mixture reaches consistency of sticky bread dough. Let stand overnight. Knead powder into clay until desired consistency.

Peanut Butter Clay

1½ c peanut butter
1 c powdered milk
1 c powdered sugar

Combine ingredients. Knead to desired consistency.

Dough-Clay

2 c flour
1 c salt
4 tsp cream of tartar
2 c water
2 T oil
Food coloring (optional)
Spice for scent (optional)

Mix flour, salt, and cream of tartar in heavy aluminum pan. Add water, oil, color, and spice. Heat on stove 3 min or until mixture pulls away from pan. Remove from heat and knead immediately. Store in airtight container. Clay keeps for several months.

Flour-Salt Dough

1½ c flour
½ c salt
½ c water
¼ c vegetable oil

Mix flour and salt. Slowly add water and oil. (Coloring is optional.) Knead well. Store in refrigerator in closed container or plastic bag. Can be baked at 225° for 2 hr. Color or decorate, if desired.

Cornstarch Dough

1 c cornstarch
2 c salt
$1\frac{1}{3}$ c cold water

Mix salt and $\frac{2}{3}$ c water in pan and bring to a boil. In separate bowl, stir cornstarch and remaining water thoroughly. Combine mixtures and knead well. Store, covered, in refrigerator.

Sawdust Clay

6 c sawdust
$5\frac{1}{2}$ c flour
2 T salt

Mix ingredients. Gradually add small amounts of boiling water. Blend thoroughly until mixture resembles stiff dough. Store in cool place in damp cloth or aluminum foil. Keeps about a week.

Papier-mâché

Tear four or five double sheets of newspaper into small pieces. Soak overnight in hot water. Knead well. Gradually add 1 c water to $\frac{1}{2}$ c flour and bring to boil over low heat. Stir until thick and glossy. Stir into paper mixture.

Fake Bread

4 c flour
1 c salt
2 c water

Knead like bread. Shape and put on cookie sheet. Mixture must be baked within 20 min or it will crack and break. Bake at 300° until toasty brown. Can be brushed with egg yolk or glue and then decorated.

Ornaments

1 c cornstarch
2 c baking soda
$1\frac{1}{4}$ c cold water

Mix dry ingredients. Add water all at once and stir until smooth. Cook over medium heat, stirring constantly until consistency of cookie dough. Roll out and cut with cookie cutters. Bake at 300° for 10 min. Paint with tube or bright water colors. If dough starts to dry out, wet hands and work the dough.

Salt Ceramic

$\frac{1}{2}$ c cornstarch
1 c salt
$\frac{1}{2}$ c boiling water

Mix ingredients in top of double boiler. Cook, stirring constantly, 2 to 3 min, until so thick that mixture follows spoon in stirring. When consistency of bread dough, dump onto waxed paper to cool. Knead with hands several minutes. Store in airtight container.

Glarch

1 c Elmer's glue
1 c liquid starch

Pour liquid starch over glue and gently fold together with a spoon. Once glue solidifies, pour off extra starch. Glarch becomes harder and more rubbery as it is worked. Once it is quite solid, rinse under cold water to remove starch.

Basic Finger Paint
Method 1

Put 3 c soap *flakes* (such as Ivory) in a medium-sized bowl. Gradually add water. Beat with a rotary or electric beater to a soft, smooth consistency that holds a peak. Color, if desired.

Method 2

Moisten 1 c laundry starch with 1 c cold water. Add 2 c hot water and cook until thick. Remove from heat and add 1 c soap flakes and a few drops of glycerin.

Method 3

Mix together in double boiler 1 c flour, 1 tsp salt, and 3 c cold water. Cook until thick, beating with an eggbeater or electric mixer.

Cornstarch Finger Paint

Dissolve ½ c cornstarch in cold water. Add to 4 c boiling water and stir. Let mixture come to boil again. Cooling causes paint to thicken slightly.

Salt and Flour Finger Paint

Stir 1 c flour and 1½ c salt into ¾ c water. Add coloring. Paint will have grainy quality.

Liquid Starch Finger Paint

Pour liquid starch on wet surface. Add color, if desired.

Starch and Gelatin Finger Paint

½ c laundry starch
1 c cold water
1 envelope unflavored gelatin
2 c hot water
½ c soap flakes

Combine laundry starch and ½ c cold water in saucepan. Soak gelatin in ¼ c cold water. Add hot water to starch mixture and cook, stirring constantly over medium heat, until mixture comes to a boil and is clear. Remove from heat and blend in softened gelatin. Add soap flakes and stir until mixture thickens and soap is thoroughly dissolved. Makes about 3 cups.

Pudding Finger Paint

Instant or cooked pudding may be used for a different experience. Danish dessert offers yet another texture, although it does stain some surfaces. When foodstuffs are used in this manner, explain to the children: "Today we're finger-painting with pudding. Another day we will have it for a snack." All finger paints should be stored in tightly covered jars and in a cool place.

Wallpaper Paste Finger Paint

Put desired amount of water into pan. Sprinkle flour on top of water, a small amount at a time. Stir until all lumps are gone. Add more flour until desired consistency (should be similar to liquid laundry starch).

RECIPES FOR FOOD

Breads

Streamlined White Bread

1¼ c warm water (not hot—110 to 115°)
1 pkg active dry yeast
2 T soft shortening
2 tsp salt
2 T sugar
3 c sifted flour

In mixer bowl, dissolve yeast in warm water. Add shortening, salt, sugar, and half the flour. Beat 2 min, medium speed on mixer, or 300 vigorous strokes by hand. Scrape sides and bottom of bowl frequently. Add remaining flour and blend with spoon until smooth. Scrape batter from sides of bowl. Cover with cloth and let rise in warm place (85°) until double, about 30 min. (If kitchen is cool, place dough on rack over bowl of hot water and cover with a towel.) Stir down batter by beating about 25 strokes. Spread batter evenly in greased loaf pan, 8½ by 4½ by 2¾ in. or 9 by 5 by 3 in. Batter will be sticky. Smooth out top of loaf by flouring hand and patting into shape. Again let rise in warm place until batter reaches ¼ in. from top of 8½-in. pan or 1 in. from top of 9-in. pan, about 40 min. Heat oven to 375°. Bake 45 to 50 min, or until brown. To test loaf, tap the top crust; it should sound hollow. Immediately remove from pan. Place on cooling rack or across bread pans. Brush top with melted butter or shortening. Do not place in direct draft. Cool before cutting. A sawtooth knife is especially good for cutting. Slice with a sawing motion rather than pressing down, making slices slightly thicker than usual. Makes one loaf.

Individual Bun Recipe (ingredients for each child)

1 tsp soft margarine
1 tsp sugar
1 T flour
1 tsp fruit (currants)
1½ T milk and egg (2 eggs to 1 pt of milk whipped together for group to share)

Blend margarine and sugar in small bowl or plastic carton. Add flour, fruit, and liquid. Stir. Put in baking papers in muffin tin. Bake at 350° until golden brown.

Whole Wheat Bread

4½ c sifted whole wheat flour
2 c sifted enriched flour (approximately)
Keep whole wheat and white flour separate until mixing.
½ cake yeast softened in ¼ c lukewarm water, *or* ½ T dry granular yeast softened in ¼ c warm water (110°)
Place in mixing bowl:
2½ c scalded milk
3 T shortening
3 T sugar
1 T salt

When milk mixture is cooled to 90°, add 3 c of the whole wheat flour. Beat well. Then add the softened yeast. Add the remaining whole wheat flour. Beat until all the whole wheat flour is thoroughly mixed into the dough. Then add enough of the white flour to make a soft dough. Mix until the dough forms an elastic, soft ball. (Whole wheat dough ferments much faster than white dough. If it gets too light, the finished bread will be coarse and crumbly.) Cover. Keep dough in a warm place away from drafts until almost tripled in bulk. Punch it down, turn it over, cover it, and let it rise 30 min. Punch it down, turn it over, cover it, and let it rise 20 min; divide into balls for loaves. Cover and rest dough 10 min. Mold into loaves and put into pans. Cover; let double in bulk. Bake in a moderate oven (375°) about 50 min. Makes 2 loaves. (The whole wheat dough will be ready for baking in a shorter time than the white dough.)

Breadsticks

1 pkg refrigerator biscuits
¼ c melted butter
Sesame seeds

Shape biscuits into 6- to 8-in. long sticks. Place half butter in 9- by 12-in. baking pan. Put sticks in butter. Pour rest of butter over sticks. Sprinkle sticks with seeds. Bake 10 min at 400°.

Cheese Biscuits

Mix together ½ c soft margarine, 2 c flour, 2 c grated cheese, and 2 c rice cereal. Roll into small balls, then flatten. Place on greased cookie sheet. Bake 8 to 10 min at 375°. Makes about 40 biscuits.

Apple Biscuits

Mix 1 c crushed Wheat Chex and ½ c grated unpeeled apples. Add ½ c apple juice. Combine 2 c biscuit mix and small amount of nutmeg and cinnamon. Stir into crumb mixture. Mix well. Spoon onto greased cookie sheet. Bake at 450° for 10 min. Makes 16 to 18 servings.

Painted Piñata Burros

1 pkg (10) 8-in. flour tortillas
1 egg yolk
2 tsp sugar
¼ tsp almond extract
Food coloring

Using cookie cutter, cut 2 cookies from each tortilla; set aside scraps. In small bowl combine remaining ingredients except food coloring; divide between 2 small bowls. Color as desired with food coloring by brushing on cookies. Bake on greased baking sheets in 425° oven 2 to 3 min until bubbly. Cool on rack. Makes 20 cookies.

Cut tortilla scraps into bite-sized pieces. Brush with melted margarine and sprinkle with sugar. Place on baking sheet; bake in 425° oven 2 to 3 min until golden.

Simple Pizza

Spread ½ English muffin with 1 T tomato sauce. Sprinkle lightly with oregano. Place one slice salami on sauce (optional). Top with slice of cheese. Place on baking sheet. Bake about 10 min at 425° or until cheese is bubbly.

Indian Fry Bread

Dissolve 1 pkg yeast (1 T) in 1 c warm milk. Add ¼ c oil and 1 T sugar. Measure and combine 3 c flour and 1 tsp salt in mixing bowl; add other ingredients. Dough should be soft but not sticky; more flour may be needed. Divide into portions and let the children knead it for 5 min. Lightly oil inside of large bowl. Make ball of all dough and place in bowl. Turn dough over so oiled side is up. Cover with plastic or damp clean towel. Let rise until double in bulk (about 2 hr). Punch down. Pull off chunks about size of table tennis ball; roll into a flat circle about ¼ in. thick. Heat ½ in. oil until hot. Fry to golden brown; turn over. Remove and drain on paper towels. Eat while warm. Serves 16 to 18 children.

Dairy

Butter

Use ½ pt cream in a pint jar. *Cream should be at room temperature and should be several days old.* Shake it until it thickens, about 10 min. Add salt to taste. Drain. Pour cold water over it and keep pouring buttermilk off. Cream with a spoon until all buttermilk is drained off. Add yellow food coloring. (Butter can also be made by putting cream in small baby food jars so more children can participate.)

Cottage Cheese

2 c whole milk (fresh or soured)
1 T vinegar

Stir and cook milk over medium heat until bubbles begin to form on top. Remove from heat and stir in vinegar. Stir gently and watch for curds, which form quickly. Liquid is whey. Stir occasionally as mixture cools. Gather curds in strainer, gently pressing curds so that whey is removed. Add salt to taste.

Homemade Yogurt

Boil ½ gal fresh milk for 4 min. Insert thermometer and cool to 100 to 125°. Add ½ c powdered milk and 1 pt plain commercial yogurt. Spoon into warm, clean jars. Put lids on. Put warm water (100 to 125°) in deep pan, put jars in (water should cover at least one half of jar). Turn to low heat (about 125°) for 2 to 4 hr. Remove when contents become firm. Refrigerate.

For additional batches, save one jar to use as next starter (can be used several times, then begin again with commercial yogurt).

At serving time, add fruit or 2 T frozen orange juice or eat plain.

The Basic Four Unit

¼ c peanut butter
½ c butter or margarine
4 c miniature marshmallows
½ c instant nonfat dried milk
1 c raisins
4 c Cheerios

Melt butter and marshmallows. Remove or turn off heat. Add nonfat dried milk and peanut butter. Stir in raisins and cereal. Put in 9- by 9-in. pan. Cut in squares. Serve.

Drop Cookies

Peanut Butter Cookies

1½ c sifted flour
1 tsp baking soda
½ c white sugar
1 c brown sugar
Dash of salt
½ c peanut butter
½ c butter or margarine, melted
1 egg

Sift flour and baking soda together once. Mix together dry ingredients. Add peanut butter, butter, and egg. Make balls the size of English walnuts, place on oiled cookie sheet 3 in. apart, and press down with fork. Bake at 375° until light brown. Makes 3 dozen cookies, mild in flavor.

Oatmeal Cookies

1 c white sugar
1 c shortening
3 eggs
½ tsp salt
2 c flour
½ tsp soda
½ tsp allspice
1 tsp cinnamon
½ tsp cloves
6 T raisin liquid
2 c oatmeal
1 c nuts
1 c raisins (covered with water and simmered for 5 min)

Cream white sugar and shortening; add eggs and beat. Sift dry ingredients and add to creamed mixture. Add raisin liquid alternately with oatmeal. Add raisins and nuts. Bake at 375° for 15 min. Makes about 5 dozen.

Snickerdoodles

1 c shortening
1½ c sugar
2 eggs
2½ c flour
2 tsp cream of tartar
2 tsp baking soda
½ tsp salt

Cream shortening and sugar. Add eggs and stir. Sift dry ingredients together and add. Mix well and roll in 1 tsp cinnamon mixed with 2 tsp sugar. Bake at 350° for 8 to 10 min. Makes about 2½ dozen.

Haystacks

Melt 2 packages butterscotch bits in a large pan. Stir in 1 can peanuts and 1 can chow mein noodles. Drop by teaspoons on waxed paper. Cool. Makes about 2 dozen.

No-Bake Cookies, Method 1

Boil for 1 min:
½ c milk
½ c butter
2 c sugar
Add:
3 c oatmeal
½ tsp vanilla
4 T cocoa
½ c nuts
½ c coconut (or raisins)

Drop from spoon onto waxed paper. Let stand until firm.

No-Bake Cookies, Method 2

2 c sugar
4 T cocoa
½ tsp salt
½ c peanut butter
½ c milk
1 tsp vanilla
2½ c quick-cooking oats

In saucepan combine sugar, cocoa, salt, peanut butter, and milk. Bring to a boil and boil 1 minute. Remove from heat and add vanilla and oats. Mix well. Drop by spoonfuls onto waxed paper. Let stand until firm. Makes about 2½ doz.

No-Bake Oatmeal Cookies

Mix together in bowl: 3 c quick oats and 3 T carob (substitute for chocolate). In saucepan, mix and boil for 1 min: 2 c sugar, ½ c milk, ½ c peanut butter, ¼ lb butter or margarine. Pour hot syrup over oat mixture and mix well. Drop by spoon onto waxed paper.

Chinese No-Bake Cookies

¼ lb. margarine (1 stick)
2 c sugar
½ c milk
½ tsp salt

Mix together in a heavy saucepan and bring to a rolling boil. Boil 1 min.
Add:

2 T peanut butter
1 tsp vanilla
2 c oats
2 c Chinese noodles

Mix and drop on wax paper or oiled cookie sheet and chill.

Chinese Chewies

Place 1 6-oz package butterscotch pieces and ½ c peanut butter in medium saucepan. Cook slowly until melted, about 6 min. Remove from heat. Add 1 13-oz can chow mein noodles and 1 c miniature marshmallows. Stir well. Spoon into pan, lined with waxed paper. Let cool. 35 servings.

Energy Cookies

4 c uncooked rolled oats
3 c unbleached white flour
2 c dates (chopped and pitted)
6 T milk
1 c brown sugar
1½ c corn or peanut oil
½ c maple syrup

Beat sugar and oil. Add oats, syrup, flour, and milk. Stir in dates. Roll into small balls, then flatten on oiled cookie sheet. Bake 15 to 20 min at 350°. Makes 5 dozen.

Aggression Cookies

3 c brown sugar
6 c uncooked oatmeal
3 c unsifted all purpose flour
3 c margarine
1 T baking soda
¾ c white sugar

Mix all ingredients in large bowl and squeeze into a well-kneaded, firm dough. Form into small (table-tennis sized) balls. Dip bottom of small glass in granular sugar and flatten each ball. Bake on ungreased cookie sheet for 10 to 12 min at 350°. Makes 5 dozen. Let cool, then pass the "aggression."

Rolled Cookies

Buttermilk Cookies

1 c shortening
2 c sugar
3 eggs, beaten
1 c buttermilk
6 c flour
1 tsp baking soda
¼ tsp nutmeg or other spice

Cream the shortening; add the sugar gradually and blend thoroughly. Add beaten eggs and buttermilk. Add sifted dry ingredients, mixing well. Chill. Roll to a thickness of about ⅛ in.; spread with sugar and cut. Place on greased cookie sheet and bake at 375° for 10 to 12 min.

Grandma Milne's Sugar Cookies

1 c shortening
2 c sugar
2 eggs
2 tsp baking soda in a little hot water
5 to 6 c flour
2 heaping tsp cream of tartar
1 c milk
2 tsp vanilla

Cream shortening and sugar; add eggs and soda. Sift flour and cream of tartar. Add dry ingredients alternately with milk. Add vanilla. Bake at 350 to 375° for 12 min.

Carolyn's Cookies

4 c flour
1 c sugar
4 tsp baking powder
½ tsp salt
1 c shortening
4 eggs, well beaten
⅓ c milk
1 tsp vanilla

Sift dry ingredients together. Cut in 1 c shortening as in pie dough. Add eggs, milk, and vanilla. Roll out and cut. Bake at 400° until brown. Makes about 5 dozen.

Coloring Sugar Cookies

Beat 1 egg yolk with 1 tsp water. Divide into containers and add different food coloring to each. Brush onto cookies before baking. If not cooked too long, the color is good.

Gingerbread Men

Simmer together for 15 min: 1 c molasses and 1 c shortening.
Cream together: 1 c sugar, 1 egg, and 1 tsp vanilla.
Dissolve: 2 tsp baking soda in ½ c hot water; add to sugar and egg.

Sift together: 6 c flour, ¼ tsp cloves, 1 tsp cinnamon, 1 tsp salt, and ½ tsp ginger. Add to molasses and sugar-egg mixtures and stir until flour is well mixed. Roll thin and cut with cookie cutter. Bake 10 min in 375° oven. This dough does not stick to the pan. Even a child can handle it. Makes about 5 dozen.

A child particularly enjoys eating cookies he has rolled out and cut himself.

Grandma's Gingerbread Dough

5½ c flour
1 tsp baking soda
1 tsp salt
3 tsp cinnamon
2 tsp ginger
2 tsp cloves
1 tsp nutmeg
⅓ tsp cardamon
1 shortening or margarine
1 c white or brown sugar
1 c molasses
1 egg

Sift flour, soda, salt, and five spices. Cream shortening and sugar until fluffy, add egg and molasses. Beat at least 8 to 10 min. Add flour mixture a little at a time. Can be rolled into log shape and frozen for up to six months. Bake at 315 to 325° for 15 to 20 min.

Popcorn
Caramel corn

Combine and bring to boil: 1 c dark corn syrup, 1 pkg brown sugar, and 1 stick butter or margarine. Add 1 c evaporated milk and ⅓ c white sugar. Cook to soft-ball stage. Pour over popped corn. Makes 2½ to 3 gal.

Popcorn Balls

1 c white Karo syrup
½ c white sugar
1 box gelatin, any flavor

Bring syrup and sugar to a boil. Add one box gelatin and let cool. Pour over popcorn. Children shape balls.

Appendix E
Additional Sources, Books for Children, Record Sources, and Publishers

CHAPTER 1. PLANNING THE CURRICULUM

Additional Sources

Berk, L. E. "How Well Do Classroom Practices Reflect Teacher's Goals?" *Young Children* 32(November 1976): 64–81.

Bruner, J. S. *The Process of Education.* Cambridge, Mass.: Harvard University Press, 1960.

Carini, P. "Building a Curriculum for Young Children from an Experiential Base." *Young Children* 33(March 1977): 14–18.

Dittman, Laura L., ed. *Curriculum Is What Happens: Planning Is the Key,* no. 119. Washington, D.C.: National Association for the Education of Young Children, 1977.

Elkind, David. "Sense and Nonsense About Preschools." *Parents Magazine,* March 1971.

Frazier, Alexander. "The State of the Art: Making a Curriculum for Children." *Childhood Education* 56(April–May 1980): 258–263.

Greenberg, Marvin. "The Male Early Childhood Teacher: An Appraisal." *Young Children* 32(January 1977): 34–38.

Highberger, Ruth, and Sharon Teets. "Early Schooling: Why Not?" *Young Children* 29(January 1974): 66–78.

Hildebrand, Verna. *Introduction to Early Childhood Education.* New York: Macmillan, 1980.

Lee, Patrick C., and Annie Lucas Wolinsky. "Male Teachers of Young Children: A Preliminary Empirical Study." *Young Children* 28(August 1973): 342–352.

Lorton, J. W., and B. L. Walley. *Introduction to Early Childhood Education.* New York: D. Van Nostrand, 1979.

Maxim, G. *The Very Young Child: Guiding Children From Infancy Through the Early Years.* Belmont, Calif.: Wadsworth Publishing, 1980.

Ramsey, Marjorie E., and Kathleen M. Bayless. *Kindergarten: Programs & Practices.* St. Louis: C. V. Mosby, 1980, pp. 29–49, 277–285.

Read, Katherine, and June Patterson. *The Nursery School & Kindergarten,* New York: Holt, Rinehart & Winston, 1980.

Robinson, Bryan. "Changing Views on Male Early Childhood Teachers." *Young Children* 36(July 1981): 27–32.
Seefeldt, C. *A Curriculum for Preschoolers.* 2d ed. Columbus, Ohio: Charles E. Merrill, 1980.
Todd, Vivian E., and Helen Heffeman. *The Years Before School: Guiding Preschool Children.* Toronto: Macmillan, 1977, pp. 159–202.
Watrin, R., and P. H. Furfey. *Learning Activities for the Young Preschool Child.* New York: D. Van Nostrand, 1978.

CHAPTER 2. THE VALUE OF PLAY

Additional Sources

Allen, Elizabeth G., and Jone P. Wright. "Just for Fun: A Creative Dramatic Learning Center." *Childhood Education* 54(February 1978): 169–175.
Baker, Katheryn R. *Let's Play Outdoors,* no. 101. Washington, D.C.: National Association for Education of Young Children, 1966.
Bogdanoff, Ruth F., and Elaine T. Dolch. "Old Games for Young Children: A Link to Our Heritage." *Childhood Education* 55(January 1979): 37–45.
Bruner, Jerome S., Alison Jolly, and Kathy Sylva, eds. *Play—Its Role in Development and Evolution.* New York: Basic Books, 1976.
Christi, James G. "Sociodramatic Play Training," *Young Children* 37(May 1982): 26–31.
Cliatt, M. J. "Play: The Window into a Child's Life." *Childhood Education* 56(February–March 1980): 218–220.
Engstrom, Georgianna, ed. *Play: The Child Strives Toward Self-Realization.* Washington, D.C.: National Association for the Education of Young Children, 1971.
Forman, George, and D. Fleet Hill. *Constructive Play: Applying Piaget in the Preschool.* Monterey, Calif.: Brooks-Cole, 1980.
Fowler, William. *Infant and Child Care.* Boston: Allyn & Bacon, 1980, pp. 187–213.
Frost, Joe L. "The American Playground Movement." *Childhood Education* 54(February 1978): 176–182.
———. "Making Playgrounds Safe for Children and Children Safe for Playgrounds." *Young Children* 55(July 1979): 23–30.
Glickman, C. D. "Problem: Declining Achievement Scores—Solution: Let Them Play." *Phi Delta Kappan* 60(1979): 454–455.
Griffin, Penelope. "Encouraging Dramatic Play in Early Childhood." *Young Children* 38(January 1983): 13–22.
Kretchevsky, Sibil, and Elizabeth Prescott. *Planning Environments for Young Children: Physical Space,* no. 115. Washington, D.C.: National Association for the Education of Young Children, 1977.
Lieberman, J. "Playfulness and Divergent Thinking: An Investigation of Their Relationship at the Kindergarten Level." *Journal of Genetic Psychology* 107(1965): 219–224.
Matterson, Elizabeth. *Games for the Very Young.* New York: Heritage Press, 1971.
Maxwell, William. "Games Children Play." *Educational Leadership* March 1983, pp. 38–41.
Mills, Belen C., ed. *Understanding the Young Child and His Curriculum.* New York: Macmillan, 1972. A variety of articles on play.
Ramsey, Marjorie E., and Kathleen M. Bayless. *Kindergarten: Programs and Practices.* St. Louis: C. V. Mosby, 1980, pp. 51–105.
Read, Katherine H., and June Patterson. *The Nursery School and Kindergarten.* New York: Holt, Rinehart & Winston, 1980.
Robinson, Helen F. "The Decline of Play in Urban Kindergartens." *Young Children* 26(1971): 333–341.
Smilansky, Sara. *The Effect of Sociodramatic Play on Disadvantaged Preschool Children.* New York: John Wiley, 1968.
Sponseller, Doris, ed. *Play as a Learning Medium.* Washington, D.C.: Association for Childhood Education International, 1974.
Strom, Robert D. "Too Busy to Play." *Childhood Education* 54(November–December 1977): 80–82.

Sutton-Smith, Brian, "The Role of Playing in Cognitive Development." *Young Children* 22(September 1967): 361–370.
Taylor, Barbara J. "Playways to a Healthy Self-Concept." In *The Self-Concept of the Young Child,* edited by Thomas D. Yawkey. Provo, Utah: Brigham Young University Press, 1980, pp. 131–50.
Wolfgang, Charles H. "An Exploration of the Relationship Between the Cognitive Area of Reading and Selected Developmental Aspects of Children's Play." *Psychology in the Schools,* July 1974, pp. 338–343.
———. *Helping Aggressive and Passive Preschoolers Through Play.* Columbus, Ohio: Charles E. Merrill, 1977.

CHAPTER 3. CREATIVE, ARTISTIC, AND SENSORY EXPRESSION

Additional Sources

Bandhofer, Marijane. "Carpentry for Young Children." *Young Children* 27(October 1971): 17–23.
Blender, Judith. "Large Hollow Blocks: Relationship of Quantity to Block Building Behaviors." *Young Children* 33(September 1978): 17–23.
Bos, B. J. *Don't Move the Muffin Tins: A Hands Off Guide to Art for the Young Child.* Nevada City, Calif.: Burton Gallery, 1978.
Brittain, W. L. *Creativity, Art, and the Young Child.* New York: Macmillan, 1979.
Day, Barbara. *Early Childhood Education: Creative Learning Activities.* New York: Macmillan, 1983.
Dudek, Stephanie A. "Teachers Stifle Children's Creativity: A Charge too Easily Made." In *Readings in Early Childhood Education 78/79.* Guilford, Conn.: Dushkin, 1978, pp. 218–221.
Flemming, Bonnie, and Darlene S. Hamilton. *Resources for Creative Teaching in Early Childhood Education.* New York: Harcourt Brace Jovanovich, 1977.
Francks, O. R. "Scribbles? Yes, They Are Art." *Young Children* 34(July 1979): 15–22.
Frost, Joe L. "Free To Be: The Arts and Child Development." *Childhood Education* 57(November–December 1980): 66–71.
Haskell, L. L. *Art in the Early Childhood Years.* Columbus, Ohio: Charles E. Merrill, 1979.
Hill, Dorothy M. *Mud, Sand, and Water.* Washington, D.C.: National Association for the Education of Young Children, 1977.
Hirsch, Elizabeth S. *The Block Book,* no. 132. Washington, D.C.: National Association for Education of Young Children, 1984.
Kane, Frances. "Thinking, Drawing—Writing, Reading." *Childhood Education* 58(May–June 1982): 292–297.
Kinsman, Cheryll A., and Laura E. Berk. "Joining the Block and Housekeeping Areas: Changes in Play and Social Behavior." *Young Children* 35(November 1979): 66–75.
Klein, Bruce. "The Hidden Dimensions of Art." *Childhood Education* 57(January–February 1982): 138–143.
Knudsen, Estelle H., and Ethel M. Christensen. *Children's Art Education.* Peoria, Ill.: C. A. Bennett, 1971.
Liepman, L. *Your Child's Sensory World.* New York: Dial Press, 1974.
Lowenfeld, Viktor, and W. L. Brittain. *Creative and Mental Growth,* 6th ed. New York: Macmillan, 1975.
Rudolph, Marguerita, and Dorothy H. Cohen. "The Many Purposes of Blockbuilding and Woodworking." *Young Children* 20(October 1964): 41–46.
Sukus, Jan. *My Toolbox Book.* Racine, Wis.: Golden Press, 1977.
Todd, Vivian D., and Helen Heffernan. *The Years Before School.* Toronto: Macmillan, 1977.
Torre, Frank D. *Woodworking for Kids.* Garden City, N.Y.: Doubleday, 1978.
U.S. Department of Health, Education, and Welfare. *How Children Can Be Creative,* no. 12. Washington, D.C.
Warren, J. "Patterns." *Young Children* 33(January 1978): 53.
Watrin, Rita, and Paul H. Furfey. *Learning Activities for the Young Preschool Child.* New York: D. Van Nostrand, 1978.
Werner, P. H., and E. C. Burton. *Learning Through Movement.* St. Louis: C. V. Mosby, 1979.

Whiren, A. "Table Toys: The Underdeveloped Resource." *Young Children* 30(September 1975): 413–419.
Whitener, Carole B., and Katharine Kersey. "A Purple Hippopotamus? Why Not!" *Childhood Education* 57(November–December 1982): 83–89.
Williams, R. M. "Why Children Should Draw: The Surprising Link Between Art and Learning." *Saturday Review,* September 3, 1977.

Books for Children

Bright, Robert. *My Red Umbrella.* New York: William Morrow, 1959.
Brooks, R. *Annie's Rainbow.* New York: Bradbury Press, 1976.
Carle, E. *My Very First Book of Colors.* New York: Harper & Row, 1974.
Johnson, C. *Harold and the Purple Crayon.* New York: Harper & Row, 1958.
Lerner, S. *Orange Is a Color: A Book About Color.* Minneapolis: Lerner, 1969.
Lionni, L. *A Color of His Own.* New York: Pantheon, 1976.
______. *Little Blue and Little Yellow.* New York: Astor-Honor, 1959.
______. *The Greentail Mouse.* New York: Pantheon, 1973.
MacDonald, G. *Red Light, Green Light.* New York: Doubleday, 1944.
McGovern, A. *Black Is Beautiful.* New York: Scholastic Book Services, 1970.
O'Neill, M. *Hailstones and Halibut Bones.* New York: Doubleday, 1961.
Provenson, A. *Roses Are Red. Are Violets Blue?* New York: Golden Press, 1970.
Reiss, J. *Colors.* Scarsdale, N.Y.: Bradbury Press, 1969.
Schneider, H., and N. Schneider. *Science Fun With a Flashlight.* New York: McGraw-Hill, 1975.
Seuss, Dr. *One Fish Two Fish, Red Fish Blue Fish.* New York: Random House, 1960.
Slobodkina, E. *Caps for Sale.* New York: Scholastic Book Services, 1976.
Tison, A., and T. Taylor. *The Adventures of the Three Colors.* Columbus, Ohio: Charles E. Merrill, 1979.
Zolotow, C. *Mr. Rabbit and the Lovely Present.* New York: Harper & Row, 1962.

CHAPTER 4. LANGUAGE ARTS

Additional Sources

Baker, A., and E. Greene. "Storytelling: Preparation and Presentation." *School Library Journal* 24(May 1981): 93–96.
Bauer, C. F. *Handbook for Storytellers.* Chicago: American Library Association, 1977.
Benninga, Jacques S., and Ruth Ann Crum. " 'Acting Out' for Social Understanding." *Childhood Education* 57(January–February 1982): 144–147.
Cawley, Magdalene. "Connecting Words With Real Ideas." *Young Children* 33(January 1978): 20–25.
Cazden, C. B., ed. *Language in Early Childhood Education.* Washington D.C.: National Association for the Education of Young Children, 1981.
Cazden, Courtney B. "Children's Questions: Their Forms, Functions, and Roles in Education." *Young Children* 25(March 1970): 202–220.
Children's Books: Awards and Prizes. New York: Children's Book Council, 1979.
Chomsky, C. "Write First, Read Later." *Childhood Education* 47(1971): 296–299.
Cohan, Dorothy H., and Marguerita Rudolph. *Kindergarten and Early Schooling.* Englewood Cliffs, N.J.: Prentice-Hall, 1977, pp. 292–312.
Corcoran, G. B. *Language Experience for Nursery and Kindergarten Years.* Itasca, Ill.: F. B. Peacock, 1976.
Davis, Hazel G. "Reading Pressures in the Kindergarten." *Childhood Education* 37(November–December 1980): 76–79.
Downing, John, and Derek Thackray. *Reading Readiness.* London: Hodder & Stoughton, 1976.
Durkin, Dolores. *Teaching Young Children to Read.* 2d ed. Boston: Allyn & Bacon, 1976.
Garcia, E. E. "Research in Review: Bilingualism in Early Childhood." *Young Children* 35(May 1980): 53–66.

Griffin, Louise. *Multi-Ethnic Books for Young Children.* Washington, D.C.: National Association for the Education of Young Children, n.d.

Gillies, Emily. *Creative Dramatics for All Children.* Washington, D.C.: Association for Childhood Education International, 1973.

Goetz, Elizabeth M. "Early Reading: A Developmental Approach." *Young Children* 34(1979): 4–11.

Haberman, Martin. "The Meaning of Reading Readiness for Young Children." *Childhood Education* 55(1979): 288.

Jensen, Mary A., and Bette A. Hanson. "Helping Young Children Learn to Read: What Research Says to Teachers." *Young Children* 36(November 1980): 61–68.

Kingman, Lee, ed. *Newberry and Caldecott Medal Books, 1966–1975.* Boston, Mass.: Horn Book, 1975.

Kovalcik, Alfred L. "Another Look at Reading Readiness." *Education Digest* 42(1977): 48–50.

Lee, D. M., and J. D. Rubin. *Children and Language: Reading and Writing, Talking and Listening.* Belmont, Calif.: Wadsworth, 1979.

Lundstan, S. W. *Listening: Its Impact on Reading and Other Language Arts.* Urbana, Ill.: National Council of Teachers of English, 1979.

McCarthy, Dorothy. "Language Development in Children." In *Manual of Child Psychology,* edited by L. Carmichael. New York: John Wiley, 1954.

Machado, J. M. *Early Childhood Experiences in Language Arts.* Albany, N.Y.: Delmar, 1979.

Magee, Mary Ann, and Brian Sutton-Smith. "The Art of Storytelling: How Do Children Learn It?" *Young Children* 38(May 1983): 4–12.

Manning, Gary, and Mary A. Manning. "Talk, Talk, Talk It Up." *Early Years* 11(January 1981): 26–27, 84.

Mattick, Ilse. "The Teacher's Role in Helping Young Children Develop Language Competence." *Young Children* 27(February 1972): 133–142.

Ostler, Renee, and Peter L. Kranz. "More Effective Communication Through Understanding Young Children's Non-verbal Behavior." *Young Children* 31(January 1976): 113–120.

"Reading and Pre-First Grade: A Joint Statement of Concerns About Present Practices in Pre-First Grade Reading Instruction and Recommendations for Improvement." *Young Children* 32(September 1977): 25–26.

Rogers, Cosby S., and Jane A. Wolfle. "Foundations for Literacy: A Building Blocks Model." *Young Children* 36(January 1981): 26–32.

Schickedanz, Judith. "Please Read That Story Again." *Young Children* 33(July 1978): 48–55.

Schimmel, J. *Just Enough to Make a Story: A Sourcebook for Storytelling.* Berkeley, Calif.: Sisters' Choice Press, 1978.

Schwartz, Judith I. "Children's Experiments With Language." *Young Children* 36(July 1981): 16–26.

Scott, Louise Binder. *Developing Communication Skills.* New York: McGraw-Hill, 1971.

______. *Talking Time.* New York: McGraw-Hill, 1971.

Seefeldt, Carol, Alice Galper, Kathy Serock, and Richard K. Jantz. "The Coming of Age in Children's Literature." *Childhood Education* 54(January 1978): 123–127.

Sherman, John Lee. "Storytelling With Young Children." *Childhood Education* 34(January 1979): 20–27.

Smith, C. A. "Puppetry and Problem-solving Skills." *Young Children* 34(March 1979): 4–11.

Smith, F. "The Language Arts and the Learner's Mind." *Language Arts* 56(February 1979): 118–125.

Sprung, B. *Non-sexist Education for Young Children. A Practical Guide.* New York: Citation Press, 1975.

Strickland, Dorothy S. "On Reading. An ACEI Position Paper." *Childhood Education* 56(1979): 67–74.

Sutton-Smith, Brian. *The Folkstories of Children.* Philadelphia: University of Pennsylvania Press, 1981.

U.S. Department of Health, Education, and Welfare. *Learning to Talk: Speech, Hearing and Language Problems in the Preschool Child.* Washington, D.C., 1969.

White, M. L. *Children's Literature: Criticism and Response.* Columbus, Ohio: Charles E. Merrill, 1976.

Williamson, Paul. "Literature Goals and Activities for Young Children." *Young Children* 36(May 1981): 24–30.

Books for Children

Aardena, V. *Why Mosquitoes Buzz in People's Ears.* New York: Dial Press, 1978.

Ahlberg, Janet, and Allen Ahlberg. *Each Peach Pear Plum: An "I Spy" Story.* New York: Viking Press, 1979.

Aliki. *Keep Your Mouth Closed, Dear.* New York: Dial Press, 1966.

Anno, M. *Anno's Alphabet: Adventure in Imagination.* New York: Harper & Row, 1975.

Aruego, Jose. *Look What I Can Do.* New York: Charles Scribner's Sons, 1971.

Bemelmans, L. *Madeline.* New York: Viking Press, 1939.

Berenstain, S., and J. Berenstain. *He Bear, She Bear.* New York: Random House, 1974.

Bishop, C. H. *The Five Chinese Brothers.* New York: Coward-McCann, 1938.

Brooke, L. L. *Ring o' Roses.* New York: Frederick Warne, 1977.

Broomfield, R. *The Baby Animal ABC.* New York: Penguin Books, 1968.

Brown, Margaret Wise. *Goodnight Moon.* New York: Harper & Row, 1947.

______. *The Important Book.* New York: Harper & Row, 1949.

Budney, Blossum. *A Kiss Is Round.* New York: Lothrop, Lee & Shepard, 1954.

Burningham, John. *The Blanket.* New York: Harper & Row, 1976.

______. *The Friend.* New York: Thomas Y. Crowell, 1976.

Burton, Virginia L. *Katy and the Big Snow.* Boston: Houghton Mifflin, 1943.

______. *Mike Mulligan and His Steam Shovel.* New York: Houghton Mifflin, 1977.

______. *The Little House.* Boston: Houghton Mifflin, 1978.

Carle, Eric. *Do You Want to Be My Friend?* New York: Harper & Row, 1971.

______. *My Very First Book of Shapes.* New York: Harper & Row, 1974.

______. *The Grouchy Ladybug.* New York: Harper & Row, 1977.

______. *The Very Hungry Caterpillar.* New York: Philomel Books, 1969.

Carrick, Carol. *The Washout.* New York: Houghton Mifflin, 1978.

Cleary, Beverly. *The Real Hole.* New York: William Morrow, 1960.

Cook, Bernadine. *The Little Fish That Got Away.* New York: Addison-Wesley, 1956.

Delton, J. *Two Good Friends.* New York: Crown, 1974.

Duvoisin, Roger. *The House of Four Seasons.* New York: Lothrop, Lee & Shepard, 1956.

Emberley, Ed. *ABC.* Boston: Little, Brown, 1978.

______. *The Wing on a Flea: A Book About Shapes.* Boston: Little, Brown, 1961.

Ets, Marie Hall. *Play With Me.* New York: Viking Press, 1955.

Field, R. *Prayer for a Child.* New York: Macmillan, 1973.

Fisher, A. *Going Places.* Glendale, Calif.: Bowmar, 1973.

Flack, Marjorie. *Angus* (series). New York: Doubleday, 1941–1977.

______. *Ask Mr. Bear.* New York: Macmillan, 1971.

Freeman, Don. *Come Again, Pelican.* New York: Viking Press, 1961.

______. *Corduroy.* New York: Viking Press, 1968.

______. *Mop Top.* New York: Viking Press, 1955.

Friskey, Margaret. *Seven Diving Ducks.* Chicago: Children's Press, 1965.

Fujikawa, G. *Gyo Fujikawa's A to Z Picture Book.* New York: Grosset & Dunlap, 1974.

Gaeddert, L. A. *Noisy Nancy Norris.* Garden City, N.Y.: Doubleday, 1965.

Gag, W. *ABC Bunny.* New York: Coward-McCann, 1933.

______. *Millions of Cats.* New York: Coward-McCann, 1928.

Green, Mary M. *Everybody Has a House.* New York: Addison-Wesley, 1961.

Greenaway, K. *A—Apple Pie.* New York: Frederick Warne, 1886.

Grossbart, Francine. *Big City.* New York: Harper & Row, 1966.

Guilfoile, E. *Nobody Listens to Andrew.* Chicago: Follett, 1957.

Hazen, Barbara. *The Me I See.* New York: Golden Press, 1978.

Hoban, Tana. *Is It Red? Is It Yellow? Is It Blue?* New York: Greenwillow Books, 1978.

Hutchins, Pat. *Rosie's Walk.* New York: Macmillan, 1971.

Iwasaki, Chihiro. *Momoko's Lovely Day.* London: Bodily Head, n.d.

______. *A Brother for Momoko.* London: Bodily Head, 1970.

______. *Momoko and the Pretty Bird.* London: Bodily Head, 1972.

Joslin, S. *What Do You Do, Dear?* New York: Addison-Wesley, 1961.

______. *What Do You Say, Dear?* New York: Scholastic Book Services, 1980.

Keats, Ezra J. *Hi Cat!* New York: Macmillan, 1970.

______. *Peter's Chair.* New York: Harper & Row, 1967.

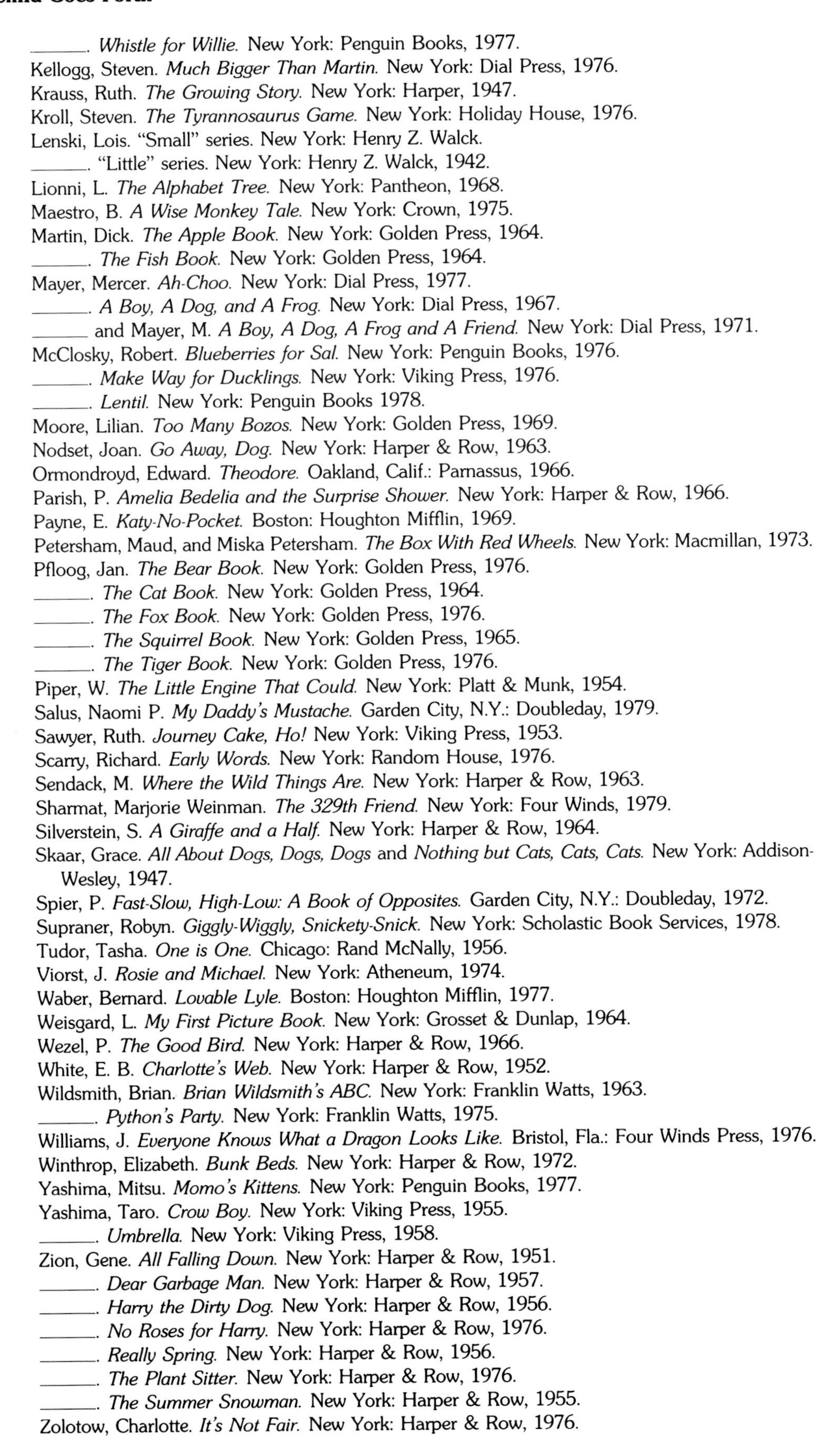

______. *Whistle for Willie.* New York: Penguin Books, 1977.
Kellogg, Steven. *Much Bigger Than Martin.* New York: Dial Press, 1976.
Krauss, Ruth. *The Growing Story.* New York: Harper, 1947.
Kroll, Steven. *The Tyrannosaurus Game.* New York: Holiday House, 1976.
Lenski, Lois. "Small" series. New York: Henry Z. Walck.
______. "Little" series. New York: Henry Z. Walck, 1942.
Lionni, L. *The Alphabet Tree.* New York: Pantheon, 1968.
Maestro, B. *A Wise Monkey Tale.* New York: Crown, 1975.
Martin, Dick. *The Apple Book.* New York: Golden Press, 1964.
______. *The Fish Book.* New York: Golden Press, 1964.
Mayer, Mercer. *Ah-Choo.* New York: Dial Press, 1977.
______. *A Boy, A Dog, and A Frog.* New York: Dial Press, 1967.
______ and Mayer, M. *A Boy, A Dog, A Frog and A Friend.* New York: Dial Press, 1971.
McClosky, Robert. *Blueberries for Sal.* New York: Penguin Books, 1976.
______. *Make Way for Ducklings.* New York: Viking Press, 1976.
______. *Lentil.* New York: Penguin Books 1978.
Moore, Lilian. *Too Many Bozos.* New York: Golden Press, 1969.
Nodset, Joan. *Go Away, Dog.* New York: Harper & Row, 1963.
Ormondroyd, Edward. *Theodore.* Oakland, Calif.: Parnassus, 1966.
Parish, P. *Amelia Bedelia and the Surprise Shower.* New York: Harper & Row, 1966.
Payne, E. *Katy-No-Pocket.* Boston: Houghton Mifflin, 1969.
Petersham, Maud, and Miska Petersham. *The Box With Red Wheels.* New York: Macmillan, 1973.
Pfloog, Jan. *The Bear Book.* New York: Golden Press, 1976.
______. *The Cat Book.* New York: Golden Press, 1964.
______. *The Fox Book.* New York: Golden Press, 1976.
______. *The Squirrel Book.* New York: Golden Press, 1965.
______. *The Tiger Book.* New York: Golden Press, 1976.
Piper, W. *The Little Engine That Could.* New York: Platt & Munk, 1954.
Salus, Naomi P. *My Daddy's Mustache.* Garden City, N.Y.: Doubleday, 1979.
Sawyer, Ruth. *Journey Cake, Ho!* New York: Viking Press, 1953.
Scarry, Richard. *Early Words.* New York: Random House, 1976.
Sendack, M. *Where the Wild Things Are.* New York: Harper & Row, 1963.
Sharmat, Marjorie Weinman. *The 329th Friend.* New York: Four Winds, 1979.
Silverstein, S. *A Giraffe and a Half.* New York: Harper & Row, 1964.
Skaar, Grace. *All About Dogs, Dogs, Dogs* and *Nothing but Cats, Cats, Cats.* New York: Addison-Wesley, 1947.
Spier, P. *Fast-Slow, High-Low: A Book of Opposites.* Garden City, N.Y.: Doubleday, 1972.
Supraner, Robyn. *Giggly-Wiggly, Snickety-Snick.* New York: Scholastic Book Services, 1978.
Tudor, Tasha. *One is One.* Chicago: Rand McNally, 1956.
Viorst, J. *Rosie and Michael.* New York: Atheneum, 1974.
Waber, Bernard. *Lovable Lyle.* Boston: Houghton Mifflin, 1977.
Weisgard, L. *My First Picture Book.* New York: Grosset & Dunlap, 1964.
Wezel, P. *The Good Bird.* New York: Harper & Row, 1966.
White, E. B. *Charlotte's Web.* New York: Harper & Row, 1952.
Wildsmith, Brian. *Brian Wildsmith's ABC.* New York: Franklin Watts, 1963.
______. *Python's Party.* New York: Franklin Watts, 1975.
Williams, J. *Everyone Knows What a Dragon Looks Like.* Bristol, Fla.: Four Winds Press, 1976.
Winthrop, Elizabeth. *Bunk Beds.* New York: Harper & Row, 1972.
Yashima, Mitsu. *Momo's Kittens.* New York: Penguin Books, 1977.
Yashima, Taro. *Crow Boy.* New York: Viking Press, 1955.
______. *Umbrella.* New York: Viking Press, 1958.
Zion, Gene. *All Falling Down.* New York: Harper & Row, 1951.
______. *Dear Garbage Man.* New York: Harper & Row, 1957.
______. *Harry the Dirty Dog.* New York: Harper & Row, 1956.
______. *No Roses for Harry.* New York: Harper & Row, 1976.
______. *Really Spring.* New York: Harper & Row, 1956.
______. *The Plant Sitter.* New York: Harper & Row, 1976.
______. *The Summer Snowman.* New York: Harper & Row, 1955.
Zolotow, Charlotte. *It's Not Fair.* New York: Harper & Row, 1976.

———. *One Step, Two . . .* New York: Lothrop, Lee & Shepard, 1981.
———. *Over and Over.* New York: Harper & Row, 1957. A book about holidays.
———. *Someday.* New York: Harper & Row, 1965.

CHAPTER 5. MUSIC AND MOVEMENT EDUCATION

Additional Sources

American Alliance for Health, Physical Education and Recreation. "Choosing and Using Phonograph Records for Physical Education, Recreation and Related Activities." Washington, D.C.: The Alliance, 1977.

Andress, Barbara. *Music Experiences in Early Childhood.* New York: Holt, Rinehart & Winston, 1980.

Andrews, Palmyra. "Music and Motion: The Rhythmic Language of Children." *Young Children* 32 (1976): 33–36.

Boardman, U., B. Landis, and B. Andress. *Exploring Music* (Kindergarten). New York: Holt, Rinehart & Winston, 1975.

Chenfeld, M. B. "Moving Movements for Wiggly Kids." *Phi Delta Kappan* 58 (November 1976): 261–263.

Commins, D. B. *The Big Book of Favorite Songs for Children.* New York: Grosset & Dunlap, 1951.

Curtis, Sandra R. *The Joy of Movement in Early Childhood.* New York: Teachers College, Columbia University, 1982.

Dalton, Arlene, Myriel Ashton, and Erla Young. *My Picture Book of Songs.* Chicago: M. A. Donohue, 1947.

Davis, B. *The Magical Child Within You.* Millbrae, Calif.: Celestial Arts, 1977.

Emerson, Peggy, and Cindy Leigh. "Movement: 'Enchantment' in the Life of a Child." *Childhood Education* 56 (November–December 1979): 85–87.

Fisher, Edward. *The Animal Song Book.* New York: St. Martin's Press, n.d.

Garretson, F. L. *Music in Childhood Education.* 2d ed. Englewood Cliffs, N.J.: Prentice-Hall, 1976.

Gerhardt, Lydia A. *Moving and Knowing: The Young Child Orients Himself in Space.* Englewood Cliffs, N.J.: Prentice-Hall, 1972.

Glazer, T. *Eye Winker, Tom Tinker, Chin Chopper.* New York: Doubleday, 1973.

Greenberg, M. *Young Children Need Music.* Englewood Cliffs, N.J.: Prentice-Hall, 1979.

Haines, B. J., and L. L. Gerber. *Leading Young Children to Music: A Resource Book for Teachers.* Columbus, Ohio: Charles E. Merrill, 1980.

Kuhmarker, Lisa. "Music in the Beginning Reading Program." *Young Children* 24 (January 1969): 157–163.

Langstaff, Nancy, and John Langstaff. *Jim Along Josie.* New York: Harcourt Brace Jovanovich, 1970.

Larrik, N. *The Wheels of the Bus Go Round and Round.* Chicago: Golden Gate, 1972.

McDonald, Dorothy T. *Music in Our Lives: The Early Years.* Washington, D.C.: National Association for the Education of Young Children, 1979.

McDonald, Dorothy T., and Jonny Ramsey, "Awakening the Artist: Music for Young Children." *Young Children* 33 (January 1978): 29–30.

McLaughlin, R., and L. Wood. *The Small Singer.* Glendale, Calif.: Bowmar, 1969.

Mettler, B. *Creative Dance in Kindergarten.* Tucson: Mettler Studios, 1976.

Mother Goose Melodies. New York: Dover, 1970.

Music in the Child's Education. New York: Ronald Press, 1970.

Nielsen, P. F., F. Sucher, and C. Carmen. *Mockingbird Flight.* Oklahoma City: Economy, 1975.

Nye, V. *Music for Young Children.* Dubuque, Iowa: William C. Brown, 1975.

Rasmus, C. J., and J. Fowler, eds. *Movement Activities for Places and Spaces.* Washington, D.C.: American Alliance for Health, Physical Education, and Recreation, 1977.

Renstrom, Moiselle. *Merrily We Sing.* Salt Lake City: Pioneer Music Press, 1962.

Richards, Mary H. *Pentatonic Songs for Young Children.* Belmont, Calif.: Fearon, 1967.

Rinehart, Carroll A. "The State of the Arts. Music: A Basic for the 1980's." *Childhood Education* 57 (January 1980): 140–45.

Seeger, Ruth. *American Folk Songs for Children.* Garden City, N.Y.: Doubleday, 1948.
Sinclair, Caroline B. *Movement of the Young Child: Ages Two to Six.* Columbus, Ohio: Charles E. Merrill, 1973.
Smith, R. B. *Music in the Child's Education.* New York: Ronald Press, 1970.
Songs to Sing With the Very Young. New York: Random House, 1966.
Stecher, M. B., and H. McEleny. *Joy and Learning Through Music and Movement Improvisation.* New York: Threshold, 1971.
Stinson, Susan W. "Movement as Creative Interaction With the Child." *Young Children* 32 (September 1977): 49–53.
Warner, Laverne. "37 Music Ideas for the Non-Musical Teacher." *Childhood Education* 58(January–February 1982): 134–136.
Wilson, H. R., and others. *Growing with Music* (Kindergarten). Englewood Cliffs, N.J.: Prentice-Hall, 1966.
Wood, Lucille F., and Louise B. Scott. *More Singing Fun.* St. Louis: McGraw-Hill, 1961.
______. *Singing Fun.* St. Louis: McGraw-Hill, 1954.
Yardley, Alice. "Movement and Learning." In *Readings in Early Childhood Education 78/79.* Guilford, Conn.: Dushkin, 1978, pp. 253–255.

Books for Children

Avery, Kay. *Wee Willow Whistle.* New York: Alfred A. Knopf, 1947.
Brown, Margaret W. *The Country Noisy Book.* New York: Harper & Row, 1976.
______. *The Indoor Noisy Book.* New York: Harper & Row, 1976.
______. *The Seashore Noisy Book.* New York: Harper & Row, 1941.
______. *The Summer Noisy Book.* New York: Harper & Row, 1951.
______. *The Quiet Noisy Book.* New York: Harper & Row, 1950.
______. *The Winter Noisy Book.* New York: Harper & Row, 1976.
Gramatky, Hardie. *Little Toot.* New York: G. P. Putnam's Sons, 1978.
Keats, Ezra. *Whistle for Willy.* New York: Penguin Books, 1977.
Lacey, Marion. *Picture Book of Musical Instruments.* New York: Lothrop, Lee & Shepard, 1942.
McGovern, Ann. *Too Much Noise.* New York: Houghton Mifflin, 1967.
Plume, Ilse. *The Bremen Town Musicians.* Garden City, N.Y.: Doubleday, 1980.
Quackenbush, Robert. *Skip to My Lou.* New York: Harper & Row, 1975.
Showers, Paul. *The Listening Walk.* New York: Harper & Row, 1961.
Silvers, Vicki. *Sing a Song of Sounds.* New York: Scroll Press, 1973.
Spier, Peter. *Crash! Bang! Boom!* New York: Doubleday, 1972.
______. *Fast-Slow, High-Low.* Garden City, N.Y.: Doubleday, 1979.
Steiner, Charlotte. *Listen to my Seashell.* New York: Alfred A. Knopf, 1959.
Tresselt, Alvin. *Rain Drop Splash.* New York: Lothrop, Lee & Shepard, 1946.
Van Woerkom, Dorothy. *The Queen Who Couldn't Bake Gingerbread.* New York: Alfred A. Knopf, 1975.

CHAPTER 6. SCIENCE

Additional Sources

Althouse, R. *The Young Child: Learning With Understanding.* New York: Teachers College Press, Columbia University, 1981.
Althouse, Rosemary, and Cecil Main. "The Science Learning Center: Hub of Science Activities." *Childhood Education* 50 (February 1974): 222–226.
Bennett, L. M., and G. Bassett. "Games and Things for Preschool Science." *Science and Children* 9 (January–February 1972): 25–27.
Bennett, Lloyd M. "Pre-Student Teaching Experience Using Science With Three- Through Five-Year-Old Children." *School Science and Mathematics.* 72 (April 1972): 301–307.
Bradbard, M., and R. C. Endsley. "How Can Teachers Develop Young Children's Curiosity? What Current Research Says to Teachers." *Young Children* 35 (July 1980): 21–32.
Carmichael, Viola S. *Science Experiences for Young Children.* Los Angeles: Southern California Association for Education of Young Children, 1969.

Croft, D., and R. Hess. *An Activities Handbook for Teachers of Young Children.* 3d ed. Boston: Houghton Mifflin, 1980.
Davis, Arnold R. "Science for Fives." *Childhood Education* 53 (February 1977): 206–210.
Day, Barbara. *Early Childhood Education: Creative Learning Activities.* New York: Macmillan, 1983.
Flemming, Bonnie, Darlene S. Hamilton, and J. D. Hicks. *Resources for Creative Teaching in Early Childhood Education.* New York: Harcourt Brace Jovanovich, 1977.
Harlan, J. D. "From Curiosity to Concepts; from Concepts to Curiosity—Science Experiences in the Preschool." *Young Children* 30 (May 1975): 249–255.
Hill, K. *Exploring the Natural World With Young Children.* New York: Harcourt Brace Jovanovich, 1976.
Kamii, C., and R. DeVries. *Physical Knowledge in Preschool Education: Implications of Piaget's Theory.* Englewood Cliffs, N.J.: Prentice-Hall, 1978.
Kamii, Constance, and Lucinda Lee-Katz. "Physics in Preschool Education." *Young Children* 34 (May 1979): 4–11.
Keyes, C. R. "A Science Open House Is Worth Copying." *Young Children* 31 (July 1976): 346–349.
Liepmann, L. *Your Child's Sensory World.* New York: Dial Press, 1973.
Margolin, Edythe. *Young Children: Their Curriculum and Learning Processes,* chaps. 6 and 7. New York: Macmillan, 1976, 1982.
Mills, Belen C., ed. *Understanding the Young Child and His Curriculum: Selected Readings.* New York: Macmillan, 1972, pp. 347–401.
National Council for the Social Studies. "Social Studies Curriculum Guidelines." Revised position statement. *Social Education* 43 (1979): 261–278.
Newman, Donald. "Sciencing for Young Children." *Young Children* 27 (April 1972): 215–226.
Ovitt, J. "Foundations of Science." In *A Creative Guide for Preschool Teachers,* edited by J. Wylie. Evanston, Ill.: Western, 1979.
Pagano, Alicia L., ed. *Social Studies in Early Childhood: An Interactionist Point of View.* Washington, D.C.: National Council for the Social Studies, 1978.
Piltz, Albert, Glenn Blough, and Ruth Roche. *Discovering Science: A Readiness Book.* A Teacher's Guide. Columbus, Ohio: Charles E. Merrill, 1973. Science for 4- and 5-year-old children.
Roche, Ruth L. *The Child and Science—Wondering, Exploring, and Growing.* Washington, D.C.: Association for Childhood Education International, 1977.
Rodell, W. C., R. G. Slaby, H. R. Robinson. *Social Development in Young Children.* Monterey, Calif.: Brooks/Cole, 1977.
Schneider, Herman, and Nina Schneider. *Got a Minute? Quick Science Experiments You Can Do.* New York: Scholastic Book Services, 1976.
______. *How Big Is Big: From Stars to Atoms.* New York: Scott, 1946.
______. *Science Fun With a Flashlight.* New York: McGraw-Hill, 1975.
Seefeldt, C. *A Curriculum for Preschoolers.* 2d ed. Columbus, Ohio: Charles E. Merrill, 1980.
Seefeldt, Carol. "Is Today Tomorrow? History for Young Children." *Young Children* 30 (January 1975): 99–106.
Shephardson, R. D. "Simple Inquiry Games." *Science and Children* 15 (October 1977): 34–36.
Smith, Robert F. "Early Childhood Science Education: A Piagetian Perspective." *Young Children* 36(January 1981): 3–11.
Sprung, B. *Non-sexist Education for Young Children: A Practical Guide.* N.Y.: Citation Press, 1975.
Thompson, G. D. "Where Do You Taste?" *Science and Children* 16 (May 1979): 25.
Walsh, Huber M. *Introducing the Young Child to the Social World.* New York: Macmillan, 1980.
Williams, D. L. "On Science for Young Children." *Science and Children* 13 (October 1975): 34–35.

Books for Children

Social Sciences

Adorjan, Carol M. *Someone I Know.* New York: Random House, 1968.
Anglund, Joan. *A Friend Is Someone Who Likes You.* New York: Harcourt Brace, 1958.
Beim, Jerrold, and Lorraine Beim. *Two Is a Team.* New York: Harcourt Brace, 1974.

Bemelmans, L. *Madeline's Rescue.* New York: Viking Press, 1953.
Berends, Polly B. *Who's That in the Mirror?* New York: Random House, 1968.
Berger, T. *I Have Feelings.* New York: Behavioral Publications, 1971.
Borack, Barbara. *Grandpa.* New York: Harper & Row, 1967.
Brenner, Barbara. *Bodies.* New York: E. P. Dutton, 1973.
Brown, Margaret Wise. *A Child's Goodnight Book.* New York: Addison-Wesley, 1943.
______. *The Little Fireman.* New York: Addison-Wesley, 1952.
Buckley, Helen E. *Grandfather and I.* New York: Lothrop, Lee & Shepard, 1959.
______. *Grandmother and I.* New York: Lothrop, Lee & Shepard, 1961.
Burningham, John. *Mr. Grumpy's Outing.* New York: Holt, Rinehart & Winston, 1971.
Burton, Virginia Lee. *Mike Mulligan and His Steam Shovel.* Boston: Houghton Mifflin, 1977.
______. *The Little House.* Boston: Houghton Mifflin, 1978.
Cohen, Miriam. *The New Teacher.* New York: Macmillan, 1974.
______. *Will I Have a Friend?* New York: Macmillan, 1967.
Crawford, Mel. *The Cowboy Book.* New York: Golden Press, 1976.
Crews, Donald. *Freight Train.* New York: Greenwillow Books, 1978.
______. *Truck.* New York: Greenwillow Books, 1980.
Delton, J. *Two Good Friends.* New York: Crown, 1974.
DeRegneirs, B. *May I Bring a Friend?* New York: Atheneum, 1964.
Eichler, M. *Martin's Father.* Chapel Hill, N.C.: Lollipop Power, 1977.
Ets, Marie H. *Just Me.* New York: Penguin Books, 1978.
______. *Play With Me.* New York: Viking Press, 1955.
Felt, S. *Rosa-Too-Little.* Garden City, N.Y.: Doubleday, 1950.
Fisher, A. *Going Places.* Glendale, Calif.: Bowmar, 1973.
Flack, Marjorie. *Wait for William.* Boston: Houghton Mifflin, 1935.
Foster, Doris V. *A Pocketful of Seasons.* New York: Lothrop, Lee & Shepard, 1960.
Francoise, A. *The Things I Like.* New York: Charles Scribner's Sons, 1960.
Freeman, Don. *Corduroy.* New York: Viking Press, 1968.
Green, Mary McBurney. *Everybody Has a House* and *Everybody Has a House and Everybody Eats.* Addison-Wesley, 1960.
______. *Is It Hard? Is It Easy?* New York: Addison-Wesley, 1960.
Greene, Carla Baker. *Doctors and Nurses.* New York: Harper & Row, 1963.
______. *Policemen and Firemen: What Do They Do?* New York: Harper & Row, 1978.
______. *Truck Drivers: What Do They Do?* New York: Harper & Row, 1967.
Hill, Elizabeth. *Evan's Corner.* Chicago: Holt, Rinehart & Winston, 1967.
Jeffrey, S. *Who Lives Here?* New York: Dandelion Press, 1979.
Keats, Ezra Jack. *A Letter to Amy.* New York: Harper & Row, 1968.
______. *Pet Show.* New York: Macmillan, 1972.
Kellogg, Steven. *Can I Keep Him?* New York: Dial Press, 1971.
Kessler, Ethel, and Leonard Kessler. *The Big Red Bus.* Garden City, N.Y.: Doubleday, 1964.
Lenski, Lois. *Davy Goes Places.* New York: Henry Z. Walck, 1961.
______. *The Little Airplane.* New York: Henry Z. Walck, 1938.
______. *The Little Farm.* New York: Henry Z. Walck, 1942.
______. *The Little Train.* New York: Henry Z. Walck, 1940.
______. *Papa Small.* New York: Henry Z. Walck, 1951.
Lerner, M. R. *Dear Little Mumps Child.* Minneapolis: Lerner, 1959.
______. *Peter Gets the Chickenpox.* Minneapolis: Lerner, 1959.
Marzollo, J. *Close Your Eyes.* New York: Dial Press, 1978.
Mayer, M. *There's a Nightmare in My Closet.* New York: Dial Press, 1968.
______. *You're the Scaredy Cat.* New York: Parents Magazine Press, 1974.
McCloskey, Robert. *Lentil.* New York: Viking Press, 1940.
______. *One Morning in Maine.* New York: Viking Press, 1952.
Merriam, E. *Mommies at Work.* New York: Scholastic Book Services, 1973.
Moncure, Jane. *People Who Help People.* Chicago: Children's Press, 1975.
Oppenheim, J. *Have You Seen Boats?* Reading, Mass.: Addison-Wesley, 1971.
______. *Have You Seen Roads?* Reading, Mass.: Addison-Wesley, 1969.
Parsons, Ellen. *Rainy Day Together.* New York: Harper & Row, 1971.
Penn, Ruth B. *Mommies Are for Loving.* New York: G. P. Putnam's Sons, 1962.
Piper, W. *The Little Engine That Could.* New York: Platt & Munk, 1976.

Puner, Helen W. *Daddies, What They Do All Day.* New York: Lothrop, Lee & Shepard, 1946.
Reich, Hans. *Children and Their Mothers.* New York: Hill & Wang, 1964.
Schlein, M. *The Way Mothers Are.* Chicago: Albert Whitman, 1963.
Sendak, M. *In the Night Kitchen.* New York: Harper & Row, 1970.
Seuss, R. *Happy Birthday to You!* New York: Random House, 1959.
Sharmat, Marjorie. *Goodnight, Andrew, Goodnight, Craig.* New York: Harper & Row, 1969.
______. *I'm Terrific.* New York: Holiday House, 1977.
Simon, Norma. *Hanukkah.* New York: Harper & Row, 1966.
______. *What Do I Say?* Chicago: Albert Whitman, 1967.
Slobodkin, L. *One Is Good, But Two Are Better.* New York: Vanguard Press, 1956.
Stanek, Muriel. *Left, Right, Left, Right.* Chicago: Albert Whitman, 1969.
Steig, W. *Sylvester and the Magic Pebble.* New York: Windmill Books, 1969.
Steptoe, J. *Train Ride.* New York: Harper & Row, 1971.
Surowiecki, S. L. *Joshua's Day.* Chapel Hill, N.C.: Lollipop Power, 1977.
Udry, J. M. *Let's Be Enemies.* New York: Harper & Row, 1961.
______. *What Mary Jo Shared.* Chicago: Albert Whitman, 1966.
Viorst, J. *Alexander and the Terrible, Horrible, No Good, Very Bad Day.* New York: Atheneum Publishers, 1976.
Waber, Bernard. *Ira Sleeps Over.* Boston: Houghton Mifflin, 1975.
Williams, B. *Albert's Toothache.* New York: E. P. Dutton, 1974.
______. *Someday, Said Mitchell.* New York: E. P. Dutton, 1976.
Yashima, Taro. *Umbrella.* New York: Viking Press, 1958.
Zaffo, G. *Airplanes & Trucks & Trains, Fire Engines, Boats & Ships, & Building & Wrecking Machines.* New York: Grosset & Dunlap, 1968.
Zolotow, Charlotte. *Big Brother.* New York: Harper & Row, 1960.
______. *Big Sister and Little Sister.* New York: Harper & Row, 1966.
______. *If It Weren't for You.* New York: Harper & Row, 1966.
______. *The Quarreling Book.* New York: Harper & Row, 1963.
______. *William's Doll.* New York: Harper & Row, 1972.

Biological Sciences

Animals

Alexander, M. *No Ducks in Our Bathtub.* New York: Dial Press, 1977.
Aliki. *My Visit to the Dinosaurs.* New York: Harper & Row, 1969.
Aruego, Jose. *Look What I Can Do.* New York: Charles Scribner's Sons, 1971.
Balian, L. *Sometimes It's Turkey—Sometimes It's Feathers.* Nashville: Abingdon Press, 1973.
Barrett, Judi. *Animal Should Definitely Not Wear Clothes.* New York: Atheneum, 1970.
Branley, F. *Big Tracks, Little Tracks.* New York: Harper & Row, 1960.
Brinckloe, J. *The Spider's Web.* Garden City, N.Y.: Doubleday, 1974.
Brown, Margaret Wise. *Wait Till the Moon Is Full.* New York: Harper & Row, 1948.
Carle, Eric. *Do You Want to Be My Friend?* New York: Harper & Row, 1971.
______. *The Very Hungry Caterpillar.* New York: Philomel, 1969.
Caudill, R. *A Pocketful of Cricket.* New York: Holt, Rinehart & Winston, 1964.
Cole, J. *A Calf Is Born.* New York: William Morrow, 1975.
Collier, Ethel. *Who Goes There in My Garden?* New York: Addison-Wesley, 1963.
Cooke, Ann. *Giraffes at Home.* New York: Harper & Row, 1972.
Crawford, Mel. *The Turtle Book.* New York: Golden Press, 1965.
Delton, Judy. *Rabbit Finds a Way.* New York: Crown, 1975.
Duvoisin, Roger. *Petunia.* New York: Alfred A. Knopf, 1950.
Eastman, P. D. *Are You My Mother?* New York: Random House, 1960.
Ets, Marie Hall. *In the Forest.* New York: Viking Press, 1976.
______. *Play With Me.* New York: Viking Press, 1976.
Fatio, Louise. *The Happy Lion.* New York: McGraw-Hill, 1964.
______. *The Happy Lion's Treasure.* New York: McGraw-Hill, 1970.
Fisher, Aileen. *Animal Houses.* Glendale, Calif.: Bowmar, 1973.
______. *Filling the Bill.* Glendale, Calif.: Bowmar, 1973.
______. *Like Nothing At All.* New York: Thomas Y. Crowell, 1979.

______. *Listen Rabbit.* New York: Thomas Y. Crowell, 1964.
______. *Sleepy Heads.* Glendale, Calif.: Bowmar, 1973.
______. *Tail Twisters.* Glendale, Calif.: Bowmar, 1973.
Flack, Marjorie. *Angus Lost.* New York: Doubleday, 1941.
______. *Ask Mr. Bear.* New York: Macmillan, 1971.
______. *The Story About Ping.* New York: Viking Press, 1977.
______. *Tim Tadpole and the Great Bullfrog.* New York: Doubleday, 1959.
Freeman, Don. *Fly High, Fly Low.* New York: Viking Press, 1957.
Friskey, Margaret. *Birds We Know.* Chicago: Children's Press, 1981.
______. *Johnny and the Monarch.* Chicago: Children's Press, 1946.
______. *Seven Diving Ducks.* Chicago: Children's Press, 1965.
Gag, W. *Millions of Cats.* New York: Coward, McCann, & Geoghegan, 1928.
Gans, Roma. *Birds at Night.* New York: Harper & Row, 1976.
______. *Birds Eat and Eat and Eat.* New York: Harper & Row, 1975.
______. *Bird Talk.* New York: Harper & Row, 1971.
______. *Hummingbirds in the Garden.* New York: Harper & Row, 1969.
Garelick, M. *What's Inside?* New York: Scholastic Book Services, 1970.
______. *Where Does the Butterfly Go When It Rains?* Reading, Mass.: Addison-Wesley, 1961.
Goldin, Augusta. *Ducks Don't Get Wet.* New York: Harper & Row, 1965.
______. *Spider Silk.* New York: Harper & Row, 1976.
Goudey, Alice. *Houses From the Sea.* New York: Charles Scribner's Sons, 1959.
Graham, M. *Be Nice to Spiders.* New York: Harper & Row, 1967.
______. *Benjy and the Barking Bird.* New York: Harper & Row, 1971.
Greene, C. *Animal Doctors, What Do They Do?* New York: Harper & Row, 1967.
Hawes, Judy. *Bees and Beelines.* New York: Thomas Y. Crowell, 1964.
______. *Fireflies in the Night.* New York: Thomas Y. Crowell, 1975.
______. *Ladybug, Ladybug, Fly Away Home.* New York: Thomas Y. Crowell, 1973.
______. *My Daddy Longlegs.* New York: Thomas Y. Crowell, 1972.
______. *What I Like About Toads.* New York: Thomas Y. Crowell, 1969.
______. *Why Frogs Are Wet.* New York: Thomas Y. Crowell, 1975.
Hazen, B. S. *What's Inside?* New York: Lion Books, 1969.
______. *Where Do Bears Sleep?* Reading, Mass.: Addison-Wesley, 1970.
Hurd, Edith T. *Starfish.* New York: Thomas Y. Crowell, 1962.
Hutchins, Pat. *Rosie's Walk.* New York: Macmillan, 1968.
Kaufmann, John. *Bats in the Dark.* New York: Thomas Y. Crowell, 1972.
Keats, Ezra Jack. *Pet Show.* New York: Macmillan, 1974.
Krauss, R. *Bears.* New York: Scholastic Book Services, 1970.
______. *Monkey Day.* Berkeley, Calif.: Bookstore Press, 1973.
Kroll, Steven. *The Tyrannosaurus Game.* New York: Holiday House, 1976.
Langstaff, J. *Over in the Meadow.* New York: Harcourt Brace Jovanovich, 1967.
Leaf, M. *The Story of Ferdinand.* New York: Viking Press, 1936.
Lenski, Lois. *The Little Farm.* New York: Henry Z. Walck, 1942.
Lerner, Marguerite. *Fur, Feathers, Hair.* Minneapolis: Lerner, 1962.
Lionni, L. *The Biggest House in the World.* New York: Pantheon, 1968.
______. *Frederick.* New York: Pantheon, 1966.
______. *The Greentail Mouse.* New York: Pantheon, 1973.
______. *Swimmy.* New York: Pantheon, 1963.
Lobel, Arnold. *Frog and Toad Are Friends.* New York: Harper & Row, 1972.
______. *Owl at Home.* New York: Harper & Row, 1975.
Mari, Iela, and Mari, Enzo. *The Apple and the Moth.* New York: Pantheon, 1970.
______. *The Chicken and the Egg.* New York: Pantheon, 1970.
Mason, George F. *Animal Sounds.* New York: William Morrow, 1948.
Mayer, Mercer. *Frog, Where Are You?* New York: Dial Press, 1969.
McCloskey, Robert. *Blueberries for Sal.* New York: Viking Press, 1976.
______. *Make Way for Ducklings.* New York: Penguin Books, 1976.
______. *One Morning in Maine.* New York: Viking Press, 1952.
Miles, Miska. *Nobody's Cat.* Boston: Little, Brown, 1969.
Mizumura, Kazue. *If I Were a Cricket.* New York: Harper & Row, 1973.
______. *The Blue Whale.* New York: Harper & Row, 1971.

______. *The Emperor Penguins.* New York: Harper & Row, 1969.
______. *The Way of an Ant.* New York: Harper & Row, 1970.
Moore, L. *Little Raccoon and the Things in the Pool.* New York: McGraw-Hill, 1963.
Nodset, J. L. *Who Took the Farmer's Hat?* New York: Harper & Row, 1963.
Parish, P. *Too Many Rabbits.* New York: Macmillan, 1974.
Payne, E. *Katy No-Pocket.* New York: Houghton Mifflin, 1969.
Petersham, M., and M. Petersham. *The Box With Red Wheels.* New York: Macmillan, 1949.
Pfloog, Jan. *Farm Book.* New York: Golden Press, 1964.
Piecewicz, A. T. *See What I Caught.* Englewood Cliffs, N.J.: Prentice-Hall, 1974.
Rojankovsky, Feodor. *Animals on the Farm.* New York: Alfred A. Knopf, 1967.
______. *The Great Big Wild Animal Book.* New York: Western, 1962.
Roy, Ron. *Three Ducks Went Wandering.* New York: Houghton Mifflin, 1979.
Schlein, Miriam. *Fast Is Not a Ladybug.* New York: Addison-Wesley, 1953.
______. *Heavy Is a Hippopotamus.* Reading, Mass.: Addison-Wesley, 1954.
Schwartz, E., and C. Schwartz. *When Flying Animals Are Babies.* New York: Holiday House, 1973.
Selsam, Millicent. *All About Eggs.* New York: Addison-Wesley, 1952.
______. *All Kinds of Babies.* New York: Scholastic Book Services, 1969.
______. *Is This a Baby Dinosaur?* New York: Harper & Row, 1972.
______. *Terry and the Caterpillars.* New York: Harper & Row, 1962.
Sharmat, Marjorie Weinman. *The 329th Friend.* New York: Four Winds, 1979.
Spier, P. *Gobble, Growl, Grunt.* Garden City, N.Y.: Doubleday, 1971.
______. *Noah's Ark.* Garden City, N.Y.: Doubleday, 1977.
Tresselt, A. *The Beaver Pond.* New York: Lothrop, Lee & Shepard, 1970.
Ungerer, T. *Crictor.* New York: Scholastic Book Services, 1969.
Ward, L. *The Biggest Bear.* New York: Houghton Mifflin, 1952.
Waters, John. *Green Turtle Mysteries.* New York: Harper & Row, 1972.
Wildsmith, Brian. *Circus.* New York: Oxford University Press, 1979.
______. *Fishes.* New York: Franklin Watts, 1968.
______. *Python's Party.* New York: Franklin Watts, 1975.
______. *Wild Animals.* New York: Oxford University Press, 1979.
Williams, G. *Baby Animals.* New York: Western, 1953.
______. *The Chicken Book.* New York: Delacorte Press, 1970.
Yashima, Mitsu. *Momo's Kittens.* New York: Penguin Books, 1977.
Young, Miriam. *Beware of the Polar Bear.* New York: Lothrop, Lee & Shepard, 1970.
Zion, Gene. *Harry the Dirty Dog.* New York: Harper & Row, 1976.
______. *No Roses for Harry.* New York: Harper & Row, 1976.

People

Alexander, M. *Nobody Asked Me If I Wanted a Baby Sister.* New York: Dell, 1971.
Aliki. *My Five Senses.* New York: Harper & Row, 1962.
______. *My Hands.* New York: Harper & Row, 1962.
Branley, F. M. *High Sounds, Low Sounds.* New York: Harper & Row, 1975.
Brown, M. W. *The City Noisy Book.* New York: Harper, 1976.
______. *The Noisy Book.* New York: Wm. R. Scott, 1939.
______. *Shhh-h-h Bang! A Whispering Book.* New York: Harper, 1943.
Freeman, Don. *Mop Top.* New York: Viking Press, 1955.
Goldin, Augusta. *Straight Hair, Curly Hair.* New York: Harper & Row, 1966.
Keats, Ezra. *Peter's Chair.* New York: Harper & Row, 1967.
______. *Whistle for Willie.* New York: Viking, 1964.
______. *A Letter to Amy.* New York: Harper & Row, 1968.
Krauss, Ruth. *The Growing Story.* New York: Harper, 1947.
Showers, Paul. *A Baby Starts to Grow.* New York: Thomas Y. Crowell, 1972.
______. *A Drop of Blood.* New York: Thomas Y. Crowell, 1972.
______. *Finding Out by Touching.* New York: Thomas Y. Crowell, 1961.
______. *Follow Your Nose.* New York: Thomas Y. Crowell, 1963.
______. *Hear Your Heart.* New York: Thomas Y. Crowell, 1968.
______. *How Many Teeth?* New York: Thomas Y. Crowell, 1962.
______. *How You Talk.* New York: Thomas Y. Crowell, 1967.

———. *The Listening Walk.* New York: Thomas Y. Crowell, 1961.
———. *Look at Your Eyes.* New York: Thomas Y. Crowell, 1976.
———. *What Happens to a Hamburger?* New York: Thomas Y. Crowell, 1976.
———. *Your Skin and Mine.* New York: Thomas Y. Crowell, 1965.
Showers, Paul, and Kay Showers. *Before You Were a Baby.* New York: Thomas Y. Crowell, 1968.
Simon, Norma. *What Do I Say?* Chicago: Albert Whitman, 1967.
Viorst, J. *I'll Fix Anthony.* New York: Harper & Row, 1969.
Wilt, J., and T. Watson. *Listen.* Waco, Tex.: Creative Resources, 1977.
———. *Look.* Waco, Tex.: Creative Resources, 1978.
———. *Rhythm and Movement.* Waco, Tex.: Creative Resources, 1977.
———. *Taste and Smell.* Waco, Tex.: Creative Resources, 1978.
———. *Touch.* Waco, Tex.: Creative Resources, 1977.
Zion, Gene. *Dear Garbage Man.* New York: Harper, 1957.
———. *The Plant Sitter.* New York: Harper, 1976.

Plants

Bancroft, Henrietta. *Down Come the Leaves.* New York: Harper & Row, 1961.
Bulla, C. R. *A Tree Is a Plant.* New York: Harper & Row, 1973.
Goldin, Augusta. *Where Does Your Garden Grow?* New York: Harper & Row, 1967.
Jordan, Helene J. *How a Seed Grows.* New York: Thomas Y. Crowell, 1960.
———. *Seeds by Wind and Water.* New York: Thomas Y. Crowell, 1962.
Krasilovsky, Phyllis. *The Shy Little Girl.* Boston: Houghton Mifflin, 1972.
Krauss, R. *The Carrot Seed.* New York: Harper & Row, 1945.
Koehler, C. *The Wonder Book of Trees.* New York: Grossett & Dunlap, 1974.
Miles, M. *The Apricot ABC.* Boston: Little, Brown, 1969.
Podendorf, Illa. *Weeds and Wild Flowers.* Chicago: Children's Press, 1981.
Selsam, Millicent E. *Play with Plants.* New York: William Morrow, 1978.
Udry, J. *A Tree Is Nice.* New York: Harper & Row, 1956.
Webber, Irma E. *Up Above and Down Below.* New York: Addison-Wesley, 1943.
———. *Travelers All: How Plants Go Places.* New York: Addison-Wesley, 1944.
———. *Bits That Grow Big.* New York: Addison-Wesley, 1949.
Zion, Gene. *Harry by the Sea.* New York: Harper & Row, 1976.

Physical Science

Alexenberg, Melvin. *Light and Sight.* Englewood Cliffs, N.J.: Prentice-Hall, 1969.
Aliki, *Fossil Tell of Long Ago.* New York: Thomas Y. Crowell, 1972.
———. *The Long Lost Coelacanth and Other Living Fossils.* New York: Thomas Y. Crowell, 1973.
———. *My Visit to Dinosaurs.* New York: Thomas Y. Crowell, 1972.
Anglund, J. *Spring Is a New Beginning.* New York: Harcourt, Brace & World, 1963.
Ardizzone, Edward. *Little Tim and the Brave Sea Captain.* New York: Oxford University Press, 1978.
Balestrino, Phillip. *Hot as an Ice Cube.* New York: Thomas Y. Crowell, 1971.
Bancroft, H., and R. Gelder. *Animals in Winter.* New York: Thomas Y. Crowell, 1963.
Bartlett, M. F. *The Clean Brook.* New York: Thomas Y. Crowell, 1960.
———. *Where the Brook Begins.* New York: Thomas Y. Crowell, 1961.
Barton, Byron. *Wheels.* New York: Thomas Y. Crowell, 1979.
Baylor, B. *Everybody Needs a Rock.* New York: Charles Scribner's Sons, 1974.
Bonsall, George. *Weather.* New York: Wonder Books, 1960.
Branley, F. M. *Air Is All Around You.* New York: Thomas Y. Crowell, 1962.
———. *The Big Dipper.* New York: Thomas Y. Crowell, 1962.
———. *The Beginning of the Earth.* New York: Thomas Y. Crowell, 1972.
———. *Gravity Is a Mystery.* New York: Thomas Y. Crowell, 1970.
———. *Flash, Crash, Rumble & Roll.* New York: Thomas Y. Crowell, 1964.
———. *Floating and Sinking.* New York: Thomas Y. Crowell, 1967.
———. *The Moon Seems to Change.* New York: Thomas Y. Crowell, 1960.
———. *North, South, East and West.* New York: Thomas Y. Crowell, 1966.
———. *Oxygen Keeps You Alive.* New York: Thomas Y. Crowell, 1972.
———. *Rain and Hail.* New York: Thomas Y. Crowell, 1963.

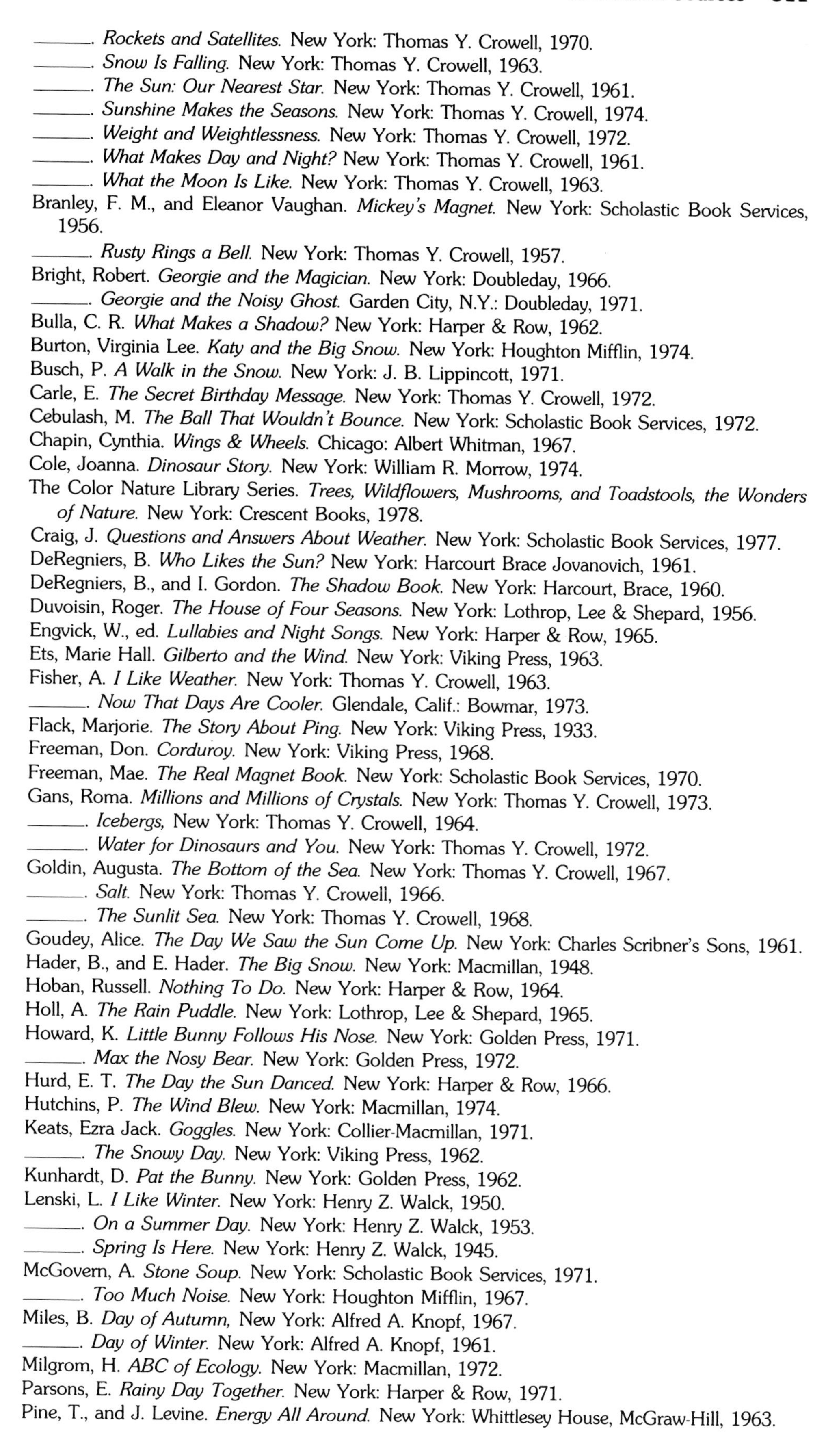

———. *Rockets and Satellites.* New York: Thomas Y. Crowell, 1970.
———. *Snow Is Falling.* New York: Thomas Y. Crowell, 1963.
———. *The Sun: Our Nearest Star.* New York: Thomas Y. Crowell, 1961.
———. *Sunshine Makes the Seasons.* New York: Thomas Y. Crowell, 1974.
———. *Weight and Weightlessness.* New York: Thomas Y. Crowell, 1972.
———. *What Makes Day and Night?* New York: Thomas Y. Crowell, 1961.
———. *What the Moon Is Like.* New York: Thomas Y. Crowell, 1963.
Branley, F. M., and Eleanor Vaughan. *Mickey's Magnet.* New York: Scholastic Book Services, 1956.
———. *Rusty Rings a Bell.* New York: Thomas Y. Crowell, 1957.
Bright, Robert. *Georgie and the Magician.* New York: Doubleday, 1966.
———. *Georgie and the Noisy Ghost.* Garden City, N.Y.: Doubleday, 1971.
Bulla, C. R. *What Makes a Shadow?* New York: Harper & Row, 1962.
Burton, Virginia Lee. *Katy and the Big Snow.* New York: Houghton Mifflin, 1974.
Busch, P. *A Walk in the Snow.* New York: J. B. Lippincott, 1971.
Carle, E. *The Secret Birthday Message.* New York: Thomas Y. Crowell, 1972.
Cebulash, M. *The Ball That Wouldn't Bounce.* New York: Scholastic Book Services, 1972.
Chapin, Cynthia. *Wings & Wheels.* Chicago: Albert Whitman, 1967.
Cole, Joanna. *Dinosaur Story.* New York: William R. Morrow, 1974.
The Color Nature Library Series. *Trees, Wildflowers, Mushrooms, and Toadstools, the Wonders of Nature.* New York: Crescent Books, 1978.
Craig, J. *Questions and Answers About Weather.* New York: Scholastic Book Services, 1977.
DeRegniers, B. *Who Likes the Sun?* New York: Harcourt Brace Jovanovich, 1961.
DeRegniers, B., and I. Gordon. *The Shadow Book.* New York: Harcourt, Brace, 1960.
Duvoisin, Roger. *The House of Four Seasons.* New York: Lothrop, Lee & Shepard, 1956.
Engvick, W., ed. *Lullabies and Night Songs.* New York: Harper & Row, 1965.
Ets, Marie Hall. *Gilberto and the Wind.* New York: Viking Press, 1963.
Fisher, A. *I Like Weather.* New York: Thomas Y. Crowell, 1963.
———. *Now That Days Are Cooler.* Glendale, Calif.: Bowmar, 1973.
Flack, Marjorie. *The Story About Ping.* New York: Viking Press, 1933.
Freeman, Don. *Corduroy.* New York: Viking Press, 1968.
Freeman, Mae. *The Real Magnet Book.* New York: Scholastic Book Services, 1970.
Gans, Roma. *Millions and Millions of Crystals.* New York: Thomas Y. Crowell, 1973.
———. *Icebergs,* New York: Thomas Y. Crowell, 1964.
———. *Water for Dinosaurs and You.* New York: Thomas Y. Crowell, 1972.
Goldin, Augusta. *The Bottom of the Sea.* New York: Thomas Y. Crowell, 1967.
———. *Salt.* New York: Thomas Y. Crowell, 1966.
———. *The Sunlit Sea.* New York: Thomas Y. Crowell, 1968.
Goudey, Alice. *The Day We Saw the Sun Come Up.* New York: Charles Scribner's Sons, 1961.
Hader, B., and E. Hader. *The Big Snow.* New York: Macmillan, 1948.
Hoban, Russell. *Nothing To Do.* New York: Harper & Row, 1964.
Holl, A. *The Rain Puddle.* New York: Lothrop, Lee & Shepard, 1965.
Howard, K. *Little Bunny Follows His Nose.* New York: Golden Press, 1971.
———. *Max the Nosy Bear.* New York: Golden Press, 1972.
Hurd, E. T. *The Day the Sun Danced.* New York: Harper & Row, 1966.
Hutchins, P. *The Wind Blew.* New York: Macmillan, 1974.
Keats, Ezra Jack. *Goggles.* New York: Collier-Macmillan, 1971.
———. *The Snowy Day.* New York: Viking Press, 1962.
Kunhardt, D. *Pat the Bunny.* New York: Golden Press, 1962.
Lenski, L. *I Like Winter.* New York: Henry Z. Walck, 1950.
———. *On a Summer Day.* New York: Henry Z. Walck, 1953.
———. *Spring Is Here.* New York: Henry Z. Walck, 1945.
McGovern, A. *Stone Soup.* New York: Scholastic Book Services, 1971.
———. *Too Much Noise.* New York: Houghton Mifflin, 1967.
Miles, B. *Day of Autumn,* New York: Alfred A. Knopf, 1967.
———. *Day of Winter.* New York: Alfred A. Knopf, 1961.
Milgrom, H. *ABC of Ecology.* New York: Macmillan, 1972.
Parsons, E. *Rainy Day Together.* New York: Harper & Row, 1971.
Pine, T., and J. Levine. *Energy All Around.* New York: Whittlesey House, McGraw-Hill, 1963.

Rockwell, Ann, and Harlow Rockwell. *Machines.* New York: Macmillan, 1972.
Sawyer, Ruth. *Journey Cake, Ho.* New York: Viking Press, 1973.
Schlein, Miriam. *Shapes.* New York: Addison-Wesley, 1952.
Schneider, Herman, and Nina Schneider. *How Big Is Big? From Stars to Atoms.* New York: Addison-Wesley, 1946.
Selsam, Millicent. *All Kinds of Babies.* New York: Scholastic Book Services, 1967.
______. *How Puppies Grow.* New York: Scholastic Book Services, 1977.
______. *Peanut.* New York: William Morrow, 1969.
______. *Plenty of Fish.* New York: Harper & Row, 1960.
Showers, P. *Find Out by Touching.* New York: Thomas Y. Crowell, 1961.
______. *Follow Your Nose.* New York: Thomas Y. Crowell, 1963.
______. *In the Night.* New York: Thomas Y. Crowell, 1961.
______. *The Listening Walk.* New York: Thomas Y. Crowell, 1961.
Shulevitz, U. *Rain, Rain Rivers.* New York: Farrar, Straus, & Giroux, 1969.
Tangborn, W. V. *Glaciers.* New York: Thomas Y. Crowell.
Tison, Annette, and Taylor, Talus. *The Adventures of the Three Colors.* New York: World, 1971.
Tresselt, Alvin. *Follow the Wind.* New York: Lothrop, Lee & Shepard, 1950.
______. *Hide and Seek Fog.* New York: Lothrop, Lee & Shepard, 1965.
______. *Rain Drop Splash.* New York: Lothrop, Lee & Shepard, 1946.
______. *Sun Up.* New York: Lothrop, Lee & Shepard, 1949.
______. *White Snow, Bright Snow.* New York: Lothrop, Lee & Shepard, 1947.
Udry, J. *Mary Jo's Grandmother.* Chicago: Albert Whitman, 1970.
Viorst, Judith. *I'll Fix Anthony.* New York: Harper & Row, 1969.
Witte, E., and P. Witte. *Who Lives Here.* New York: Golden Press, 1961.
Wyler, Rose, and Gerald Ames. *Secrets in Stones.* New York: Four Winds Press, 1971.
Zaffo, George, and Charles Black. *Big Book of Airplanes.* New York: Grossett & Dunlap, 1977.
Zolotow, C. *The Sky Was Blue.* New York: Harper & Row, 1963.
______. *The Storm Book.* New York: Harper & Row, 1952.
______. *Summer Is . . .* New York: Abelard-Schuman, 1967.
______. *Summer Night.* New York: Harper & Row, 1974.
______. *When the Wind Stops.* New York: Harper & Row, 1975.

CHAPTER 7. TRANSITION ACTIVITIES

Additional Sources

Planning Transition Activities

Curtis, Sandra R. *The Joy of Movement.* New York: Teacher's College Press, Columbia University, 1982.
Hildebrand, Verna, and Rebecca P. Hines. "The Pied Pipers of Poetry." *Young Children* 36(January 1981): 12–18.
Hirsch, E. S. "Transition Periods: Stumbling Blocks of Education." New York: Early Childhood Education Council of New York City, 1972.
Kounin, Jacob S., and Sylvia Obradovic. "Managing Emotionally Disturbed Children in Regular Classrooms: A Replication and Extension." *Journal of Special Education* 2(1968): 129–135.
Mugge, D. J. "Taking the Routine out of Routines." *Young Children* 31(March 1976): 209–217.
Vartuli, Sue, and Carol Phelps. "Classroom Transitions." *Childhood Education* 57 (November–December 1980): 94–96.

Activities

Finger Plays

Cromwell, Liz, and Dixie Hibner. *Finger Frolics: Fingerplays for Young Children.* Livonia, Mich.: Partner Press, 1978.
Glazer, Tom. *Eye Winker, Tom Tinker, Chin Chopper.* Garden City, N.Y.: Doubleday, 1973.
Grayson, Marion. *Let's Do Fingerplays.* Washington, D.C.: R. B. Luce, 1967.
Matterson, Elizabeth. *Games for the Very Young.* New York: American Heritage, 1971.
Poulsson, Emilie. *Finger Plays for Nursery and Kindergarten.* New York: Dover, 1971.

Scott, Louise B. *Rhymes for Learning Times.* Minneapolis: T. S. Denison, 1983.
Scott, Louise B., and J. J. Thompson. *Rhymes for Fingers and Flannelboards.* St. Louis: Webster, 1969.
Steiner, Violette J., and Roberta E. Pond. *Finger Play Fun.* Columbus, Ohio: Charles E. Merrill, 1970.

Mother Goose and Nursery Rhymes

Battaglia, Aurelius. *Mother Goose.* New York: Random House Picturebook, 1973.
Fujikawa, G. *Mother Goose.* New York: Grossett & Dunlap, 1975.
Greenaway, Kate. *Mother Goose: or the Old Nursery Rhymes.* New York: Frederick Warne, 1882.
Hennings, Dorothy G. "Waddle Away With Mother Goose." *Early Years* 6 (March 1976): 38–39.
Lobel, Arnold. *Gregory Griggs and Other Nursery Rhyme People.* New York: Greenwillow Books, 1978.
Mother Goose Melodies. New York: Dover, 1970.
O'Bruba, William S. "Mother Goose Remembered." *Early Years* 6 (March 1976): 40.
Rao, Anthony. *The Highlights Book of Nursery Rhymes.* Columbus, Ohio: Highlights for Children, 1974.
Tudor, T. *Mother Goose.* New York: Henry Z. Walck, 1944, 1976.
Wright, B. P. *The Real Mother Goose.* Chicago: Rand McNally, 1916, 1978.

Poetry

Alderson, Brian, ed. *Cakes and Custard.* New York: William Morrow, 1975.
Chukovsky, Kornei. *From Two to Five.* Berkeley: University of California Press, 1968.
Conklin, Hilda. *Poems by a Little Girl.* New York: Frederick A. Stokes, 1923.
Chute, Marchette. *Around and About.* New York: E. P. Dutton, 1957.
Counting Out Rhymes. New York: Dover, 1970.
De la Mare, Walter. *Peacock Pie.* New York: Holt, 1924.
DeRegniers, B., E. Moore, and M. M. White. *Poems Children Will Sit Still For.* New York: Scholastic Book Services, 1973.
Eenie, Meenie, Minie, Mo. New York: Dover, 1970.
Farjeon, Eleanor. *Poems for Children.* New York: Frederick A. Stokes, 1951.
Field, Rachel. *Taxis and Toadstools.* New York: Doubleday, Doran, 1926.
Fisher, Aileen. *Feathered Ones and Furry.* New York: Thomas Y. Crowell, 1971.
Frank, Josette, ed. *Poems to Read to the Very Young.* New York: Random House, 1961.
———. *More Poems to Read to the Very Young.* New York: Random House, 1968.
Fujikawa, Gyo. *A Child's Book of Poems.* New York: Grosset & Dunlap, 1969.
Geismer, B., and A. Suter. *Very Young Verses.* Boston: Houghton Mifflin, 1975.
Greenaway, Kate. *Under the Window.* New York: Frederick Warne, 1910.
Hoberman, Mary Ann. *Nuts to You and Nuts to Me.* New York: Alfred A. Knopf, 1974.
Hopkins, Lee B., comp. *Good Morning to You, Valentine.* New York: Harcourt Brace Jovanovich, 1975.
Jacobs, Leland B. *Just Around the Corner.* New York: Holt, Rinehart, 1964.
Lawrence, Marjory. *A Beginning Book of Poems.* Reading, Mass.: Addison-Wesley, 1967.
Lear, Edward. *The Quangle-Wangle's Hat.* New York: Franklin Watts, 1969.
Lenski, Lois. *City Poems.* New York: Henry Z. Walck, 1971.
Miller, M., ed. *One Misty Moisty Morning.* New York: Farrar, Straus & Giroux, 1971.
Milne, A. A. *The World of Christopher Robin.* New York: E. P. Dutton, 1958.
———. *When We Were Very Young.* New York: E. P. Dutton, 1924.
O'Neill, Mary. *Hailstones and Halibut Bones.* Garden City, N.Y.: Doubleday, 1961.
Richards, Laura E. *Tirra Lirra.* Boston: Little, Brown, 1955.
Rosetti, Christina. *Sing-Song.* New York: Macmillan, 1952.
Rothman, Joel, and Argentina Palacios. *This Can Lick a Lollipop/Esto Coza Chupando Un Caramelo.* Garden City, N.Y.: Doubleday, 1979.
Sandburg, Carl. *Early Moon.* New York: Harcourt, Brace, 1958.
Stevenson, Robert Louis. *A Child's Garden of Verses.* London: Henry Z. Walck, 1947; Collins, 1973.
Tippett, James S. *Crickety, Cricket.* New York: Harper & Row, 1973.
Zuromski, Diane. *The Farmer in the Dell.* Boston: Little, Brown, 1978.

Puppets

Cole, Ann, Carolyn Haas, Edith Bushnell, and Betty Weinberger. *I Saw a Purple Cow.* Boston: Little, Brown, 1972, pp. 26–28.

Vermeer, Jackie, and Marian Lariviere. *The Little Kid's Craftsbook.* New York: Taplinger, 1973, pp. 78–96.

CHAPTER 8. FIELD TRIPS

Additional Sources

Buschoff, Lotte K. "Going on a Trip." *Young Children* 26(March 1971): 224–232.

Cohen, Shirley. "Planning Trips for Vulnerable Children." *Childhood Education* 48(1972): 192–196.

Croft, D., and R. Hess. *An Activities Handbook for Teachers of Young Children.* 3d ed. Boston: Houghton Mifflin, 1980.

Hildebrand, Verna. "Trips for Preschoolers." *Childhood Education* 43(May 1967): 524–528.

______. *Introduction to Early Childhood Education.* New York: Macmillan, 1976, pp. 357–372.

Kelsey, K. W. "A Neighborhood Field Trip." *Science and Children* 16(April 1979): 14–15.

Moore, Sallie, and Phyllis Richards. *Teaching in the Nursery School.* New York: Harper, 1959, pp. 53–69.

Russell, Helen R. *Ten-Minute Field Trips: A Teacher's Guide.* Chicago: J. G. Ferguson, 1973. Mainly for grade school children, but some ideas can be adapted.

Seefeldt, Carol. *Social Studies for the Preschool-Primary Child.* Columbus, Ohio: Charles E. Merrill, 1977, pp. 316–324.

CHAPTER 9. SPECIAL OCCASIONS

Additional Sources

Baker, Donald, and James Last. "Celebration!" *Childhood Education* January 1978, pp. 131–134.

Crystal, Frances H. "The Holiday Dilemma: Celebrating the Holidays in Preschool and Kindergarten." *Young Children* November 1967, pp. 66–73.

Moore, Sallie, and Phyllis Richards. *Teaching in the Nursery School.* New York: Harper, 1959, pp. 100–124.

Ramsey, Patricia G. "Beyond Ten Little Indians and Turkeys." *Young Children* 34(September 1979): 28–51.

Schmidt, V. E., and E. McNeill. *Cultural Awareness: A Resource Bibliography.* Washington, D.C.: National Association for the Education of Young Children, 1978.

Timberlake, Pat. "Classroom Holidaze." *Childhood Education,* January 1978, pp. 128–130.

Todd, Vivian E., and Helen Heffernan. *The Years Before School.* Toronto: Macmillan, 1977, pp. 302–318.

Selected Jewish Sources

American Association for Jewish Education. "Jewish Education: The Early Years." *Pedagogic Reporter* 24(Fall 1972):3.

Chanover, Hyman. *A Curriculum Guide for the Kindergarten.* New York: United Synagogue Book Service, n.d.

Chicago Board of Jewish Education. *Manual for the Nursery School and Kindergarten.* n.p., n.d.

Edidin, Ben M. *Jewish Holidays and Festivals.* New York: Hebrew Publishing, 1940.

Siegel, R., M. Strassfeld, and S. Strassfeld. *The First Jewish Catalog: A Do-It-Yourself Kit.* Philadelphia: Jewish Publication Society of America, 1973.

Strassfeld, M., and S. Strassfeld, eds. *The Second Jewish Catalog.* Philadelphia: Jewish Publication Society, 1976.

———. *The Third Jewish Catalog.* Philadelphia: Jewish Publication Society, 1980. Includes index for all three volumes.

Books for Children

Aichinger, Helga. *The Shepherd.* New York: Thomas Y. Crowell, 1967.
Anglund, Joan Walsh. *Christmas Is a Time of Giving.* New York: Harcourt Brace Jovanovich, 1961.
Barry, Robert. *Mr. Willoby's Christmas Tree.* New York: McGraw-Hill, 1963.
Brown, Margaret Wise. *Christmas in the Barn.* New York: Thomas Y. Crowell, 1949.
———. *On Christmas Eve.* Reading, Mass.: Addison-Wesley, 1975.
———. *The Golden Egg Book.* New York: Golden Press, 1947.
Brown, Myra B. *Birthday Boy.* New York: Franklin Watts, 1963.
Bruna, Dick. *Christmas Book.* New York: Methuen, 1976.
Buckley, Helen. *The Little Boy and the Birthdays.* New York: Lothrop, Lee & Shepard, 1965.
Carle, Eric. *The Secret Birthday Message.* New York: Thomas Y. Crowell, 1972.
Dalgleish, A. *The Thanksgiving Story.* New York: Charles Scribner's Sons, 1954.
———. *The Fourth of July Story.* New York: Charles Scribner's Sons, 1956.
Devlin, W., and H. Devlin. *Cranberry Christmas.* New York: Scholastic Book Services, 1980.
Duvoisin, Roger. *Easter Treat.* New York: Alfred A. Knopf, 1954.
Fern, Eugene. *Birthday Presents.* New York: Farrar, Straus, & Giroux, 1967.
Flack, Marjorie. *Ask Mr. Bear.* New York: Macmillan, 1958.
Geffner, Anne. *A Child Celebrates: The Jewish Holidays.* Sepulveda, Calif.: Double M. Press, 1979.
Hoffman, Felix. *The Story of Christmas.* New York: Atheneum, 1975.
Kahl, V. *Plum Pudding for Christmas.* New York: Charles Scribner's Sons, 1956.
Kaufman, Joe. *The Christmas Tree Book.* New York: Golden Press, 1965.
Keats, Ezra Jack. *The Little Drummer Boy.* New York: Macmillan, 1968.
Klein, Leonore. *Picnics and Parades.* New York: Alfred A. Knopf, 1976.
Krahn, F. *April Fools.* E. P. Dutton, 1974.
Kraus, Ruth. *Birthday Party.* New York: Harper & Row, 1957.
Kroeber, Theodora. *A Green Christmas.* Oakland, Calif.: Parnassus Press, 1967.
Massey, Jeanne. *Littlest Witch.* New York: Alfred A. Knopf, 1959.
Schatz, Letta. *When Will My Birthday Be?* New York: McGraw-Hill, 1962.
Seuss, Dr. *How the Grinch Stole Christmas.* New York: Random House, 1957.
Showers, Paul. *Indian Festivals.* New York: Thomas Y. Crowell, 1969.
Slobodkin, Louis. *Trick or Treat.* New York: Macmillan, 1972.
Thayer, Jane. *Gus Was a Christmas Ghost.* New York: William Morrow, 1970.
Tresselt, Alvin. *The World in the Candy Egg.* New York: Lothrop, Lee & Shepard, 1967.
Wells, Rosemary. *Morris's Disappearing Bag.* New York: Dial Press, 1978.
Zolotow, Charlotte. *The Bunny Who Found Easter.* Oakland, Calif.: Parnassus Press, 1959.

CHAPTER 10. FOOD: NUTRITION, PREPARATION, AND ENJOYMENT

Additional Sources

Bruno, J., and P. Dakan. *Cooking in the Classroom.* New York: Golden Press, 1970.
Church, Marilyn. "Nutrition: A Vital Part of the Curriculum." *Young Children* November 1979, pp. 61–66.
Cobb, V. *Science Experiments You Can Eat.* Philadelphia: J. B. Lippincott, 1974.
Cook, R., and others. "Nutritional Status of Head Start and Nursery School Children." *Journal of American Dietetic Association* 68(February 1976): 120–126.
Cooper, T. T., and M. Ratner. *Many Hands Cooking: An International Cookbook for Girls and Boys.* New York: Thomas Y. Crowell, 1974.
The Children's Cookbook: A Beginner's Guide to Cooking. 1980. Available from Favorite Recipes Press, P.O. Box 77, Nashville, TN 37202
Feingold, F. "Hyperkinesis and Learning Disabilities Linked to Artificial Food Flavors and Colors." *American Journal of Nursing* 75(1975): 797–803.

Foster, Florence P., comp. *Adventures in Cooking: A Collection of Recipes for Use in Nursery Schools, Day Care Centers, Head Start Programs, Kindergartens, and Primary Classrooms.* Westfield, N.J.: New Jersey Association for the Education of Young Children, 1971.

Galen, Harlene. "Cooking in the Curricula." *Young Children* 33(January 1977): 59–69.

Goodwin, M., and G. Pollen. *Creative Food Experiences for Children.* Washington, D.C.: Center for Science in the Public Interest, 1974, 1980.

Herr, Judith, and Winifred Morse. "Food for Thought: Nutrition Education for Young Children." *Young Children* 38(November 1982): 3–11.

Kahn, Ellen H. *Cooking Activities for the Retarded Child.* New York: Abingdon, 1974.

Katz, D., and M. T. Goodwin. *Food: Where Nutrition, Politics and Culture Meet: An Activities Guide for Teachers.* Washington, D.C.: Center for Science in the Public Interest, 1976.

Kelley, Lynn. *Classroom Cooking. It's as Easy as Pie.* 1975. Available from Arizona Center for Education, Research and Development, College of Education, University of Arizona, Tucson, AZ 85721.

Kerr, G. "The Nutritional Correlates of Life: Growth and Learning." *Journal of School Health* 42(April 1972): 191–196.

Kositsky, Val. "What in the World Is Cooking in Class Today—Multiethnic Recipes for Young Children." *Young Children* 33(November 1977): 23–31.

Lombardi, Felipe Rojas. *The A to Z No-Cook Cookbook.* New York: R. L. Creations, 1972.

Marbach, Ellen S., Martha Plass, and Lily H. O'Connell. *Nutrition in a Changing World: A Curriculum for Preschool.* Provo, Utah: Brigham Young University Press, 1979.

McClenahan, Pat, and Ida Jaqua. *Cool Cooking for Kids: Recipes and Nutrition for Preschoolers.* Belmont, Calif.: Fearon, 1976.

McIntyre, M. "Science Is Eating." *Science and Children* 12, no. 5(1975): 38.

Parents' Nursery School. *Kids Are Natural Cooks—Child Tested Recipes for Home and School Using Natural Foods.* Boston: Houghton Mifflin, 1974.

Pittsburgh AEYC. *Children in Contemporary Society: Special Issue: Nutrition and Young Children* 12(November 1978). Available from Pittsburgh AEYC, P.O. Box 11173, Pittsburgh, PA 15237.

Raman, S. P. "Role of Nutrition in the Actualization of the Potentialities of the Child: An Anisa Approach." *Young Children* 31(November 1975): 24–32.

Stein, Sara. *The Kids' Kitchen Takeover.* New York: Workman, 1975.

Stori, M. *I'll Eat Anything If I Can Make It Myself.* Available from CBH Publishers, 464 Central, Northfield, IL 60093.

Sunderlein, S., and B. Wills. *Nutrition and Intellectual Growth in Children.* Washington, D.C.: Association for Childhood Education International, 1969.

Twardosz, S., M. F. Cataldo, and T. Risley. "Menus for Toddler Day Care: Food Preference and Spoon Use." *Young Children* 30(January 1975): 129–144.

U.S. Department of Agriculture. Yearbook. *What's to Eat? and Other Questions Kids Ask About Food.* Washington, D.C.: GPO, 1979.

U.S. Department of Agriculture. *Food Buying for Child Care Centers.* FNS-108, Washington, D.C.: GPO, 1974.

U.S. Department of Health, Education, and Welfare, Head Start Bureau. *Nutrition Education for Young Children.* Pub. no. (OHDS) 76–31015. Washington, D.C.: Administration for Children, Youth and Families, OCD, 1976.

Wainwright, A. *Girls and Boys Easy to Cook Book.* New York: Grosset & Dunlap, 1979.

Wanamaker, N., K. Hearn, and S. Richarz. *More Than Graham Crackers. Nutrition Education and Food Preparation with Young Children,* no. 316. Washington, D.C.: National Association for the Education of Young Children, 1979.

Warren, Jean. *Super Snacks: Sugarless, Seasonal Snacks.* Available from Warren Publishing, 1004 Harborview Lane, Everett, WA 98203.

Books for Children

Asch, F. *Sand Cake.* New York: Parents Magazine Press, 1979.

Atwood, A. *The Little Circle.* New York: Scribner, 1967.

Baldwin, A. N. *Sunflowers for Tina.* New York: Scholastic Book Services, 1973.

Brown, M. W. *Nibble, Nibble.* Reading, Mass.: Addison-Wesley, 1959.

Carle, E. *The Tiny Seed and the Giant Flower.* New York: Thomas Y. Crowell, 1976.

———. *The Very Hungry Caterpillar.* Philomel, 1969.
———. *Pancakes, Pancakes.* New York: Pantheon, 1975.
———. *Walter the Baker.* New York: Alfred A. Knopf, 1972.
Collier, Ethel. *Who Goes There in My Garden?* New York: Addison-Wesley, 1963.
Cook, Bernadine. *The Little Fish That Got Away.* New York: Scholastic Book Services, 1956.
Goffstein, M. B. *Fish for Supper.* New York: Dial Press, 1976.
Goldin, A. *Salt.* New York: Thomas Y. Crowell, 1966.
Greenaway, K. *A—Apple Pie.* London: F. Warne, 1886.
Hall, R. *The Bright & Shining Breadboard.* New York: Lothrop, Lee & Shepard, 1969.
Ipcar, D. *Hard Scrabble Harvest.* Garden City, New York: Doubleday, 1976.
———. *Bring in the Pumpkins.* New York: Scholastic Book Services, 1978.
Kahl, V. *The Dutchess Bakes a Cake.* New York: Charles Scribner's Sons, 1955.
Krauss, Ruth. *The Growing Story.* New York: Harper & Row, 1947.
———. *The Carrot Seed.* New York: Scholastic Book Services, 1971.
Martin, Dick. *The Apple Book.* New York: Golden Press, 1964.
———. *The Fish Book.* New York: Golden Press, 1976.
McCloskey, Robert. *Blueberries for Sal.* New York: Viking Press, 1966.
Pape, D. L. *A Bone for Breakfast.* Champaign, Ill.: Garrard, 1974.
Scheer, J. *Rain Makes Applesauce.* New York: Holiday House, 1964.
Selsam, M. *The Apple and Other Fruits.* New York: William Morrow, 1973.
———. *The Carrot and Other Root Vegetables.* New York: William Morrow, 1970.
———. *More Potatoes.* New York: Harper & Row, 1972.
———. *Peanut.* New York: William Morrow, 1969.
———. *Popcorn.* New York: William Morrow, 1976.
———. *Seeds and More Seeds.* New York: Harper, 1959.
———. *The Tomato and Other Fruit Vegetables.* New York: William Morrow, 1970.
Sendak, M. *In the Night Kitchen.* New York: Harper & Row, 1970.
Supraner, R. *Giggly-Wiggly, Snickety-Snack.* New York: Scholastic Book Services, 1978.
Tresselt, A. *Autumn Harvest.* New York: Lothrop, Lee & Shepard, 1951.
Webber, Irma E. *Up Above and Down Below.* New York: Addison-Wesley, 1943.

CHAPTER 11. MATHEMATICS

Additional Sources

Ashlock, Robert B. "Planning Mathematics Instruction for Four- and Five-Year-Olds." In *Understanding the Young Child and His Curriculum,* edited by Belen Mills. New York: Macmillan, 1972, pp. 341–345.
Baratta-Lorton, Mary. *Workjobs . . . for Parents.* Menlo Park, Calif.: Addison-Wesley, 1975.
Barbe, Walter B. *Basic Skills in Kindergarten: Foundation for Formal Learning.* Columbus, Ohio: Zane Bloser, 1980.
Barron, L. *Mathematics Experiences for Early Childhood Years.* Columbus, Ohio: Charles E. Merrill, 1979.
Cahoon, Owen W. *A Teacher's Guide to Cognitive Tasks for Preschool.* Provo, Utah: Brigham Young University Press, 1974.
Charlesworth, R., and D. Radeloff. *Experiences in Math for Young Children.* Albany, N.Y.: Delmar, 1978.
Cruikshank, Douglas E., David L. Fitzgerald, and Linda R. Jensen. *Young Children Learning Mathematics.* Boston: Allyn & Bacon, 1980.
Dawes, Cynthia. *Early Maths.* New York: Longman, 1977.
Day, Barbara. *Early Childhood Education: Creative Learning Activities.* New York: Macmillan, 1983, pp. 232–258.
Flood, James, and Diane Lapp. *Language/Reading Instruction for the Young Child.* New York: Macmillan, 1981.
Friedman, F., and B. Fink. "Piaget in the Classroom." *Science and Children* 10(September 1972): 13–15.
Frost, Joe. *The Young Child and the Educative Process.* New York: Holt, Rinehart & Winston, 1976.

Gelman, R. "Counting in the Preschooler: What Does and Does Not Develop?" In *Children's Thinking: What Develops?* edited by R. S. Siegler. Hillsdale, N.J.: Lawrence Erlaum, 1978.

Ginsburg, Herbert. *Children's Arithmetic: The Learning Process.* New York: D. Van Nostrand, 1977.

Ginsburg, R. *Mathematical Concept Learning by the Pre-School Child. Final Report.* ERIC document #ED065171. Washington, D.C.: National Center for Education, Research and Development, 1971.

Green, R. T., and V. J. Laxon. *Entering the World of Number.* New York: Thames-on-Hudson, 1977.

Heard, Ida Mae. "Number Games With Young Children." *Young Children* 24(January 1969): 147–150.

Hucklesby, Sylvia. *Opening Up the Classroom: A Walk Around the School.* Urbana, Ill: University of Illinois. ERIC Clearing House on Early Childhood Education, 1971. Ideas to teach math and science using stones and sticks.

Johnson, Martin L., and John W. Wilson. "Mathematics." In *Curriculum for the Preschool-Primary Child: A Review of the Research,* edited by Carol Seefeldt. Columbus, Ohio: Charles E. Merrill, 1976, pp. 153–174.

Kamii, Constance. *Number in Preschool and Kindergarten,* no. 103. *Educational Implications of Piaget's Theory.* Washington, D.C.: National Association for the Education of Young Children, 1982.

Kennedy, Leonard M. *Guiding Children to Mathematical Discovery.* 3d ed. Belmont, Calif.: Wadsworth, 1980.

Lorton, Mary B. *Mathematics Their Way.* Menlo Park, CA: Addison-Wesley, 1976.

Maffel, Anthony C., and Patricia Buckley. *Teaching Preschool Math Foundations and Activities.* New York: Human Sciences Press, 1980.

McCarthy, Melodie, and John P. Houston. *Fundamentals of Early Childhood Education.* Cambridge, Mass: Winthrop, 1980.

McIntyre, Margaret. "Books Which Give Mathematical Concepts to Young Children: An Annotated Bibliography." *Young Children* 24(June 1969): 287–291.

Mills, Belen, ed. *Understanding the Young Child and His Curriculum.* New York: Macmillan, 1972, pp. 332–346. Contains bibliography and selected readings.

Montessori, Maria. *The Montessori Method.* New York: Schocken Books, 1964.

Nuffield Mathematics Project. *Mathematics Begins.* New York: John Wiley, 1967.

Piaget, Jean. "How Children Form Mathematical Concepts." *Scientific American* 189, no. 20 (1953): 74–79.

Rea, R. E., and R. E. Reys. "Mathematics Competence of Entering Kindergarteners." *Arithmetic Teacher 17,* no. 1 (1970): 701–705.

Schwartz, Sydney L., and Helen F. Robison. *Designing Curriculum for Early Childhood.* Boston: Allyn & Bacon, 1982, pp. 185–211.

Scott, L. B., and J. Garner. *Mathematical Experiences for Young Children: A Resource Book for Kindergarten and Primary Teachers.* New York: McGraw-Hill, 1978.

Spodek, Bernard. *Teaching in the Early Years.* Englewood Cliffs, N.J.: Prentice-Hall, 1978, pp. 152–176.

Steffe, Leslie P., ed. *Research on Mathematical Thinking of Young Children.* Reston, Va.: National Council of Teachers of Mathematics, 1975.

Uprichard, E. "The Effects of Sequence in the Acquisition of Three Set Relations: An Experiment with Preschoolers." *The Arithmetic Teacher* 17(1970): 597–604.

Vance, Barbara. *Teaching the Prekindergarten Child.* Monterey, Calif.: Brooks/Cole, 1973, pp. 269–282.

Walter, Marion. "Geometry for Young Students in the 80's." *Teacher,* February 1981, pp. 45–49.

Watrin, R., and P. H. Furfey. *Learning Activities for the Young Preschool Child.* New York: D. Van Nostrand, 1978, pp. 372–400.

Weikart, David P., Linda Rogers, Carolyn Adcock, and Donna McClelland. *The Cognitively Oriented Curriculum.* Washington, D.C.: National Association for the Education of Young Children, ERIC, 1971, pp. 94–145.

Wilderman, Ann. "The Metrics Are Coming." *Early Years.* 5(April 1975): 8.

Willert, Frederick. "Centimeter by Centimeter." *Early Years* 5(April 1975).

Withers, Carl. *Counting Out Rhymes.* New York: Dover, 1970.

Zaslavsky, Claudia. "The Shape of a Symbol/The Symbolism of a Shape." *Teacher* 99(February 1981): 36–43.

Books for Children

Allen, Robert. *Numbers: A First Counting Book.* New York: Platt & Munk, 1968.
Berkley, E. *Big and Little, Up and Down.* Reading, Mass.: Addison-Wesley, 1950.
Blegvad, L. *One Is for the Sun.* New York: Harcourt Brace Jovanovich, 1968.
Brewer, Mary. *Which Is Biggest?* Chicago: Children's Press, 1976.
Bright, R. *My Red Umbrella.* New York: William Morrow, 1959.
Budney, Blossom. *A Kiss Is Round.* New York: Lothrop, Lee & Shepard, 1954.
Carle, Eric. *The Very Hungry Caterpillar.* New York: Philomel, 1969.
Cook, Bernadine. *The Little Fish That Got Away.* New York: Scholastic Book Services, 1956.
Emberly, E. *The Wings on a Flea.* Boston: Little, Brown, 1961.
Francoise, J. *Marie Counts Her Sheep.* New York: Charles Scribner's Sons, 1963.
______. *What Time Is It, Jeanne Marie?* New York: Charles Scribner's Sons, 1963.
Froman, Robert. *Angles Are Easy as Pie.* New York: Thomas Y. Crowell, 1976.
Gag, Wanda. *Millions of Cats.* New York: Coward, 1928.
Hoban, Tana. *Big Ones, Little Ones.* New York: Greenwillow Books, 1976.
______. *Count and See.* New York, Macmillan, 1972.
______. *Over, Under and Through and Other Spatial Concepts.* New York: Macmillan, 1973.
______. *Push-Pull, Empty-Full.* New York: Macmillan, 1972.
______. *Circles, Triangles and Squares.* New York: Macmillan, 1974.
Hoberman, M. A., and N. Hoberman. *All My Shoes Come in Twos.* Boston: Little, Brown, 1957.
Holl, A. *Let's Count.* Reading, Mass: Addison-Wesley, 1976.
Hutchins, Pat. *Changes, Changes.* New York: Macmillan, 1971.
______. *Clocks and More Clocks.* New York: Macmillan, 1970.
Kaufman, J. *Big and Little.* New York: Golden Press, 1967.
Keats, E. J. *Over in the Meadow.* New York: Scholastic Book Services, 1972.
Kohn, B. *Everything Has a Shape & Everything Has a Size.* Englewood Cliffs, N.J.: Prentice-Hall, 1966.
Kredenser, Gail, and Stanley Mack. *One Dancing Drum.* New York: S. G. Phillips, 1971.
Langstaff, John. *Over in the Meadow.* New York: Harcourt Brace Jovanovich, 1967.
Lionni, Leo. *Inch by Inch.* New York: Astor-Honor, 1962.
McLeod, E. *One Snail and Me.* Boston: Little, Brown, 1981.
Miller, J. P. *Big and Little.* New York: Random House, 1975.
Moncure, Jane B. *Magic Monsters Count to Ten.* Mankato, Minn.: Child's World, 1979.
Ogle, Lucille. *I Spy With My Little Eye.* New York: McGraw-Hill, 1970.
Poulet, Virginia. *Blue Bug's Treasure.* Chicago: Children's Press, 1976.
Reiss, J. J. *Numbers.* Scarsdale, N.Y.: Bradbury Press, 1971.
Rowan, D. *Everybody In.* Englewood Cliffs, N.J.: Bradbury Press, 1968.
Ruben, Patricia. *What Is New? What Is Missing? What Is Different?* Philadelphia: J. B. Lippincott, 1978.
Sazer, Nina. *What Do You Think I Saw?* New York: Pantheon, 1976.
Schlein, M. *Shapes.* New York: Addison-Wesley, 1952.
Schneider, Herman, and Nina Schneider. *How Big Is Big?* New York: Addison-Wesley, 1946.
Shapp, Martha, and Charles Shapp. *Let's Find Out About What's Big and What's Small.* New York: Franklin Watts, 1975.
Sugita, Yutaka. *Good Night—1, 2, 3.* New York: Scroll Press, 1971.
Tudor, T. *One Is One.* Chicago: Rand, 1956.
Ungerer, Tomi. *Crictor.* New York: Harper & Row, 1958.
Walter, Marion. *Look at Annette.* New York: M. Evans, 1972.
______. *The Magic Mirror Book.* New York: Scholastic Book Services, 1976.
______. *Make a Bigger Puddle, Make a Smaller Worm.* New York: M. Evans, 1972.
Weiss, Malcolm E. *666 Jellybeans! All That?* New York: Thomas Y. Crowell, 1976.
Yeoman, John. *Sixes & Sevens.* New York: Macmillan, 1971.
Zolotow, Charlotte. *One Step, Two . . .* New York: Lothrop, Lee & Shepard, 1981.

CHAPTER 12. GUIDANCE TECHNIQUES FOR TEACHERS AND PARENTS

Additional Sources

Anderson, Luleen S. "The Aggressive Child." *Children Today* (January–February 1978): 11–14.

Caldwell, Bettye M. "Aggression and Hostility in Young Children." *Young Children* 32(January 1977): 4–13.

Erikson, Erik. *A Healthy Personality for Your Child.* Midcentury White House Conference on Children and Youth. Washington, D.C.: GPO, 1950.

Essa, Eva. *Practical Guide to Solving Preschool Behavior Problems.* Delmar, 1983.

Gross, Beatrice, and Ronald Gross. "Parent-Child Development Centers: Creating Models for Parent Education." *Children Today* 6 (November–December 1977): 7–12.

Harms, Thelma O., and Deborah Cryer. "Parent Newsletter: A New Format." *Young Children* 33 (July 1978): 28–32.

Helms, Donald B., and Jeffrey S. Turner. *Exploring Child Behavior: Basic Principles.* Philadelphia: W. B. Saunders, 1978.

Hildebrand, Verna. "Parents: A Good Energy Resource." *Forecast for Home Economics* 21(January 1976): F13, F36.

———. "Developing Children Need Developing Adults." *Dimensions* 5(June 1977): 99–104.

Hymes, James L., Jr. *Behavior and Misbehavior.* Englewood Cliffs, N.J.: Prentice-Hall, 1955.

Kelly, Francis. "Guiding Groups of Parents of Young Children." *Young Children* 37(November 1981): 29–31.

Marion, Marian C. "Create a Parent-Space—A Place to Stop, Look and Read." *Young Children* 28(April 1973): 221–224.

Nedler, Shari, and O. D. McAfee. *Working With Parents: Guidelines for Early Childhood and Elementary Teachers.* Belmont, Calif.: Wadsworth, 1979.

Swick, Kevin, and R. Eleanor Duff. *The Parent-Teacher Bond: Relations, Responding, Rewarding.* Dubuque, Iowa: Kendall/Hunt, 1978.

Veach, David M. "Choice with Responsibility?" *Young Children* 32(May 1977): 22–25.

Washington, Kenneth R. "Success! A Parent Effectiveness Approach for Developing Urban Children's Self-Concepts." *Young Children* 32(July 1977): 5–10.

Of Special Interest to Parents

Andres, Palmyra. "What Every Parent Wants to Know." *Childhood Education 52,* no. 6 (1976): 304–305.

Bell, T. H. *Your Child's Intellect—A Guide to Home-Based Preschool Education.* Salt Lake City: Olympus, 1972.

Cahoon, O. W., A. H. Price, and A. L. Scoresby. *Parents and the Achieving Child.* Provo, Utah: Brigham Young University Press, 1979.

Croft, D. J. *Parents and Teachers: A Resource Book for Home, School and Community Relations.* Belmont, Calif.: Wadsworth, 1979.

Gordon, I. *Baby Learning Through Baby Play.* New York: St. Martin's Press, 1973.

Gordon, I., Barry Guinagh, and R. Emile Jester. *Child Learning Through Child Play: Learning Activities for Two and Three Year Olds.* New York: St. Martin's Press, 1972.

Gordon, Ira J., and William F. Breivogel. *Building Effective Home/School Relationships.* Boston: Allyn & Bacon, 1978.

———. "Parenting, Teaching and Child Development." *Young Children* 31(March 1976): 173–183.

Hogan, Jane. "Getting Parents Involved in Their Children's Education." *Phi Delta Kappan* 22 (July–August 1978).

Honig, A. *Parent Involvement in Early Childhood Education.* Washington, D.C.: National Association for the Education of Young Children, 1975.

Honig, Alice. *Parent Involvement in Early Childhood Education,* no. 135. Washington, D.C.: National Association for the Education of Young Children, 1977.

Leavitt, Edith, and Shirley Cohen. "Educating Parents of Children With Special Needs—Approaches and Issues." *Young Children* 21(May 1976): 263–272.

Nedler, Shari. "Working With Parents on the Run." *Childhood Education* 53(January 1978): 128–132.

O'Brien, Marion, J. Porterfield, E. Herbert-Jackson, and T. R. Risley. *The Toddler Center: a Practical Guide to Day Care for One- and Two-Year-Olds.* Baltimore: University Park Press, 1979.

Rich, D. "Family-Community Involvement in Teacher Education." In *Early Childhood Education,* edited by L. G. Golubcheck and V. Persky. Wayne, N.J.: Avery, 1977, pp. 325–330.

Schickedanz, J. A. "Parents, Teachers and Early Education." In *Early Childhood Education,* edited by L. H. Golubcheck and B. Persky. Wayne, N.J.: Avery, 1977, pp. 331–333.

Stone, Jeannette G. *A Guide to Discipline,* rev. ed. Washington, D.C.: National Association for the Education of Young Children, 1978.

Wenig, M., and M. L. Brown. "School Effort + Parent/Teacher Communications = Happy Young Children." *Young Children* 30 (July 1975): 373–376.

RECORD SOURCES

Bowmar/Noble Records
4563 Colorado Blvd.
Los Angeles, CA 90039

Camden-RCA Records
Educational Sales
P.O. Box RCA 1000
Indianapolis, IN 46291

Capital Records, Inc.
1290 Avenue of the Americas
New York, NY 10019

Childcraft Education Corp.
20 Kilmer Rd.
Edison, NJ 08817

Children's Book & Music Center
5373 West Pico Blvd.
Los Angeles, CA 90019

Columbia Records
51 West 52nd St.
New York, NY 10019

Decca Records
445 Park Ave.
New York, NY 10022

Disneyland Records
800 Sonora Ave.
Glendale, CA 91201

Educational Activities, Inc.
1937 Grand Avenue
Baldwin, NY 11510

Educational Record Sales
157 Chambers Street
New York, NY 10007

Educational Recordings of America
P.O. Box 210
Ausania, CT 06401

Folkways Records
43 West 61st St.
New York, NY 10023

Folkways/Scholastic Records
906 Sylvan Avenue
Englewood Cliffs, NJ 07632

Ginn and Co.
191 Spring St.
Lexington, MA 02173

Golden Records Educational Division
Michael Brent Pub., Inc.
Port Chester, NY 10573

Hap Palmer Record Library
Educational Activities, Inc.
1937 Grand Avenue
P.O. Box 87
Baldwin, NY 11510

Honor Your Partner Records
P.O. Box 392
Freeport, NY 11520

Kimbo Educational
P.O. Box 477
86 South 5th Ave.
Long Branch, NJ 07740

A. B. LeCrone Co.
819 N.W. 92nd St.
Oklahoma City, OK 73114

Lyons Band
530 Riverview Ave.
Elkhart, IN 46514

Marlo Thomas and Friends
Arista Records
1776 Broadway
New York, NY 10019

MCA Records, Inc.
70 Universal City Plaza
Universal City, CA 91608

Melody House Publishing Co.
819 N.W. 92nd St.
Oklahoma City, OK 73114

RCA Music Service
Educational Department
1133 Avenue of the Americas
New York, NY 10036
RCA Records
Educational Sales
P.O. Box RCA 1000
Indianapolis, IN 46291
Rhythms Productions
Whitney Bldg.
Box 34485
Los Angeles, CA 90034
Scott, Foresman & Co.
1900 East Lake Ave.
Glenview, IL 60025
Sing 'N Do Records
P.O. Box 55
Deal, NJ 07723
Tom Thumb Records
Rhythms Productions
Whitney Bldg.
Box 34485
Los Angeles, CA 90034
Weston Wood Studios
Weston, CT 06883
Youngheart Records
Box 27784
2413½ Hyperion Avenue
Los Angeles, CA 90027
Young People's Records
Children's Record Guild
100 Avenue of the Americas
New York, NY 10017
Vox Productions Inc.
211 East 43rd St.
New York, NY 10017

Sources for Ordering Instruments

Children's Music Center, Inc.
2500 Santa Monica Blvd.
Santa Monica, CA 90404
Lyons Band
530 Riverview Ave.
Elkhart, IN 46514
Magnamusic-Baton, Inc.
10370 Page Industrial Blvd.
St. Lewis, MO 63132
Oscar Schmidt-International, Inc.
Garden State Rd.
Union, NJ 07083
Peripole, Inc.
P.O. Box 146
Brown Mills, NJ 08015
Rhythm Band, Inc.
P.O. Box 146 (or 126)
Fort Worth, TX 76101

PUBLISHERS OF CHILDREN'S BOOKS

Atheneum Publishers
Books for Children
122 East 42d Street
New York, NY 10017
Bradbury Press
2 Overhill Road
Scarsdale, NY 10583
Columbia Children's Book and Record Library
51 West 52d Street
New York, NY 10019
Thomas Y. Crowell Co.
Department of Books for Children
666 Fifth Avenue
New York, NY 10019
T. S. Denison & Co., Inc.
5100 West 82d Street
Minneapolis, MN 55437
Dover Publications, Inc.
180 Varick Street
New York, NY 10014
Basic Books, Inc.
10 East 53d Street
New York, NY 10022
Children's Book Press
76 Castro Street
San Francisco, CA 94114
Coward, McCann & Geoghegan, Inc.
200 Madison Avenue
New York, NY 10016
Jonathan David Publishers, Inc.
68-22 Eliot Avenue
Middle Village, NY 11379
Dodd, Mead & Co.
79 Madison Avenue
New York, NY 10016
E. P. Dutton & Co., Inc.
201 South Park Avenue
New York, NY 10003
Follett Publishing Co.
1010 West Washington Bd.
Chicago IL 60607

Grosset & Dunlap, Inc.
51 Madison Avenue
New York, NY 10010
Harper & Row, Publishers
Library Department
10 East 53d Street
New York, NY 10022
Holt, Rinehart & Winston, Inc.
383 Madison Avenue
New York, NY 10017
Lawrence Publishing Co.
c/o Borden Publishing Co.
1855 West Main Street
Alhambra, CA 91801
J. B. Lippincott Co.
521 Fifth Avenue
New York, NY 10017
Macmillan Publishing Co.
866 Third Avenue
New York, NY 10022
Grolier, Inc.
575 Lexington Avenue
New York, NY 10022
Harcourt Brace Jovanovich, Inc.
757 Third Avenue
New York, NY 10017
Holiday House, Inc.
18 East 53d Street
New York, NY 10022
Alfred A. Knopf, Inc.
201 East 50th Street
New York, NY 10022
Little, Brown & Co.
Children's Books
34 Beacon Street
Boston, MA 02106
Lothrop, Lee & Shepard Co.
105 Madison Avenue
New York, NY 10016
Melmont Publishers, Inc.
1224 West Van Buren Street
Chicago, IL 60607
William Morrow & Co., Inc.
105 Madison Avenue
New York, NY 10016
Platt & Munk, Publishers
51 Madison Avenue
New York, NY 10010
G. P. Putnam's Sons
200 Madison Avenue
New York, NY 10016
Random House, Inc.
201 East 50th Street
New York, NY 10022
Scholastic Book Services
50 West 44th Street
New York, NY 10036
The Seabury Press
Books for Young People
815 Second Avenue
New York, NY 10017
Oxford University Press, Inc.
200 Madison Avenue
New York, NY 10016
Prentice-Hall, Inc.
Englewood Cliffs, NJ 07632
Rand McNally & Co.
P.O. Box 7600
Chicago, IL 60680
St. Martin's Press, Inc.
175 Fifth Avenue
New York, NY 10010
Scott Foresman & Co.
1900 East Lake Avenue
Glenview, IL 60025
Charles Scribner's Sons
597 Fifth Avenue
New York, NY 10017
Viking Press, Inc.
40 West 23d Street
New York, NY 10010
Henry Z. Walck, Inc.
2 Park Avenue
New York, NY 10016
Franklin Watts, Inc.
387 Park Avenue South
New York, NY 10016

Index

Student Survey

Barbara J. Taylor

A CHILD GOES FORTH, 6th Ed.

Students, send us your ideas!

The author and the publisher want to know how well this book served you and what can be done to improve it for those who will use it in the future. By completing and returning this questionnaire, you can help us develop better textbooks. We value your opinion and want to hear your comments. Thank you.

Your name (optional) ______________________ School ______________________

Your mailing address ______________________ City ______________________

State ________ ZIP ________ Instructor's name (optional) ______________________

Course title ______________________ Department ______________________

1. How does this book compare with other texts you have used? (Check one)

   ☐ Superior ☐ Better than most ☐ Comparable ☐ Not as good as most

2. Circle those chapters you especially liked:

   Chapters: 1 2 3 4 5 6 7 8 9 10 11 12

   Comments:

3. Circle those chapters you think could be improved:

   Chapters: 1 2 3 4 5 6 7 8 9 10 11 12

   Comments:

4. Please rate the following. (Check one for each line)

	Excellent	Good	Average	Poor
Readability of text material	( )	( )	( )	( )
Logical organization	( )	( )	( )	( )
General layout and design	( )	( )	( )	( )
Up-to-date treatment of subject	( )	( )	( )	( )
Match with instructor's course organization	( )	( )	( )	( )
Illustrations that enhance the text	( )	( )	( )	( )
Selection of topics	( )	( )	( )	( )

(Over, please)

5. List any chapters that your instructor did not assign. ____________________

____

6. What additional topics did your instructor discuss that were not covered in the text? ____________________

____

7. How much have you used the material in the appendixes? (Check one response for each appendix.)

		Used Regularly	Used Occasionally	Did Not Use
Appendix A.	Characteristics of Young Children	( )	( )	( )
Appendix B.	Suggested Curriculum Topics	( )	( )	( )
Appendix C.	Lesson Plans	( )	( )	( )
Appendix D.	Recipes	( )	( )	( )
Appendix E.	Additional Sources, Books for Children, Record Sources, and Publishers	( )	( )	( )

8. Did you buy this book new or used? ☐ New ☐ Used
Do you plan to keep the book or sell it? ☐ Keep it ☐ Sell it
Do you think your instructor should continue to assign this book? ☐ Yes ☐ No

9. After taking the course, are you interested in taking more courses in this field? ☐ Yes ☐ No
Did you take this course to fulfill a requirement, or as an elective? ☐ Required ☐ Elective

10. What is your major? ____________________
Your class rank? ☐ Freshman ☐ Sophomore ☐ Junior ☐ Senior ☐ Other, specify:

11. GENERAL COMMENTS:

May we quote you in our advertising? ☐ Yes ☐ No

Please remove this page and mail to:

Mary L. Paulson
Burgess Publishing Company
7108 Ohms Lane
Minneapolis, MN 55435

THANK YOU!